NINTH EDITION

Literature *for* Children

A SHORT INTRODUCTION

David L. Russell

Ferris State University

330 Hudson Street, NY 10013

Vice President and Editor in Chief: Kevin M. Davis
Portfolio Manager: Drew Bennett
Content Producer: Yagnesh Jani
Managing Content Producer: Megan Moffo
Portfolio Management Assistant: Maria Feliberty
Executive Product Marketing Manager: Christopher Barry
Executive Field Marketing Manager: Krista Clark
Procurement Specialist: Deidra Smith
Cover Designer: Studio Montage
Cover Art: LSC Communications/Crawfordsville
Media Producer: Allison Longley
Editorial Production and Composition Services: SPi Global
Editorial Project Manager: Clara Bartunek
Full-Service Project Manager: Sasibalan Chidambaram, SPi Global
Text Font: Sabon LT Pro 10.75 pt

For related titles and support materials, visit our online catalog at www.pearsonhighered.com.

Every effort has been made to provide accurate and current Internet information in this book. However, the Internet and information posted on it are constantly changing, so it is inevitable that some of the Internet addresses listed in this textbook will change.

Library of Congress Cataloging-in-Publication Data
Names: Russell, David L., 1946- author.
Title: Literature for children : a short introduction / David L. Russell,
    Ferris State University.
Description: Ninth edition. | NY, NY : Pearson Education, 2017. | Includes
    bibliographical references, appendix, and glossary.
Identifiers: LCCN 2017046759| ISBN 9780134800455 | ISBN 0134800451
Subjects: LCSH: Children's literature—History and criticism. |
    Children—Books and reading.
Classification: LCC PN1009.A1 R87 2017 | DDC 809/.89282—dc23 LC record available at
https://lccn.loc.gov/2017046759

1   18

 **Pearson**

ISBN 10: 0-13-480045-1
ISBN 13: 978-0-13-480045-5

Dedication

This is for my grandchildren,
Mason, Mariya, Emily, Sarah, Lily, Ella,
and *Gabriella*, and to the memory of *Tookie*
and Bryan Woods

About the Author

David L. Russell is a professor of English at Ferris State University in Big Rapids, Michigan, where he teaches children's literature and folk literature. He is the author of *Patricia MacLachlan* and *Scott O'Dell*, both published by Twayne Publishers, as well as *Stuart Academic Drama: An Edition of Three University Plays* by Garland Publishing. He has also published numerous scholarly articles on children's literature, and was a contributor to *The Oxford Encyclopedia of Children's Literature*, *The Continuum Encyclopedia of Children's Literature*, and *The Cambridge Guide to Children's Books in English*. He is currently co-editor of *The Lion and the Unicorn*.

Contents

CHAPTER **3**   Experiencing Literature
Reading, Writing, Talking, and Doing   61

CHAPTER 4   The Art and Craft of Fiction

The Medium and the Message   83

CHAPTER 7 Folk Narratives
The Oldest Stories 189

CHAPTER **8**   Fantasy

The World of -Make-Believe   221

APPENDIX

Preface

Revisions always pose both opportunities and risks. Certainly, just being asked to do a revision is an honor, but it is more importantly a responsibility. One wants to preserve the features valued by loyal users of the previous edition while making changes that might appeal to a wider audience. Perhaps most importantly, a revision allows for the updating of material to keep pace with the dynamic world of children's literature.

As so often happens, this revision turned out to be more dramatic than I had originally envisioned, and a generous publisher has made it possible to have full color throughout the book. This, I trust, will make the overall design more visually appealing. The chapters have been reshuffled, and, more importantly, reduced in number. Logic and efficiency were my motives for these changes. Katherine Paterson famously said, "I love revision. Where else can spilled milk be turned into ice cream?" It is with this spirit that I have entered into this ninth edition.

New to This Edition

Perhaps most noticeably, the entire book is now illustrated in color, which I hope makes for a livelier and more pleasing presentation.

- All chapters have been rewritten and updated where necessary to keep abreast of developments in the field.
- All resource lists have been updated.
- Chapter 1 (The History of Children's Literature) now includes material on twentieth-century theories of child development (Piaget, Erickson, and Kohlberb), which were formerly in a separate chapter. This move is to emphasize the development of modern children's literature as it addresses new attitudes toward childhood.
- Chapter 2 (Reading the World: Issues in Children's Literature) combines materials from former chapters 3 and 4, including the social issues of diversity and inclusion, the personal issues of sexuality and death, and the harsh realities of war and violence. In addition, the chapter concludes with a discussion of intellectual freedom, which is often called into play with books on all these issues.

- The new Chapter 4 constitutes a shifting of the literary and critical materials originally in Chapter 9. Because this information applies to all children's literature, its placement near the beginning of the text probably makes the most sense. Additionally, the discussion of critical approaches has been enhanced considerably.

- The new Chapter 5 (Picture Books), which begins Part II, combines the discussions of all picture books, which in previous editions had been divided between two chapters. This should avoid some redundancy, and the inclusion of more full-color illustrations should strengthen the discussions on art.

- The new Chapter 6 (Poetry) opens with a discussion of Mother Goose rhymes, which had originally been placed in a chapter on books for the very young. Using Mother Goose as an entrée to the discussion of poetry may make more sense.

In my own classes, students spend most of their time reading the primary material—the picture books, the poetry, the folktales, the fantasies, the realistic fiction, the nonfiction—which is as it should be. This book is intended as a supplement to that reading, and the focus is always, I hope, on the literature itself. Finally, I offer no apology for my approach, which is decidedly literary, reflecting my own background as a teacher of English literature. My hope is that all who use this book come away with more than just ideas about how to make reading fun in the classroom (however important that is). Children's literature provides an excellent opportunity for us to develop an appreciation for the art of literature and an understanding of how literature reflects our world and ourselves.

As always, I close with a quotation from *Ecclesiasticus*, a question that goes to the heart of education:

If thou hast gathered nothing in thy youth, how canst thou find anything in thine age?

The History of Children's Literature

How We Got Here

"We are not makers of history. We are made by history."

–Martin Luther King, Jr.

Introduction

On the 18th of July in 1744, John Newbery's *A Little Pretty Pocket Book* first went on sale in his bookshop near St. Paul's Cathedral in London. Over the next few years, he would publish nearly 100 books for children, earning for himself the epithet "Father of Children's Literature." That title may be something of an overstatement—Newbery himself never wrote anything remotely memorable for children. However, Newbery's bookstore proved that writing books for children could become a profitable pursuit. And since that time, the children's book market has flourished.

But of course, children have always enjoyed good stories, whether they be told around the tribal fires of the earliest civilizations or shared in dramatic form in ancient theaters or passed along by word of mouth through the generations (see Jonathan Gottschall's *The Storytelling Animal* and Brian Boyd's *On the Origin of Stories*). For thousands of years, little distinction was made between stories for children and stories for adults; everyone enjoyed the same stories, and some stories were simply diluted for the very young (just as today). But over time, and for a variety of reasons, children's literature began to be separated from adult literature, until children's literature finally came to occupy its own niche in the literary canon. Let's see how that happened.

The Earliest Children's Literature

History is important because it tells us where we have been—as individuals, we each have our own history; our society has a history that has shaped us as does our culture as a whole. In Western culture, we can trace our roots to Judaeo-Christianity and to the ancient Greeks (ca. 850–150 BCE) and Romans (ca. 150 BCE–476 CE). For many in our society, the Old Testament stories are among the earliest literary experiences. Regardless of personal beliefs or religious convictions, we cannot deny that the stories of the Creation, the Garden of Eden, the Flood, the stories of Abraham and Moses, David and Goliath, and others form the inescapable foundation of our cultural heritage. It is difficult to fully appreciate modern culture without some knowledge of this seminal well of story.

The same is true of the literature of classical Greece and Rome. Around the eighth century BCE, the Greek poet Homer wrote *The Iliad*, the story of the Trojan War, and *The Odyssey*, the story of Odysseus' travels back home to Ithaka following the war. Even though Homer clearly had adults in mind, these stories have long been popular with children (and it is almost certain that young people were in those early Greek audiences listening to these fabulous stories being recited). After all, they contain exotic adventures, wondrous creatures with magical powers, and some of the world's first superheroes—the forerunners of Superman, Batman, and Wonder Woman. These tales have long been retold for children, and many modern versions are available—including Padraic Colum's *The Children's Homer* (1918), Marcia Williams's *Greek Myths* (1992), Jeanne Steig's somewhat daring *A Gift from Zeus: Sixteen Favorite Myths* (2001), and Heather Anderson's *Child's Introduction to Greek Mythology* (2011), a lively retelling for very young children.

The Greeks also gave us Aesop's *Fables*, brief talking animal stories, each with a pointed moral. These include such famous tales as "The Wolf in Sheep's Clothing" (its moral being "Things aren't always what them seem"), "The Tortoise and the Hare" ("Slow and steady wins the race"), and "The Ant and the Grasshopper" ("Always be prepared"). Tradition has it that they were written by a teacher named Aesop in Greece around 600 BCE, presumably as lessons for his students. They quickly became a staple of European cultural heritage, and William Caxton's version, *The Fables of Aesop* (1484), was among the first books to come off the early printing presses. Even today, new versions (either in collections or as individual tales) continue to appear regularly, such as Jerry Pinkney's 2009 Caldecott Medal–winning *The Lion and the Mouse*, a wordless adaptation; and Beverley Naidoo's 2011 *Aesop's Fables,* illustrated by Piet Grobler, which is given an African setting.

Another popular storyteller from the ancient world was the Roman poet Ovid (ca. 43 BCE–17/18 CE) who wrote down many of the ancient Greek and Roman myths and legends in his book *Metamorphoses*. He retells, among others, the tales of Hercules, of the famed lovers Pyramus and Thisbe (an inspiration for *Romeo and Juliet*), and of Pygmalion, who fell in love with a statue he sculpted of a beautiful woman. Adrian Mitchell's *Shapeshifters: Tales from Ovid's Metamorphoses* (2010) is one of many recent adaptations for children of these ancient stories—*metamorphosis* means "transformation" and is derived from the fact that quite often the stories recount individuals being transformed (from human to animal, or vice versa). Many of the ancient myths have inspired modern variations, notably Rick Riordan's popular Percy Jackson series, including the books *Percy Jackson and the Olympians* and *The Heroes of Olympus*. So you see, children are not immune to ancient tales; in fact, these oldest of stories remain among the most powerful and most popular.

The Middle Ages

The Middle Ages (approximately the period from the fall of the Roman Empire in 476 to around 1450) was a rather rough-and-tumble period that was kept civilized through the efforts of the Roman Catholic Church. Medieval life was precarious. Some estimate that one-third of all children died before they were 5 years old, and about one-third of the entire population of Medieval England was under the age of 14—it was a youthful society. Although childhood was often brief and teenagers were generally treated as adults, the evidence of medieval toys suggests that the young did enjoy a childhood and were doted on by their parents. Although after the fall of Rome, education dramatically declined and few people could read, the oral tradition was kept alive. Naturally, all children would have been familiar with the biblical stories—Adam, Eve, and the forbidden fruit; Noah and the flood; Jonah and the great fish; Moses and the parting of the Red Sea; David's killing of Goliath. In addition, a wealth of other adventure stories and hero tales emerged. Favorites included the adventures of King Arthur, Charlemagne, Roland, and Beowulf. The epic of *Beowulf*, composed sometime between 900 and 1100, tells of the struggles between a great king and a dreadful monster, Grendel, and the monster's even more dreadful mother. It is rather a grizzly tale, as monster stories usually are, which may account for its lasting popularity. Many children's versions are in print, including Rosemary Sutcliff's *Dragon Slayer: The Story of Beowulf* (originally published in 1961, but reissued) and James Rumford's strikingly illustrated *Beowulf*, in 2007.

As the Middle Ages progressed, society became more sophisticated—education became important and the first European universities were founded in this period. The University of Bologna (in Italy) came first in 1088, followed by the University of Paris (c. 1150) and Oxford University (1167). Although most of the literate people were from the aristocracy, general literacy gradually rose over the course of years. As in ancient times, literature specifically for children was comparatively rare. Nevertheless, children must have been captivated by many of the adventure tales that were circulating about, most famously those of King Arthur and his Knights of the Round Table.

Arthur may have been a British leader who lived in the fifth century CE and fought against Germanic invaders in Britain. Absolutely nothing for certain is known about him, but he and his knights have found their way into countless legends that became increasingly popular during the High Middle Ages (about 1200–1450)—Arthur the ideal king, his knights all paragons of valor and virtue (usually). The unusual feature about these Arthurian knights is that they were both skilled warriors and gallant lovers. Their stories recount both heroic battles and tender romances, and this combination seems to have ensured their continued popularity over the centuries. The stories of King Arthur have been retold for children many times over the years. Among the many modern children's versions of these medieval tales are Michael Morpurgo's *Sir Gawain and the Green Knight* (2004), illustrated by Michael Foreman; *Sir Gawain and the Loathly Lady*, by Selina Hastings and illustrated by Juan Wijngaard (1987); Benedict Flynn's *King Arthur and the Knights of the Round Table* (2008), and Gerald Morris's *Sir Gawain the True* (2011), one of a series of books containing loose, but lively, adaptations of Arthurian legends. You will notice that we have not mentioned the folktales—tales of Cinderella, Beauty and the Beast, Little Red Riding Hood, Rapunzel, tales that seem so quintessentially medieval. That is because, despite their medieval, preindustrial settings, few of them can be traced undeniably back to the Middle Ages. And we may presume that medieval children knew some versions of many of these stories, but no one bothered to record them. So the stories we know today come to us from a much later time—the eighteenth and nineteenth centuries—and we will come to that shortly.

The greatest English writer of the Middle Ages was Geoffey Chaucer (1343–1400), who is most famous for his *Canterbury Tales,* a collection of stories allegedly told by pilgrims as they travelled on the road to Canterbury Cathedral to worship at the great shrine of St. Thomas Beckett. Most of Chaucer's work is for adults, but many pieces can be found that are entertaining for children as well. A modern-day version of Chaucer's tale, *Chanticleer and the Fox,* illustrated by Barbara Cooney and winner of the 1959 Caldecott Medal, is an example of a charming medieval story of the clever underdog (should we say "under-rooster") that is quite appealing to children. If nothing else, it reminds us that children the world over have similar tastes regardless of time and place.

The Renaissance

*R*enaissance literally means "rebirth," and the historical period known as the Renaissance (from about 1400–1700) represented a rekindling of the interest in the learned, sophisticated cultures of ancient Greece and Rome. This did not happen overnight. In fact, the first European universities were founded in the eleventh and twelfth centuries, signaling an interest in learning; and then around 1440, the invention of the movable-type printing press, attributed to Johannes Gutenberg (although the Chinese came up with it long before), would change the world. No longer did books have to be laboriously copied by hand, but they could be mass

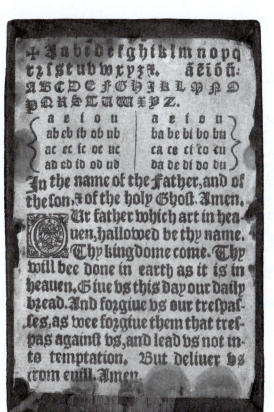

FIGURE 1.1 ■ This typical hornbook from the time of Shakespeare illustrates the religious nature of education at that time. It is simply parchment fastened to a wooden paddle and laminated with animal horn for durability. Very young students in the sixteenth and seventeenth centuries would have learned to read using such a teaching device.

produced. Books became cheaper and more plentiful, literacy increased, learning advanced, and ideas spread more quickly than ever before. Few inventions in history have had the impact of the printing press.

Still, the Renaissance produced very few books specifically for children. Among the earliest were hornbooks (see Figure 1.1), which were not really books but sheets of parchment attached to wooden slabs and covered with transparent horn (from cattle, sheep, and goats), an early form of lamination to make them durable. Hornbooks were used by very young children in school and usually contained simple language lessons (the alphabet, numbers, the Lord's Prayer). In the 1700s, the hornbook was supplanted by the battledore, which was made of cardboard (again, for durability) and usually folded in three. The battledore contained the alphabet,

CXXXVI.

Ludi Pueriles.

Boyes-Sport

Boys used to play either with *Bowling-stones* 1. or throwing a *Bowl*, 2. at *Nine-pins*, 3. or striking a *Ball*, through a *Ring*, 5. with a *Bandy*, 4. or scourging a *Top*, 6. with a *Whip*, 7. or shooting with a *Trunk*, 8. and a *Bow*, 9. or going upon *Stilts*, 10. or tossing and swinging themselves upon a *Merry-totter*, 11.

Pueri solent ludere vel *Globis fictilibus*, 1. vel jactantes *Globum*, 2. ad *Conas*, 3. vel *mittentes* Sphærulam per *Annulum*, 5. *Clava*, 4. versantes *Turbinem*, 6. *Flagello*, 7. vel jaculantes *Sclopo*, 8. & *Arcu*, 9. vel incidentes *Grallis*, 10. vel super *Petaurum*, 11. se agitantes & oscillantes.

FIGURE 1.2 ■ John Comenius's *Orbis Sensualium Pictus* is often considered the first children's picture book. It first appeared in 1658 as a German/Latin textbook and was an immediate success. It revolutionized Latin instruction, a necessity in a society in which Latin was still the language of scholarship. The English/Latin version, from which this illustration is taken, appeared in 1659. Although the woodcut illustrations are crude, they provide a wealth of information about seventeenth-century European life.

often along with other instructional material, sometimes even a short story, and some included illustrations. But what is often considered the first true illustrated book for children was John Comenius's *Orbis Sensualium Pictus* (see Figure 1.2), which appeared in 1658. It is not a storybook but a textbook designed to teach

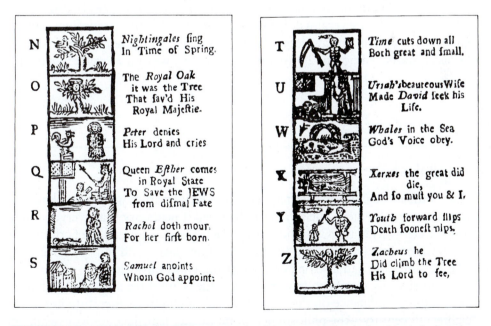

FIGURE 1.3 ■ The *New England Primer* was one of the longest-lived school texts in American history, flourishing from approximately 1690 to 1830. The earliest surviving copy is from 1727, from which these illustrations are taken. Intended to teach the children of the early Puritans how to live a godly life, the book is unabashedly didactic, which is evident even in its rhyming alphabet, recalling a time when church and state were not as separate as they are now.

Latin vocabulary—a sort of Latin through pictures. (Every educated person in Europe knew Latin in those days; professors even delivered college lectures in Latin.) One of the most famous schoolbooks of the period was the *New England Primer*, which first appeared sometime around 1690 and continued in print in one form or another until 1886. It introduced young Puritan children to the alphabet through rhymes ("In Adam's fall/We Sinned all" for the letter *A*) and moved to increasingly sophisticated reading material—all with a religious intent (see Figure 1.3).

But when literate children wanted to read books for pleasure, they had to turn to adult books, one of the favorites being John Bunyan's *The Pilgrim's Progress* (1678). Although it is a serious religious allegory about human salvation, it is filled with thrilling adventures and terrifying monsters (much as in *Beowulf*). These features appealed to young readers from the very beginning. Today hundreds of editions remain in print, including many retold for children, such as that by Geraldine McCaughrean (2001). Equally popular was Daniel Defoe's *Robinson Crusoe* (1719), about a man surviving on a strange deserted island. Defoe's story is still found in many modern children's versions, including one beautifully illustrated by N. C. Wyeth (1920). It has also become the prototype for modern survival stories (such as Scott O'Dell's *Island of the Blue Dolphins* and Jean Craighead George's *Julie of the Wolves*). Survival stories involving young heroes and heroines remain enormously popular with children. Jonathan Swift's *Gulliver's Travels* (1726) is also a journey tale, one that visits several wildly fanciful lands filled with extraordinary adventures. Gulliver's story remains available to children in many adapted versions (such as the "Classic Starts" edition of 2006) and has found its way into several film adaptations.

The Eighteenth Century

The Philosophers

One of the more important outcomes of the Reformation was its emphasis on education and literacy. The reformers believed it necessary that everyone (not just the clergy as in the Catholic Middle Ages) be able to read the Scriptures. This emphasis on literacy extended to children of all classes and to both boys and girls. The Reformation had a strong democratizing effect on society.

Contributing significantly to these new ideas are three men who had an extraordinary influence on the emerging field of children's literature in the eighteenth century—the philosophers John Locke, Jean-Jacques Rousseau, and a bookseller named John Newbery. In 1693, the English philosopher John Locke (1632–1704) wrote a famous essay called *Thoughts Concerning Education*. Here, he described the minds of young children as blank slates (in Latin, *tabula rasa*) waiting to be written upon. All children, he argued, had equal capabilities to learn, and adults needed to provide the proper learning environment and suitable material to fill the youthful minds. For Locke, heredity was unimportant, for he believed that everyone began life on an equal intellectual footing, with the same capacity to learn and understand. Thus began the perennial argument over the relative influence of heredity and the environment (that is, nature versus nurture). Today, Locke's ideas have been seriously challenged by human genetic studies (see Chapter 2; let's face it, we are not all born with equal abilities), but his belief in the importance of education still drives our schools and universities.

The French philosopher Jean-Jacques Rousseau (1712–1778) wrote an influential book called *Emile* (1762). This work describes Rousseau's notion of an ideal education, which he believed should emphasize moral development through a simple lifestyle, preferably lived in the country, away from the corrupting influence of the city. Curiously, Rousseau did not encourage reading, which he feared would propagate immoral behavior—a belief rather unfortunately held by some people yet today (see "Intellectual Freedom" in Chapter 2). However, he did admire *Robinson Crusoe* and its argument for self-sufficiency. Rousseau inspired many followers who wrote didactic and moralistic books to teach children how to be good and proper human beings.

The Bookseller and Moral Writers

This chapter began with a reference to John Newbery (1713–1778), who was neither philosopher nor writer (really), but would have great influence on children's reading. He was, in fact, a clever businessman who hit upon the idea of marketing books especially written for children. Newbery owned a bookshop near St. Paul's Cathedral in London in the mid-eighteenth century. In 1744, he wrote and published *A Little Pretty Pocket Book* (see Figure 1.4), a curious collection of verse, fables, games, and jingles for children (in which, interestingly, we find the first-known reference to a game called "base-ball"). As an added incentive, boys were given a ball and girls a pincushion when they bought the book (marketing was Newbery's real genius). This book is the first children's book we know of ever sold in a bookshop. Although Newbery wrote and compiled other books for children— none of them very good—his most important contribution is that he provided a market for other writers. Now there was a place where children's books could be purchased, and writing books for children could be lucrative. Newbery's shop was run by his nephew's widow, Elizabeth Newbery, well into the nineteenth century, and she continued to expand the business of publishing children's books, eventually listing over 400 titles for children. Without the Newberys, children's literature as we know it today could never have come about. John Newbery's contribution was at last recognized when the American Library Association established, in 1922, the famous medal that bears his name and is given each year to what is judged the best children's book published in the United States.

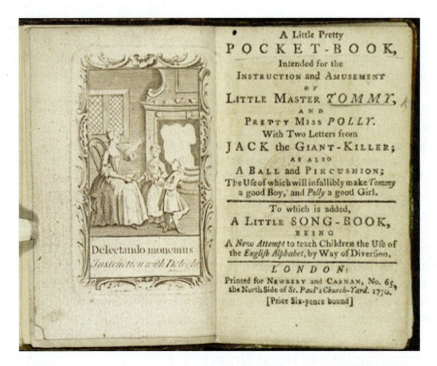

FIGURE 1.4 ■ The title page of John Newbery's *Little Pretty Pocket-Book* demonstrates the eighteenth-century penchant for exhausting titles. This is considered the first book published for children that was neither for educational nor religious purposes, but for entertainment.

In the latter half of the eighteenth century a flurry of writers, mostly women, were creating books for children. Many were followers of Rousseau, writing "moral" books, extolling the virtues of the simple life, of kindness, of Christian charity and humility. Among the earliest was Maria Edgeworth (1744–1817), who wrote a popular book titled *Simple Susan* (1796), about a country girl whose goodness helps her to triumph over an ill-intentioned city lawyer. Another disciple of Rousseau was Sarah Trimmer (1741–1810), who wrote *The Story of the Robins* (originally called *Fabulous Histories*, 1786), about a family of robins living side-by-side with a human family who learn from the robins the virtue of kindness. The story was unusual in a time that frowned on tales of talking animals. The eighteenth-century rationalists thought talking animal tales were illogical, and religious zealots thought them unholy. Covering her bases, Mrs. Trimmer carefully pointed out to her young readers that her story is a fable and that animals cannot really talk. She is also famous for condemning fairy stories for children because they were sacrilegious and lacked moral purpose. Mary Martha Sherwood (1775–1851), another of the moral writers, wrote *The History of the Fairchild*

Family (1818), which includes frighteningly vivid stories about the souls of impious children moldering in cold graves or being consigned to the fires of hell—these were presumably more appropriate for young readers than silly tales with talking animals.

The Discovery of the Folktales

Alongside the moralistic tales came something rather refreshing—the revival of the old folktales from the quickly fading oral tradition. Actually, folktales were printed in England as early as 1729. At that time, *Tales of Mother Goose*, originally retold by the Frenchman Charles Perrault (1628–1703), was first translated and published in English. Although they were not originally for children, these tales, which included "Cinderella," "Little Red Riding Hood," and "Sleeping Beauty in the Wood," soon became staples in English nurseries. In 1791, Elizabeth Newbery published the first children's edition of the Middle Eastern *Tales from the Arabian Nights*, including the stories of Sinbad the sailor, Aladdin and his lamp, and Ali Baba and the forty thieves.

At the beginning of the nineteenth century, two brothers, Jacob (1785–1863) and Wilhelm (1786–1859) Grimm, collected and published a great number of European folktales, and the Grimms' tales are still the most famous of all collections. The Grimms also inspired a number of European folktale collectors, including Asbjörnsen and Moe in Norway, and Joseph Jacobs (*English Fairy Tales*) and Andrew Lang (*The Blue Fairy Book*, *The Red Fairy Book*, and so on) in Great Britain. In 1835 in Denmark, Hans Christian Andersen published the first of his original fairy tales, which carry the unmistakable imprint of the traditional folktale and remain enduringly popular to this day. It was also at this time that collections of the old folk rhymes, variously called Mother Goose rhymes or nursery rhymes, began to appear in book form (see Figure 1.5).

The Victorian Golden Age

In 1865, Lewis Carroll (pseudonym for Charles Dodgson) published *Alice's Adventures in Wonderland*, usually considered the first English children's story written purely for entertainment with no thought toward moral rectitude. The sequel, *Through the Looking-Glass*, appeared in 1871–1872. These wild fantasies continue to fascinate children (and moviegoers) today, and their unforgettable characters (Alice, the Mad Hatter, the Cheshire Cat, the Jabberwock, Tweedledum and Tweedledee, the Red Queen, the White Knight, and many others) are indelibly fixed in English-speaking culture. Carroll's works helped to establish the trend away from eighteenth-century didacticism in children's literature. No longer were

9

The man in the moon came down too soon
To inquire the way to Norridge;
The man in the south, he burnt his mouth
With eating cold plum-porridge.

FIGURE 1.5 ■ Abel Bowen's woodcut illustration of "The Man in the Moon," from *Mother Goose's Melodies*, dramatically depicts the contrast between the ridiculous and the sublime that underlies much of children's literature. On the left side, with grace and elegance, a youth descends from the crescent moon; on the right side, a buffoonish character is engaged in a nonsensical act. Dating from 1833, this publication is among the earliest American children's books designed purely for the pleasure of young readers.

children's books viewed as merely vehicles for lessons in living or moral and religious guides. Children's literature was beginning to be seen as entertainment in addition to (or rather than) moral and spiritual education.

Alice's Adventures in Wonderland heralded things to come. Encouraged by increasing prosperity, a rising middle class, the broadening of public education, and the development of technology, children's literature began to flourish in the later nineteenth century. Soon, high-quality books were appearing in both Great Britain and the United States. They covered a broad literary spectrum, including

- *Adventure stories* (R. M. Ballantyne's *The Coral Island*, 1857, and Mark Twain's *The Adventures of Tom Sawyer*, 1876)—often set in exotic places in the far-flung British Empire or in the vastness of the American landscape;

- *Series books* (Oliver Optic's *Outward Bound; or, Young America Afloat*, 1867, and Horatio Alger Jr., *Ragged Dick; or, Street Life in New York*, 1867)—also adventure stories for boys, but usually with an educational or moral purpose, which were very popular in America, and they tend to be formulaic, each book in the series following a very similar pattern;

- *Historical novels* (Robert Louis Stevenson's *Kidnapped*, 1886, and Howard Pyle's *Otto of the Silver Hand*, 1888)—usually adventure stories, but set in some romantic or exotic past, eighteenth-century Scotland in the case of *Kidnapped* or the Middle Ages as in Pyle's book;

- *Domestic and family stories* (Charlotte Yonge's *The Daisy Chain*, 1856, and Louisa May Alcott's *Little Women*, 1868)—usually intended as fare for girls, about the joys, trials, and tribulations of family life;

- *School stories* (Thomas Hughes's *Tom Brown's School Days*, 1857, and Edward Eggleston's *The Hoosier Schoolmaster*, 1871)—a counterpart to domestic and family stories but for boys and with a school setting where boys could have adventures beyond the watchful eyes of their parents (many of these stories take place in boarding schools);

- *Fantasies* (George MacDonald's *The Princess and the Goblin*, 1872, and L. Frank Baum's *The Wonderful Wizard of Oz*, 1900)—following in the path of *Alice's Adventures in Wonderland*, stories set in magical lands or about magical encounters in our own world;

- *Poetry* (Edward Lear's *A Book of Nonsense*, 1846, and Robert Louis Stevenson's *A Child's Garden of Verses*, 1885)—some delightfully nonsensical (Lear), others charming and sentimental (Stevenson); and

- *Folktales* (Andrew Lang's *The Blue Fairy Book*, 1889, and Joseph Jacobs's *English Fairy Tales*, 1890)—collected and retold from the rich oral repository, following in the tradition of the brothers Grimm.

In addition, by the mid-1800s, printing technology had perfected color printing, and this attracted many fine illustrators to the field of children's books. Earlier illustrations tended to be rather crude woodcuts and few talented artists were willing to use their talents for the cheaply printed volumes for children. But with the introduction of color printing, many very fine artists began to see the possibilities that children's stories held. Walter Crane (see Figure 1.6) and George Cruikshank were among the pioneers in this arena. Randolph Caldecott (1846–1886) brought a lively humor to his illustrations (see Figure 1.7). Kate Greenaway (1846–1901) depicted a charming and carefree Victorian childhood in her illustrations of popular nursery rhymes and poems (see Chapter 5, Figure 5.3). Their illustrations set the standard for the age and are admired today. Beatrix Potter became a sensation with the publication of *The Tale of Peter Rabbit* (1901), which she both wrote and illustrated (see Figure 5.5). As the twentieth century progressed, more and more

FIGURE 1.6 ■ Walter Crane's sophisticated use of line and composition can be seen in his portrayal of Jack and Jill carrying the bucket of water down the hill, from *The Baby's Opera* (1877).

FIGURE 1.7 ■ Randolph Caldecott, the great nineteenth-century English illustrator, was one of the pioneers of children's book illustration. His art is characterized by an economy of line and a playfulness of manner that make his work appealing today, more than a century after his death. The American Library Association annually awards the Caldecott Medal, named in his honor, to what it judges the most distinguished picture book published in the United States. This illustration from *The Frog He Would A-Wooing Go* (1883) depicts Caldecott's lively sense of humor.

artists would follow her lead and both write and illustrate their own works. Potter's books are still in print and much loved, perhaps in part because she followed her own advice: "I think the great point in writing for children is to have something to say and to say it in simple, direct language" (quoted in Hunt, *An Introduction to Children's Literature*, 88). The later nineteenth century is widely regarded as the golden age of children's literature—and certainly it was the period during which children's literature came into its own.

The Twentieth Century

The early twentieth century continued the rich tradition of the nineteenth and gave us such classic fantasies as J. M. Barrie's *Peter Pan* (first a play in 1904 and then a novel called *Peter and Wendy* in 1911), about the boy who would not grow up; Kenneth Grahame's *The Wind in the Willows* (1908), about the irrepressible Rat, Mole, Badger, and Mr. Toad of Toad Hall; and A. A. Milne's ever-popular *Winnie-the-Pooh* (1926). Realistic novels continued to gain a foothold. Frances Hodgson Burnett's *The Secret Garden* (1911) is the story of Mary Lennox, initially a rather unappealing heroine, who ultimately finds her redemption on the bleak English moors. In America the semi-autobiographical series by Laura Ingalls Wilder, beginning with *The Little House in the Big Woods* (1932), remained popular for many years and inspired a popular television series. Wilder's popularity endures, although her works have come under criticism for their rather heavy-handed celebration of the pioneer spirit and the negative portrayal of Native Americans.

Through much of the twentieth century, realistic fiction for children remained rather conservative, but fantasy, perhaps by its very nature, more easily challenged the status quo. P. L. Travers's *Mary Poppins* (1934), a collection of wildly fanciful stories about an eccentric nanny, has raised many an adult eyebrow because of the title character's outrageous behavior. And Theodore Geisel challenged much about modern society with his unorthodox picture books under the pseudonym Dr. Seuss. J. R. R. Tolkien's fantasy, *The Hobbit; or, There and Back Again* (1937), is the prequel to his great trilogy, *The Lord of the Rings*, a fantasy for young adults and adults that explores philosophical questions (in the same way C. S. Lewis's *Narnia Chronicles* explores religious beliefs). Of course, all of these can be enjoyed as pure adventure stories and flights of fancy, without the reader's pondering the deeper motives, which is one of the great advantages of fantasy.

Children's Literature Around the World

Children's literature is, of course, a worldwide phenomenon and we would be remiss not to mention a few of the international works that have played a prominent role in the development of the field.

Canada, Australia, and New Zealand have all made significant contributions to children's literature, particularly in the twentieth century. Among the early Canadian writers are the naturalists Ernest Thompson Seton (*Wild Animals I Have Known*, 1898) and Charles G. D. Roberts (*Red Fox*, 1905), who are usually credited with inventing the realistic animal story. Perhaps the most famous Canadian writer, Lucy Maud Montgomery (*Anne of Green Gables*, 1908), wrote domestic stories about life on Prince Edward Island. Modern trends include literature by and about the native peoples of Canada (Basil Johnston's *Tales the Elders Told: Ojibway Legends*, 1981). One of the most famous contemporary Canadians in children's literature is author/illustrator Jon Klassen, who has won the Canadian Governor General's Award for illustration (for *Cat's Night Out* by Carolyn Stutson, 2010) and the Caldecott Medal (for *This Is Not My Hat*, 2012).

Kate Langloh Parker's *Australian Legendary Tales* (1896) was one of the first books to explore aboriginal legends. Among the best-known modern Australian children's writers are Patricia Wrightson, much of whose work is based on aboriginal traditions (*The Ice Is Coming*, 1977), and Ivan Southall, a writer of vivid survival stories, often with bleak endings (*Ash Road*, 1965), and more recently Mem Fox and illustrator Bob Graham. And New Zealand's most celebrated children's author, Margaret Mahy, twice won the prestigious Carnegie Medal (for *The Haunting*, 1981, and *The Changeover*, 1983).

Happily, through translation, children can also access the great store of children's books from non-English speaking lands—which is where our journey actually began. Children's literature, in fact, has long been an international phenomenon, drawing on stories from the world over. Germany, in addition to the brothers Grimm, also boasts Heinrich Hoffmann, who wrote *Struwwelpeter* (1845), a collection of cautionary tales that some view as hilarious and others as horrifying. Felix Salten's *Bambi* (1923) and Erich Kästen's *Emil and the Detectives* (1929) are two modern German works that have become classics. *The Adventures of Pinocchio* (1883), by the Italian author Carlo Collodi, is the world's most famous puppet story, with its familiar theme of a toy wishing to be alive. France has given us Jean de Brunhoff, the creator of *The Story of Babar, the Little Elephant* (1931), the first of a series of picture books (seven in all) about a little elephant who becomes a wise and benevolent ruler. And Antoine de Saint-Exupéry's *The Little Prince* (1943), also French, remains a fantasy classic for all ages. Sweden's Selma Lagerlöf, who won the Nobel Prize for Literature in 1909, wrote *The Wonderful Adventures of Nils* (in two volumes, 1906–1907), a highly imaginative work of fantasy. In 1945, Astrid Lindgren, the best-known Swedish children's author, wrote *Pippi Longstocking*, the fanciful story of a remarkable girl with superhuman strength, unconventional values, and complete independence—in other words, every child's hero. The Finnish writer Tove Jansson created the Moomin family in a popular series of books beginning with *Comet in Moominland* (1946). These books about the gentle Moomins and their eccentric friends contain a healthy dose of philosophy as their adventures and misadventures unfold in a delightfully amorphous way.

Asia is now a ripe source of excellent books for children, and the study of children's literature is becoming more prominent in places such as China, Japan, and the Middle East, although children's books in English translation from these lands are still rare. On the other hand, English-speaking children can enjoy works such as Grace Lin's Newbery Honor books *Where the Mountain Meets the Moon,*

2009, and *Starry River of the Sky,* 2012, lyrical works that celebrate her Chinese heritage. And young adults will be moved by Aisha Saeed's *Written in the Stars,* 2015, a riveting teenage love story that takes us to modern-day Pakistan. Children's literature can provide an excellent bridge between us and distant lands and cultures.

Modern Theories of Child Development

So we have seen a veritable explosion of children's books throughout the twentieth- and into the twenty-first centuries, and these works will be the subject of much of the rest of this book. However, the last hundred years have also been a time of dramatic changing social attitudes toward children—and particularly toward their intellectual, emotional, and social development. Advancements in the field of child psychology and a greater understanding of child development have greatly impacted our understanding of children, their abilities, desires, and needs. And this, in turn, has affected the writing of children's literature, not to mention our opinions about certain children's books of the past.

During the twentieth century, among the most notable contributions to the study of childhood were the theories of child development. For the first time, science tried to explain how humans progressed (intellectually, psychologically, and socially) from infancy to adulthood. For our purposes, the most significant are probably Jean Piaget, who studied intellectual or cognitive development, and Erik Erikson, who studied social development. Both viewed human development as occurring in a series of stages through which children pass on their way to maturity. Lawrence Kohlberg studied a different type of human development— moral development, or how we learn right from wrong. Let's briefly examine these theories, keeping in mind that the age spans mentioned here are only approximations (not everyone develops at the same pace). We should note that these theories have been criticized for ignoring female development, which, some argue, is not the same as male development. Males, for example, generally value competition, self-assertiveness, individual rights, and social rules. Females, on the other hand, tend to value human relationships, responsibility to others, cooperation, community values, and tolerance for opposing viewpoints. In addition, some argue that females reach these developmental stages more quickly than males do. Another criticism of these theories is that they neglect minority groups, whose values are often different from those of the majority. Nevertheless, these theories are helpful as a general guide—so long as we remember their limitations.

Piaget and Cognitive Development

The Swiss psychologist Jean Piaget (1896–1980) outlined four major periods of intellectual development through which humans progress from birth to adulthood.

First is the **sensorimotor period** (from birth to about 2 years of age), when children are entirely egocentric (they are unaware of the needs of others), and they experience the world entirely through the senses (what they can see, hear, taste, touch, and smell). At this stage, books are objects to feel and manipulate with their hands—once they've learned that books are not to eat. Some children's writers learned early on that cloth books, board books, books with movable parts (such as pop-up books, called by some "mechanical books") are all appealing at this stage. Mechanical books actually appeared in Victorian England—although they were not always intended for 2-year-olds.

However, children quickly outgrow these books, which function as often as toys as they do books. By about the age of 2, they move into the second stage—the **preoperational period,** when they begin to acquire and refine motor skills, become less egocentric, and start making friends. This period lasts until about the age of 7 years—or about second grade. Although they do not use logic yet at this stage, children can use symbols to represent ideas. For example, they learn the alphabet and numbers (after all, that's what written language is—a symbolic representation of ideas). And, although they can grasp certain concepts—colors, shapes, opposites—everything is seen in concrete terms. Also, they tend to give human qualities to everything (a concept known as *animism*), which helps explain their fondness for books about talking animals and animated toys and machines. They also grasp the sense of story—using characters to work through a plot. They understand mood (the anxiety of Potter's Peter Rabbit as he tries to escape MacGregor's garden or the approaching quiet restfulness in Margaret Wise Brown's *Good Night Moon*). Picture books can be especially good at establishing a mood through well-planned illustrations as well as effective language (see Chapter 5).

The third period, **concrete operations,** lasts from about 7 to 12 years of age when children still have difficulty with abstract ideas, but are able to apply a kind of logic to their thinking. They are capable of understanding these basic concepts of logic: **conservation** (that quantity is not affected by appearance), **reversibility** (that some actions, like knotting a shoestring, can be undone), **assimilation** (using what we already know to explain new information—a St. Bernard and a Chihuahua are both dogs), and **accommodation** (revising what we already know to explain new information—not all four-legged creatures are dogs). It is during this period that children move away from picture books and into more complex storybooks. Chapter books are usually introduced in about second grade. Plots can now be more complicated and characters can display greater depth by having more than one side. We also see characters getting more involved in the adult world—even when those characters are talking animals (think of the characters in E. B. White's *Charlotte's Web*).

Finally, the fourth period, **formal operations,** occurs between the ages of about 12 and 15 or 16 (when most children reach full cognitive maturity). In these early teen years, young people begin to use formal logic and engage in a true exchange of ideas, comprehending the viewpoints of others and understanding what it means to live in a society. Having entered adolescence, most are ready for more mature topics, such as love, sexuality, social issues, and even politics. Today, many of these issues arise in the middle school years, and later we will examine some of the topics explored in books for these readers (see Chapters 8, 9, and 10).

Erikson and Psychosocial Development

Piaget's interest was in intellectual development, whereas Erik Erikson (1902–1994) explored how we develop socially and psychologically. He saw growing up as a series of psychosocial conflicts that we must overcome. Erikson's theory complements, it does not compete with, Piaget's. For our purposes, just the first five stages are important (altogether, Kohlberg identified eight stages through life). During the first stage from birth to about 18 months, which he termed the **trust versus mistrust** stage, the helpless must trust the caregiver, but at the same time is fearful of abandonment. So building trust becomes essential. We turn again to Margaret Wise Brown's *Goodnight Moon*, which remains popular with the very young in part because its repetitious pattern (a little bunny saying "Goodnight" to everything in the room) is reassuring.

From about 18 months to 3 years, children are in Erikson's **autonomy versus doubt** stage. They begin to walk and talk and experiment with their newfound independence. At the same time, however, they are wary of their abilities. Look at Crockett Johnson's *Harold and the Purple Crayon*, about a boy who creates his own world with a magical crayon. Harold is inventive when he extricates himself from some interesting dilemmas (such as drawing a hot air balloon to keep him afloat after he falls from a cliff—which he also drew).

In the third stage, **initiative versus guilt**, children from about 3 to 6 years realize they have responsibilities (potty training springs to mind). Most children now want to take the initiative ("I want to do it myself!"). But also, they may feel guilt and shame if they believe they have failed or disappointed. This is a theme in Maurice Sendak's classic, *Where the Wild Things Are*, about a naughty boy sent to his room without supper. Just as in *Harold and the Purple Crayon*, childhood imagination is celebrated as an essential feature in human growth and development.

The fourth stage, **industry versus inferiority**, from about 7 to 11 years, is when children begin to seek success, but not just for their own satisfaction, but to gain the approval of others. This is the state when peer pressure becomes significant. Books such as Beverly Cleary's *Henry Huggins* and *Ramona the Pest* help young readers explore these desires for both personal achievement and acceptance and friendship.

As they move toward adolescence at about 11 years of age, young people begin to discover who they are (individually, socially, and culturally), the stage Erikson called **identity versus role confusion**, which lasts through most of the teen years. Adolescents are torn between the familiar security of childhood and the natural, if uneasy, desire to become adults. Judy Blume's popular *Are You There, God? It's Me Margaret*, the story of a girl facing her first menses along with a crisis in religious belief, is a perennial favorite for girls at this stage. Most readers at this stage crave openness and honesty, preferring stories about others like themselves (realism), but many also find pleasure in escapist tales (fantasy, science fiction, and so on).

Kohlberg and Moral Development

Finally, it is worth a brief look at the work of Lawrence Kohlberg (1927–1987), who studied the development of moral reasoning and moral judgment—that is, how individuals determine what is right and wrong. Like Piaget and Erickson, he saw development occurring in a series of stages through which an individual passes to moral maturity (at least, ideally). Kohlberg identifies three levels of development—preconventional, conventional, and postconventional—each subdivided into two stages, which he called "orientations." The first two levels are most important for our purposes.

The **preconventional level**, which Kohlberg places roughly from birth to about 9 years of age, is when children are just learning social conventions—being polite, using manners, obeying elders, and so on. Initially, right and wrong are simply a matter of what does and does not result in punishment or what pleases others. The first stage, *punishment/obedience orientation*, is when children obey rules because the rules come from some authority figure (a parent or a preschool teacher) or because they wish to avoid punishment. For example, in Beatrix Potter's *The Tale of Peter Rabbit*, the title character suffers the consequences of not listening to his mother. The second stage of the preconvention level is *self-interest orientation*, when children believe that "right" behavior is any action that helps or rewards them. A good example is Templeton the rat in E. B. White's *Charlotte's Web*, a thoroughly self-centered creature who helps out only if he is promised food. Presumably, readers see Templeton as selfish and unattractive, in contrast to the caring, magnanimous Wilbur. Most children's books for readers in the preconventional level share these themes.

The next stage, the **conventional level**, is not reached until around the age of 9 or 10. This is when individuals finally understand and observe (we hope) social conventions. It is the stage in which most adults operate, and it also has two parts. The first part, *interpersonal concordance* (or *"good boy/good girl"*) *orientation*, is when youths long to have the approval of others. Suddenly they want to be in "cliques" and everyone wants to belong—no one wants to be an outsider. The second part, *"law and order" orientation*, comes when individuals conform not for reasons of identity, but simply in order to abide by the law and accept their obligations as members of society. In other words, individuals at this stage are aware of their place in the world and demonstrate concern for others—two important signs of maturity. Mildred Taylor's *Roll of Thunder, Hear My Cry*, about an African American girl coming of age in the 1930s in the Deep South where she encounters hateful racial discrimination, is a good example of this orientation. Robert Cormier's *The Chocolate War*, about unscrupulous behavior in a private school, explores the issue of maintaining personal integrity when it comes up against peer pressure and social conformity.

(The final level, **postconventional**, is one that Kohlberg felt most people never achieve, for this is when individuals act in the interest of the welfare of others or of society as a whole; this is usually called the *social contract orientation*. And a very select few achieve *principled conscience orientation*, when people act out of regard for ethical principles or their own conscience—that is, saints and martyrs.)

Understanding how individuals develop is useful in selecting books for young readers. It is helpful to realize the varying capacities of young minds and how children see the world around them. As children develop, they put aside certain books and move on to others that are both more challenging and better suited to their developmental needs. In very young children, these transitions occur rapidly, and in the course of a very few years, they outgrow the nursery rhymes and picture books and require more complex stories, more compelling characters, and more probing themes. By the time they reach adolescence, most readers are capable of reading all but the most technical and esoteric of books. Ideally, our goal as educators should be to instill in children the desire to want to read and read, and read some more. We want them to know what is out there to read and how to read intelligently with a critical mind. These are lofty, but very worthwhile, goals.

Summary

Children's literature has been around for a long time and has enjoyed a wide variety of influences, from the ancient Greeks, whose wondrous mythological tales still enthrall us, to the rich diversity of the twenty-first century. We have also seen that the good stories never grow old and, significantly, children do not seem to care how old a story is—they just know a good one when they hear it. But, of course, we have seen decided changes as well, particularly from the day when John Newbery was selling children's books from his London shop in the eighteenth century. Beginning in the mid-nineteenth century, children's literature became far broader in its interests and more inclusive in its appeal, as well as more experimental. It was then that truly talented writers and illustrators turned to creating books for children. The twentieth century saw the development of the psychological study of childhood, which gave us a clearer understanding of children's needs, capabilities, and desires. This, in turn, helps us understand their response to children's books. Although it is not necessary to label all the various stages identified by Piaget, Erickson, and Kohlberg, it is good to understand the basic concepts—that a human being's development passes through stages over time through intellectual, emotional, and physical growth. And each stage brings with it new challenges, challenges that help determine a reader's needs and interests.

As we move through the twenty-first century, we trust that the demand for excellence in children's literature continues, for without reading, our civilization would disintegrate in a single generation. The ideas of our past would be lost forever, forcing humanity once again naked into the world. As students of children's literature, our great purpose is to bring the joy of reading to the next generation, giving them the tools they will need to build a better world than their parents have known.

Recommended Resources

Adams, Gillian. "Medieval Children's Literature: Its Possibility and Actuality." *Children's Literature,* 26 (1998): 1–24.

Aries, Philippe. *Centuries of Childhood: A Social History of Family Life.* New York: Knopf, 1962.

Boyd, Brian. *On the Origin of Stories: Evolution, Cognition, and Fiction.* Cambridge, MA: Harvard University Press, 2009.

Carpenter, Humphrey. *Secret Gardens: A Study of the Golden Age of Children's Literature.* Boston: Houghton Mifflin, 1985.

Carpenter, Humphrey, and Mari Prichard. *The Oxford Companion to Children's Literature.* Oxford: Oxford University Press, 1984.

Cullinan, Bernice, and Diane G. Person, eds. *The Continuum Encyclopedia of Children's Literature.* New York: Continuum, 2001.

Darton, F. J. Harvey. *Children's Books in England: Five Centuries of Social Life.* Cambridge: Cambridge University Press, 1982.

Demers, Patricia. *Heaven Upon Earth: The Form of Moral and Religious Children's Literature, to 1850.* Knoxville: University of Tennessee Press, 1993.

Demers, Patricia, and Gordon Moyles, eds. *From Instruction to Delight.* Toronto: Oxford University Press, 1982.

Erikson, Erik. *Childhood and Society.* New York: Norton, 1950.

Gottschall, Jonathan. *The Storytelling Animal: How Stories Make Us Human.* New York: Houghton Mifflin Harcourt, 2012.

Greven, Philip. *Spare the Child: The Religious Roots of Punishment and the Psychological Impact of Physical Abuse.* New York: Alfred A. Knopf, 1990.

Griswold, Jerry. *Feeling Like a Kid: Childhood and Children's Literature.* Baltimore, MD: The Johns Hopkins University Press, 2006.

Hunt, Peter, ed. *Children's Literature: An Illustrated History.* Oxford: Oxford University Press, 1995.

_____. *An Introduction to Children's Literature.* Oxford: Oxford University Press, 1994.

Healy, Jane. *Your Child's Growing Mind: Brain Development and Learning from Birth to Adolescence.* New York: Three Rivers Press, 2004.

Jackson, Mary V. *Engines of Instruction, Mischief, and Magic: Children's Literature in England from Its Beginnings to 1839.* Omaha: University of Nebraska, 1990.

Kohlberg, Lawrence. *The Philosophy of Moral Development.* San Francisco: Harper & Row, 1981.

_____. *Essays on Moral Development. Vol. II: The Psychology of Moral Development, the Nature and Validity of Moral Stages.* San Francisco: Harper & Row, 1985.

Kozulin, Alex, and others, eds. *Vygotsky's Educational Theory in Cultural Context.* Cambridge: Cambridge University Press, 2003.

Lane, Frederick S. *The Decency Wars: The Campaign to Cleanse American Culture.* Amherst, NY: Prometheus, 2006.

Lerer, Seth. *Children's Literature: A Reader's History from Aesop to Harry Potter.* Chicago: University of Chicago Press, 2009.

Lystad, Mary. *From Dr. Mather to Dr. Seuss: 200 Years of American Books for Children.* Cambridge, MA: Harvard University Press, 1980.

MacDonald, Ruth. *Literature for Children in England and America from 1646 to 1774.* Troy, NY: Whitston, 1982.

MacLeod, Anne Scott. *A Moral Tale: Children's Fiction and American Culture, 1820–1860.* Hamden, CT: Archon, 1975.

Marcus, Leonard. *Minders of Make-Believe: Idealists, Entrepreneurs, and the Shaping of American Children's Literature.* New York: Houghton Mifflin Harcourt, 2008.

Meigs, Cornelia, Elizabeth Nesbitt, Anne Thaxter Eaton, and Ruth Hill. *A Critical History of Children's Literature: A Survey of Children's Books in English.* New York: Macmillan, 1969.

Morrison, Susan S. "Introduction: Medieval Children's Literature." *Children's Literature Association Quarterly* 23.1 (1998): 2–6.

National Coalition Against Censorship, www.ncac.org.

Nikolajeva, Maria, ed. *Aspects and Issues in the History of Children's Literature.* Westport, CT: Greenwood, 1995.

Neubauer, John. *The Fin-De-Siecle Culture of Adolescence.* New Haven, CT: Yale University Press, 1992.

Orme, Nicholas. *Medieval Children.* New Haven: Yale UP, 2001.

Piaget, Jean. *The Language and Thought of the Child.* New York: Harcourt, Brace, 1926.

_____. "Piaget's Theory." In P. H. Mussen. *Handbook of Child Psychology. Book I: History, Theory, and Methods,* 4th ed. Ed. W. Kessen. New York: John Wiley & Sons, 1983.

Pickering, Samuel F., Jr. *John Locke and Children's Books in Eighteenth-Century England.* Knoxville: University of Tennessee Press, 1981.

_____. *Moral Instruction and Fiction for Children, 1749–1820.* Athens: University of Georgia Press, 1993.

Pinker, Steven. *The Blank Slate: The Modern Denial of Human Nature.* New York: Viking, 2002.

_____. *How the Mind Works.* New York: Norton, 1998.

_____. *The Language Instinct.* New York: HarperCollins, 2000.

Ravitch, Diane. *The Language Police: How Pressure Groups Restrict What Students Learn.* New York: Knopf, 2003.

Schorsch, Anita. *Images of Childhood: An Illustrated Social History.* New York: Mayflower, 1979.

Sugarman, Susan. *Piaget's Construction of the Child's Reality.* Cambridge: Cambridge University Press, 1987.

Summerfield, Geoffrey. *Fantasy and Reason: Children's Literature in the Eighteenth Century.* Athens: University of Georgia Press, 1983.

Thwaite, Mary F. *From Primer to Pleasure in Reading: An Introduction to the History of Children's Books in England.* Boston: The Horn Book, 1972.

Townsend, John Rowe. *Trade and Plum-Cake for Ever, Huzza! The Life and Work of John Newbery, 1713–1769.* Cambridge, UK: Colt, 1994.

_____. *Written for Children: An Outline of English-Language Children's Literature,* 5th rev. ed. London: Kestrel, 1990.

Tucker, Nicholas. *The Child and the Book: A Psychological and Literary Exploration.* Cambridge: Cambridge University Press, 1981.

Vidal, Fernando. *Piaget before Piaget.* Cambridge, MA: Harvard University Press, 1994.

Vygotsky, L. S. *Mind in Society: Development of Higher Psychological Processes,* rev. ed. Cambridge, MA: Harvard University Press, 2006.

Watson, Victor, ed. *The Cambridge Guide to Children's Books in English.* Cambridge: Cambridge University Press, 2001.

Wooden, Warren W. *Children's Literature of the English Renaissance.* Lexington: University of Kentucky Press, 1986.

Zipes, Jack, ed. *The Oxford Encyclopedia of Children's Literature.* Oxford: Oxford University Press, 2006.

Reading the World

Issues in Children's Literature

"Once you learn to read you will be forever free."

–Frederick Douglass

Introduction

Love of reading is one of the greatest gifts we can pass along to children. Rudine Sims Bishop summed up the reading process in this evocative way:

> *Books are sometimes windows, offering views of worlds that may be real or imagined, familiar or strange. These windows are also sliding glass doors, and readers have only to walk through in imagination to become part of whatever world has been created or recreated by the author. When lighting conditions are just right, however, a window can also be a mirror. Literature transforms human experience and reflects it back to us, and in that reflection we can see our own lives and experiences as part of the larger human experience. Reading, then, becomes a means of self-affirmation, and readers often seek their mirrors in books.*

Undeniably literature can give us pleasure. But perhaps more importantly, it also gives us wisdom and insight. Books are filled with ideas, ideas that can shape our thinking and alter our lives, ideas that can recreate society and impact the world at large. We naturally understand the value of the Bible, the Torah, and the Qur'an, but the power of literature is reflected in books like Tom Paine's *Common Sense* (which fueled the American Revolution), Harriet Beecher Stowe's *Uncle Tom's Cabin* (to which Lincoln attributed the start of the Civil War), Harper Lee's *To Kill a Mockingbird* (which urged on the civil rights movement), and Rachel Carson's

Silent Spring (which helped launch the environmental movement), to name just a few. Reading both fiction and nonfiction opens new vistas, reveals the multifaceted human condition, and helps us to see our place in the world.

In this chapter, will be considering some of the more important issues that children's books address—particularly the social, psychological, and political issues. It is also crucial that we understand the role of literature in a free society. A society without readers is a society in trouble, because it must necessarily be a society of followers. And finally, we should remind ourselves that among the first acts of history's most notorious tyrants has been to burn the books. And what are these despots afraid of? The free exchange of ideas is always a threat to an oppressor. So we will close the chapter with a discussion of the critical, and sometimes contentious, issue of censorship and intellectual freedom.

Cultural Diversity and Inclusion

Among the most important issues of our time are the twin concerns of diversity and inclusion. Diversity, of course, refers to recognizing and celebrating our individual differences. Inclusion refers to bringing together individuals of varying cultural backgrounds in order to build a stronger and more vibrant society. A diverse society is one that offers a broader range of experiences and ideas. And an inclusive society is one that embraces and takes advantage of its diversity. So what does this have to do with children's literature? Reading itself reinforces social norms and attitudes. In short, it has the power to shape our view of society. And, since social attitudes are formed at a very early age, children's literature can play a significant role in nurturing a prosperous and dynamic culture.

Unfortunately, world history often reveals an unending saga of the powerful subduing and oppressing the weak. And in too many cases, human suffering and tragedy result from an irrational fear of the "other" and an equally irrational belief in the superiority of one's own people. In the United States, particularly, the powerful and weak (the rulers and the ruled) were often identified by physical traits, beginning when white Europeans tried to supplant the Indigenous people (who happened to have had copper skin tones) and then imported people from Africa (who happened to be black) to do the hard labor. In time, Asians would be added to the mix. Racism, which has long been a characteristic of human beings, became a disease with inhuman consequences. Here we will examine the representation in children's books of the four principal cultural groups that have suffered discrimination in the United States: American Indians, African Americans, Latinos/as, and Asian Americans. But the general principles can be applied to anyone who is, for any reason, looked upon as an "outsider."

American Indians

Some estimates place the death rate of Indigenous inhabitants of the Western Hemisphere at 95 percent (some 100 million people) in the century after Columbus landed. A great many of these deaths inadvertently resulted from diseases the Europeans carried and against which the Indigenous peoples had no immunity, but wholesale slaughter was not beyond the pale for the European conquerors. In the United States, the scars still remain in the form of decimated Indigenous nations whose descendants live impoverished lives on remnants of their former land reserved for them by the U.S. government (the reservation or the "Rez," as many American Indians term it). The nomenclature used to describe ethnic populations is often problematic. "Native Americans" was once preferred, but "Indigenous Peoples" has become increasingly popular, and in Canada they are called "First Nations." The forged term, Amerindian, has not caught on widely. In fact, many prefer to be identified by their tribal affiliation—Cherokee, Navajo, Ojibwa, Sioux, and so on. Here we will opt for "American Indian," simply for clarity and simplicity, if not for accuracy.

American Indians have long been the subject of a mythology that continues to cloud the general public's perception. In the past, and all too often, the image of an American Indian was that of a beaded, feathered warrior in animal skins and moccasins. For a long time, children's picture books either ignored the American Indian altogether or fell back on the stereotypes. Perhaps many still do. American Indians argue that even today's picture books rely too heavily on these old images and fail to portray the modern American Indian realistically. Indeed, by and large, picture books about American Indians still feature the traditional conceptions and ignore the fact that currently in the United States about 2 million American Indians live like everyone else with homes, televisions, computers, cars, careers, and hobbies. But they also enjoy a rich and ancient heritage, which many celebrate in rituals such as the tribal powwow, a colorful and engaging experience that should not be missed. Unfortunately, far too many are still subject to racial discrimination and lack the social advantages accorded to white America. And all these facets of the American Indian experience are important subject matter in books for children and young adults.

The most authentic examples of American Indian literature are found in the folktales that have been collected over the years (including those by Joseph Bruchac, Craig Kee Strete, and others). The best of these children's versions of the folktales identify the specific American Indian tribal affiliations (e.g., Iroquois, Shoshone, Osage) and the Native tellers themselves. (For a fuller discussion of folktales, see Chapter 7.)

Two important and popular types of American Indian literature are historical fiction and nonfiction. Since about 1970, the predominant theme of this literature has been the correction of misconceptions (about the relationships between whites and American Indians, for example). Of course, children are keen to learn about the legendary American Indians—particularly those who resisted (without ultimate success) the encroachment of the white settlers and the U.S. Calvary. Some of the best books are the factual accounts (as we will see, truth is often stranger and sometimes more fascinating than fiction) or fictionalized history (see chapters 9 and 10 for a further discussion of these literary genres). Scott O'Dell was one of the earliest children's writers to offer the Indigenous point of view of historical events. His *Sing Down the Moon*, first published in 1970, is a fictionalized account of a factual event, the brutal, forced relocation of the Navajo in the nineteenth century. Russell Freedman's nonfictional *Indian Chiefs* describes an equally tragic story. It is a history of six of the celebrated leaders of the nineteenth-century American Indians facing overwhelming odds in their struggle against the encroaching white American government. This is a view Americans seldom got when watching the 1950s and 1960s television Westerns. In the realm of fiction, one of the earliest stories to explore the plight of modern-day Indigenous peoples is Margaret Craven's *I Heard the Owl Call My Name* (1967), a story for older readers about a dying priest sent to work in a First Nations parish on the coast of British Columbia. The sparse, elegant prose describes the quickly vanishing way of life. The priest, while coming to terms with his own mortality, grows to love and respect the traditional native culture, as it struggles to survive in the modern world. Although O'Dell, Freedman, and Craven are not of Indigenous heritage, they perceptively and movingly portray the dilemma of the clash of cultures and its effect on individuals.

Joseph Bruchac, who, like so many of us, is of mixed ethnicity, part of which is native Abenaki, has written many award-winning books about Indigenous culture in America. His novel, *Code Talker*, is based on the true story of how Navajo Marines used their unbreakable language code to dispatch military messages during the Second World War. On a more personal level is Ignatia Broker's *Night Flying Woman: An Ojibway Narrative*, describing the life of the author's great-great-grandmother and the uprooting of her people by nineteenth-century whites. And Sherman Alexie's *The Absolutely True Diary of a Part-Time Indian* is a coming-of-age story (partly autobiographical) that frankly portrays the struggles of a teenager growing up on a modern-day reservation. Alexie is one of the most popular of the Indigenous writers publishing today. Among the other significant writers of Indigenous heritage who have emerged in the last few decades are Louise Erdrich, Virginia Driving Hawk Snede, and, more recently, Canadian writer Jan Bourdeau Waboose.

So you see, books about American Indian culture come in a wide variety and reveal the many facets of native life and history. What we should look for in culturally conscious books are portraits of American Indians as individuals, sensitive descriptions of American Indian cultural traditions, and an awareness that each American Indian society is a distinctive cultural entity—that there are Creek, Iroquois, Sioux, and so on. The best books reject demeaning vocabulary, artificial dialogue, and cruel and insensitive Indian stereotypes. Donnarae MacCann suggests that we ask ourselves, "Is there anything in the book that would make a Native American child feel embarrassed or hurt to be what he or she is? Can the child look at the book and recognize and feel good about what he or she sees?" (quoted in Harris 161). This is a yardstick we can use with all stories about other cultures.

African Americans

The Spanish first brought enslaved Africans from western Africa as early as 1526, and the first recorded Africans arrived in Jamestown, Virginia, in 1619, as indentured servants. (Slavery would come later.) So, in other words, Africans have been in the Americas almost from the beginning of European settlement. Again, terminology is important to understand. In the seventeenth and eighteenth centuries, most Black Americans, proud of their African heritage, preferred to be called "African." By the early nineteenth century, freed Black Americans, seeking wider acceptance in America, preferred the term "Negro" (just as European Americans would prefer being called "white" to "European"). "Negro" remained acceptable well into the twentieth century, but has been largely replaced. By the 1960s and the emergence of protest movements, "Black" became a signal of pride and many still prefer that term (the Congressional Black Caucus, for example, and, more recently, the "Black Lives Matter" movement). Others, still, prefer "people of color," which has not entirely caught on perhaps because it is not easily turned into an adjective. We will use the term "Black" for our purposes here, but we need to be always mindful that words matter and connotations are frequently in flux.

Helen Bannerman's *Little Black Sambo*, first published in 1899, is the simple tale of a boy who outwits four ferocious tigers who are intent on eating him. He triumphs in the end and is rewarded with a huge stack of pancakes. It sounds pretty harmless, doesn't it? However, Bannerman, a Scotswoman living in British India, regrettably decided to illustrate the book herself, resulting in unfortunate caricatures of black people with huge round eyes and thick red lips (see Figure 2.1). To make matters worse, she chose to name her main character and his parents, "Little Black Sambo," "Black Mumbo" and "Black Jumbo"—demeaning names for persons of African descent. (Curiously, Bannerman's title character is not African at all, but from southern India, where Bannerman lived for a time—Africa may have people with dark skin tones, but it has no tigers.) And, the text of the book, far from being racist, is a very positive portrait of a clever and resourceful boy of color who has loving and caring parents. Nevertheless, by the mid-twentieth century in America, the book had become a symbol of racism and was removed from schools and libraries—for years it was virtually impossible to find in libraries and bookstores. Eventually it reemerged in new garb, notably in Julius Lester's retelling, *Sam and the Tigers* (2000), which alters the text and provides new illustrations, and Fred Marcellino's *The Story of Little Babaji* (1996). Marcellino's book is interesting

FIGURE 2.1 ■ An illustration from Helen Bannerman's 1899 book *The Story of Little Black Sambo*. Although unintended, Bannerman's artless portrait of her little hero would become the poster child for American racism.

THE STORY OF LITTLE BLACK SAMBO

in that it retains Bannerman's text verbatim, with the exception of the names of the characters, who are renamed Little Babaji, Mamaji, and Papaji, which are a little more Indian sounding. And Marcellino has substituted for Bannerman's rather naïve pictures his own elegant illustrations that give the story a great deal of class (see Figure 2.2). The result has redeemed Bannerman's classic, which we can all now enjoy without discomfort.

When it comes to the characterization of Black Americans in children's books, the history is not always very flattering. In the past when Black Americans were portrayed in literature (which was not all that frequently) they were often stereotypical caricatures; but, there are interesting exceptions. In Mark Twain's classic *Huckleberry Finn*, first published in 1884/1885, we find that Huck, a boy from the wrong side of the tracks as it were, is constantly in trouble, and his best friend is a runaway slave referred to as "Nigger Jim." Modern readers may wince at this appellation, but it is historically faithful to the time and place—the early-nineteenth century mid-America. But more important is the fact that Jim is, arguably, the most honorable character in the book, a sharp contrast to the white thugs, ruffians, crooks, and fools that populate Huck's world.

Of course, this sensitivity to symbols is the result of the tremendous burden of conscience the United States bears from the historic treatment of the millions of Africans brought to America in servitude. Throughout most of American history,

THE STORY of LITTLE BABAJI

FIGURE 2.2 ■ Fred Marcellino's stylish reillustrations for Bannerman's *Little Black Sambo* and a new name for the hero transform what has long been regarded as an icon of politically incorrect literature into the classic tale it really is.

racial and cultural divides have been the norm. This deplorable history has left scars that remain to this day, which is why it is important that we speak specifically to this issue of racial and cultural injustice, discrimination, and maltreatment. But is also important that we try to raise our children without the prejudices that have so long been a shameful part of our national character.

Aside from *Huckleberry Finn*, few mainstream literary works included important and positive Black characters until well into the twentieth century. And the overwhelming majority of the country's authors were white. The earliest significant body of literature from African Americans came in the 1920s with the so-called Harlem Renaissance, Langston Hughes being the most prominent among writers for children—his poetry remains much loved today. The literature of the 1920s sought to give Black Americans pride and a sense of their history. In 1945, Jesse C. Jackson (not the preacher-activist) published *Call Me Charley*, one of the earliest adolescent books with a Black protagonist, Charley, who must gain acceptance when he attends an all-white school. Although today African American readers may object because Charley eventually fits in and is accepted because he adopts the ways of his white classmates, we have to recognize the book as a landmark. And, for the time period, the sentiments ring true, perhaps because the story was based on the author's own experiences. In the 1960s came the Black Arts Movement, a more revolutionary effort comprised of politically involved Black artists, poets, novelists, and others. This movement, through a variety of artistic forms, emphasized the injustices of the past, greater realism, and the empowerment of Black Americans. The movement itself eventually dissipated, in part due to its stridency, but it inspired writers like James Baldwin, Nikki Giovanni, and Maya Angelou, all of whom wrote, at one time or another, books for children. These influences continue to dominate children's literature featuring Black American characters to this day.

Interestingly, one of the first picture books featuring an African American protagonist was by a white Jewish illustrator/storyteller, Ezra Jack Keats. *The Snowy Day* (1962) is the quiet portrait of a very young boy, dressed in a bright red snow suit, exploring his city neighborhood following a heavy snowstorm. Only the illustrations indicate he is Black—the text never mentions it. And his actions are simply those of a typical 5-year-old. In other words, it is clear that his color is not supposed to matter. However, later picture books with Black characters are more likely to focus on the Black community. Lucile Clifton's touching poetic picture book series featuring a young Black boy, Everett Anderson (*Some of the Days of Everett Anderson*, *Everett Anderson's Good-bye*, and others), describe a working-class Black family, complete with realistic dialogue—a working mother, an absent father (who eventually dies), and a young boy's fears, longings, hopes, and dreams.

By the end of the twentieth century, children's literature by African Americans had come into its own, with many award-winning writers, including Christopher Paul Curtis, Virginia Hamilton, Walter Dean Myers, John Steptoe, Mildred Taylor, and Jacqueline Woodson. The trend in today's books about African Americans is to portray what is distinctive about African American life—rather than to emphasize the mythical melting pot that was once supposed to be the American dream. Christopher Paul Curtis's *Bud, Not Buddy*, portrays life in the Black community in Depression-era Michigan, and his *The Watsons Go to Birmingham—1963* takes us to Alabama to witness the dreadful church bombing that killed four innocent children and was a turning point in the civil rights movement. And Carolivia Herron's *Nappy Hair* is a lively picture book about a young Black girl's unruly, "nappy" hair—a feature that was once a source of ridicule from racist whites. But in Herron's story, the hair becomes a proud symbol of the girl's Black heritage, reaching all the way back to Africa. Herron deftly recreates the joyous Black dialect with its pattern of call and response (also an echo of African roots).

In 1970, the American Library Association began awarding the Coretta Scott King Award, specifically for African American authors and illustrators of children's books. Despite these great strides, books by and about African Americans continue to be underrepresented in American publishing (as do those of all other non-European white ethnic groups). There is still work to be done.

Latinos/as

Over the years, the cultural group now known as Latinos has been referred to as Mexican American, Chicano, and Hispanic. These terms are not interchangeable, and no single term captures the true diversity of this culture. *Hispanic*, for example, refers to individuals from the Spanish-speaking cultures of Mexico, Central America, and South America, whereas *Latino* includes all of Latin America, including Portuguese-speaking Brazilians. However, none of the terms really accommodates the Indigenous people of these regions (such as the Zapotec in Mexico.) So, with these caveats, in this text we use the term Latino (Latina is the feminine form) because it is slightly more inclusive.

Latinos now constitute the largest "minority" group in the United States—and the fastest-growing. Traditionally, the Latino culture in the United States has been characterized by the Spanish language, the Roman Catholic Church (but not exclusively), and the folk traditions of Latin America (which includes Mexico, Central America, and South America). This group is still vastly underrepresented in children's books, and its portrayal has been controversial. Unfortunately, we still find in the modern media the unfair and negative stereotypes of the criminal alien or the helpless victim, the volatile Latin temperament, the male machismo, and so on. Although children's books usually avoid these stereotypes, earlier books portray an overabundance of poor migrant workers or other rural laborers. This image is quite contrary to the reality. Today, most Latinos are city dwellers, and they can be found in all walks of life.

We are now seeing more and more writers of Latino heritage producing some very fine works for young readers. One popular Latino author, Gary Soto, has distinguished himself as both a poet and a storyteller, with prose works like *Baseball in April* and *Buried Onions* and poetry collections including *A Fire in My Hands* and *Canto Familia*. His subjects are modern-day Latino children pursuing their hopes and dreams like all other children. Pat Mora has published several poetry collections, including *Borders*, *Chants*, and *Communion*, in addition to several family stories for young children, such as *A Birthday Basket for Tia*. Mora's poems for young children are filled with images of the Southwest and Latino culture, and throughout she scatters Spanish expressions, reminders that the Latino culture is often a bilingual culture. Sandra Cisneros gained fame for her book for older children, *The House on Mango Street*. And Pam Muñoz Ryan's Belpré Award–winning *Esperanza Rising* is an historical novel set in Mexico and California in the early twentieth century. This is a moving account of a young girl's coming of age after she, her widowed mother, and her grandmother (her *abuela*) are cheated out of their vast Mexican landholdings and forced to flee to California, where Esperanza learns what it is like to be part of an oppressed working class. All these writers focus on the importance of the family—especially the extended family—which is key to Latinos' personal identity. The characters also tend to be bilingual, which allows them to hold on to their traditional heritage as well as function successfully in the English-speaking culture. In fact, the prevalence of the Spanish language in the United States has inspired a new trend in modern picture books—the dual-language book, such as Carmen Lomas Garza's *Family Picture/ Cuadros de Familia*.

In 1996, the American Library Association established the Pura Belpré Award for the Latino/a author and illustrator whose work "best portrays, affirms, and celebrates the Latino cultural experience in an outstanding work of literature for children and youth." (Pura Belpré was the first Puerto Rican librarian in New York City who, when she could find no stories portraying Latino children, wrote her own.) Past winners include authors Julia Alvarez, Margarita Engle, and Pam Muñoz Ryan for their writing, and Yuyi Morales and Joe Cepeda for their illustrations. Like African Americans, Latinos have become a significant social and political force in American society. There has never been a greater need for sensitive, honest, and intelligent children's books representing Latino culture than there is today.

Asian Americans

The term *Asian American* is another catch-all word; it includes Chinese Americans, Japanese Americans, as well as those from other Asian nations—Korea, Cambodia, Thailand, and so on. Asian Americans, like the other groups we have discussed so far, have been subjected to unkind stereotypes—misogynistic males and submissive females, all speaking English very poorly and being reticent and docile. A controversial example of this tendency to stereotype is Claire Huchet Bishop's *The Five Chinese Brothers*, first published in 1938. For years this book was celebrated as a minor children's classic, but in the aftermath of the civil rights movement, when society began to question all stereotypes, the book, most particularly for its illustrations, was criticized as promoting ethnic stereotypes. The text tells us, for example, that the five brothers "all look alike," and Kurt Wiese's illustrations portray caricatures of Oriental stereotypes. (This story has also been faulted for its violence, but as we will see, many folktales are riddled with violence—and they get away with it.) Similar criticism has been leveled toward the more recent award-winning *Tikki-Tikki Tembo*, retold by Arlene Mosel and illustrated by Blair Lent. In this case, a Japanese folktale is given a Chinese setting (although, oddly, some of the clothing is clearly Japanese)—the implication apparently being that American children would not know the difference or care. Certainly a writer of fiction can exercise some license—unlike the writer of nonfiction (see Chapter 10)—but the prevailing attitude today is that cultures, when portrayed in children's books, should be depicted with both sensitivity and accuracy. Children's books should not be in the business of perpetuating offensive or insensitive cultural stereotypes. In fact, children's books should seize the opportunity they have to provide young readers with positive and accurate impressions of the world's rich cultural heritage.

One excellent way to introduce children to Asian culture is through myths and legends. Many of these are now being illustrated for young children. For a good example, see Sanjay Patel and Emily Haynes's *Ganesha's Sweet Tooth*, a brightly illustrated picture book, and Amy Novesky's *Elephant Prince: The Story of Ganesh*, both stories from the Hindu. Kashmira Sheth's *Monsoon Afternoon*, illustrated by the Japanese artist Yoshiko Jaeggi (a truly international collaboration) focuses on the customs of Hindu India. A Chinese folktale is the subject of Ai-Ling Lui's *Yeh Shen*, a Chinese Cinderella beautifully illustrated by Ed Young. Young has written and illustrated many children's books that display his passion for his native China, and his art reflects the influence of traditional Chinese painting. His *Lon Po Po: A Red-Riding Hood Story from China* won the 1990 Caldecott Medal.

In addition to traditional folktales, we can find many very fine picture books that accurately evoke Asian and Asian American cultures. Allen Say's books—such as *Grandfather's Journey* (winner of the 1994 Caldecott Medal), which tells the story of Japanese American immigrants—are fine examples of culturally sensitive narratives. Sandhya Rao's award-winning picture book, *My Mother's Sari*, relates the simple story of a child learning the meaning and mystery of the traditional Indian garment, the sari.

Laurence Yep's *Dragonwings*, a work for older children, describes life as it was lived in San Francisco's Chinatown in the early 1900s. In *Coolies*, Rosanna Yin describes the experiences of the earliest Chinese immigrants, the workers who helped lay the transcontinental railroad in the nineteenth century. *A Step from Heaven*, by An Na, describes the difficult experiences of a young Korean girl growing up in America. The harrowing story of the Japanese American internment during the Second World War has been the subject of several moving books, both fiction and nonfiction. Perhaps the most famous is the autobiographical *Farewell to Manzanar* by Jeanne Wakatsuki and James D. Houston.

Finally, Grace Lin, who built a reputation as a popular picture book author/illustrator, has recently gained fame as a novelist. And her *The Year of the Dog* is the first of a popular series, the Pacy Lin series, about Pacy, the young daughter of Taiwanese immigrants growing up in America. These books, which are semi-autobiographical, have been celebrated for portraying the reality of living in a multicultural world, where each individual must find his or her place, far from ethnic stereotypes. Her recent Newbery Honor Book, *Where the Mountain Meets the Moon*, and its companion, *The Starry River of the Sky*, beautifully weave Chinese folk legends into a magical adventure narrative. (Incidentally, I fully realize the absurdity of grouping Indian, Chinese, Japanese, Korean, Vietnamese, and the rest into one overarching category. Chinese and Indian cultures, for example, are no more alike than North American and South American. We live in a complex world, and we cannot do it justice in a brief discussion such as this. The best we can do is to raise awareness of the complex issues.)

Other Cultures

It is now possible to find children's books on a wide variety of world cultures, from virtually every continent. Among the most prominent, perhaps, are books on the Jewish experience. Judaism as a culture transcends national boundaries. Jewish Americans have long played crucial roles in American culture, in the arts, business, education, and politics. However, anti-Semitism has been a blot on Western civilization, in the United States as well as Europe. Of course, when we think of anti-Semitism, most of us see visions of the Holocaust and the slaughter of 6 million innocent victims of the Nazi regime. Indeed, when it comes to children's literature about Judaism, stories of the Holocaust dominate the list. Anne Frank's *The Diary of a Young Girl*, a teenager's firsthand account of the horrors of the Nazi occupation of the Netherlands, is the most famous. Other memoirs include Aranka Siegal's *Upon the Head of a Goat: A Childhood in Hungary, 1939–1944*, which describes the atrocities perpetrated in eastern Europe, and Judith Kerr's *When Hitler Stole Pink Rabbit*.

Aside from books about the Holocaust, books about Jewish culture tend to fall into three categories: folktales, informational books, and contemporary novels. Nobel Laureate Isaac Bashevis Singer recorded many tales of Jewish life, including *Shlemiel Went to Warsaw and Other Stories*, *Zlateh the Goat and Other Stories*, and *Mazel and Shlimazel*. These are partly his own original stories and partly retellings of traditional Jewish folktales that he heard as a child. They are filled with a rich sense of humanity and the warm humor often associated with Jewish culture. Informational books generally describe Jewish customs and religious rituals. Michele Lee Meyer's *My Daddy Is Jewish and My Mommy Is Christian* is a picture book that describes circumstances becoming increasingly familiar in U.S. society. Among the novelists, one of the most celebrated is Chaim Potok, whose *My Name Is Asher Lev* is the story of a young Hasidic Jew, an artist engaged in the conflict between his faith and his art, as well as tradition and modernity.

Not surprisingly, one culture that has attracted tremendous interest in the past few years is Islam. (We should perhaps say "cultures," though, since, like

Christianity and Judaism, the Muslim faith is practiced in many variations.) Recent books about the Muslim culture reveal several tendencies. Demi's *Muhammad* is a picture book describing the life of the prophet who founded the faith in the seventh century. Joelle Stoltz's *The Shadows of Ghadames* is a novel set in Libya in the nineteenth century that provides some historical perspective on Islam. And Elizabeth Fama's *Overboard*, which is set in Indonesia (the world's most populous Muslim country), is a contemporary story that brings together Muslims and Western Christians. Aisha Saaed's *Written in the Stars* is a rather sensational book for older readers, about an American Muslim teenager, whose conservative immigrant parents force her into an arranged marriage while on a family visit in Iran. To reveal the outcome would be a disservice.

The Importance of Diversity and Inclusion

Naturally, it is impossible to cover all cultures and ethnic groups, and any omission here is not intended as a slight. Combing the Internet can produce some interesting results. Any good book about a culture or a place or a people we do not know can make us better world citizens—tolerant, understanding, and empathetic. Rosa Guy, a distinguished writer of books for young adults (*The Friends*, *Ruby*, and others) and a native of the former British colony of Trinidad, has issued this call to arms for all cultural groups:

> *I reject the young of each succeeding generation who dare to say: "I don't understand you people . . . " "I can't stand those people . . . " or, "Do you see the way they act . . . ?" They are us! Created by us for a society which suits our ignorance.*
> *I insist that Every child understand this. I insist that Every child go out into the world with this knowledge: there are no good guys. There are no bad guys. We are all good guys. We are all bad guys. And we are all responsible for each other.* (34)

Another troubling issue is the relatively few number of authors from these various ethnic groups who are publishing books—and the relatively few books about these ethnic groups that are being published. The Cooperative Children's Book Center (CCBC) at the University of Wisconsin-Madison has been, since 1985, monitoring books by and about people of color and First/Native Nations (as mentioned, in Canada, Native Americans are known as First Nations). The CCBC reports that out of the 4,300 books published in 2015, which it reviewed, only 492 were about these four ethnic groups—African American, American Indian, Asian-Pacific American, and Latino/a (see Table A). That is less than 11.5 percent—even though, according to the 2015 U.S. census estimates, these groups make up over 35

TABLE A   This table indicates the total number of children's books received in the year 2015 by the Cooperative Children's Book Center (CCBC) at the University of Wisconsin-Madison, and identifies those books by and about African Americans, American Indians/First Nations, Asian Pacific/Asian Pacific Americans, and Latinos/as. We may assume the bulk of the remaining books were by and about Americans and Canadians of European descent (in other words, "whites"). The disparity is remarkable and indicates the dramatic underrepresentation of these populations in the published works.

Total Books Received	4,300
By African Americans	16
About African Americans	269
By American Indians/First Nations	19
About American Indians/First Nations	42
By Asian-Pacifics/Asian-Pacific Americans	23
About Asian-Pacifics/Asian-Pacific Americans	113
By Latino/as	8
About Latino/as	2

percent of the population. And the disparity is even greater when we look at how relatively few authors are identified as belonging to these ethnic categories.

Some critics insist that only members of an ethnic group can honestly write about that group. August Wilson, the celebrated African American playwright (and perhaps the foremost American playwright of the last half of the twentieth century), argues that "someone who does not share the specifics of a culture remains outside, no matter how astute a student or well meaning the intentions" (quoted in Harris 42). Thus, Wilson insists that only African Americans should write about African Americans, only American Indians about American Indians, and so on. However, another African American, the critic Henry Louis Gates, Jr., disagrees: "No human culture is so inaccessible to someone who makes the effort to understand, to learn, to inhabit another world" (Gates 30). In other words, Gates believes that a writer does not have to be African American to write about African Americans, but that a writer does have to know a lot about them and has to be able to empathize with them, to walk in their shoes. Let us hope that Gates is correct, for that offers us the promise of a better world.

This discussion barely scratches the surface of the issue of race and culture in children's books. What is most important is that we are aware of our rich and diverse racial and cultural heritage and that we consciously keeping looking for ways to inform young readers, to broaden their minds, and foster their acceptance and understanding of those who come from backgrounds different from theirs. Mark Twain wrote, "Travel is fatal to prejudice, bigotry, and narrow-mindedness." In the absence of travel, wide and varied reading is perhaps the next best thing.

Social Diversity and Inclusion

In addition to the need for cultural diversity and inclusion are a number of issues that we might describe as matters of social diversity and inclusion. These affect everyone, regardless of ethnic background or place of origin, and most are, quite simply, the problems we all face growing up. And, not unexpectedly, they are the subjects of many children's and YA books—both fiction and nonfiction.

Sexual Development

Sexuality has always been one of the most difficult issues for adults to broach with children. Naturally, most people think that these are issues that should be handled in the home by parents and guardians—and that would be ideal. Unfortunately, for a variety of reasons, this does not always happen. Fortunately, a large number of honest and accurate books are now available to assist diffident adults in getting the necessary information to children. Take, for example, the light-hearted (but effective) *Mommy Laid an Egg* by Babette Cole, or, for older readers, *It's Perfectly Normal: Changing Bodies, Growing Up, Sex, and Sexual Health* by Robie Harris (illustrated by Michael Emberley). Both books employ humor to remove the stigma of discussing bodily functions with children. But, at the same time, neither book sugarcoats the issues. Adults have to face the uncomfortable fact that children are going to learn about sex with or without their parents' or guardians' help—ideally, it is with their help.

Sexual Preference and Gender Identity

Two other issues that we should not ignore are sexual preference and gender identity. When teenagers, for example, face questions concerning sexual preference and gender identity, one of the most comforting things to know is that one is not alone, odd, or out of the ordinary. Fortunately, LGBTQ (lesbian, gay, bisexual, transgender, and questioning) themes are becoming more common in books for YA readers and a wide range of topics can be found, from David Levithan's *Boy Meets Boy* (2008), which can be described as a romantic comedy, and the same author's *Two Boys Kissing* (2014), a novel based on a true story, to Julie Anne Peters' *Luna* (2004), about a transgender teen, to Francesca Lia Block's *Weetzie Bat* (1989), a groundbreaking work of magical realism for YA readers that deals with a variety of lifestyles and sensitive issues.

Although, as we might expect, most books dealing with sexuality are for YA readers, it is possible to find gay-themed stories intended for very young readers. And, you may ask, why is that necessary? Michael Willhoite's *Daddy's Roommate*, first published in 1991, helps to answer that question. This is a picture book for preschoolers describing the weekends a young boy spends with his father and his father's male partner. The situation described is idealized, of course, with the boy's mother accepting of her ex-husband's choices. But the fact is that, today, many children are raised by gay and lesbian couples. Why should they be made to feel their family arrangements are any less acceptable than anyone else's? Some of the reasons we read books are to broaden our minds, enrich our experiences, help us understand difficult things, and give us empathy. *Daddy's Roommate* provides honest, sensitive treatment of a subject many people find difficult to discuss. The simple illustrations and straightforward story told by a child narrator provide just the right amount of information for very young readers, and the book concludes with the statement that being gay is just "one more kind of love." Leslea Newman and Diana Souza's *Heather Has Two Mommies* is a sort of counterpart to Willhoite's book, in which a lesbian couple is raising a child. It is never too early to begin the campaign to stamp out bigotry and prejudice.

No one is suggesting that these books should become part of the classroom curriculum (although that may come in time). Nor were these books ever intended for that. But it is important for us to realize that these issues are not isolated, and they affect a broad spectrum of our population. Knowing about some of these titles, being aware that these subjects are dealt with in good children's books, will come in handy at some point—for everyone. When the appropriate time comes, you will know it and you will have the resources you need. Learning about the difficult issues of life through reputable books, sensitively written, and under the guidance of a caring and knowledgeable adult is surely preferable to picking up rumor and misinformation from the streets and playgrounds.

The Physically, Emotionally, and Intellectually Challenged

Another change taking place in our society is a more receptive attitude toward individuals with special needs. These individuals were once virtually ignored in children's books, undoubtedly a holdover from the time when people with physical, emotional, or intellectual differences were largely hidden away from society—either institutionalized or secluded at home. Society is now more sensitive to the needs of these individuals. Our laws now recognize the existence of individuals with physical disabilities, and our schools seek to include and accommodate all children. Although this is a subject still not widely addressed in children's books, a few titles deserve mention. Perhaps the most famous of these books is Robert Kraus's *Leo the Late Bloomer*, about a young tiger who develops more slowly than others. Taro Yashima's *Crow Boy* is about a Japanese boy suffering from shyness; Lucille Clifton's *My Friend Jacob* describes the relationship between a young black boy and his older white friend who is intellectually challenged. Virginia Hamilton's *Sweet Whispers, Brother Rush* is about a family coping with an inherited mental disorder.

And physical disabilities are featured in such books as Carolyn Meyer's *Killing the Kudu*, which tackles stereotypes about people in wheelchairs. It is fairly safe to say that there is virtually no disability—from autism to speech disorders—that is not addressed in some children's book. The best books present their subjects with sensitivity and emphasize the need for society to embrace all individuals. And many stories reveal that disabilities do not prevent one from becoming a good friend and productive member of society.

Transition and Tragedy

In many ways, human beings are always in a state of transition—life circumstances rarely remain static for long. And for children, particularly, change is practically the only constant—moving through the stages of development, advancing through the grades in school, acquiring new siblings, making new friends, moving to new homes. And most children adjust to these changes readily. Other changes are more difficult. All too frequently, young children have to make serious adjustments in their lives—parents divorce, a friend or relative dies, tragedy strikes. There was a time when adults thought that children needed to be sheltered from the tragedies of life. But leaving children in ignorance of what is happening may be more frightening to them—what is mysterious and unknown to us is almost always worse than the reality. (The scariest part of a horror film is often the part when we don't know what is lurking behind the door or hiding in the attic.) Fortunately, a lot of excellent children's books are available that introduce young readers in intelligent and sensitive ways to some of the hard knocks of life. In this section we will look specifically at books dealing with divorce, death, and war and violence—issues that sadly affect children more than we would like to think. The best children's books on these subjects are those that present the issues as transitional—part of the passage of life to which we must adjust. This means that we expect books that are open and honest, wise and compassionate. In addition to the books mentioned here, see Chapter 9 for further discussion of these issues.

Divorce

It does not seem to matter what the age, children are sorely impacted by their parents' divorce. Even in unhappy homes, a family breakup can be devastating. Children are likely to see it as the end their world—which, in some ways, it is. Things will never be quite the same again. Some will blame themselves. Some will hate one or the other parent—or, just as likely, they will hate both. They are going to be very angry. And they are going to be very sad.

What books can do is help them see that the fault is not with them, that their parents still love them, that they can survive the turmoil in their lives, and even that good things often do come out of bad things. Books about divorce can be found for all ages of young readers. Laurie Krasny Brown and Marc Brown's *Dinosaurs Divorce* is unusual in that it is really a handbook for very young children—perhaps through first grade—whose parents divorce. It is ostensibly a picture book, but with chapters on topics like stepparents, stepsiblings, and sharing holidays. The fact that the characters are dinosaurs helps to broaden the appeal of this book—it is every child's book on divorce. Sandra Levins' *Was It the Chocolate Pudding?: A Story for Little Kids about Divorce*, also for very young children, is told from the point of view of a child and deals with the many complicated adjustments that divorce entails—and the title, of course, is a reference to the self-blame that haunts many children.

A great number of novels for older readers deal with divorce—either directly or tangentially—which suggests how common divorce is in our society. A long-time favorite is Beverly Cleary's *Dear Mr. Henshaw*, a Newbery Award–winning book, dealing with a sixth-grade boy's anger with his father after his parents' divorce. And Paula Danziger's *The Divorce Express*, for readers in their early teens, describes the hectic life of a girl who must commute by bus between her divorced parents' homes and deal with the crises in their lives—as well as in her own. Of course, what matters most is that children's books address the issues surrounding divorce with honesty and openness. (See Chapter 9 for a further discussion of family issues in children's literature.)

Death

Accepting death is often the first of life's hard hurdles that children must confront—the death of a pet, a grandparent, and even, sadly, a parent, a sibling, or a friend. As much as we would like to shelter our children from this greatest of life's sorrows, it just is not possible—nor is it wise to try. But it is helpful if we are aware of good books on the subject, books that can help the very young deal with these issues. Some of the best books on dying deal in metaphors young readers can grasp and these books also resist the temptation to offer simple platitudes.

It is important to remember that not everyone shares our own spiritual outlook and that there are many different ways to look at death. Not everyone is assuaged by the promise of an afterlife, as in Christianity or Islam. Some cultures, like Hinduism and Buddhism, embrace the concept of reincarnation. Other cultures, like Judaism, place the emphasis on this life and daily living—and not an afterlife. Some deny any afterlife at all. So when approaching the idea of death with children other than our own, it is wise for us to be aware of other beliefs, to respect their differences, and to honor other cultures.

Regardless of one's personal convictions about death, such a loss is painful. The sorrow is difficult and necessary, but it is not permanent. And that is probably the best message for very young readers. Margaret Wise Brown's classic *The Dead Bird* is a simple picture book about a group of children who find a dead bird and proceed to give it a burial. After the obsequies, which are solemn and touching, the children are soon back at play—going about the business of their lives, as they should be. Death is presented as part of the natural cycle of life, as *The Book of Common Prayer* correctly tells us, "In the midst of life, we are in death." Although, perhaps Brown's more important message is that "Life goes on."

One effective way to deal with the concept of death is metaphorically—that is, using symbols to convey our ideas about death. A metaphor is simply a comparison, usually to help to make an abstract or complex idea more concrete and therefore more easily understood. An example is Oliver Jeffers's *The Heart and the Bottle*, in which a young girl's grief over the death of her father—which is only implied, never obliquely stated—causes her to "bottle up" her heart—quite literally. But keeping her heart in the bottle also prevents her from moving on with her own life and experiencing other feelings, such as happiness or wonder. Only when she has accepted the loss and recognizes that beauty and joy still exist in the world is she able to let her heart out of the bottle and once again embrace life—while still keeping the good memories.

Wolf Erlbruch's *Duck, Death and the Tulip* is, at first glance, a rather startling book. It tells the story of Death, personified as a skeletal figure clad in a long plaid coat, who courts a relationship with an inquisitive Duck, who wants to know what death is like. They share several experiences and, at one point, Death experiences a sudden chill and Duck offers comfort and cradles Death in her arms. Later, when her own end approaches and Duck herself suddenly feels cold, she asks Death to help keep her warm. It is a profoundly touching scene. Duck then dies quietly, and Death, after laying a tulip on her lifeless body, gently places Duck in the great river (the book does not broach the subject of an afterlife) and nudges her on her way. The river suggests the constant ow of time, of course. Death itself is almost moved by Duck's passing but then utters the nal line: "But that's Life." The book presents life and death as seamless parts of a beautiful process (perhaps symbolized by the tulip, which is never actually referred to in the text). Its message is that we all walk with death and that death itself, rather than an adversary to be feared, is part of life, as natural as birth, growth, and love. Without speculating on religious implications or diminishing the sense of loss, Erlbruch offers a simple, straightforward view of this inscrutable subject and makes it accessible for even very young children. (See Chapter 9 for a further exploration of death and dying in children's literature.)

War and Violence

Another controversial issue that often arises in discussions of children's book is the place of war and violence. Surprisingly, we can find books for very young children on such unlikely subjects as war and its grim effects and even street violence. Why introduce such elements into a child's book? Sadly, as with the other controversial issues we have discussed, we cannot shelter children from the effects of these dreadful experiences. Today in America, far too many children know the tragedy of losing a parent to war or a sibling to street violence. We would not expect children to understand the politics of war, or its history, or its purpose. (Do we understand that ourselves?) Instead, children's books on war deal with its effects on society, on families, on individuals. One profoundly moving book is Roberto Innocenti and Christophe Gallaz's *Rose Blanche*, a story of a young German girl who discovers a Nazi concentration camp during the Second World War and, risking her own life, secretly brings food to the prisoners. The uncompromising ending in which the girl is killed during a battle is sensitively handled and, although very sad, is not without hope for a better world. The stunning illustrations capture both the chilling and the poignant aspects of the time period (see Figure 2.3).

Toshi Maruki's *Hiroshima No Pika* is a children's picture book that describes the August morning in 1945 when the atomic bomb was dropped on Hiroshima. The simple but frank descriptions from a little girl's point of view, illustrated by stark, expressionistic paintings, provide a moving portrayal of an event that children should not have to experience. But children did experience that, and many more children today experience the tragedies of disease, war, starvation, and neglect. And this is why these books and others like them, despite their horrifying subjects, remain appropriate for children. If told with the proper sensitivity—common sense must always be our guide—these stories might encourage a more humane world in the future. It is never too early for children to learn empathy for others.

Violence is no stranger to children's literature (see the discussion on Mother Goose rhymes in Chapter 6). And, in addition to the violence of war, children's picture books have tackled such subjects as street violence and, yes, domestic violence. Eve Bunting's *Smoky Night* describes the violent events witnessed by a young boy and his family during the 1992 street riots in Los Angeles. The controversial illustrations by David Diaz won the Caldecott Medal in 1995. And Taylor Clark's 1992 picture book, *The House That Crack Built*, illustrated by Jan T. Dicks, deals with the tragedy of illegal drugs and drug addicts, described in poetry that mimics both the Mother Goose verse ("This Is the House That Jack Built") and hip-hop and rap music. It is a clever way to approach a very difficult subject, particularly for its intended audience, teenagers. In recent years, many YA novels, particularly, have appeared that deal with violence on many levels, beginning with the street gangs in S. E. Hinton's 1967 ground-breaking novel, *The Outsiders*, and going up to Suzanne Collins's *The Hunger Games* series. This is not

FIGURE 2.3 ■ The illustration by Roberto Innocenti from *Rose Blanche* (by Innocenti and Christophe Gallaz) depicts Rose Blanche, a German girl who has been bringing food to the prisoners in a concentration camp, when she discovers they have all been transported away. She stands, a solitary figure holding a purple flower, in marked contrast with the drab and desolated landscape, a poignant symbol of bravery and compassion.

to mention the violence found in Victorian novels for young readers—take a look at Stevenson's *Treasure Island* (how could we have a book about pirates without violence?).

Sadly, domestic violence is a reality in the lives of some children and even this topic has found its way into children's books—some, surprisingly, for very young children. Margaret Holmes's *A Terrible Thing* (2000) approaches the subject in a very general way—never describing the "terrible thing"—but it attempts to put the experience into some perspective and help a child through the unpleasant process. Carol McCleary's *My Daddy Lost His Temper* (2014) is clearly intended as a handbook for children in desperate situations.

It is pointless to deny that violence is a regrettable part of life. Children experience violence on the playground. And sibling disputes too often end in fisticuffs. Do we even have to mention the daily news? It's a pretty good bet that violent acts will play a major role in any half-hour news program. Until human nature undergoes a dramatic change, violent acts will continue to be an unfortunate part of our culture. Perhaps this is the best argument for children's books that deal with violence—particularly those that treat it with frankness and honesty, with all its shame and horror. And many experts today suggest that violence in books can be therapeutic, providing a much-needed outlet for pent-up emotions (an outlet far more socially acceptable than a rumble on the playground). Also, if the violence in literature is portrayed with its unfortunate consequences, then it becomes less glamorous. In the end, facing the truth will always triumph over living with ignorance and deception. Violence portrayed with its moral consequences may, therefore, provide a healthy outlet (see Creasey). Furthermore, it is doubtful that the children who are reading such literature are the bullies on the playground.

Bibliotherapy

Related to all these controversial issues is the concept of bibliotherapy—the use of books as therapy for good mental health. The term itself goes back to the 1930s, but the idea that reading books can be part of the healing process for both mind and body is very old indeed. Above the entrance to the library at Thebes in ancient Greece was an inscription that announced: "A Healing Place for the Soul."

For very young children, some of the most famous examples of books used for bibliotherapy are the Berenstain Bears books by Stan and Jan Berenstain. The characters are a typical family—mother, father, daughter, son—except, of course, they are bears. Each book addresses a very specific childhood experience and shows typical responses from both children and parents to these situations (*The Berenstain Bears and the Bad Dream* and *The Berenstain Bears Go to the Doctor* are two examples). The Berenstains, who began writing in the 1960s and whose work has been continued by their son, Mike, have evolved with society, writing stories about children who are physically challenged and children who encounter drug dealers. As with most other didactic literature, the plots of these books are predictable and contrived, and the characters a bit flat, since all else is sacrificed for the lesson being taught.

Also popular are books such as those found in the Good Behavior Series, written for preschoolers, such as Marine Agassi's *Hands Are Not for Hitting* (2002), Elizabeth Verdick's *Feet Are Not for Kicking* (2008), and, for older readers, Pamela Espeland's *Hey, Dude, That's Rude! (Get Some Manners)* (2007). Espeland's book, which employs a somewhat more sophisticated humor, including sarcasm, seems more appropriate for older readers (from about fourth grade and up) who are often resistant to heavy-handed didacticism. However, life lessons can be also found in books that simply tell good and wise stories, without resorting to didacticism. (Previously we mentioned Ezra Jack Keats's *The Snowy Day*, which is the first of a series of books about Peter, a young boy growing up in the inner city and dealing with bullies, a new baby sister in *Peter's Chair*, and a first "crush" on a girl in *A Letter to Amy*. Also mentioned was Lucille Clifton's series of picture books in poetry, describing the transitions in a young child's life, including the death of a parent in *Everett Anderson's Goodbye*, a mother's new boyfriend in *Everett Anderson's 1, 2, 3*, and, boldly, child abuse in *One of the Problems of Everett Anderson*—all for children between the ages of about 4 and 6 years.)

The problem with bibliotherapy is not whether it works—people have been assuaged and emboldened by books for centuries—but how it should be used. Do we wait until a grandparent dies to hunt down a children's book on death? And does the book have to be specifically about the death of a grandparent to do any good? Do we wait until a crisis occurs before sharing books about broken families? And does the book's crisis have to mirror our own? One librarian, Maeve Visser Knoth, has suggested that the best use of bibliotherapy is to encourage wide and deep reading that prepares children for life's eventualities—rather than to scramble for the perfect antidotal book when a difficult occasion arises. She writes:

> *I would rather inoculate children than treat the symptoms of the emotional trauma. We give children vaccinations against measles. We can't vaccinate against divorce, but we can give children some emotional knowledge to use when their families, or other families they know, do go through a divorce. I advocate that we read picture books about death and divorce and new babies when no one is dying, when a marriage is strong, before anyone is pregnant.* (273–274)

Reading is for enjoyment, but it is also for enlightenment. In young children, especially, what they read will strongly influence what they feel, what they come to believe. This chapter, admittedly, has come with an agenda—the belief that the best way to address an issue is head on, that to ignore a problem is no solution, and that social justice for everyone should be our priority. In other words, children should be prepared for life, not sheltered from it.

Intellectual Freedom

Finally, we should say a word about censorship—which is the act of suppressing what people can read or even say. Censorship is usually exercised for moral, social, religious, political, or military purposes. Authoritarian governments are notorious for censoring written or spoken ideas that oppose them, and throughout history dictators and scoundrels have resorted to burning books they deemed threatening. History is filled with famous incidents of book burning. The First Emperor of China not only burned the books, but killed the scholars. Jewish manuscripts were destroyed by the Christians in thirteenth-century France. The conquering Spaniards destroyed much of the literature of the Mayans and Aztecs in the sixteenth century. Perhaps most famously, Adolf Hitler ordered the burning of books in Germany in 1933. And in the 1970s the Pinochet regime burned books in Chile. Indeed, America's founders realized the importance of protecting the written word. The First Amendment to the U.S. Constitution declares: "Congress shall make no law respecting an establishment of religion, or prohibiting the free exercise thereof; or abridging the freedom of speech, or of the press . . . ." Nevertheless, educators not infrequently encounter attempts to limit this freedom when it comes to choosing books for the classroom. Of course, any time an adult chooses a book for a child, a certain amount of discretion is involved (we call this taste or judgment). The problem occurs when a few individuals with strongly held beliefs attempt to dictate what everyone else should read. In this chapter we have mentioned a number of books that might raise concerns for some people—books about sex, about alternative lifestyles, about religious beliefs, or books with graphic violence are all potential targets. And, indeed, teachers daily face the persistent efforts by parents or by social, political, or religious organizations to ban certain books, certain subjects, certain points of view from the classroom.

Censorship of children's books is rooted in society's desire to protect the "innocence" of childhood. Its goal is to guard against elements deemed inappropriate for young readers—harsh language, sexual innuendos, death and dying, violence, and alternative religious beliefs or philosophies. But who in society makes these judgments? Adults? And which adults? What is their agenda? These are all legitimate questions. The following books have all been banned by some authority at one time or another: Mark Twain's *The Adventures of Huckleberry Finn*, Anne Frank's *Diary of a Young Girl*, Dr. Seuss's *If I Ran the Zoo*, Maurice Sendak's *Where the Wild Things Are* and *In the Night Kitchen*, Shel Silverstein's *A Light in the Attic*, and all of J. K. Rowling's Harry Potter books, to name just a few. Indeed, a list of the most frequently banned books almost suggests that if a book has not been banned somewhere, it may not be any good at all.

In February 2007, a news item swept the nation when several librarians around the country announced that they were going to remove Susan Patron's Newbery Award–winning *The Higher Power of Lucky* from their libraries. And why? On the very first page, the book's female protagonist, 10-year-old Lucky Trimble, overhears a character describing a rattlesnake biting his dog on the "scrotum." Because they thought that term inappropriate in a book for 10-year-olds, or, more likely, they feared community backlash, some nervous librarians took the book off the shelves. Ignored was the fact that the book is an uplifting and beautifully told story of a young girl's finding her inner strength, her "higher power." Happily, most professionals take a more reasonable approach to these matters and realize that attempts to shelter children from reality never work. In fact, they often backfire—if you want to make something enticing or exciting, forbid it. Doesn't it seem better that children learn about sensitive and controversial topics from responsible adults rather than from their friends—or worse, through ill-informed experiences?

All this is not to say that some subjects do not demand more mental and emotional maturity than others. It would be foolish to share with preschoolers a story about a teenage girl's first menses. On the other hand, many preschoolers have had to deal with deaths in the family, child abuse, divorce, and other traumas. So, well-written books on these topics may fill an important need for these children. Common sense is every educator's best asset. It is appropriate that the fight against censorship is now formally referred to as the fight for intellectual freedom. Here is the statement of principles on intellectual freedom from the National Council of Teachers of English:

> The following principles support the inclusion of agency, fairness, and multiple perspectives in the process of defending intellectual freedom in education:
>
> - The preservation of intellectual freedom in education depends upon the fostering of democratic values in the classroom, critical thinking stances and practices among teachers and students, open inquiry methods and access to information, and the exploration of multiple points of view.
> - As trained professionals, educators are qualified to select appropriate classroom materials and resources from a variety of sources given their teaching goals and the needs and interests of the students they serve.
> - Professional educators, drawing upon their training and content knowledge, should play an integral role in the curriculum design process at the district and school levels.
> - Educational communities should prepare for challenges to intellectual freedom with clearly defined policies and procedures that guide the review of classroom materials and resources called into question. In the creation and enactment of these policies and procedures, educators' knowledge and expertise should be solicited as integral, valuable, and necessary.

The teacher's responsibility is a heavy and multifaceted one, for the teacher must act in the best interest of the students, foster the ideals of a just and democratic society, and be respectful of the prevailing standards of the community—which can be a challenging juggling act at times. See Figure 2.4 for some guiding principles to protect intellectual freedom in the classroom.

FIGURE 2.4 ■ A Brief Guide to Preserving Intellectual Freedom in the Classroom

1. **Know your rationale for using a book in the classroom. Answer these questions:**
   - Is the book appropriate for this age level?
   - Does the book meet your objectives in the class, and how?
   - Does the book appear on recommended lists, and what have been the reactions of critics?
   - What possible objections could be raised to the book—language, tone, theme, subject matter—and how can you best address these objections?
   - As a last resort, what alternative readings can you offer in place of this book?

2. **Have guidelines for handling community and parental objections. Carefully organized procedures can do much to stem the tide of emotionalism. Include the following:**
   - A complaint form on which specific objections are to be recorded
   - A clearly designated procedure for dealing with the complaint
   - A broad-based committee of teachers, administrators, and community representatives for hearing the complaints
   - A clear philosophical statement articulating the school's educational principles

3. **Join with other teachers and the administration to protect students' right to read (and teachers' right to teach).**

4. **Actively support other teachers when they encounter censorship challenges.**

5. **Educate the community about the importance of intellectual freedom.**
   - Write letters or articles for the local newspaper.
   - Lobby the school board members and other community leaders.
   - Conduct or sponsor community workshops on censorship.

6. **Keep informed about censorship issues through professional journals, reports, association meetings, and new media.**

Summary

The call for an acceptance of diversity in society, which initially focused almost exclusively on skin color, has since expanded to include not simply racial equality, but cultural acceptance of religious, gender, and sexual preference distinctions. The issues of diversity and inclusion, of cultural sensitivity and intellectual and social awareness, are complicated, but the good news is that prejudice is not innate.

Studies have shown that prejudice is a learned behavior—in other words, we are taught to be prejudiced and it is reinforced by our isolation from those different from us. It is easier to hate an entire group than a single individual. It is also easier to hate a group we do not know or know only superficially. And so the most effective ways to combat prejudice are through education and human interaction. This is where children's literature enters.

As human beings, our ability to flourish in the world has depended greatly on our diversity and our ability to adapt to changing environments. Wide reading can help make us more adaptable, for books enrich our personal experiences, enlarge our horizons, nurture tolerance, and help us to understand who we are. Reading books from and about a wide variety of cultures may help us achieve one of society's most important goals—to acknowledge the tenet in the *Universal Declaration of Human Rights* that "All human beings are born free and equal in dignity and rights."

It is important to realize that reading can serve as both a window and a mirror—like a window, it allows us to see the wider world around us, and, like a mirror, it helps us to reflect on ourselves and better understand who we are. Reading should broaden a child's view of the world—not obscure it. And that ultimately results in our embracing the whole of humanity. The American poet Edwin Markham articulated this in his poem "Outwitted":

> *He drew a circle that shut me out—*
> *Heretic, rebel, a thing to flout.*
> *But Love and I had the wit to win:*
> *We drew a circle that took him in.*

Works Cited

Bishop, Rudine Sims. "Mirrors, Windows, and Sliding Glass Doors." *Perspectives: Choosing and Using Books for the Classroom* 6.1 (Summer 1990).

Gates, Henry Louis Jr. " 'Authenticity,' or The Lesson of Little Tree." *The New York Times* 24 (November 1991): 1, 26–30.

Guy, Rosa. "Innocence, Betrayal, and History." *School Library Journal* (November 1985): 33–34.

Harris, Violet, ed. *Teaching Multicultural Literature in Grades K–8*. Norwood, MA: Christopher-Gordon, 1993.

Knoth, Maeve Visser. "What Ails Bibliotherapy?" *The Horn Book Magazine* (May/June 2006): 273–276.

Lindberg, L. D., et al. "Changes in Adolescents' Receipt of Sex Education, 2006-2013." *Journal of Adolescent Health* (2016). doi:10.1016/j.jadohealth.2016.02.004

Maruki, Toshi. *Hiroshima No Pika*. Boston: Lothrop, Lee, & Shepard, 1982.

Publishing Statistic on Children's Books about People of Color and First/Native Nations and by People of Color and First/Native Nations

Authors and Illustrators. Madison, WI: Cooperative Children's Book Center. School of Education. University of Wisconsin-Madison. Ongoing publication updated 2016.

Rochman, Hazel. *Against Borders: Promoting Books for a Multicultural World*. Chicago: American Library Association, 1993.

Wilson, Edward O. *On Human Nature*. Cambridge, MA: Harvard University Press, 1978.

Recommended Resources

American Library Association website, www.ala.org. A good place to look for a list of recently censored books.

Belensky, Mary Field, and others. *Women's Ways of Knowing*. New York: Harper, 1986.

Benes, Rebecca C. *American Indian Picture Books of Change: The Art of Historic Children's Editions*. Santa Fe: Museum of New Mexico Press, 2004.

Botello, Maria José, and Masha Kabakow Rudman. *Critical Multicultural Analysis of Children's Literature: Mirrors, Windows, and Doors*. New York: Routledge, 2009.

Creasy, Megan. "Does Violence Have a Place in Children's Literature?" *Onaota Reading Journal* (2010).

Day, Frances A. *Lesbian and Gay Voices: An Annotated Bibliography and Guide to Literature for Children and Young Adults*. Westport, CT: Greenwood, 2000.

Derman-Sparks, Louise. "Revisiting Multicultural Education: What Children Need to Live in a Diverse Society." *Dimensions of Early Childhood* 22 (1993): 6–10.

Dowd, F. S. "Evaluating Children's Books Portraying American Indian and Asian Cultures." *Childhood Education* 68.4 (1992): 219–224.

Fox, Dana L., and Kathy G. Short, eds. *Stories Matter: The Complexity of Cultural Authenticity in Children's Literature*. Urbana, IL: NCTE, 2003.

Gebel, Doris. *Crossing Boundaries with Children's Books*. Lanham, MD: Scarecrow, 2006.

Giorgis, Cyndi, and Janelle Mathis. "Visions and Voices of American Indians in Children's Literature." *The New Advocate* 8.2 (Spring 1995): 125–142.

Gopalakrishnan, Ambika G. *Multicultural Children's Literature: A Critical Issues Approach*. Washington, DC: SAGE Publications, 2010.

Harada, V. H. "Issues of Ethnicity, Authenticity, and Quality in Asian-American Picture Books, 1983–93." *Journal of Youth Services in Libraries* 8.2 (1995): 135–149.

Harris, Violet J. "Continuing Dilemmas, Debates, and Delights in Multicultural Literature." *The New Advocate* 9.2 (Spring 1996): 107–122.

Lindgren, Merri V. *The Multicultural Mirror: Cultural Substance in Literature for Children and Young Adults*. Fort Atkinson, WI: Highsmith Press, 1991.

Lo, Suzanne, and Ginny Lee. "Asian Images in Children's Books: What Stories Do We Tell Our Children?" *Emergency Librarian* 20.5 (May–June 1993): 14–18.

Manna, Anthony L., and Carolyn S. Brodie, eds. *Many Faces, Many Voices: Multicultural Literary Experiences for Youth*. Fort Atkinson, WI: Highsmith, 1992.

McCann, Donnarae, and Gloria Woodard. *The Black American in Books for Children: Readings in Racism*. Metuchen, NJ: Scarecrow, 1985.

McIntosh, Peggy. "White Privilege: Unpacking the Invisible Knapsack." *Peace and Freedom* (July/August 1989): 10–12.

Norton, Donna E. *Multicultural Children's Literature: Through the Eyes of Many Children*, 3rd ed. Boston: Pearson, 2008.

Pang, V. O., C. Colvin, M. Tran, and R. H. Barba. "Beyond Chopsticks and Dragons: Selecting Asian-American Literature for Children." *The Reading Teacher* 46.3 (1992): 216–224.

Pratt, Linda, and Janice J. Beaty. *Transcultural Children's Literature*. Upper Saddle River, NJ: Merrill/Prentice Hall, 1999.

Sims, Rudine. *Shadow & Substance: Afro-American Experience in Contemporary Children's Fiction*. Urbana, IL: NCTE, 1982.

_____. "Walk Tall in the World: African-American Literature for Today's Children." *Journal of Negro Education* 58 (1990): 556–565.

Smith, Katherine Capshaw. *Children's Literature of the Harlem Renaissance*. Bloomington, IN: Indiana University Press, 2004.

_____. "Introduction: The Landscape of Ethnic American Children's Literature." *MELUS* 27.2 (Summer 2002): 3–8.

Children's Books on Culture and Ethnicity: A Selected and Annotated Booklist

This list includes only books focusing on culture and ethnicity. For additional books on diversity, see the booklists at the end of Chapter 9.

American Indian and Native Heritage

Andrews, Jan. *Very Last First Time*. Illus. Ian Wallace. Vancouver, BC: Douglas & McIntyre, 2002.
- A picture book about an Inuit girl finding mussels on the ocean floor, under ice.

Broker, Ignatia. *Night Flying Woman: An Ojibwa Narrative*. St. Paul: Minnesota Historical Society Press, 1983.
- An account of the lives of several generations of Ojibwa people in Minnesota.

Bruchac, Joseph. *Squanto's Journey: The Story of the First Thanksgiving*. Illus. Greg Shed. New York: Harcourt, 2000.
- A familiar tale told from the American Indian perspective.

_____. *Wabi*. New York: Dial, 2006.
- A shape-shifter tale woven into a novel of self-discovery and young love. Just one of many great books by the famed Abenaki writer.

Dorris, Michael. *Morning Girl*. Logan, IA: Perfection Learning, 1999.
- A historical novel set in the Bahamas in 1492, when a young girl sees Columbus arrive.

Erdrich, Louise. *The Game of Silence*. New York: HarperCollins, 2005.
- Sequel to *Birchbark House* (1999), a story about nineteenth-century Ojibwe people whose way of life is threatened by European settlers.

Frost, Helen. *Diamond Willow*. New York: Farrar, Straus & Giroux, 2016.
- A verse novel about an Alaskan girl, part Athabascan and part white, who must draw on her cultural roots for survival when she and her blind dog are trapped in a blizzard.

Highwater, Jamake. *Anpao: An American Indian Odyssey*. New York: Harper, 1977.
- A mystical tale of a young American Indian's journey across many time periods.

Lacapa, Michael. *The Flute Player*. Menomonie, WI: Northland, 1990.
  • An Apache *pourquoi* tale about lost love. A picture book for early elementary children.

Manitonquat (Medicine Story), reteller. *The Children of the Morning Light: Wampanoag Tales*. New York: Macmillan, 1994.
  • A collection of tales from the American Indians of New England.

McDermott, Gerald. *Arrow to the Sun: A Pueblo Indian Tale*. New York: Viking, 1974.
  • A strikingly illustrated retelling of a cultural origins tale.

_____. *Raven: A Trickster Tale from the Pacific Northwest*. New York: Harcourt, 1993.
  • A beautifully illustrated tale about Raven's bringing light to the world.

Mikaelsen, Ben. *Touching Spirit Bear*. New York: HarperCollins, 2002.
  • The wrenching story of a juvenile delinquent who is transformed by a traditional Native American custom, banishment to an isolated Alaskan island for one year.

Nelson, S. D. *Buffalo Bird Girl: A Hidatsa Story*. New York: Abrams, 2012.
  • The true story of a Hidatsa Indian girl in the Dakotas in the nineteenth century.

O'Dell, Scott. *Sing Down the Moon*. Boston: Houghton Mifflin, 1970.
  • The story of the cruel relocation of the Navajo in the nineteenth century.

Pearsall, Shelley. *Crooked River*. New York: Knopf, 2005.
  • Set in 1812, the story of a young girl who befriends an Ojibwe Indian enslaved by her father. A moving tale of injustice and inhumanity.

Savageau, Cheryl. *Muskrat Will Be Swimming*. Illus. Robert Hynes. Menomonie, WI: Northland, 1996.
  • A story of a young girl coming to appreciate her native heritage through the help of her grandfather and the art of storytelling. For early elementary children.

Sherman, Alexie. *The Absolutely True Diary of a Part-Time Indian*. New York: Little Brown, 2007.
  • A story of a modern teenager from the Spokane Indian Reservation attending an all-white school. Wonderfully told and based on the author's life.

Sneve, Virginia Driving Hawk. *The Christmas Coat: Memories of My Sioux Childhood*. Illus. Ellen Beier. New York: Holiday House, 2011.
  • A charming tale from the author's own childhood in South Dakota.

Sneve, Virginia Driving Hawk, selector. *Dancing Teepees: Poems of American Indian Youth*. Illus. Stephen Gammell. New York: Holiday House, 1989.
  • Poems from both the oral tradition and contemporary Indian poets.

Speare, Elizabeth George. *The Sign of the Beaver*. Boston: Houghton Mifflin, 1983.
  • A survival story of two eighteenth-century boys, one white and one Indian, who become reluctant friends.

Tingle, Tom. *Crossing Bok Chitto: A Choctaw Tale of Friendship and Freedom*. Illus. Jeanne Rorex Bridges. El Paso, TX: Cinco Puntos Press, 2006.
  • A picture book that portrays a cross-cultural friendship in Mississippi in the 1800s.

Vaughan, Richard Lee. *Eagle Boy: A Pacific Northwest Native Tale*. Illus. Lee Christiansen. Seattle, WA: Sasquitch Books, 2000.
  • A story of a young boy befriending an eagle and saving his people. A retelling of a tale told among several native peoples of the Pacific Northwest.

Wyss, Thelma Hatch. *Bear Dancer: The Story of a Ute Girl*. New York: Margaret K. McElderry, 2005.
- A tale of cultural clashes in which a nineteenth-century Ute girl encounters white people for the first time.

Yellow Robe, Rosebud. *Tonweya and the Eagles and Other Lakota Stories*. Illus. Jerry Pinkney. New York: Dial, 1979.
- A collection of animal tales from the Plains Indians.

African American and African Heritage

Brooks, Gwendolyn. *Bronzeville Boys and Girls*. 1967. Illus. Faith Ringgold. New York: Amistad, 2006.
- Poems originally written by Pulitzer Prize–winner Brooks in 1956, now newly illustrated.

Coles, Robert. *The Story of Ruby Bridges*. Illus. George Ford. New York: Scholastic, 1995.
- The story of a 6-year-old girl who becomes the first African American in an integrated New Orleans school in 1960.

Curtis, Christopher Paul. *Bud, Not Buddy*. New York: Delacorte, 1999.
- A narrative of a young Canadian black boy, son of former slaves, who learns about slavery in the United States in the mid-nineteenth century.

Draper, Sharon M. *Stella by Starlight*. New York: Atheneum, 2015.
- A young African American girl, growing up in a segregated town during the Depression, encounters the Ku Klux Klan.

Duncan, Alice Faye. *Honey Baby Sugar Child*. Illus. Susan Keeter. New York: Simon & Schuster, 2005.
- A simple warm depiction of the bond between an African American mother and her child.

Feelings, Tom. *Soul Looks Back in Wonder*. New York: Dial, 1993.
- A collection of poems on black themes for all ages.

Gibney, Shannon. *See No Color*. Minneapolis, MN: Carolrhoda Books, 2015.
- The experiences of a 16-year-old African American girl who is adopted by a white family.

Giovanni, Nikki. *Shimmy Shimmy Shimmy Like My Sister Kate: Looking at the Harlem Renaissance Through Poems*. New York: Holt, 1996.
- Poems for young people by a celebrated African American poet.

Guy, Rosa. *The Friends*. New York: Viking, 1973.
- The story of a difficult friendship between two girls of color—one from the West Indies and one from New York.

Hamilton, Virginia. *M. C. Higgins, the Great*. New York: Macmillan, 1974.
- A black teenager in the Appalachian Mountains must choose between tradition and change.

Herron, Carolivia. *Nappy Hair*. Illus. Joe Cepeda. New York: Knopf, 1997.
- A lively picture book celebrating a young black girl's wondrous hair.

Johnson, Angela. *The First Part Last*. New York: Simon & Schuster, 2010. (Part 2 of the "Heaven" Trilogy including *Heaven* and *Sweet Hereafter*)
- The moving story of an African American teenager's life as a single father.

King, Martin Luther Jr. *I Have a Dream*. Illus. various artists. New York: Scholastic, 2007.
- One of the most inspiring speeches of the twentieth century, beautifully illustrated by award-winning artists.

Lester, Julius. *To Be a Slave*. Illus. Tom Feelings. New York: Dial, 1998.
- A celebrated nonfiction work, first published in 1968, that describes the life of a slave in the words of slaves themselves.

Levine, Ellen. *Henry's Freedom Box: A True Story from the Underground Railroad*. Illus. Kadir Nelson. New York: Scholastic, 2007.
- A slave in the early nineteenth century mails himself to freedom. A brief story, beautifully illustrated.

Long, Mark, and Jim Demonakos. *The Silence of Our Friends*. Illus. Nate Powell. New York: First Second, 2012.
- A graphic novel for teenage readers about a racial incident at a Texas university in 1968.

Mathis, Sharon Bell. *Teacup Full of Roses*. New York: Viking, 1972.
- The story of a troubled African American family with a child on drugs.

McKissack, Patricia. *Goin' Someplace Special*. Illus. Jerry Pinckney. New York: Atheneum, 2001.
- A touching picture book set in the segregated South in the 1950s.

Nelson, Kadir. *We Are the Ship: The Story of Negro League Baseball*. New York: Hyperion, 2008.
- A well-told and beautifully illustrated history of the Negro baseball leagues in the early twentieth century.

Raven, Margot Theis. *Circle Unbroken*. Illus. E. B. Lewis. New York: Farrar, Straus & Giroux, 2004.
- African American history told through a woman teaching her granddaughter the ancient art of basket weaving.

Rhodes, Jewell Parker. *Ninth Ward*. New York: Little Brown, 2010.
- A story of the tragedy of Hurricane Katrina in New Orleans and an African American girl's will to survive.

Rhuday-Perkovich, Olugbemisola. *Eighth-Grade Superzero*. New York: Arthur A. Levine, 2010.
- The trials and tribulations of a boy adjusting to a Brooklyn middle school.

Ringgold, Faith. *Tar Beach*. New York: Crown, 1991.
- A picture book with a Depression-era setting in Harlem. A magical tale with a comment on social injustice.

Robinson, Sharon. *Safe at Home*. New York: Scholastic, 2006.
- A story in which baseball helps to fill the void left when a young boy's father dies. Well-drawn characters by the daughter of baseball legend Jackie Robinson.

Scattergood, Augusta. *Glory Be*. New York: Scholastic, 2012.
- A story seen through the eyes of a 12-year-old girl, when the civil rights movement reaches a small Mississippi town in 1964.

Steptoe, John. *Mufaro's Beautiful Daughters*. New York: Lothrop, 1974.
- A beautifully illustrated picture book version of a traditional Zimbabwean folktale.

Williams-Garcia, Rita. *One Crazy Summer*. New York: Amistad, 2011.
- A powerful story of three black sisters who find themselves involved in the social upheaval of 1968.

Woodson, Jacqueline. *If You Come Softly*. New York: Putnam, 1998.
- A moving teenage love story about an African American boy and a Jewish girl.

Latinos/as and Latino Heritage

Ada, Alma Flor, and F. Isabel Campoy. *Yes! We Are Latinos: Poems and Prose about the Latino Experience*. Illus. David Diaz. Watertown, MA: Charlesbridge, 2013.
- Portraits in poetry and prose telling the stories of Latina/os from many points of view.

Alvarez, Julia. *Return to Sender*. New York: Knopf, 2009.
• A story about the struggle of illegal migrant workers in Vermont.

Anaya, Rudolfo. *Maya's Children: The Story of La Llorona*. Illus. Maria Baca. New York: Hyperion, 1997.
• Based on the tragic Hispanic folktale "Crying Woman," a strikingly illustrated version modified for younger readers.

Canales, Viola. *Tequila Worm*. New York: Paw Prints, 2008.
• A story in which a teenage Latina must fit in at an elite Texas boarding school.

Cisneros, Sandra. *Hairs/Pelitos*. Illus. Terry Ybáñez. New York: Knopf, 1994.
• A bilingual picture book celebrating diversity.

_____. *The House on Mango Street*. Houston: Arte Público, 1984.
• A coming-of-age story of a girl growing up in a Hispanic neighborhood in Chicago.

De Treviño, Elizabeth Borton. *I, Juan De Pareja*. New York: Bell Books, 1965.
• Set in seventeenth-century Spain, the story of a slave of the painter Velasquez who teaches himself painting.

Dorros, Arthur. *Abuela*. New York: Dutton, 1991.
• A picture book story of a young girl's magical bond with her grandmother, her *abuela*.

Galarza, Ernesto. *Barrio Boy*. Notre Dame, IN: University of Notre Dame Press, 1971.
• An early-twentieth-century story of a boy from rural Mexico adjusting to city life in the United States.

Garza, Carmen Lomas. *Family Picture/Cuadros de Familia*. San Francisco: Children's Book Press, 1990.
• A celebration of the author's girlhood. A bilingual text with outstanding illustrations.

Griego, M. C., Betsy L. Bucks, Sharon S. Gilbert, and Laura H. Kimball. *Tortillitas para Mama and Other Nursery Rhymes, Spanish and English*. Illus. Barbara Cooney. New York: Square Fish, 1987.
• Latin American nursery rhymes in a bilingual edition with lovely illustrations.

Herrera, Juan Felipe. *Calling the Doves/El Canto de las Palomas*. Illus. Elly Simmons. 1990. San Francisco: Children's Book Press, 2001.
• A biographical account of a boy growing up as a migrant farm worker. Bilingual text beautifully illustrated.

Lopez, Diana. *Confetti Girl*. New York: Little Brown, 2009.
• The story of a Latina girl in a bilingual Texas community dealing with the tribulations of middle school, complete with sorrow, anger, and joy.

Marcantonio, Patricia Santos. *Red Ridin' in the Hood and Other Cuentas*. Illus. Renato Alarcão. New York: Farrar, Straus & Giroux, 2005.
• Retellings of familiar tales with a Latino twist. Great fun.

Martinez, Victor. *Parrot in the Oven: Mi Vida*. New York: HarperCollins, 1996.
• The story of a Hispanic boy from a dysfunctional family coming of age in a small California town.

Mora, Pat. *Confetti: Poems for Children*. Illus. Enrique O. Sanchez. New York: Lee and Low, 1996.
• Narrative poems about the culture of the American Southwest. Colorfully illustrated.

_____. *Tomás and the Library Lady*. Illus. Raul Colón. New York: Knopf, 1997.
• Based on the true story of the son of itinerant farm workers who learns to love reading.

Rice, David. *Crazy Loco*. New York: Dial, 2001.
• A collection of short stories about life in a small south Texas town.

Ryan, Pam Muñoz. *The Dreamer*. New York: Scholastic, 2010.
• A fictionalized portrait of the childhood of the great poet Pablo Neruda.

_____. *Esperanza Rising*. St. Louis, MO: Turtleback, 2002.
- The story of a 13-year-old girl from Mexico adjusting to a new way of life during the Depression of the 1930s.

Soto, Gary. *Chato's Kitchen*. Illus. Susan Guevara. New York: Putnam, 1995.
- The story of Chato the cat, who lives in the barrio and invites the mice to dinner (as guests or meal?).

_____. *A Fire in My Hands*. New York: Harcourt, 2006.
- Poems for teenage readers inspired by the poet's own youth.

_____. *Snapshots from the Wedding*. Illus. Stephanie Garcia. New York: Putnam, 1997.
- A Mexican American wedding described with free verse and imaginative illustrations.

Tafolla, Carmen. *What Can You Do with a Paleta?* Illus. Magaly Morales. New York: Tricycle, 2009.
- A playful picture book illustrating life in the barrio while celebrating the Mexican popsicle.

Torres, Leyla. *Subway Sparrow/Gorrión del Metro*. New York: Farrar, Straus & Giroux, 1993.
- A story of four people who speak different languages coming together to help a trapped bird.

Asian American and Asian Heritage

Crew, Linda. *Children of the River*. New York: Bantam, 1989.
- The story of a Cambodian refugee coping with haunting memories as she adjusts to life in America.

Fritz, Jean. *Homesick: My Own Story*. New York: Putnam, 1982.
- The story of a famed American author recalling her childhood in China.

Houston, Jeanne Wakatsuki, and James D. Houston. *Farewell to Manzanar*. New York: Bantam, 1973.
- Based on the true story of the Japanese American relocation during the Second World War.

Kadohata, Cynthia. *Weedflower*. New York: Atheneum, 2006.
- The story of a Japanese American girl befriending a Mohave boy during the Second World War.

Lawson, Julie. *White Jade Tiger*. Toronto: Dundurn, 2017.
- A time-travel fantasy about a modern-day Chinese girl transported back to 1881 and the building of the Canadian railroad (by Chinese laborers), where a mystery arises.

Lin, Grace. *Where the Mountain Meets the Moon*. New York: Little Brown, 2011.
- A Newbery Honor book about a girl's adventure to save her family. This enchanting tale is set in China and draws on Chinese folktales.

_____. *Dim Sum for Everyone*. New York: Dragonfly, 2003.
- A story about traditional Chinese food.

Lord, Bette Bao. *In the Year of the Boar and Jackie Robinson*. New York: Harper, 1984.
- A very funny and ultimately uplifting story of a Chinese girl moving to America in 1947 and adapting to a new culture.

Louie, Ai-Ling. *Yeh-Shen: A Cinderella Story from China*. Illus. Ed Young. New York: Philomel, 1982.
- A beautifully illustrated folktale.

Mahy, Margaret. *The Seven Chinese Brothers*. Illus. Jean and Mou-Sein Tseng. New York: Scholastic, 1990.
- A retelling of an old Chinese folktale about brothers with extraordinary gifts.

Pung, Alice. *Lucy and Linh*. (Australia: Black, 2014.) New York: Random House, 2016.

- A girl from a poor Chinese family in Australia is accepted to an elite school where she drifts away from her heritage and must face tough decisions. Although not technically about Asian Americans, the message about cultural ties remains valid.

Say, Allen. *Grandfather's Journey*. Boston: Houghton Mifflin, 1994.
- A picture book portrait of the author's grandfather's immigration to America.

Uchida, Yoshiko. *A Jar of Dreams*. New York: Atheneum, 1991.
- The story of a Japanese girl growing up in America during the Depression who learns the importance of her heritage.

Vaughan, Marcia K. *The Dancing Dragon*. Illus. Stanley Woo Hoo Foon. New York: Mondo, 1996.
- The Chinese New Year, described in rhymed couplets and colorfully illustrated.

Wang, Rosalind C. *The Fourth Question*. Illus. Ju-Hong Chen. New York: Holiday House, 1991.
- A retelling of a Chinese folktale in which a simple man seeks wisdom.

Wong, Janet S. *Good Luck Gold and Other Poems*. New York: Margaret K. McElderry, 1994.

- A collection of poems about a young Chinese American girl's experiences.

Yacowitz, Caryn. *The Jade Stone*. Illus. Ju-Hong Chen. New York: Holiday House, 1992.
- A retelling of a traditional Chinese tale about an artist and his devotion to art.

Yagawa, Sumiko. *The Crane Wife*. Tr. Katherine Paterson. Illus. Suekichi Akaba. New York: Mulberry, 1987.
- A retelling of a traditional Japanese folktale of animal transformation.

Yep, Laurence. *Angelfish*. New York: Putnam, 2001.
- The story of a young Chinese American ballet student uncovering the secret of an unpleasant man.

_____. *Dragon Prince: A Chinese Beauty and the Beast Tale*. Illus. Kam Mak. New York: HarperCollins, 1997.
- Lovely illustrations accompany the retelling of a traditional tale.

Yin Lau, Rosanna. *Coolies*. Illus. Chris Soentpiet. New York: Penguin, 2001.
- A story of the Chinese railroad workers of the 1860s.

Young, Ed. *Lon Po Po: A Red-Riding Hood Story from China*. New York: Philomel, 1990.
- A Chinese folktale beautifully illustrated by an award-winning artist.

Other Cultures

Boyne, John. *The Boy in the Striped Pajamas*. New York: David Fickling, 2006.
- A narrative of the Holocaust, as viewed through the eyes of a 9-year-old boy.

Cohen, Barbara. *Molly's Pilgrim*. Illus. M. J. Deraney. New York: Lothrop, Lee, and Shepard, 1983.
- The story of a young Russian Jewish immigrant showing her American classmates a new meaning of Thanksgiving.

Cunnane, Kelly. *For You Are a Kenyan Child*. Illus. Ana Juan. New York: Atheneum, 2006.

- A picture book describing a day in the life of a Kenyan boy.

Demi. *Buddha*. New York: Henry Holt, 1996.
- A beautifully illustrated picture book about the life and legends of the Buddha.

_____. *Muhammad*. New York: Margaret K. McElderry, 2003.
- A picture book narrative of the prophet's life, with an explanation of Islam.

Fama, Elizabeth. *Overboard*. Peru, IL: Cricket, 2002.

- The story of a shipwreck that leaves an American girl and an Indonesian boy struggling to survive in the ocean.

Frank, Anne. *The Diary of a Young Girl: The Definitive Edition.* New York: Doubleday, 1995.
  - The famed diary of a young Jewish girl in hiding from the Nazis in the Second World War.

Innocenti, Roberto, and Christophe Gallaz. *Rose Blanche.* Illus. Roberto Innocenti. New York: Creative Education, 1985.
  - A striking picture book about a young German girl aiding Jews in a concentration camp during the Second World War.

Katz, Karen. *My First Ramadan.* New York: Henry Holt, 2007.
  - A picture book about a young boy observing the Muslim holy month with his family.

Kerr, Judith. *When Hitler Stole Pink Rabbit.* New York: Coward McCann & Geoghegan, 1971.
  - The adventures of a Jewish girl forced to flee Hitler's Germany.

Kherdian, David. *The Road from Home: The Story of an Armenian Girlhood.* New York: Greenwillow, 1979.
  - A powerful memoir of the Armenian holocaust.

Lasky, Kathryn. *The Night Journey.* New York: Warne, 1981.
  - The story of a Jewish girl learning about her grandmother's experiences in Czarist Russia.

McCormick, Patricia. *Sold.* New York: Hyperion, 2006.
  - The harrowing tale of a 13-year-old Nepalese girl whose father sells her into prostitution in India.

Naidoo, Beverley. *The Other Side of Truth.* New York: HarperCollins, 2001.
  - The story of a young Nigerian girl caught up in the violence plaguing her country.

Novesky, Amy. *Elephant Prince: The Story of Ganesh.* Illus. Belgin K. Wedman. San Rafael, CA: Mandala, 2004.
  - A picture book about one of Hinduism's most endearing gods.

Patel, Sanjay, and Emily Haynes. *Ganesha's Sweet Tooth.* Illus. Sanjay Patel. San Francisco: Chronicle, 2012.
  - The story of how the beloved elephant god of Hinduism came to write one of India's most important epics.

Polacco, Patricia. *The Keeping Quilt.* New York: Simon & Schuster, 1988.
  - A picture book about an immigrant Jewish family attempting to keep Russian traditions.

Potok, Chaim. *My Name Is Asher Lev.* New York: Knopf, 1972.
  - The story of a Hasidic Jew struggling with his commitment to his faith and to his art.

Staples, Suzanne Fisher. *Shabanu: Daughter of the Wind.* New York: Knopf, 1989.
  - The story of a modern Pakistani girl struggling with the conflict between tradition and modernity.

Stolz, Joelle. *The Shadows of the Ghadames.* New York: Delacorte, 2004.
  - The story of a Muslim girl in nineteenth-century Libya being introduced to a changing world.

Wolk, Bernard. *Coming to America: A Muslim Family's Story.* New York: Lee & Low, 2003.
  - A photo essay describing a Muslim family's immigration to America and the subsequent adjustment.

Yolen, Jane. *The Devil's Arithmetic.* New York: Perfection, 1990.
  - The story of a girl being transported back through time to Poland in the 1940s, where she witnesses the horrors of the Holocaust.

Experiencing Literature

Reading, Writing, Talking, and Doing

"The mind is not a vessel to be filled but a fire to be kindled."

–Plutarch

Introduction

One of the greatest gifts we can give to a child is a love for reading. This love is usually developed early in life. A 6-year-old, extolling the virtues of reading, once told me, "I could read a hundred chapter books in a day. I always thought my life was great because of reading." Although such enthusiasm in the very young is heartening, it is never too late to acquire a love of reading. Several years ago, a college student told me he had been a reluctant reader all his life until, as a teenager, he spent a summer roughing it in the Michigan woods. There was no running water and no electricity (and this was before Wi-Fi). So, out of desperation, he turned to books borrowed from a local library. By the end of the summer, he was a convert. "Now," he said, "I can't get enough of reading!" Instilling this kind of passion in young people should be the goal of every teacher. Unfortunately, our technology-driven world makes it easier and easier for people to find excuses not to read. Our concern in this chapter is what can be done in the classroom to encourage reading and to stimulate thinking about reading. Elementary teachers particularly have a golden opportunity, for many of their students are not likely to have been seduced by the allure of the computer in its myriad incarnations. And, of course, what is done in the classroom is also dictated by external mandates—and we will briefly examine the role of these mandates in the overall education of our children.

Language Acquisition

We begin with an overview of how language is acquired—for language is the foundation of storytelling and, subsequently, reading. In the last chapter we looked at developmental theories of general human growth and development and how they impact reading, and now it might be helpful if we consider the one human ability that makes literature itself possible: the ability to use language to communicate. One area in which children seem to excel beyond the expectations of adults is language acquisition. It is amazing that in five short years, children can master the abstract concept of attaching meanings to certain sounds (words) and to organize those sounds into intelligible patterns (sentences) to convey those meanings.

Steven Pinker, a psychologist who has studied human thought and language, is convinced that language acquisition is innate. He argues that we are born with the ability to memorize the meanings of words and their various forms (such as singulars, plurals, possessives, and verb tenses) and to assimilate the rules of grammar and syntax of the language that we hear on a daily basis. Very young children possess a linguistic plasticity, or malleability, that extends to their abilities to create sounds. Despite the popular notion that pronunciation is difficult for children, they often have a much easier time of it than do most adults. (Many English-speaking preschoolers have little problem pronouncing Mandarin Chinese, for instance, and Spanish pronunciation comes easy for them.) Indeed, the time for children to start learning a second language is when they're in preschool or the early elementary grades—when it's easier to memorize, to make new sounds, and to adapt to new language patterns. It is a wasted opportunity that the American educational system has largely failed to advocate serious foreign language study for elementary schoolchildren. Waiting until high school is too late—the native language patterns are too firmly imbedded and the linguistic habits are difficult to break.

All this research shows that as adults—and as teachers—we should build on children's language abilities and their natural curiosity about sound, sense, and language. The books they read or that we read to them should be expanding their vocabulary—not accommodating it. Most children love language and love practicing it. Even the simplest Mother Goose rhymes offer exciting and challenging vocabulary, with their nonsense words and archaisms. Children are not intimidated by big words or unusual words. Take, for example, the nursery rhyme of Old Mother Hubbard, who successively went to the "joiner's," the "fishmonger's," the "cobbler's," and the "hosier's"; or the crooked man who went a crooked mile and "found a crooked six-pence against a crooked stile"; or Jack who was "nimble"; or Mary who was "contrary"; or little Nancy Etticoat who wore a white "Petticoat." The 3-year-olds who enjoy these old rhymes seldom complain that the vocabulary is too difficult for them. Indeed, young children are eager to learn new words, and equally eager to pronounce them. If only we could prolong this fascination, dare we say love, of language into adulthood.

Educational Theories

The conundrum over how children best learn new concepts has faced humans from the very beginning of civilization. For centuries, simple rote learning or memorization was the accepted path to knowledge—but not always a very interesting or effective one. It was not until the twentieth century that truly new approaches to learning were suggested. Many of these build on the work of Piaget, Erickson and Kohlberg, which we discussed in Chapter 1. Today our educational system is still being influenced by two theories developed in the early and mid-twentieth century—those of Lev Vygotsky and Louise Rosenblatt. As with all useful theories, they have undergone many adaptations over the years, but many of the basic premises remain relevant. What follows is but a very brief overview.

Lev Vygotsky and Social Interaction

Lev Vygotsky (1896–1934) was a Russian psychologist whose ideas on child development sharply parted with those of Piaget and his followers (see Chapter 1). Vygotsky discarded the stage theory of development and, instead, believed that human development is a continuing and never-ending process—that we have no developmental "goals" to reach, only a series of lifelong transformations to experience. In other words, we are all lifelong learners. He also believed that human beings are essentially social creatures and that it is through our social interaction that we grow intellectually. For Vygotsky, community plays a central role in education (something that Piaget did not consider). Consequently, and unsurprisingly, Vygotsky believed that the environment in which one grows up greatly influences learning (something else Piaget neglected to consider). And, important for our purposes, Vygotsky saw language as humans' greatest tool, for it permits communication beyond oneself.

Vygotsky believed that learning fell into three categories: There are things we can learn on our own (by practice or through reading), things we can learn with the help of others (through guidance and explanation), and things we just cannot learn (not all of us can learn to sing grand opera or write prize-winning novels or play professional hockey). Formal education deals with the second category: things we can learn with the help of others. Vygotsky developed a concept called the *zone of proximal development* (ZPD). The ZPD is that area between what we can learn on our own and what we are simply not capable of learning (see Figure 3.1),

FIGURE 3.1 ■ Vygotsky's Zone of Proximal Development

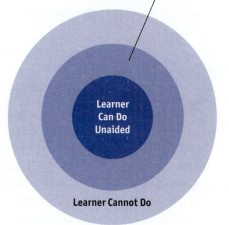

and this, he believed, is what education must focus on. This idea may seem like a "no-brainer" to us today, but it revolutionized education because it suggested that learning is a give-and-take process in which the teacher and the students have a shared responsibility: Students learn from teachers, teachers learn from students, and students learn from each other.

Vygotsky's ideas rejected the traditional classroom, in which the teacher delivers information to attentive students sitting quietly in neat rows. In its place is a room of clustered desks, workspaces for small groups, and specialized learning stations. This is a place where everyone is responsible for teaching as well as learning, and education is a cooperative, shared experience. Small group discussions replace lectures; team projects replace individual examinations. Students assume responsibility for helping each other. The teacher relinquishes the authoritarian grip over the classroom in exchange for a cooperative community of learning. For many teachers, this switch requires a great deal of faith and a fair amount of risk. But for those able to make this leap, the teaching experience—if more challenging—is often more enjoyable and more rewarding.

Reader Response Theory

Louise Rosenblatt (1904–2005) is most famous for two books, *Literature as Exploration* (1938) and *The Reader, the Text, the Poem: The Transactional Theory of the Literary Work* (1978). In these works she reacted against the prevailing notion of teaching literature, which seemed to suggest that there is a right way and there is a wrong way to interpret literature (and that the teacher always knows the "right way"). Rosenblatt, instead, argued that reading literature is a process of give-and-take between the reader and the text and that no two readers interpret a text in the same way. Each of us comes from a unique set of experiences—personal, familial, psychological, social, educational, intellectual, religious, and so on—and these help determine how we react to a text.

One of the most famous results of Rosenblatt's ideas is what we call reader response theory. Reading a literary text is, according to this theory, part of a complex process that includes a collaboration of the writer (who has a message), the text (the symbols the writer uses to convey the message), and the reader (who receives the message and then interprets it according to his or her own experiences, thoughts, and beliefs). And, each time we reread a text, we may find our attitudes and interpretations changing, since our life experiences and knowledge are always changing. So the text acts on the reader, and the reader interacts with the text. (Some call this *transaction*, and hence this method is often referred to as *transactional analysis*.)

Using reader response theory when studying a literary text, readers share their feelings about the text and then attempt to explain and defend those feelings. It becomes highly personal, for, according to Rosenblatt, our personal reactions to a text depend upon our life experiences, the values we hold, what we have been taught—and no two people are going to view a text in exactly the same way (and certainly not for exactly the same reasons).

Let's use a simple example. The familiar folktale "Rumpelstiltskin," you will remember, is about a miller who lies to the king about his daughter's ability to spin straw into gold. The king agrees to marry the daughter if she spins a roomful of straw into gold each night for a year. Fortunately, a mysterious stranger appears, offering to help her if she promises him her firstborn child—and she agrees. Eventually the time comes for her to make good on her bargain, which she now regrets. So the stranger agrees to yet another bargain. She can keep her child if she can guess his name. She does so through the help of a spy, and, presumably, lives happily ever after.

If we ask readers to rank the main characters—Rumpelstiltskin, the miller, the daughter, the king—according to who acts most and least ethically, we find a wide range of attitudes and little general agreement. Sometimes readers cannot even agree on who is the hero and who is the villain. How can so many interpretations be possible? And which one is valid? The reason we find such conflicting opinions is because all readers bring to the story different sets of experiences and respond through those experiences, and every interpretation is valid for the one who expressed it. Consequently, for some, the miller's daughter is an innocent victim, a pawn of her father and the king. But others fault the daughter for bargaining with the life of her own child. Some readers see Rumpelstiltskin as villainous and opportunistic, but others believe he was only acting fairly, in accordance with the agreement (and he did save her life). Some dislike the miller for his dishonesty, which puts his daughter's life in jeopardy. Others say he was simply trying to give his daughter a break in life (he wanted more for her than he had). Many people regard the king as merely greedy, but others see him as a victim, deceived by the miller and his daughter, and a man of his word. So we see that reader response often points out the complexity of human behavior and the difficulty in determining right and wrong. Of course, what causes such a variation in judgment is quite simply the variation in individual experiences and perspectives—we are, all of us, different; we grew up in different circumstances and environments; and we were influenced by different experiences and people. Naturally we are not all going to think about life or a literary text in the same way.

Reader response theory opens up many doors for discussion. Rather than finding the one "correct" reading for a work of literature (which likely does not exist), it allows for a variety of simultaneous interpretations and encourages us to see the complexity and the richer fabric of the work. This makes reader response theory different from the critical theories we will examine in Chapter 4. Feminist or archetypal or psychoanalytical critics may feel compelled to argue their cases to us, to convince us their ideas are valid. But reader response theory automatically assumes that no two people are going to respond in exactly the same way. Indeed, we may even react to a text differently upon a second or third reading. Reader response theory can also explain why the reputations of books change over time. Some works lose their appeal, and others grow in popularity. People change with the times. Reader response theory helps us as readers to discover why we feel the way we do about a novel, a poem, or a play. And it respects individual differences; however, it is most effective when we are able to think about and explain why we feel the way we do—for then we learn more about ourselves.

Using Literature in the Classroom

Reading Experiences

The purpose of this text is not to be an activity guide for teaching literary texts. Many excellent sources and teaching suggestions can be found online and in pedagogical textbooks. Following are just a few ideas for bringing about a connection between children and the books they read—and, we hope, for nuturing a love of reading in all children. This list of suggestions is certainly not exhaustive—so always be on the lookout for fresh ideas. And don't forget, a teacher's own imagination is often the best resource.

READING ALOUD From a parent's gentle singing of a lullaby while rocking an infant to sleep to the reading of such childhood classics as *Alice's Adventures in*

Wonderland or *Pinocchio*, sharing literature orally with children can be one of the most fulfilling human experiences. The relaxing moments of story time with young children are among the most cherished memories of parenthood. And the times are equally magical when young children want to read the stories to us. However, we should not think that only small children like being read to. I've found that even college students enjoy listening to stories. Effective reading aloud can be modeled by observing a few guidelines:

- Read stories you enjoy (unless you are a very good actor and can pretend to like the story). Your own enthusiasm will be contagious.
- Choose stories that fit the children's intellectual, emotional, and social developmental levels (see Chapter 1). Don't be afraid of a few challenging words—they never bother children—but make sure you know how to pronounce the words and what they mean. (Young children don't let you get away with much.)
- If the book is a picture book, make sure everyone can see the pictures. This is easy when you're reading to a single child but trickier when reading to a class of 25. Remember that it is most effective if your audience can see the pictures as you are reading—not before or afterward.
- Keep the reading experience an interactive one. Depart from the text when doing so seems necessary. Allow for questions and comments as you read—and you should feel free to ask questions as well.
- Rehearse your reading and be sure to use the proper inflections, the appropriate cadence, and the right tone (some books are "quiet" books; some are "noisy"). If there is dialogue, try reading in different voices. Children love this.

The reward for you is a grateful and delighted audience—and that is well worth the effort you put into reading aloud.

STORYTELLING   Storytelling is the art of narrating a tale from memory rather than reading it, and involves two elements: selection and delivery. This is a talent that not everyone possesses—we are not all born actors. To do it effectively, you have to rid yourself of inhibitions and not be afraid of looking foolish at times. But if you can let loose and sink into your story, it can be great fun. First, you need to choose good stories—ones with interesting characters, lively action, good dialogue, and perhaps an unusual twist at the end. Pick your personal favorites and prepare a repertoire of stories to draw on. To be a good storyteller, you must also be a performer (and, admittedly, this is not for everyone). Practice your delivery. Assume voices for the various characters. Remember that timing is everything—speeding up, slowing down, and pausing at the right times. And most importantly, rehearse, rehearse, rehearse.

Folktales are natural fodder for storytellers. They include easily memorized patterns and ample dialogue to enliven the story, and they are brief enough to be relayed in a single sitting. Also, they lend themselves well to adaptation, so you can adjust the tale to the audience and to your own tastes. Some storytellers like to create their own tales, sometimes from their own experiences or from their imaginations. All stories work best when they gradually build to a climax and quickly end while the audience's interest is still at a peak.

Of course, a rich and beautiful voice is an asset to any would-be storyteller. However, if you don't have such a voice, don't worry. Develop some other assets—effective body movement, facial expressions, eye contact, clear enunciation, meaningful inflection, and appropriate pauses—or maybe fancy dress. And, with practice, you can develop a greater vocal range and a voice that will project. Pacing and dynamics are crucial. You have to know when to slow down, when to speed up, when to talk in near whispers, when to shout, and so on. And do not overlook physical movement. Natural body gestures (and at times even exaggerated ones, depending on the story) and direct eye contact will help engage the audience. Finally, don't be afraid to ham it up. This is no time to be shy.

BOOK TALKS   A book talk, which should result in a free-flowing group discussion of a book, can work very well with older students (upper elementary and above). And it is a welcome replacement for those set questions from the teacher and the expected "correct" answers from the students.

A good book discussion requires serious preparation. Also, a good book discussion evolves and transforms as it proceeds. Be sure that you are well prepared before beginning a book discussion. This means not only reading the book carefully but also finding out what other readers (including critics) have said about it. (You can find a lot of information online. Just make sure your sources are reliable and consult the works listed in "Children's Literature Resources" at the back of this book.) You might want to include visual aids, photographs, a geographical map, a time line, a web, a story map, and anything else that might give readers some useful insight.

Integral to most book discussions are the questions asked by the leader. The following types of questions progress from least to most sophisticated and can be useful in most elementary school settings:

- *Memory or factual questions* are the simplest type of questions and make good icebreakers. These questions ask us to recall facts about the setting, plot, and characters. However, memory questions that dwell on insignificant details are a waste of time. In a discussion of E. B. White's *Charlotte's Web*, for example, questions like "What was Wilbur's favorite food?" or "What was Charlotte's oldest child's name?" seem a bit silly. Instead, ask questions like, "Why was Wilbur's life in danger?" and "How did Fern save Wilbur?"

In other words, your questions should have a good purpose and lead to further discussion.

- *Interpretation or analytical questions* ask us to draw conclusions from the facts in the story. Many readers are anxious to offer their own opinions; however, opinions ought to be based on facts from the text. For example, after a reading of *Charlotte's Web*, you might ask such questions as "How does the relationship between Fern and Wilbur change over the course of the book?" and "How does Wilbur's character change from the beginning to the end of the book?"

- *Application questions* ask us to apply knowledge received from a book to real-life situations or to other books. These questions help readers see the relationships between literature and life and require deeper thinking. A discussion of *Charlotte's Web* might include a question such as "In what ways do Templeton, Charlotte, and Wilbur remind you of people you know?" and "Do you have friends who remind you of Charlotte, Wilbur, or Templeton, and in what ways?"

All these questions attempt to help readers understand why they feel the way they do about a piece of literature.

Writing Experiences

As early as second grade, most children are capable of responding to literature through writing. Certainly by the time they reach the middle elementary grades, children should be writing as a regular part of their total curriculum. Several possibilities are available at all grade levels.

WEBBING AND MAPPING   Webbing and mapping, which are sometimes as much art as writing, help us to think about the connections in a text and to analyze the text as a whole. Webbing is a visual means of demonstrating relationships between story elements or concepts. A web consists of a figure (the simplest resembles a spider's web, which is where the term comes from) on which labels are placed to show the connections between aspects of a literary work. For example, the web in Figure 3.2 illustrates the ways in which the principal characters in the folktale "Cinderella" are opposites. Almost any image can be a potential tool for webbing or mapping a story. The petals of a flower, the steps of a stairway, the points of a star, or the branches of a tree are just some of the images that can be used to demonstrate the connections in a work of literature. For example, we might label the petals of a flower with a character's personality traits to show how the individual grows (or "blossoms") throughout the course of a story. Since many people are visual learners and grasp ideas more quickly if they can see them illustrated, webbing is an effective tool for examining relationships in a poem, story, or play.

FIGURE 3.2 ■ Web for "Cinderella"

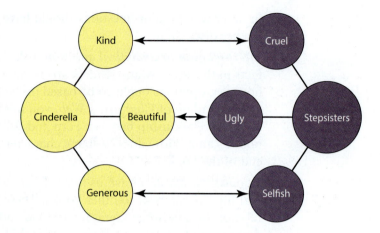

Very much like a web, a story map charts the progress of a book's plot in a visual manner. Figure 3.3 is a very simple story map that illustrates the circular journey of Hansel and Gretel from their home to the witch's cottage and back. The labels suggest possible character development that might occur in the main characters along the way. In addition to being educational, a webbing exercise can be fun for children.

FIGURE 3.3 ■ Story Map for "Hansel and Gretel"

RESPONSE JOURNALS   When we write down our thoughts, we usually think them through more thoroughly. Having young readers write in a response journal, in which they can freely record their feelings, is one way to get them to ponder their reading experiences. One approach to a useful response journal is to have students write a paragraph after completing each chapter of a book. In that paragraph they may express whatever they wish about the characters, the plot, the setting, the theme, and so on. A more directed approach is to give students a set of questions to respond to in their journals. (Review the various types of questions just discussed.) Sharing journals (with other students, with teachers, or with parents) can also be a rewarding experience. Of course, it goes without saying that we should never share private journals with others without the writer's consent. (See Sharon Creech's, *Walk Two Moons*, in which a teacher reads aloud to his class passages from the students' private journals—resulting in some unhappy consequences.)

BOOK REPORT ALTERNATIVES   For many, book reports conjure up dreary memories of dull and rambling plot summaries, often inflicted on an entire classroom of students on an appointed day. However, many interesting variations can actually be stimulating. See Figure 3.4 for some ideas.

Dramatic Experiences

Dramatic responses to literature offer opportunities for individual creativity and cooperative achievement. Most of the following dramatic exercises can be adapted to folktales or to chapters from favorite books.

STORY CIRCLE   A story circle is an experience in which participants sit in a circle (on chairs, on the floor, whatever works) and take turns reading or simply telling stories, poems, memories, and songs. This can be a nonthreatening and very rewarding experience. This could be a fine way to begin or end the school week. The secret is to keep everything informal and relaxed and not to force participation. You may have to make a few rules—you don't want the same handful of people doing all the talking, for example. But it may be best to keep things as fluid as possible, at least at the beginning. You might want to announce a theme—family, holidays, sports, hobbies, and so on. It will take time for some to become at ease with the process, but most will come around—and at the very least, even the observers will gain something from the experience.

STORY THEATER   Story theater is a pantomime accompanied by a narrator who reads or tells the story while others act out the plot. Since even inanimate objects (such as a tree) might be portrayed by an actor, story theater allows for a very flexible number of performers. (Some children may enjoy portraying objects like the moon or a door, for example.) The performance can be as simple or elaborate as the

FIGURE 3.4 ■ Twenty-Five Things to Do with a Book

1. Create a story map for the book.
2. Prepare a two-minute radio spot promoting the book.
3. Write a biographical sketch of the author.
4. Turn one chapter into a child's picture book.
5. Create a collage or montage emphasizing the plot or theme.
6. Write a three- or four-paragraph book review for the local newspaper.
7. Create a dust jacket for the book.
8. Make a list of your 10 favorite things about the book.
9. Create a poster advertising the book.
10. Write a defense for the villain's actions.
11. Pick a favorite scene or chapter and prepare a dramatic reading.
12. Create a diorama of your favorite scene.
13. Create a mobile or stabile representing the theme or a character.
14. Make a cast list of well-known actors for a film of the book.
15. Create a geographical map of the setting based on evidence from the book.
16. Prepare a timeline for events in the story.
17. Write a news article reporting an event in the story, as if it just happened.
18. Write a new episode for the book using the same characters.
19. Create a bulletin board display to entice others to read the book.
20. Rewrite an episode from a different point of view.
21. Write a poem about the book.
22. Create a web illustrating the interactions of the main characters.
23. Rewrite a scene to include yourself as a new character.
24. Write a fictional biographical sketch of your favorite character.
25. Rewrite one chapter as a one-act play.

means and story dictate. Pantomime, because it does not require memorization, is one of the simpler dramatic forms for children. It does require one good reader, however, and some uninhibited actors. Often younger children have few inhibitions, so story theater is a good exercise to begin in the elementary years. The best tales for a story theater presentation are those with plenty of action; otherwise, the performers will be little more than furniture. Many folktales are good sources for story theater, particularly the farcical tales, such as "Clever Gretel," where action rather than dialogue dominates.

READER'S THEATER   True reader's theater is traditionally performed without any physical action whatsoever. Instead, the readers are usually seated, and each takes one of the speaking parts in a script. The old-time radio dramas were, in essence, reader's theater. All the audience's attention is directed to the language, so the readers must be expressive and read with clarity and precision. To avoid distraction from the reading, performers might want to wear uniform clothing—usually in black or black and white. But a reader's theater performance does not have to be a formal affair. It can be readily adapted to the classroom—even on an impromptu basis. It requires no memorization, physical movement, scenery, or props—just a lively script. The best stories are those with several speaking parts, ample dialogue, a fairly easy vocabulary but with expressive language, and, finally, a good conflict. "Hansel and Gretel," for example, would involve at least five characters (Hansel, Gretel, father, wicked stepmother, and witch) and a narrator. To increase the number of parts so more readers can participate, it is easy to divide the narrator's part among several readers. The real fun in reader's theater happens when the readers themselves become engaged in their roles and begin to read with feeling and conviction. (See Recommended Resources at the end of this chapter for a good website for reader's theater resources.)

PUPPET THEATER   Combining both dramatic and artistic responses to literature, puppet theater is a favorite medium of young (and sometimes old) children. Puppet making is an elaborate and time-honored art form, and it can easily be simplified. Puppets can be made from old socks, paper bags, construction paper and sticks, cardboard cylinders, vegetables (they make wonderful puppets, but don't wait too long to do the show), or, for the truly creative, string-operated marionettes with movable hands, feet, eyes, and mouths. The puppet theater itself can be as simple as a table draped with a sheet to hide the puppeteers. Large appliance boxes open up many possibilities. Once the puppet is made, the dramatic part of the experience begins. Stories with ample dialogue and action work best. And, since lines need not be memorized and the puppeteers are hidden from the audience's view, puppet theater can be an ideal form for beginning thespians. It is also perfect for shy children who, behind the mask of the puppet, may find an exhilarating outlet for their creativity.

Artistic Experiences

Another popular means of exploring literature is through art. As soon as they can handle a crayon or pencil, even the youngest children can be asked to draw pictures in response to a story. And for older children, the possibilities are limitless.

GRAPHIC ART   Children love working with paints, watercolors, crayons, and pencils. Drawings and paintings require the simplest of art supplies and minimal initial instruction, yet they allow for a great deal of originality. Having children draw pictures suggested by picture storybooks can be a means of getting them to explore different artistic styles, such as the Art Nouveau style of Kay Nielsen's illustrations for *East of the Sun, West of the Moon*, Beatrix Potter's delicate representational style in *The Tale of Peter Rabbit*, and Ludwig Bemelmans's expressionism in *Madeline*. (Illustrations from these and other works can be seen in Chapter 5.) Encouraging children to draw pictures after hearing stories read to them can result in some of the most highly individualistic creations, for they do not have another artist's work to imitate.

For those who have limited graphic skills, a collage or montage is a viable alternative. A collage is a picture created from various materials (cloth, wood, cotton, leaves, rocks, and so on) that can be fixed to a poster board or other surface to make a unified work. Quite similar is the montage, which is composed entirely of pictures (cut from magazines, newspapers, and so on). Creating a collage or a montage about a favorite story can be both enjoyable and enlightening, since it requires a certain amount of synthesis and analysis. Posters can be made to represent a theme, a character, plot details, or even a mood, using the collage or montage method.

PLASTIC ART   The plastic arts include three-dimensional works (unlike graphic works, which generally are two dimensional). Although sculpture and pottery can be unwieldy to create in a typical classroom, figures can be made from clay, paper, or wood to represent story characters or objects. Another artwork that can be accomplished in the classroom is a mobile, a free form usually cut from paper or cardboard and interconnected and suspended by string or wire so that when hung, the parts turn freely in the breeze. A mobile can demonstrate the relationships between plot elements or characters of a story. A diorama is a three-dimensional scene often created from a shoebox or another carton (an unused fish aquarium, with its glass sides, provides some interesting opportunities as well) and decorated with cardboard cutouts, plastic figures, or other suitable objects.

BOOK CREATION   Making their own books is a rewarding activity for children of all ages, and it is an activity that combines a variety of literary experiences. Very young children can create alphabet, counting, or concept books, or they can do takeoffs on favorite nursery rhymes or poems. Older children might want to experiment with ghost stories, adventure stories, family stories, or poetry. Books can be illustrated with a variety of media—crayon, watercolor, collage, montage, pencil, and so on. Binding the books can be as simple as fastening them in a loose-leaf folder or as elaborate as sewing the pages together and making cloth-covered cardboard covers. Not only does such a project give children firsthand experiences in designing books and laying out pages, but it can also result in an attractive finished product suitable for a gift or a keepsake. Creating a book is a rewarding way of bringing a writing exercise to a satisfying climax.

Regardless of the art project, it is important to remember that the art is an extension of the literature and not an end in itself. In other words, we are not reading *Pinocchio* for the purpose of making our own puppet when we are finished. And the art should not be simply gratuitous ("Now that we have read *Pinocchio*, let's all draw a picture of his nose"). The art project should become a meaningful part of the study of the literature, helping children to understand and appreciate the literature.

Technology in the Classroom

It is possible to find studies that both praise and excoriate technology's effect on our children. Outside the classroom, teenagers are spending an average of nine hours a day using online media in its various incarnations (Common Sense Media). Other statistics show that the amount of time everyone spends reading has declined dramatically in the past generation. One poll found that nearly 25 percent of adult Americans did not read a single book in the course of a year (see Weissman). It is easy to blame this on technology—but it is not that simple. Nor will blame make the technology go away.

In the classroom, particularly in the language arts classroom, technology can be seen as the enemy. After all, our object is to get children to read books, not to encourage further use of their computers, iPads, or cell phones. We should be under no illusion that technology will magically transform our classrooms into stimulating theaters of learning or that it will cause our students to hunger and thirst for knowledge. It is not a silver bullet; it is not a magic potion. Learning remains hard work, it requires discipline and determination, and no amount of visual stimulation will change that.

However, technology in the classroom can be a positive thing and presents a number of advantages. Perhaps most obviously, technology is already a part of our students' lives—even preschoolers can maneuver through a number of educational websites ("ABCmouse," "ABCya!" "FunBrain," "Gameaquarium," "Game Classroom," "Kahn Academy," "Toddler Fun Learning," to name just a few of the more popular). So even the youngest children will be familiar with technology—and many will be skilled at it.

Also, technology allows us to adapt our teaching to the individual students—permitting students to work at their own pace. And studies suggest that information acquired through the use of technology is more readily retained—undoubtedly because the students themselves are active participants in the learning process.

Technology can liven up classroom presentations and activities, making them more colorful, more interactive, and appealing to today's technology-savvy children. (How many of us have sought the help of someone younger to resolve a computer glitch?) Technology can make research easier—answers to all sorts of questions can readily be found with an intelligent Google search during class, for example. But the keyword here is "intelligent"—for unfortunately, the fingertip access to a wealth of information does little good if we don't evaluate that information. We have to be our own gatekeepers. We should maintain a healthy skepticism and know how to draw the line between accurate and useful facts and figures and incorrect, skewed, or blatantly false and misleading information. In other words, computers won't replace our brains. And illustrating the flaws, the misinformation, the propaganda, the oversimplification—all of which are readily found online—is an important, a crucial, part of a child's education.

Although many innovative ways of incorporating technology into the classroom exist—particularly for subjects such as the sciences, history, mathematics, and geography (if that subject is still taught)—when it comes to reading and literature, the important thing is that students read. You don't need a computer to do that. You need a good book (okay, maybe the book is on an iPad). But technology can help bridge the gap between a good book and students' life experiences. Here are just a few options available to teachers who wish to incorporate particularly computer technology into the literature or reading classroom:

- Online video interviews with favorite authors (see Reading Rockets at readingrockets.org)
- Film clips of historical events (see YouTube for fascinating archival materials)
- Film clips of movie versions of children's stories and books (many are available online)
- Interactive websites (such as those mentioned)
- Student-created comics (see the Student Interactive Comic Creator at readwritethink.org)
- Recorded student performances (puppet theater, reader's theater, creative dramatics)
- Student-created presentations (Having students create their own PowerPoint presentations can help them with communication, organization, and creativity—and they are more likely to retain the information than by simply reading it. And second graders can create PowerPoints.)
- Classroom access to the Internet can be used to answer questions, explore options, keep up-to-date with news, connect with the outside world—all right in the classroom.

This list does not begin to scratch the surface of opportunities for incorporating technology into the classroom. And all of these experiences can provide insights into a work of literature—so long as we don't allow them to replace the work of literature.

In sum, technology can give us easy access to a wealth of information. And technology can provide entertainment along with learning. But technology is simply a tool (or a host of tools) that places knowledge at our fingertips. In the end it is the human brain that still must do the real processing, the analysis, the unraveling, the interpreting, the judging, and, ultimately, the creating.

The Common Core Curriculum

In 2014, a new set of educational standards in English Language Arts and Mathematics was implemented across the United States, and the overwhelming majority of states have officially adopted them. These standards, prepared by the Common Core State Standards Initiative, are designed to provide consistent educational outcomes from state to state and, in the words of the initiative's mission statement, "to be robust and relevant to the real world, reflecting the knowledge and skills that our young people need for success in college and careers" (www.corestandards.org). Beginning in 2014, the standardized tests required by the No Child Left Behind Act of 2001 now assess student progress in attaining the goals of the Common Core.

Although most people agree that schools should be held accountable, the implementation of standardized testing has long been controversial. Some fear that teachers will only "teach to the test," that the pressure to perform often results in cheating, and that students from poorer schools are at a disadvantage. And, indeed, the government has given waivers to "failing" schools across the country, based on their disproportionately large number of poor and/or minority students. Nevertheless, it seems likely that most of you who are planning to be teachers will be required to address state and national standards in your classroom—and in most cases that will mean the Common Core Standards.

The documents outlining the Common Core Standards in English Language Arts (including reading, writing, speaking/listening, and language) are complex and detailed. But the most salient features, for our purposes, are these describing the reading component:

Students (in both elementary and high schools) should be able to

- Read closely (understand what they read, the vocabulary, the syntax, and the organization)
- Make logical inferences (draw conclusions from what they read, connect it to other texts they have read, and apply it to their personal lives)
- Cite specific textual evidence (use written material to support an argument or a point of view)

● Read complex literary and informational texts (comprehend a range of reading material—novels, plays, poetry, and the wide range of nonfiction, from science to history to business and beyond) (www.corestandards.org)

This last point is a significant one, since the goal is that the assigned reading for elementary school students should be at least 50 percent nonfiction (purely informational material) and in high school that percentage should increase to 70 percent. The argument for this is that most adults, from college students to people on the job, read primarily nonfiction—letters, memos, technical manuals, and reports. This element in the Common Core Standards has been a source of concern for some experts.

One concern is the list of recommended (but not mandated) nonfiction. The suggested readings include the Preamble to the Constitution, George Washington's "Farewell Address," Lincoln's "Gettysburg Address," and Martin Luther King Jr.'s "Letter from Birmingham Jail"—all relatively short works. (It is interesting that only the Constitution's Preamble is cited—and not the whole Constitution.) The problem is that all of these works were written in a specific historical context and can be fully understood only within that framework. One critic notes:

> The New Common Core Standards are meant to prepare our students to think deeply on subjects they know practically nothing about, because instead of reading a lot about anything, they will have been exercising their critical cognitive analytical faculties on little excerpts amputated from their context. So they can think "deeply," for example, about Abraham Lincoln's Second Inaugural Address, while knowing nothing about the nation's Founding, or Slavery, or the new Republican Party, or, of course, the American Civil War. (Fitzhugh, n.p.)

We should also keep in mind that reading excerpts from historical documents is not the same as reading an entire book of history, in which an argument is supported (if the book is good) by reliable facts that lead to a reasonable conclusion. So if nonfiction reading is to be emphasized in high school, for example, wouldn't it make sense that students read *good* nonfiction? And wouldn't it make sense that they read entire books of nonfiction and not just bits and pieces? It seems unlikely that reading mundane memos, banal reports, and numbing encyclopedia articles will stimulate interest in reading.

But perhaps the more serious concern is why these informational texts, nonfiction, and even technical manuals (from the sciences and technology) should be preferred over the literary classics (novels, plays, poems, and essays), which have long been at the core of humanistic education. In other words, the Common Core seems to argue that English education should be adapted to train students for the workforce rather than to develop their basic intellectual, critical, and aesthetic faculties. We often hear the argument that reading Shakespeare won't get you a job.

(I could argue that my taking high school trigonometry did little to prepare me for teaching English!) Education is not job training. It is mind training. And, contrary to the belief that reading factual, informational texts will improve student reading, studies indicate that reading good literature (such as Shakespeare, Emily Dickinson, Mark Twain, George Orwell, Toni Morrison) develops vocabulary, critical thinking, alternative points of view, aesthetic awareness, social consciousness, and political acumen better than informational texts (and often with a great deal more enjoyment).

As a case in point, in 1993, the Commonwealth of Massachusetts adopted a reading curriculum founded on classic and quality literature. For the next 13 years, Massachusetts SAT scores rose, with Massachusetts students scoring first in national reading tests (Chieppo and Gass). But when Massachusetts adopted the new Common Core Curriculum and dropped much of its emphasis on literature, scores immediately began to plummet.

Further, this approach to reading devalues the intellectual challenges that good literature offers readers. In other words, teaching reading should go beyond simple reading competency. The best literature—from Shakespeare to Jane Austen to Mark Twain to George Orwell (all of whom have been traditionally taught in high school)—offers a cultural and intellectual broadening that readers will not get from snippets in the daily news, memos from the boss, and how-to manuals. The role of the language arts teacher is not only to teach competence in reading but also to teach the accompanying thinking and reasoning skills and the insight into life that great books give us.

Toddlers are enticed to read by their love of language and love of story. And we all know that our favorite books from childhood are the great fictional stories—*Charlotte's Web*, *The Secret Garden*, *Charlie and the Chocolate Factory*, *The Lion, the Witch and the Wardrobe*, *Treasure Island*, *The Adventures of Huckleberry Finn*, *Island of the Blue Dolphins*. These are the stories young readers fall in love with, and these are the stories that encourage them to read more. Moreover, recent scholarship suggests that storytelling fosters learning, cooperation, and creativity. Storytelling is fundamental to human nature—even our dreams come in the form of stories, complete with characters, plots, and settings. (See Boyd, *On the Origin of Story*, and Gottschall, *The Storytelling Animal*, cited in Chapter 1.) When early humans attempted to make sense of the world they inhabited, they created stories—creation stories, heroic epics, cautionary tales, proverbs—they did not write factual manuals describing survival techniques. The concept of story—and its literary offspring, fiction, drama and poetry—is deeply imbedded in our being. And these are the works that will transform young readers into lifelong readers and, more importantly, into critical thinkers with cultural awareness and intellectual insight, and into creative thinkers.

And finally, the Common Core Curriculum standards often encourage the reading of excerpts over complete works—or reading shorter works over longer ones. Perhaps this is a response to an overpacked curriculum, or to the shortened attention spans encouraged by our technology-driven world. Or, it just may be that adults are underestimating children's intellectual capacity. The phenomenal success of the Harry Potter books have belied the notion that modern children cannot tackle long books—I know of second graders who have happily pushed through the 500–600-page books—and look eagerly for more. Too often, as teachers, we get what we expect from our students. Education should open doors, broaden vistas.

When choosing classroom books for both children and young adults, we may want to think more about challenging students—pushing the envelope. Young readers will, more often than not, surprise us. The elementary students who plough through the lengthy Harry Potter books are also the ones who relish the outrageous adventures of Pippi Longstocking, the little Swedish heroine with extraordinary strength and an imitable personality. Nor should we overlook the many engaging informational books—books on history, astronomy, nature, distant lands. At every opportunity, we, as teachers, should be opening doors for our students by sharing books—both fiction and nonfiction. Reading should be a crucial part of our daily classroom routine. And we should be encouraging (and requiring) our students to read on their own. In the elementary years, curiosity needs to be nourished. Older students need to be challenged to read. And we, as adults, need to keep challenging ourselves and continue to grow as readers, so that we don't fall into complacency. This brings us back to the epigraph from Plutarch at the beginning of this chapter: The mind is not a vessel to be filled but a log to be set afire.

Summary

As adults, we understand that we must attend to the physical and emotional well-being of children, but just as important is attending to their intellectual well-being. Today we live in a world beset by media—mostly visual, from computers to movies to television—all competing to see which can produce the wildest stimulation. This makes our encouragement of reading and of the love of books all the more important. Reading books, unlike watching television, requires us to think, to interact mentally. This is why reading is so vital to intellectual development.

Reading should be at the center of the learning experience. But we also should look for ways to keep children engaged in their reading. The reader response approach to literature is a method that encourages children to go beyond merely reading the words in a book; it invites them to bring their own personal responses to the reading, to find in the reading what is meaningful to them, and to explore the responses of others.

Our goal in the classroom should be to enrich the reading experience and stimulate critical reading. Some ways to achieve these goals include reading aloud, storytelling, book discussions, writing experiences (including webbing, mapping, journal writing, and various written responses to books), dramatic experiences (including story circles, reader's theater, puppetry, and creative dramatics), artistic responses in both the graphic and plastic arts, creation of original books, and the extensive possibilities of today's technology. All these can broaden children's understanding, stimulate their imagination, and embolden their passion. Eventually, some of them, with our encouragement, may subscribe to the motto posted prominently in my favorite local bookstore: "Eat, Sleep, Read."

Works Cited

Chieppo, Charles, and Jamie Gass, "Education as Work Force Development Falls Short," *SouthCoast Today* (July 28, 2011). Web.

Common Sense Media at commonsensemedia. com.

Fitzhugh, Will. "Turnabout" (August 28, 2012), educationviews.org.

Giannetti, Louis, and Scott Eyman. *Flashback: A Brief Film History*. Englewood Cliffs, NJ: Prentice Hall, 1986.

Weissman, Jordan. "The Decline of the American Book Lover." *The Atlantic* (January 21, 2014). Web.

Recommended Resources

This list barely scratches the surface, but it is intended only to provide examples of some of the methods discussed in the chapter. There is no shortage of ideas. Hundreds and hundreds of education books are in print, and more are coming out each year. Thousands of websites provide instructional materials as well.

"Aaron Shepherd's RT Page: Scripts and Tips for Reader's Theater," www.aaronshep.com/rt/index.htm. (A fine source for free reader's theater scripts for elementary and middle school use.)

Bromley, Karen D'Angelo. *Webbing with Literature: Creating Story Maps with Children's Books*, 2nd ed. New York: Simon & Schuster, 1995.

"Carol Hurst's Children's Literature Site by Carol Otis Hurst and Rebecca Otis," www.carolhurst.com. (A compendium of book lists and classroom ideas on a wide range of subjects.)

Champlin, Connie. *Storytelling with Puppets*, 2nd ed. Chicago, IL: ALA, 1997.

Dawes, Lyn. *Talking Points: Discussion Activities in the Primary Classroom*. London: Routledge, 2011.

Engler, Larry, and Carol Fijan. *Making Puppets Come Alive: How to Learn and Teach Hand Puppetry*. New York: Dover, 1997.

Gottschall, Jonathan. *The Storytelling Animal: How Stories Made Us Human*. New York: Houghton Mifflin Harcourt, 2012.

Kennedy, John. *Puppet Planet: The Most Amazing Puppet-Making Book in the Universe*. Cincinnati, OH: North Light Books, 2006.

McCaslin, Nellie. *Creative Drama in the Classroom and Beyond*, 8th ed. Boston: Allyn & Bacon, 2006.

Mikkelsen, Nina. *Powerful Magic: Learning from Children's Responses to Literature*. New York: Teachers College Press, 2005.

Norfolk, Sherry, Jane Stenson, and Diane Williams. *The Storytelling Classroom: Applications across the Curriculum.* Westport, CT: Libraries Unlimited, 2006.

Pellowski, Ann. *The Storytelling Handbook: A Young People's Collection of Unusual Tales and Helpful Hints on How to Tell Them.* New York: Simon & Schuster, 1995.

Pitler, Howard, Elizabeth R. Hubbell, and Matt Kuhn. *Using Technology with Classroom Instruction That Works,* 2nd ed. Alexandria, VA: Association for Supervision and Curriculum Development, 2012.

Purves, Alan, et al. *How Porcupines Make Love: Teaching a Response-Centered Literature Curriculum.* White Plains, NY: Longman, 1990.

Salem, Linda C. *Children's Literature Studies: Cases and Discussions.* Westport, CT: Libraries Unlimited, 2005.

Sawyer, Ruth. *The Way of the Storyteller.* New York: Penguin, 1942. (A classic introduction to storytelling from a noted storyteller and author of children's books.)

Schickedanz, J. A., and Renee Casberque. *Writing in Preschool: Learning to Orchestrate Meaning and Marks,* 2nd ed. Newark, DE: International Reading Association, 2009.

Shedlock, Marie. *The Art of the Storyteller.* New York: Dover, 1951. (Advice on storytelling from a celebrated storyteller, a classic work.)

Simon, Fran, and Karen Nemeth. *Digital Decisions: Choosing the Right Technology Tools for Early Childhood Education.* Lewisville, NC: Gryphon House, 2012.

Sloan, Glenna Davis. *The Child as Critic: Developing Literacy through Literature, K–8,* 4th ed. New York: Teachers College Press, 2003.

Trelease, Jim. *The Read-Aloud Handbook,* 7th ed. New York: Penguin, 2013.

Vasquez, Vivian Maria, and Carol Branigan Felderman. *Technology and Critical Literacy in Early Childhood.* New York: Routledge, 2012.

Yopp, Ruth Helen, and Hallie Kay Yopp. *Literature-Based Reading Activities,* 5th ed. Boston: Allyn & Bacon, 2009.

CHAPTER 4

The Art and Craft of Fiction

The Medium and the Message

"Prose is architecture not interior decoration."

–Ernest Hemingway

Introduction

Why is it that we are enthralled by some books and bored by others? Why do some books stick with us our entire lives and others are forgotten before the day is through? Part of the answer, of course, has to do with our individual tastes, interests, and life experiences—not everyone likes the same books. And, in fact, our tastes are constantly changing. Old favorites can lose their appeal and we sometimes find ourselves fascinated by books we once avoided. What makes us respond to literature as we do? Is there such a thing as good literature? Or is it all merely personal opinion? A work of literature—whether it is a short story, a novel, a play, a poem—is the product of a writer with a good idea who is able to express that idea through skillful use of language, imagery, and structure. A good piece of literature forces us both to think and to feel. In this chapter we will examine how authors bring that miracle about. And we will look at some ways of thinking about literature and how and why we respond to books the way we do—a subject we call literary criticism. A chapter like this necessarily relies on a certain amount of terminology, but that is merely convenience so we can carry on discussions. The important parts are the ideas, so keep your eyes focused on the larger picture. Our subject in this chapter is fiction; poetry includes an entirely different vocabulary and we will discuss that in Chapter 6.

Literary Elements: Tools of the Trade

First, let's consider what makes up a story—a story needs a narrator (someone to tell the story), a plot (something has to happen), one or more characters (to enact the plot), a setting (a place for things to happen), an idea or theme (a point the author is trying to make), and, of course, language or style (with which to convey ideas). Knowing something about these features gives us a leg up in understanding the story. For prospective teachers, these tools are indispensable in choosing books and leading discussions. And let's not forget the budding writers who will want to examine this literary architecture to hone their own skills. At the very least, this chapter will provide us with a vocabulary with which we can talk about books.

Narrator

Every story has to have a storyteller, whom we call the narrator. Never think of the narrator as the author—rather, think of the narrator as a mask or persona that the author is adopting. How we respond to a story depends in large degree upon who is telling it. It is crucial that we do not mistake the narrator for the author. In fact, some writers use a device that Wayne C. Booth (1961) calls the "unreliable narrator," a storyteller who cannot always be believed. One of the most famous is found in Agatha Christie's early mystery, *The Murder of Roger Ackroyd*, in which the first-person narrator (spoiler alert) turns out to be the killer. And in Edgar Allan Poe's story, "The Tell-Tale Heart," the narrator turns out to be a lunatic.

So our response to a story depends a great deal on the narrative approach the author uses. We usually find one of three common narrative approaches in children's fiction: first-person narrator, limited narrator, and omniscient narrator.

FIRST-PERSON NARRATOR   Sometimes the narrator is also a character in the story, and this is called a first-person narrator. This is easy to identify, since the narrator refers to him- or herself as "I." Richard Peck opens his Newbery Honor book *A Long Way from Chicago* this way: "It was always August when we spent a week with our grandma. I was Joey then, not Joe: Joey Dowdel, and my sister was Mary Alice. In our first visits we were still just kids, so we could hardly see her town because of Grandma. She was so big, and the town was so small" (1). Naturally, a first-person narrator can only tell us what he or she knows, feels, or experiences, but this is also the most intimate narrator and we come to feel as if we know the narrator personally. Alice Childress's *A Hero Ain't Nothin' but a Sandwich* is about the plight of Benjie, a 13-year-old African American boy struggling with heroin addiction. The story is told in the first person, but each chapter has a different narrator, including Benjie, his mother, grandmother, mother's boyfriend, teachers, and others. So we get the story from multiple points of view, and we, the readers, have to piece together the truth from the often-contradictory observations of several witnesses. It is important to remember that, in many respects, the first-person narrator may be the most unreliable—but also the most interesting.

LIMITED NARRATOR The limited narrator is an outside storyteller—one who is not a character in the story but whose viewpoint is limited to that of a single character. In other words, the limited narrator tells us only what that one character knows and feels. In the first chapter of *Little House in the Big Woods*, Laura Ingalls Wilder introduces her characters like this:

> So far as the little girl could see, there was only the one little house where she lived with her Father and Mother, her sister Mary and baby sister Carrie. A wagon track ran before the house, turning and twisting out of sight in the woods where the wild animals lived, but the little girl did not know where it went, nor what might be at the end of it.
>
> The little girl was named Laura and she called her father, Pa, and her mother, Ma. In those days and in that place, children did not say Father and Mother, nor Mamma and Papa, as they do now. (2–3)

And so the entire story is told through Laura's eyes—but not in her words. The narrator's viewpoint is limited to Laura's, and we will not learn where the wagon track goes until she does. Like the first-person narrator, the limited narrator provides intimacy, but it is not restricted, for example, by the vocabulary or grammar of a 5-year-old Laura.

OMNISCIENT NARRATOR The omniscient narrator is also an outside narrator, but one who can know the thoughts and feelings of all the characters in a story. *Omniscient*, in fact, means "all-knowing." Since both the omniscient narrator and the limited narrator are outside storytellers, it is not always obvious which is being used at first. E. B. White's *Charlotte's Web* opens with the exclamation of the young girl, Fern, "Where's Papa going with that axe?" and then goes on to describe Fern's feelings about the newborn runt who will be Wilbur the pig. We might suspect that this story is being told from Fern's point of view. But in the second chapter, the focus shifts to that of Wilbur. Later on, we see events described through the eyes of the farmer and hired hand and then through Fern's parents' eyes. This shifting viewpoint clearly identifies an omniscient narrator. The omniscient narrator is typically the most detached narrative viewpoint, but it also allows the reader to see the story from a variety of perspectives.

Setting

The setting of a story includes the time, the place, and the social atmosphere. A well-drawn setting helps establish the mood of a story. Wilder's *Little House on the Prairie*, for example, is set on the Great Plains in the latter half of the nineteenth century. So, we read descriptions of the daily activities of the Ingalls family—poor settlers eking out a living in a place where wells are dug by hand, the nearest neighbor is miles away, and the family huddles in a log cabin behind a blanket for a door while wolves lurk perilously close outside.

Sometimes the setting almost becomes a character, challenging the protagonist to show his or her mettle. Setting is crucial in survival stories, such as Scott O'Dell's *Island of the Blue Dolphins* or Jean Craighead George's *Julie of the Wolves*, in which the protagonists are struggling to survive in hostile environments— inhospitable weather, dangerous wildlife, and tormenting isolation.

The setting can also be crucial when the story takes place in foreign lands (Lois Lowry's *Number the Stars* recreates the atmosphere of Denmark during the Second World War), or in imaginary lands (remember Dorothy's observation in *The Wizard of Oz*, "Toto, I have a feeling we're not in Kansas anymore"), or in science fiction, where a future world must be envisioned. Indeed, one of the reasons these stories are so popular is because their settings permit readers to escape to imaginary places, where life is more exciting and where they may forget for a while the cares of their everyday lives.

Character

A story is not likely to stick if it does not have believable and memorable characters. We often remember the characters long after we have forgotten a book's title or the specific details of its plot. Who can forget irascible Pinocchio? Or irrepressible Huck Finn? Or endearing Wilbur and Charlotte? The creation of interesting characters is an essential part of any successful fictional story. Let's consider the role of character in a story.

CHARACTER TYPES   Most stories include a protagonist (the main sympathetic character) and an antagonist (the chief opponent of the protagonist). We sometimes call these characters the hero and villain; however, protagonists are not always heroic, and antagonists are not always villainous. Protagonists might be strong, compassionate, and fearless, but they may also be bullheaded and rash. Antagonists might be dastardly, but they might also have an unexpected streak of generosity.

Usually a story includes several minor or supporting characters, who can be interesting in their own right—Long John Silver in *Treasure Island* or the Scarecrow in *The Wonderful Wizard of Oz*, for example. Many times these minor characters are stock characters representing types rather than individuals—the flatterer, the show-off, the conceited, the tight-fisted, the addle-brained, the snob, and so on. When a character possesses the opposite traits of another character, we call him or her a foil character. "Foil" is a jeweler's term for a setting designed to make a jewel look bigger and brighter. So Templeton, the self-centered rat in *Charlotte's Web*, is a foil to Charlotte, and makes her kind and selfless nature seem all the more attractive.

CHARACTER DEVELOPMENT   Each character may possess specific personality traits, but not all characters are as completely fleshed out as others. Some characters reveal fully developed personalities; these are the round characters. Charlotte, for example, is wise, compassionate, determined, and resourceful; Wilbur is at times happy, sad, frightened, loving, and so on. Other characters are only partially developed; these are the flat characters. We usually see just one side of them (the selfish rat Templeton, the stuttering goose, and the dim-witted farmhand are all examples of flat characters in *Charlotte's Web*).

In addition, some round characters may change through the course of the story; these are called dynamic characters. For example, at the beginning of *Charlotte's Web*, Wilbur is immature, self-absorbed, timid, and fearful, but by the end he becomes brave, selfless, and compassionate. Wilbur's transformation, his intellectual and psychological growth, is what makes him a dynamic character.

Dynamic characters are restricted to the main characters. Any more than that would take a very long book, indeed. Most characters are what we call static characters—that is, their personalities really do not change. The selfish rat, Templeton, is just the same rapscallion at the end of the story as at the beginning— he does a good deed only when there is something in it for him. Templeton is a flat and static character. It could be argued that Charlotte, on the other hand, is a well-rounded character, but one who does not really change. She is wise, kind, and compassionate from the very beginning—and she remains that way. In fact, we don't want her to change. This would make her a round but static character.

CHARACTER REVELATION   And finally, we should consider how we learn about characters in a book. We gain our knowledge of characters in several ways:

- *What the narrator says about the character*—Although reliable, this usually is the least memorable way of getting to know a character (it's like learning about someone from a lecture).

- *What the other characters say about the character*—This evidence is, of course, only as reliable as the source; we must be wary of hidden motives or prejudices. Do we really trust what Templeton the rat says about someone?

- *What the character says about him- or herself*—This information can be reliable, but characters do not always mean what they say, they do not always tell the truth, nor do they always understand themselves. At the beginning of *Charlotte's Web*, for instance, can Wilbur really explain why he is so timid and so self-absorbed?

- *What the character actually does*—Actions, we all know, speak louder than words, and it is through actions that some of the most convincing evidence about character is revealed. The actions of Wilbur, Charlotte, and Templeton really tell us what these characters are like.

Plot

The novelist E. M. Forster once said, "The king died and then the queen died is a story. The king died, and then the queen died of grief is a plot" (86). The point is that the plot is not just a series of events; it is a series of *interrelated* events. In life, for example, you get someone else's mail by mistake, your phone rings and it's a wrong number, your neighbor cancels a luncheon engagement, and a friend asks you to take her to the dentist. This is not a plot—it's just a series of unfortunate events. In life, things don't always make sense. However, in literature, we expect every action to have a purpose, to make some meaningful contribution to the plot. So, in a book or story, the seemingly random events just described might actually turn out this way: The mail was deliberately switched so you wouldn't see the birthday cards that came. The so-called wrong number was a ruse to see if you were home. And your friend doesn't really need a dentist—it's only a ploy to get you out of the house so your neighbors can decorate for your surprise birthday party. The point is that a plot is a deliberate artifice, a carefully woven design. Nothing occurs without a purpose. Let's now look at three common plot patterns—dramatic, episodic, and parallel—and the journey device.

DRAMATIC PLOT A dramatic plot focuses on a conflict that must be resolved. The characters, setting, and conflict are introduced near the beginning. Then the action intensifies over the course of the story until it finally reaches a peak—called the climax. This could be a fierce confrontation, an emotional reaction by one or more characters—it is usually the most exciting part of the story. Following the climax, the story usually moves rather quickly to the end, tying up any loose ends—this is called the denouement (meaning "unraveling") (see Figure 4.1). This structure is probably the most familiar storyline; it is commonly found in mysteries, adventures, romances, folktales, and most picture book stories. E. B. White's *Charlotte's Web* is a good example.

EPISODIC PLOT An episodic plot consists of a series of chapters, each of which acts as a dramatic story in itself. An episodic book often reads like a series of short stories rather than like a unified novel. However, the episodes are tied together by a common set of characters, setting, and theme, and they are usually brought to a satisfying closure at the end. Weekly television sitcoms and dramas are often episodic, each episode being complete in itself. The typical episodic novel is given unity by its theme and perhaps by an overarching problem. Eleanor Estes's *The Moffats* is a series of vignettes about four siblings and their widowed mother who, over a year's time, must adjust to leaving their beloved home. Laura Ingalls Wilder's *The Little House in the Big Woods* uses an episodic plot to relate a series of largely unrelated events during a year in the life of a Midwestern pioneer family. The physical and emotional growth of the child protagonist is often a unifying

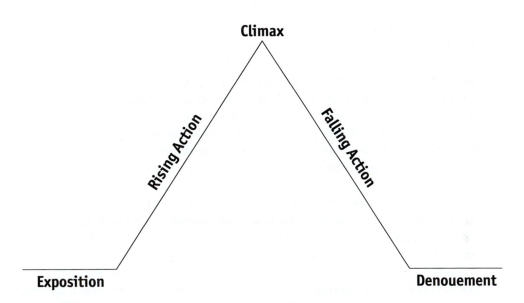

FIGURE 4.1 ■ Freytag's Pyramid, depicting the five major parts of most fictional stories.

element (much as it is in the simple dramatic plot). If we were to diagram the episodic plot, it would look like a series of connected dramatic plots (see Figure 4.2).

PARALLEL PLOT   When an author weaves two or more dramatic narratives throughout a single book, the result is a parallel plot structure. Typically, the chapters will alternate between the adventures of sets of characters—in some cases, there may be three or four sets of characters engaged in their separate activities. Eventually, all the various narratives come together, bringing the adventures to a common conclusion. As with the episodic plot, the parallel plots are usually linked by some common characters and a similar theme. Robert McCloskey's picture book *Blueberries for Sal* (see Chapter 5) is an unusual example of a parallel plot in a picture book. A good example of a parallel plot for older readers is Tove Jansson's *Moominsummer Madness*, in which we follow three sets of characters engaged in different activities on a series of wacky adventures, all leading them to the same place at the end,

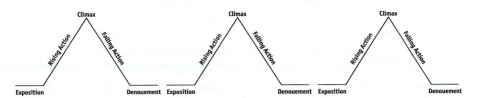

FIGURE 4.2 ■ An episodic plot usually functions like a series of dramatic plots, each part of the series being one episode or chapter.

where everything is happily resolved. (The story is inspired in part by Shakespeare's *A Midsummer Night's Dream,* a dramatic example of a parallel plot.)

THE JOURNEY   It has been said that in literature, there are really only two kinds of stories to tell: In one, a stranger comes to town; in the other, someone goes on a journey. Think of all the heroes and heroines you know who set off on journeys—Peter Rabbit, Alice, Dorothy, the Pevensie children in *The Lion, the Witch, and the Wardrobe,* and Harry Potter, to name but a few. Journeys make good plot devices because, on a journey, the protagonist can meet new people, see new places, and experience new adventures.

Journeys are of two principal kinds—circular or linear. In a circular journey, the hero departs from home, experiences an adventure, and then returns home in the end—older and wiser, presumably. The tale of Hansel and Gretel and their adventures into the woods and back home is a classic circular journey (see the visual representation in Chapter 3, Figure 3.3.). It is not surprising that most journeys in books for young readers are circular. In those early years, children still think returning home is best. *Alice's Adventures in Wonderland* and *The Wonderful Wizard of Oz* are among the best-known examples.

In a linear journey, the hero leaves home, but does not return, making a new home instead. As we might expect, this journey is more common in fiction for older readers. One example involving a very young hero is Roald Dahl's *James and the Giant Peach.* James leaves his home in England and floats across the Atlantic Ocean (in a very large peach), accompanied by an assortment of oversized insects and one worm, and he makes himself a new home in New York City's Central Park. But whether the journey is circular or linear, the protagonist is always transformed as a result of the journey—for having gained knowledge and experience—and this makes the journey an ideal metaphor for life. This happens in the journeys of Ged, the hero of Ursula Le Guin's fantasy *A Wizard of Earthsea,* who travels throughout his world of Earthsea in search of himself. In realistic fiction, Mark Twain's *The Adventures of Huckleberry Finn* is one of the classic journey stories.

Conflict

What makes a plot gripping is the conflict. Conflicts are sometimes depicted in terms of good versus evil or right versus wrong. For a story to hold our interest, something must be at stake. Peter Rabbit's very life is at stake when he ventures into Mr. McGregor's garden. It is usually the conflict that urges us to keep reading. But conflict has another important role, for it is the means by which the protagonist is allowed to transform, to grow, to mature. Conflicts come in several forms, and the four most prevalent in children's fiction are protagonist against another, protagonist against society, protagonist against nature, and protagonist against self. (A fifth, protagonist against fate, is rarely found in children's books.)

PROTAGONIST AGAINST ANOTHER   The protagonist-against-another conflict occurs when two characters—the protagonist and the antagonist—are pitted against each other (see Figure 4.3). They may want the same thing (Cinderella and her wicked stepsisters all want to marry Prince Charming). Or perhaps they have conflicting desires (in *Charlotte's Web*, Wilbur wants to live, and the humans want to eat him). Or perhaps one character is determined to prevent another from achieving a goal (in Natalie Babbitt's *Tuck Everlasting*, the heroine, Winnie, must stop the villain from finding the spring of immortality and selling its water for profit).

PROTAGONIST AGAINST SOCIETY   The protagonist-against-society conflict occurs when the protagonist is pitted against mainstream society and its values and mores (see Figure 4.4). We find this struggle in many stories of racial prejudice, such as Mildred Taylor's *Roll of Thunder, Hear My Cry*, depicting the struggle of an African American family against a community of white racists. But society can offer other challenges as well. Robert Cormier's *I Am the Cheese* depicts an innocent family in a hopeless struggle against government corruption. And Alice Childress's *A Hero Ain't Nothin' but a Sandwich* portrays a teenage character, Benjie, plagued by drug addiction and at odds with his family, the school, and even his peers.

PROTAGONIST AGAINST NATURE   The protagonist-against-nature conflict occurs when the protagonist is engaged in a struggle for survival, usually alone in some natural wilderness or forbidding landscape (see Figure 4.5). For example, Scott O'Dell's *Island of the Blue Dolphins* is the story of a young woman abandoned

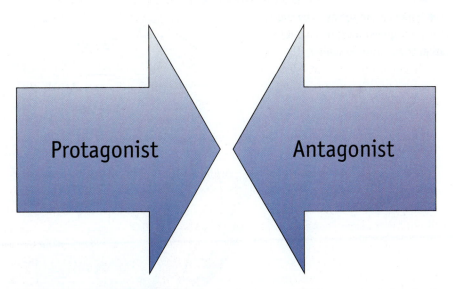

FIGURE 4.3 ■ The simplest conflict is that between good (the protagonist) and evil (the antagonist). The antagonist may be another person, or it may be nature itself.

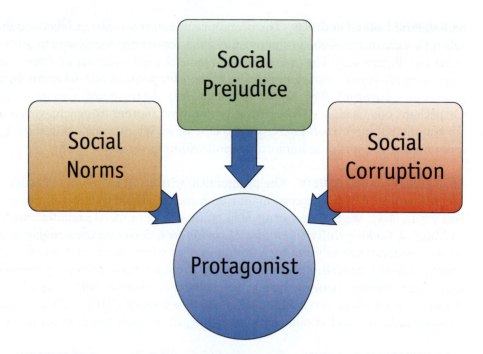

FIGURE 4.4 ■ Sometimes the protagonist is up against society as a whole, and society becomes the antagonist. The protagonist cannot defeat society, so he or she must try to change it, or be changed by it.

FIGURE 4.5 ■ When nature seems to be the antagonist, the protagonist must reach out to embrace it rather than struggle against it.

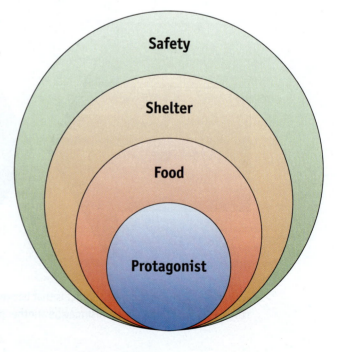

on a deserted island and how she manages to live for 18 years. In Jean Craighead George's *Julie of the Wolves*, a young girl must survive the harsh climate of the Alaskan wilderness. In most modern treatments of this conflict, the protagonists usually survive because they learn how to live with nature—not fight against it.

PROTAGONIST AGAINST SELF   The protagonist-against-self conflict is an emotional or intellectual struggle within the protagonist him- or herself (see Figure 4.6). Max in Sendak's *Where the Wild Things Are* (see the discussion in Chapter 5) is torn between wanting to be a monster (that is, doing exactly as he pleases) and obeying his mother and accepting boundaries (which are literally represented in the illustrations). Max's real enemy is not his mother. It is himself. Judy Blume's *Are You There God? It's Me, Margaret* exposes the various emotional conflicts facing a girl in her early teens. In Patrick Ness's *A Monster Calls*, which we will examine more thoroughly later in this chapter, a young protagonist, Conor, encounters a strange monster's nightly visits, which are metaphorical of Conor's inner struggles with his mother's impending death and his reluctance to let her go.

Style

Have you ever noticed how two people can tell the very same story, but evoke very different responses from the listeners? Some people have a knack for setting the scene, choosing details, organizing ideas, building suspense, and finding the

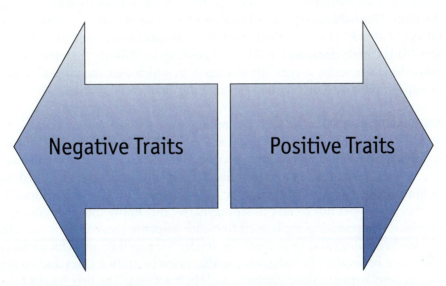

FIGURE 4.6 ■ Sometimes the protagonist's struggle is internal. His or her desires, hopes, and dreams pulling against doubts, anxieties, and fears—and right and wrong are not always clear.

right words. This knack we call a writer's style. What follows are some of the most frequently used storytelling techniques, techniques that a good storyteller has mastered.

EXPOSITION AND DIALOGUE   Every story requires some background information—even if it is nothing more than a simple statement such as "Once upon a time." The narrator's explanations and descriptions are referred to as *exposition*. Exposition may be used to set the scene, introduce a character, and move the action along, as in this example from Laura Ingalls Wilder's *Little House in the Big Woods*:

> When Laura and Mary had said their prayers and were tucked snugly under the trundle bed's covers, Pa was sitting in the firelight with the fiddle. Ma had blown out the lamp because she did not need its light. On the other side of the hearth she was swaying gently in her rocking chair and her knitting needles flashed in and out above the sock she was knitting. (236)

With just a few well-chosen details, Wilder evokes the feeling of the pioneering life—trundle bed, fireplace, oil lamp, knitting needles, and a fiddle for entertainment.

But to give a scene a sense of immediacy and drama, writers often turn to dialogue. Dialogue refers to the words exchanged by the characters in a story. (It is called monologue if only one character is involved.) Dialogue not only furthers the action, it also allows the author to convey individual peculiarities, such as the goose's quirky speech in *Charlotte's Web* when she replies to Wilbur's inquiry about the time: "Probably-obably-obably about half-past eleven. . . . Why aren't you asleep, Wilbur?" (33). Charlotte's intellectual superiority over the other barnyard animals is clearly demonstrated by her greeting to Wilbur: "Salutations!" (35). In a play, the entire script is typically dialogue, in which case the necessary background or exposition has to be revealed through the characters' words.

FORESHADOWING AND FLASHBACK   But telling a story is not merely relating a series of facts with some dialogue. A good storyteller knows how to build suspense, set up expectations, and organize details. Two methods for accomplishing these effects are foreshadowing and flashback. Foreshadowing refers to the dropping of hints about what is to come in the future, as when Little Red Riding Hood's mother warns her not to talk to strangers (we just know the girl's going to do the opposite!). Foreshadowing is used to create suspense (horror films are addicted to foreshadowing) and to prepare the reader for possibilities, which makes the plot more believable. Foreshadowing also helps to unify a story and to make connections between the characters and their actions. The first line in *Charlotte's Web* is Fern's disarming question, "Where's Papa going with that axe?" And these, it turns out, foreshadow the principal conflict—saving Wilbur's life.

Another example of foreshadowing can be found in the opening paragraph of Natalie Babbitt's *Tuck Everlasting*. This is the story of a lonely girl's encounter with a strange family who accidentally stumbled on a magical spring that bestows immortality on all who drink from it:

> *The first week of August hangs at the very top of summer, the top of the live-long year, like the highest seat of a Ferris wheel when it pauses in its turning. The weeks that come before are only a climb from a balmy spring, and those that follow a drop to the chill of autumn, but the first week of August is motionless, and hot. It is curiously silent, too, with blank white dawns and glaring noons, and sunsets smeared with too much color. Often at night there is lightning, but it quivers all alone. There is no thunder, no relieving rain. These are strange and breathless days, the dog days, when people are led to do things they are sure to be sorry for after.* (3)

In this description of the novel's setting, the references to motionlessness, blank dawns, glaring noons, lightning quivering "all alone," and breathless days are all examples of foreshadowing, for this is a tale of high tension, dastardly deeds, and difficult choices. In the well-constructed story, everything has a purpose; there are usually no loose ends, nothing is left undone.

The flashback is rather like the opposite of foreshadowing. It is a device by which the narrator takes the reader back to a time and place before the story's present time. This is often used in books for older readers but is unusual in stories for preschoolers, whose concept of time is not yet sophisticated enough to grasp the subtleties of the device. However, one example that children are familiar with is in Charles Dickens's *A Christmas Carol,* when the Ghost of Christmas Past takes Scrooge back to his youth. The flashback is usually used to reveal necessary background information, such as explaining why a character behaves in a certain way.

Theme

The plot is what happens in a story; the theme is what the story is really about. But the theme should not be regarded as a lesson to be learned. Recall the eighteenth-century moral writers (see Chapter 1), who insisted on hammering home their lessons, and see the upcoming discussion about didacticism. The theme is the fundamental principle or idea that the author is trying to convey. And an idea implies a complete thought. "Friendship" is a topic—it is not a theme. However, "friendship requires us to make sacrifices" expresses a theme. Today's readers prefer the theme to be woven into the fabric of the text—to emerge organically from the events of the story and the actions of the characters.

It is also important to remember that a book may have more than one theme—although one may predominate. *Charlotte's Web*, for example, explores the importance of friendship, the instinct for survival, and the inevitability of the

FIGURE 4.7 ■ Themes Found in Popular Children's Books

Pippi Longstocking by Astrid Lindgren	"To be yourself in a world that is constantly trying to make you something else is a great achievement."—Ralph Waldo Emerson
Charlotte's Web by E. B. White	"There is nothing on this earth to be prized more than true friendship."—Thomas Aquinas
The Moffats by Eleanor Estes	"You don't choose your family. They are God's gift to you, as you are to them."—Desmond Tutu
Are You There, God? It's Me, Margaret by Judy Blume	"It takes courage to grow up and become who you really are."—e. e. cummings
Island of the Blue Dolphins by Scott O'Dell	"It's not the strongest or the most intelligent who will survive, but those who can best manage change."—Charles Darwin
Number the Stars by Lois Lowry	"Courage is being scared to death . . . and saddling up anyway."—John Wayne
Bridge to Terabithia by Katherine Paterson	"Grief is the price we pay for love."—Queen Elizabeth II
A Monster Calls by Patrick Ness and Siobhan Dowd	"If you speak the truth . . . you will be able to face whatever comes."—Ness and Dowd, *A Monster Calls*

cycle of life. The accompanying chart (see Figure 4.7) lists some popular children's books along with some possible themes, expressed through quotations from books or well-known people. The important thing is to note that the theme is an idea and that the idea is universal—applying to all people everywhere.

Another thing to keep in mind is that themes are similar whether they are found in fantasy fiction or realistic fiction—that is, there is no "fantasy" theme or "realistic" theme. All themes address the human condition—even when the novels are set in a galaxy far, far away and are populated with the most fantastical of creatures. It is the theme that gives the story its ultimate meaning. Let's look more closely at *A Monster Calls*, which we referred to in the discussion of conflict. The book, written by Patrick Ness but based on an idea by Siobhan Dowd, who did not live to see it realized, is set in modern-day England. Ten-year-old Conor refuses to face the fact that his mother is dying. His divorced father now lives with his new family in America, and his only other relative is his maternal grandmother, who seems cold and controlling, and entirely unable to comprehend Conor's world. Then, in the middle of the night, a terrifying monster, in the form of an ancient yew tree, comes to Conor's room and announces that he has some stories to tell Conor. Logic tells the boy that this is a dream (or nightmare), but telltale signs keep appearing (his bedroom floor is inexplicably strewn with poisonous yew berries, for example). The story moves between the mysterious midnight encounters with the monster and Conor's troubled life—his inability to cope in school, his mother's rapidly deteriorating condition, personal conflicts with his grandmother and father—all leading to the inevitable climax. In the course of the book we see Conor behave outrageously—in ways that even he cannot understand, until the end, when we all understand. The book's ultimate message, reinforced by the Monster's stories, is finally revealed: *Accepting death means letting go.*

It is a powerful story of love, sacrifice, and redemption—and even when we've finished the book, we are at a loss to describe it as either fantasy or realistic fiction. But it does not matter—for the theme addresses the universal human condition. The novels we remember the longest are the ones in which we discover a reflection of ourselves and our experiences—including the demons that haunt us and the unexpected angels that rescue us. And sometimes the demons and angels are ambiguous figures—and perhaps one in the same. Finally, it is the monster who reveals the theme when he tells Conor, "If you speak the truth . . . you will be able to face whatever comes" (203).

Tone

A story may be serious, humorous, satirical, passionate, sensitive, zealous, caustic, poignant, and warm, among other things. This quality of fiction is referred to as tone. It suggests the author's attitude toward the subject. Here are some of the most common tones found in children's books.

DIDACTICISM   To be didactic simply means to teach, to be instructive. There is nothing wrong with didacticism. In fact, we expect didacticism in a textbook—like this one. But in a novel or story or poem, didacticism can sound preachy and intrusive. Most fiction writers today generally try to avoid it. Beatrix Potter avoids a didactic tone in *The Tale of Peter Rabbit* by resisting the temptation to tell us how bad Peter has been (she doesn't have Peter confess his sins to his mother or promise to be a good bunny from now on, for example).

Too often in didactic stories, the message overtakes the tale and we end up with stereotyped and underdeveloped characters, silly and contrived plots, and phony language. In the eighteenth century (see Chapter 1), adults thought that all children's books should teach moral lessons. Consequently, these books all turned out to be didactic. Take one of the most famous examples, *The History of Little Goody Two-Shoes* (1765)—published by Newbery and written by an unknown author (see Figure 4.8). This is the story of an orphan girl who has but one shoe. When a sympathetic rich man gives her a new pair, she goes about rejoicing that she now has "two shoes." As it turns out, the girl's name is Margery Meanwell, whose father had been ruined by two wicked men, Timothy Gripe

FIGURE 4.8 ■ This is the cover to a nineteenth-century edition of *Goody Two-Shoes*, the didactic and sentimental story published (and perhaps written by) John Newbery in the eighteenth century. The illustration emphasizes the heroine's easy relationship with the animals, suggesting both her simplicity and innate goodness.

(Source: Wikisource, the Free Online Library)

and Farmer Graspall—well, you get the picture. Margery eventually becomes a popular teacher "who had the Art of moralizing and drawing Instructions from every Accident," and when her students lose a favorite pet, she reads "them a Lecture on the Uncertainty of Life, and the Necessity of being always prepared for Death." Eventually, her goodness brings her to the attention of a widowed lord who marries her, proving that virtue does, indeed, pay off. Not only is the tale didactic, instructing us that we should all be more like Goody Two-Shoes, but it is sentimental as well, which brings us to another subject.

SENTIMENTALISM Sentimentalism is the outward show of excessive emotion—or of emotion that is inappropriate to the circumstances. Expressing emotion in a story is perfectly fine—but we usually don't like it when the emotion is out of proportion. (It's sort of like the reactions of small children to the excessive hugging and kissing from Aunt Bertha.) In other words, sentimentalism is the expression of feeling without substance. Let's return to *The History of Little Goody Two-Shoes*, a story both didactic and sentimental. Little Goody Two-Shoes's death is described as "the greatest Calamity that ever was felt in the Neighbourhood," and a monument "was erected to her Memory in the Church-yard, over which the Poor as they pass weep continually, so that the Stone is ever bathed in Tears." A later example of sentimentalism in children's books is found in the Elsie Dinsmore series, written by Martha Finley, beginning in 1867. Throughout the series, sweet Elsie Dinsmore bravely overcomes many heartbreaks and tribulations. But one critic complained, as far back as 1896, "nothing can be more dreary than the recital of Elsie's sorrows and persecutions. Every page is drenched with tears." "Even," the critic continues, "on comparatively cheerful nights [Elsie] is content to shed 'a few quiet tears upon her pillow' " (Repplier, n.p.). This is a sure sign of a sentimental work.

Eleanor Porter's *Pollyanna*, made famous by a 1950s Disney film, is another example of sentimentalism. The young heroine, through her incessant cheerfulness, transforms a perennially gloomy town into a place of irrepressible "gladness." The problem with sentimentalism, as with most other excesses, is that it smacks of phoniness or insincerity, and is often simply silly.

HUMOR   Unlike didacticism and sentimentalism, humor is a welcome feature in all literature. Rare is the child who does not like a funny story. Most scholars agree that incongruity is the foundation of humor. We laugh at the tension resulting from something out of the ordinary. But humor is also elusive; whether or not we laugh at a joke depends on the teller (wording and timing are important) and on us (what we find hilarious others may find offensive or silly). Humor is age specific; what we find funny when we are 3 years old is seldom funny when we are 21. Katharine Kappas identifies various types of humor most commonly found in books for children up through early adolescence. They include exaggeration, incongruity, surprise, slapstick, absurdity, uncomfortable situations, ridicule, defiance, violence, and verbal humor. But it is the child's penchant for physical humor that makes Roald Dahl's controversial works popular. In Dahl's *Charlie and the Chocolate Factory*, for example, several disagreeable children meet their ends in bizarre ways while touring a candy factory. Books such as these allow children to release social and psychological tensions and give them a way of coping with uncomfortable, out-of-the-ordinary situations. It is unlikely that any child ever became violent from reading Roald Dahl—although evidence suggests that seeing violence in the visual media may have adverse effects (see Huesmann).

Humor is how people express latent hostility. Take, for example, a familiar comic situation: A man steps on a banana peel, his heels go straight up in the air, and he lands on his behind. People laugh at this for several reasons. The movement is incongruous and unexpected, and it contains a touch of slapstick. It also makes the observers feel superior (they weren't the ones who fell), and they are relieved the man was not hurt. One of the important prerequisites for laughter provoked by someone else's misfortune is that the victim must seem to deserve the fate or the harm must not be critical. The banana peel mishap is funnier if the victim is a pompous bore, but it is not so funny if the victim is a sweet, old lady—or if the victim dies, which results in dark or gallows humor. A good example of this is Edward Gorey's *The Gashlycrumb Tinies*, the morbidly funny alphabet book briefly discussed in Chapter 5, and see the gruesome illustration from Heinrich Hoffmann's *Struwwelpeter*, a popular nineteenth-century children's book in Figure 4.9.

It is through laughter that we learn to survive. Because it puts everyone on the same human level, laughter becomes the salve of the oppressed and the balm of the weak and vulnerable. And who in our society feels weaker and more vulnerable than a child? It is little wonder children find humor so indispensable to their well-being.

PARODY   Parody is a literary imitation of another piece of literature, usually for comic effect. Parody is to literature what cartoon caricature is to art. Both exaggerate in order to ridicule. For a good antidote to sentimentalism, we can turn to Mark

FIGURE 4.9 ■ This illustration from Heinrich Hoffmann's *Struwwelpeter: Merry Tales and Funny Pictures,* from the mid-nineteenth century, clearly demonstrates the difference in sensibilities between the nineteenth and twenty-first centuries. This rather gruesome depiction of the punishment of a thumbsucker was considered perfectly suitable for 5- and 6-year-olds.

(Source: Project Gutenberg EBook.)

Twain's *The Adventures of Huckleberry Finn*, which contains a parody of nineteenth-century sentimentalism just described. Huck describes the character of Emmeline Grangerford, a young girl obsessed with death, who "kept a scrap-book . . . and used to paste obituaries and accidents and cases of patient suffering in it . . . and write poetry after them out of her own head" (Twain 144). Commenting on Emmeline's early death, Huck utters the classically unsentimental remark: "I reckoned that with her disposition she was having a better time in the graveyard." Twain's comic satire foreshadows the decline of sentimentalism in modern children's stories.

Parody implies a degree of sophistication; after all, if we are not familiar with the original work, we will not get the joke. Mark Twain's parody in his description of Emmeline Grangerford is funnier if we know about Elsie Dinsmore, for example. Once rare in children's fiction, parodies are becoming especially popular in children's picture books. Jon Scieszka's *The True Story of the Three Little Pigs* is a popular retelling of the familiar tale from the wolf's point of view (he was framed!). Another reversal is found in Eugene Trivizas's *The Three Little Wolves and the Big Bad Pig*, which has a heavy-handed but very funny message about nonviolence. David Wiesner's *The Three Pigs* is a sophisticated tale that cleverly deconstructs the story and depicts the characters forming alliances with characters from other nursery stories. And in recent years political parodies of children's picture books have appeared, such as *Pat the Politician* by Julie Marcus and Susan Carp, a spoof on Dorothy Kunhardt's popular tactile book, *Pat the Bunny*. Of course, many of these parodies are intended for adult readers. Parodies demonstrate the vitality of literature and can suggest to children new ways of interpreting old tales.

IRONY You may recall in *The Wonderful Wizard of Oz* that Dorothy undertakes a journey to seek the help of a wizard so she can get back home. On the way, she meets three new friends—Scarecrow, who wishes for brains; Tin Woodsman, who wishes for a heart; and Cowardly Lion, who wishes for courage. On the journey, each friend learns that he already possesses what he longed for—Scarecrow is wise, Tin Woodsman is kind and tender, and Cowardly Lion is bold and fearless. On the other hand, the "all-powerful" Wizard of Oz is revealed to be a phony, an eccentric humbug. In the end, Dorothy finds that she had the ability to get home on her own all along (through the magic of her slippers, which are actually silver shoes in the book).

These are all examples of irony. Irony occurs when the reality turns out to be different from the appearance. It can be intentional (as with the wizard, who knows he's a fraud) or circumstantial (as with Dorothy and her friends, who really are unaware of their own strengths). Irony adds layers to a story's meaning. It can be humorous. It can be tragic. It reminds us that the world is not always what it seems.

Sometimes irony can devolve into cynicism, which is the opposite of sentimentalism. The cynic believes that human nature is fundamentally corrupt and the world is a rotten place to be. Obviously, this is not a tone that is normally found in children's fiction. However, it is a feature of many of the works for adolescents written by Robert Cormier—*The Chocolate War, I Am the Cheese,* and others. Cormier deals with dark topics: a religious boy's school in which the priests are all corrupt, a government that betrays its own citizens. The characters in Cormier's books are thoroughly depraved, and society itself is utterly debased. Frankly realistic, Cormier offers no happy endings or even hopefulness, which, as you might imagine, has led to considerable controversy over his writings.

Literary Criticism: Thinking About Books

Literary criticism examines, evaluates, and interprets works of literature. From time to time, as an educator, you may turn to articles or books about children's or young adult literature as a way to explore a work with young readers. Literary criticism often helps us understand a story or a novel or to see it in a different way. Although critics are often accused of ruining a literary text by overanalyzing it (and this does happen), if we don't think about the text at all and what it means, then we are probably not getting a lot out of it. And part of the enjoyment of sharing ideas about literature is to get different "takes" on it, to discover things we missed, to see how other readers react to a work. In this section, we will briefly look at several ways of reading and thinking about a text, with specific references to some familiar children's texts, to demonstrate how literary criticism can expand our views.

Historical Criticism

Historical criticism is so called because it looks at the world—the society, the time, and place—from which a literary work came and how that world affected the literature. Historical criticism asks such questions as these:

- Who is the author, where did he or she come from, and what was his or her object in writing the work?
- How did the political and social events of the time influence the author and how are they reflected in the work?
- How did the religious or philosophical attitudes of the time influence the author and how are they reflected in the work?
- How does the work reflect the influence of other writers, in form, style, or thinking? How does it reject those influences?
- What did the work mean to the writer's contemporaries? Would they read it differently from how we read it?

Let's take, for example, the familiar folktale of "Hansel and Gretel." One of the troubling aspects of this story is how parents can be so callous as to abandon their children. Of course, we do not know who wrote "Hansel and Gretel" nor exactly when it was first written, but we know it was European and from the preindustrial era (that is, before the eighteenth century), so we will begin there. Preindustrial Europe was a time of widespread famine, and peasants lived on the verge of starvation. The overwhelming emphasis on food in the tale—the children drop bread crumbs, they are enticed by a gingerbread house from which they eat delicious candies, the witch is killed in her own oven, where she had planned to bake Hansel—may be partly explained by the difficult times from which the story arose. Some argue that the abandonment of children might not have been so unusual a thing in a society that often lived in desperation and on the verge of starvation. The historian Barbara Tuchman writes that during the fourteenth century "reports spread of people eating their own children, of the poor in Poland feeding on hanged bodies taken down from the gibbet" (24). However, recent research contradicts the notion that medieval parents did not love their children sufficiently, and tells us infanticide was condemned (see Orme). Knowledge about the historical times in which a work was written can inform our understanding, but we have to take care where we gather our facts. Furthermore, the historical approach often overlooks the literary elements and structure as well as the author's individual contributions.

Structuralism and Formalism

In the early 1900s, two new critical movements began to supplant historical criticism—structuralism and formalism. For our purposes, we will consider the structuralist and formalist movements at the same time (probably a gross oversimplification, but it will serve for our purposes). The structuralist movement is cross disciplinary and can be found in anthropology, sociology, psychology, and architecture, among other disciplines, whereas formalism is strictly applied to literature. The formalists abandon the concerns of the historical critic and are interested in a text as a work of art with characters, plot, setting, symbols, organization, and so on. What the author's intentions or purpose might have been (the so-called "intentional fallacy") is of no concern to the formalists, nor do they care about the reader's emotional response (the "affective fallacy"). What matters is the structure of a work, how the various parts fit together. So, the formalists might ask questions like these:

- What pattern, or underlying structure, is revealed in the plot elements (and what about flashbacks, shifting points of view, rearrangement of chronology)?
- How do the various elements in a text relate to each other and how do they all work together to form a united whole?
- Is there a pattern of images or symbols evident in the work that help unify it? How does that pattern expand the work's meaning?

- Do the characters portray recognizable types? Are they symbols of larger concepts? Do the characters play off each other, reflecting opposites or complements, for example?
- Can the structure of the work be compared to that of other works? And, if so, what are the distinctive differences?

A formalist interpretation of "Hansel and Gretel," for example, would consider the structure of the tale—a circular journey that also contains repetitive elements (the children go into the forest with their parents twice; the nearsighted witch, after caging Hansel, feels his finger daily to see if he is fattening up). It is also tempting to compare the two houses—one cold and impoverished, the other replete with good things to eat and a treasure chest (not to mention a warm oven!). The formalist might examine the parallel roles of the two women (does the stepmother foreshadow the witch?) and of the two children (each one has an opportunity to shine). The overall structure of a text and how the parts relate to each other are the chief concerns of the formalist. But there is so much more to a text than this, as we will see in other critical approaches.

Archetypal Criticism

Archetypal criticism also finds its roots in structuralism (with its attention to literary form) and in the thinking of psychologist and physician Carl Gustav Jung (1875–1961), who believed in a collective unconscious shared by all human beings. Something deep within us contains the "cumulative knowledge, experiences, and images of the entire human race" (Bressler 92). Jung argued that this explains why people the world over respond to similar myths and stories (we find Cinderella stories in virtually every culture on Earth). Jung identified certain character types called archetypes, and these are found in both life and literature, types such as *the innocent youth or dreamer, the warrior, the caregiver, the wanderer, the rebel, the companion, the helper, the scapegoat, the villain, the wise counselor, the magician.* You can probably think of many more. These archetypes appear over and over again in stories from around the world, and the characters of one type engage in similar patterns of behavior. In addition, we can also find situational archetypes in literature, including:

- the **journey** (in which the hero leaves home, encounters trials, triumphs over adversity, and either returns home—a *circular journey*—or finds a new home—a *linear journey*),
- the **initiation or coming-of-age** (which tells of the hero's self-discovery and growing up); and
- the struggle between **Good and Evil** (one of the world's oldest stories—take Adam and Eve for example).

The archetypal critic interprets a literary work as a reflection of a great mythic cycle—which in one sense represents the human lifespan (from innocence to maturity), but also the pattern of human society and civilization in general (the history of the United States is often characterized as a coming-of-age story). The great proponent of archetypal criticism was Northrop Frye, who categorized literature into four great genres—comedy, romance, tragedy, and satire. These he compared to the cycle of seasons. Spring represented comedy and the birth of the hero; summer represented romance, the fruition of love and marriage; autumn represented tragedy and the death of the hero; and winter represented irony or satire, coping with loss. The journey through the year recalls the journey of life. It is a very tidy way to classify literature—perhaps too tidy.

Questions an archetypal critic might ask include these:

- Are there archetypal characters portrayed in the text? If so, what archetypes do they fit?
- Are there archetypal structures? Again, the circular and linear journey come to mind, but now they become symbolic passages. What does the journey represent?
- What recurring symbols or images (objects, actions, or ideas) are found in the text and what is their significance?
- As a result of these archetypal patterns, what larger message is implied by the text? Are the characters enacting great mythic themes?

The tale of *Hansel and Gretel* affords an opportunity to see the archetypal circular journey, during which the young hero and heroine encounter horrifying experiences involving an archetypal figure (the witch). Through wit and cunning they overcome the evil and receive a boon in the form of the witch's jewels. Then, with the help of yet another archetypal figure, the white duck (the helper and, perhaps, a symbol of nature?), they return home triumphantly to the open arms of their penitent father. Of course, this is a folktale and it lacks the character depth of a novel, but the pattern is quite clear. Archetypal criticism invites us to see these larger patterns of literature, and it seeks the common threads that run through all human experiences. But it also can overlook some of the more intimate human aspects of literature.

Psychoanalytical Criticism

Psychoanalytical criticism finds its roots in the work of Sigmund Freud, the father of psychoanalysis, who believed our characters were shaped by the experiences of our childhood, many of which we have forgotten or repressed but remain as part of our unconscious mind. To examine a literary work psychoanalytically is to probe the unconscious of the characters, to determine what their actions really

FIGURE 4.10 ■ Gustave Dore's LITTLE RED RIDING-HOOD invites a psychoanalytical interpretation of the folktale.

reveal about them—or, as often, about the author. (Psychoanalytical criticism is very unlike formalist criticism, which ignores the author's role in the creation of a text.) For Freud, one of the great human motivators is sex, which, in Freud's day at least, was quite often repressed and the source of many neuroses. Figure 4.10 is a nineteenth-century engraving by Gustave Doré depicting the story of "Little Red Riding Hood," which a Freudian critic might find provocative. Some might see the illustration charged with latent sexuality. And is it coincidence that the preying animal is a wolf, the figure our culture also associates with a sexually predatory male? This is the sort of symbolic reading that might be taken by a psychoanalytical approach to a children's text. Other questions that might be asked from a psychoanalytical point of view include the following:

- What is the psychological motivation for a character's behavior? (Dreams? Fears? Obsessions? Unconscious desires?)
- What hidden psychological messages can be found in the language or structure of the text?

- What symbols does the author use and how do they reinforce the theme?
- What does the work suggest about the author's intent? Is the author's own psychological makeup reflected in the work? (Unlike formalist criticism, this approach is keenly interested in the author's imprint—intentional or otherwise—on the literature.)

The most famous modern example of psychoanalytical reading of children's literature is perhaps Bruno Bettelheim's study of folktales, *The Uses of Enchantment* (1976). Take, for example, Bettelheim's analysis of "Hansel and Gretel." He interprets the story as a symbolic representation of the child emerging from the developmental stage of oral fixation—when children want to put everything in their mouths. The tale is rife with food references. The children must be abandoned because of lack of food, they find a gingerbread house that they begin to eat, the house is inhabited by a cannibal witch. The gingerbread house, Bettelheim contends, "stands for oral greediness and how attractive it is to give in to it" (161). He goes yet a step further with the Freudian suggestion that the house is also a symbol of the human body, and that the children's devouring of the house symbolically represents their nursing. The witch personifies "the destructive aspects of orality" and also represents the threatening mother. On the other hand, the witch has jewels that the children inherit, but only when they have reached a higher stage of development, represented by the wisdom they use in deceiving and killing the witch. Bettelheim concludes, "This suggests that as the children transcend their oral anxiety, and free themselves from relying on oral satisfaction for security, they can also free themselves of the image of the threatening mother—the witch—and rediscover the good parents, whose greater wisdom—the shared jewels—then benefit all" (162). As you can probably guess, one danger in psychoanalytical criticism is the tendency to overanalyze, to see every object as a symbol and every word as an expression of an unconscious desire or fear.

Of course, all this psychoanalytical criticism will be of little interest to the child readers, but it can be very helpful for adults who choose books for children. Roderick McGillis argues that if "psychic health depends upon confronting, ordering, and understanding the subconscious, then a psychoanalytic approach allows [adults] to defend certain aspects of children's books that might offend or disturb some adult readers" (100). McGillis points to the notable example of Maurice Sendak's classic, *Where the Wild Things Are*, which was criticized by many adults when it first appeared, for they thought the monsters would scare young readers. Quite the opposite, the monsters captivated, perhaps even comforted, children who recognized their own fears and aggressive impulses transformed and tamed in these tantalizing creatures.

Feminist Criticism

An offspring of the feminist movement of the mid-twentieth century, feminist criticism actually combines other critical methods while placing its focus on the questions of how gender affects a literary work, writer, or reader. The feminist approach might ask such questions as these:

- How are women and men portrayed in the text? What roles do they play and are the roles gender-biased?
- What assumptions are made about the relationship between men and women?
- How are masculinity and femininity defined? Consider the workplace, the home, and society in general.
- Is male superiority or female subservience either assumed or implied in the text? If so, what is the justification?
- What gender conflicts are depicted in the text? How are they resolved, if they are?
- How are readers of different gender likely to respond to the text?

A major concern of feminist criticism is the masculine bias in literature. Historically, most works (including those written by women) were written from a masculine point of view and for male audiences. Literature has traditionally celebrated the masculine traits and portrayed the feminine as weak and subservient. Among the first works to come under attack were the folktales, with their stereotypically beautiful, helpless princesses who needed only a good man to set their lives aright and enable them to live happily ever after. In "Hansel and Gretel," we can see that the feminist critic might object to the portrayal of a woman as either a selfish wife or a cannibalistic witch. The mother/wife is, on the other hand, simply taking a desperate situation in hand, assuming authority where her ineffectual husband will not. And, Hansel also proves equally ineffectual, marking the path with breadcrumbs that are quickly eaten by the birds and then finding himself imprisoned by the witch. It is Gretel who must take the decisive action and rescue them by cleverly deceiving the witch and then killing her. Gretel is, of course, an exception to the rule and refuses to fit into the traditional feminine mold.

The point is that we need to challenge the way we have traditionally read literature. Looking at a literary text from a feminist point of view can enrich a reading, making us aware of the complexity of human interaction. To read a text as a woman, according to some theorists, is to read it with "the skeptical purity of an outcast from culture" (Auerbach 156). To read a text as a woman "means questioning its underlying assumptions about differences between men and women that usually posit women as inferior" (Waxman 150). Feminist criticism therefore ultimately becomes cultural criticism.

Ecocriticism

Among the newest of critical approaches, ecocriticism (ecology + criticism) is an interdisciplinary approach to thinking about literature, particularly focusing on the nonhuman world and humanity's relationship to it. Ecocriticism is a product of the environmental movement, often traced to the 1962 publication of Rachel Carson's *Silent Spring*, which warned of the widespread hazardous effects of pesticides on our environment. After that book, we could no longer take the natural world for granted, and the terms *ecology*, *environmentalism*, *natural*, and *green* have taken on special meaning in our society. So it is not surprising that readers would begin looking at literature in a new way. As a consequence, it is also an ethical criticism in the same way that feminist criticism is ethical—both seeking redress, as it were, for past transgressions and justice for the future. Much like feminist criticism, ecocriticism often argues a social agenda. And, like the feminist critic, the ecocritic is faced with the fact that social attitudes on these issues have dramatically changed in past few decades, and modern literature may hold strikingly different values from the literature of the past. Here are some questions an ecocritic might ask when thinking about a work of literature:

- How is nature represented in the literature?
- What is the role of the physical setting in the text?
- What language is used to describe nature and what does that tell us?
- What is the relationship between nature or the physical setting and the characters?
- Does the literature consider the effect of human exploitation of the environment?
- Does the text argue for humanity's responsibility to protect the environment?

Although this may be a stretch, a possible ecocritical reading of "Hansel and Gretel" might examine the role of the forest—a place that humans have not yet exploited or destroyed (although, remember, Hansel and Gretel's father is a woodcutter, whose job entails the potential destruction of the natural world). The forest, in traditional folktales, is always depicted as a place of mystery and of danger, but the children are much safer in the wild wood (that is, the natural world) than either at their father's home within the clutches of their wicked stepmother or in the cannibal witch's gingerbread house. And we should not overlook the fact that when Hansel spreads the stone pebbles (natural materials) he and Gretel find their way safely home. But on the second foray into the woods, Hansel is forced to resort to breadcrumbs (a human concoction) and they prove ineffective. The natural world of the forest, interestingly, poses them no harm. It is only when they encounter the gingerbread house, which is very much an aberration of the natural world, that they are in real danger. The very materials of the house—cakes, cookies, and candies—are again all human concoctions. (We don't want to press this too far, but the house contains no "natural" foods!) That incongruity alone should bode the potential dangers. After escaping the witch's clutches and heading for home, Hansel and Gretel encounter a natural obstacle—a lake to cross—but once again, nature comes to their rescue, this time in the form of the white duck, who carries them safely over the water to their home. It would seem the natural world, for all its unpredictability, is far more accommodating to Hansel and Gretel than the human world. In fact, their joy over the reunion with their father is curious, for he was deeply complicit in the abandonment plot—so we are left with a problematic ending.

Biologist Barry Commoner, an early environmental activist, summed up the issue with his four laws of ecology:

1. *Everything is connected to everything else.* Whatever we do will have consequences beyond us.

2. *Everything must go somewhere.* Nature does not have waste; nothing can be really "thrown away."

3. *We cannot improve upon Nature.* We can either learn to live with it or suffer the consequences of our foolishness.

4. *For everything there is a cost ("There is no free lunch").* When we take something from Nature, we invariably convert something useful into something useless. (Paraphrased from *The Closing Circle,* 1971)

Ecocritical readings of children's books do have an agenda, but it is an agenda that more and more people feel cannot be ignored.

Summary

Our understanding of literature is enriched when we are acquainted with the writer's tools. Consequently, it is helpful to know about the role of the narrator, the setting, the use and development of character and plot. Equally important are the conflict and the theme, as well as such storytelling techniques as exposition, dialogue, foreshadowing, and flashback. The universal motif of the journey is pervasive in children's books and serves as a metaphor for our life's journey. Children fairly early on become aware of a writer's tone—is the story sad, happy, funny? And although young children will care little about literary criticism, it is helpful for those teaching children of all ages to know as much about the books they are teaching as possible. And, for those working with older readers, the various critical approaches can provide starting points for discussion and alternative ways of thinking about a work of fiction. The more we know about how literature works—how it is put together—the better we will appreciate its accomplishment.

You may rightly ask, what does a young child need to know about literary analysis or critical approaches to literature? The answer is, probably, nothing. But as adults who help make choices in children's reading and who wish to help children become sophisticated and insightful adult readers, we ourselves need to be insightful readers. And, as children mature, we want them to become insightful readers as well. Certainly, the more we know about psychoanalytical readings, for example, the better able we are to understand how a story affects us. And once we become attuned to a feminist or an ecocritical approach to literature, we can see how even subtle literary references can shape our thinking. Reading is not merely entertaining; it is broadening, challenging, enriching, and fulfilling. It is food for the mind and soul.

Works Cited

Auerbach, Nina. "Engorging the Patriarch." In *Feminist Issues in Literary Scholarship.* Ed. Shari Benstock. Bloomington: Indiana University Press, 1987: 150–160.

Babbitt, Natalie. *Tuck Everlasting.* New York: Farrar, Straus & Giroux, 1975.

Bettelheim, Bruno. *The Uses of Enchantment: The Meaning and Importance of Fairy Tales.* New York: Knopf, 1976.

Bressler, Charles E. *Literary Criticism: An Introduction to Theory and Practice.* Englewood Cliffs, NJ: Prentice Hall, 1994.

Forster, E. M. *Aspects of the Novel.* 1927. New York: Harcourt Brace, 1954.

The History of Little Goody Two-Shoes, 5th ed. London: Newbery and Carnan, 1768.

Kappas, Katherine H. "A Developmental Analysis of Children's Response to Humor." *The Library Quarterly* 37 (January 1967): 67–77.

MacLachlan, Patricia. *Sarah, Plain and Tall.* New York: Harper & Row, 1985.

McGillis, Roderick. *The Nimble Reader: Literary Theory and Children's Literature.* New York: Twayne, 1996.

Ness, Patrick, and Siobhan Dowd. *A Monster Calls.* Illus. by Jim Kay. Somerville, MA: Candlewick Press, 2011.

Peck, Richard. *A Long Way from Chicago.* New York: Dial, 1998.

Repplier, Agnes. "Little Pharisees in Fiction." *Scribner's Magazine* (December 1896). www. readseries.com.

Tuchman, Barbara. *A Distant Mirror: The Calamitous 14th Century.* New York: Knopf, 1978.

Twain, Mark. *The Adventures of Huckleberry Finn.* 1884. New York: Random House, 1996.

Waxman, Barbara Frey. "Feminist Theory, Literary Canons, and the Construction of Textual Meanings." In *Practicing Theory in Introductory College Literature Courses.* Ed. James M. Calahan and David B. Downing. Urbana, IL: National Council of Teachers of English, 1991.

White, E. B. *Charlotte's Web.* New York: Harper, 1952.

Wilder, Laura Ingalls. *Little House in the Big Woods.* Illus. Garth Williams. New York: Harper & Row, 1953.

Recommended Resources

Booth, Wayne C. *The Rhetoric of Fiction.* Chicago: University of Chicago Press, 1961.

Boyd, Brian. *On the Origin of Stories: Evolution, Cognition, and Fiction.* Cambridge, MA: Belknap, 2009.

Cameron, Eleanor. *The Green and Burning Tree.* Boston: Little, Brown, 1969.

Cart, Michael. *What's So Funny? Wit and Humor in American Children's Literature.* New York: HarperCollins, 1995.

Dobrin, Sidney I., and Kenneth B. Kidd, eds. *Children's Culture and Ecocriticism.* Detroit, MI: Wayne State University Press, 2004.

Hearne, Betsy, and Roger Sutton, eds. *Evaluating Children's Books: A Critical Look.* Urbana: University of Illinois Press, 1993.

Horning, Kathleen T. *From Cover to Cover: Evaluating and Reviewing Children's Books,* rev. ed. New York: Collins, 2010.

Huesmann, L. Rowell. "The Impact of Electronic Media Violence: Scientific Theory and Research." *Journal of Adolescent Health* 41.6 (December 2007): S6–S13.

Hunt, Peter. *Understanding Children's Literature,* 2nd ed. New York: Routledge, 2005.

May, Jill P. *Children's Literature and Critical Theory.* New York: Oxford University Press, 1995.

Nodelman, Perry. *The Hidden Adult: Defining Children's Literature.* Baltimore: The Johns Hopkins University Press, 2008.

Orme, Nicholas. *Medieval Children.* New Haven: Yale UP, 2001.

Rudd, David, ed. *The Routledge Companion to Children's Literature.* New York: Routledge, 2010.

Tatar, Maria. *Enchanted Hunters: The Power of Stories in Childhood.* New York: Norton, 2009.

Picture Books

The Union of Story and Art

"What is the use of a book . . . without pictures or conversations in it?"

–Lewis Carroll, *Alice's Adventures in Wonderland* (1865)

Introduction

We dare say that most children—at least up until the age of about 7 or so—feel just as Alice when she asked the question in the epigraph above. And the picture books we read as children—books like Beatrix Potter's *The Tale of Peter Rabbit*, Margaret Wise Brown's *Goodnight Moon*, Maurice Sendak's *Where the Wild Things Are*, and Chris Van Allsburg's *The Polar Express*—are books we never forget. In a picture book, the visual and the verbal elements are equally important in conveying the message. Virtually all books for the very young are picture books. The best are almost magical creations that stimulate the imagination and please the senses. In this chapter, we will look at this collaboration of art and storytelling that has produced some of the classic works of our culture, beginning with books for toddlers and moving through those sophisticated picture books that intrigue both young and old readers.

Beginning Books

Tactile and Movable Books

Among the first books we buy for young children are cloth books, board books, and movable or pop-up books, often called "tactile" books because their physical makeup begs to be patted, caressed and squeezed. For one- and two-year-olds, cloth books have long been very popular. They are almost indestructible (they're even washable), and there is no danger that the children will eat the pages. However, they lack the feel of books, and they do not store very easily—unless we put them in sock or underwear drawers. Board books are also quite durable—although they are not so good to chew on. And if they do not exactly feel like books, they are useful for showing children what a book is, how it is laid out, how to handle it, and how to turn the pages. Many classic picture books have been converted into board books (sometimes with abridged texts), including Margaret Wise Brown's *Good Night Moon* and *Runaway Bunny*, and many of Eric Carle's books. Children quickly outgrow both cloth and board books and are happy to get on to the real thing.

Movable books, which incorporate movable parts within the pages (anything from lift-the-flap or pull-the-tab devices to pop-up mechanisms of extraordinary refinement), are very popular, and come from a long tradition. Movable books have been around for hundreds of years—they reach back to the Middle Ages and the Renaissance, although those books were not for children. For example, in the Renaissance, pages with movable parts were used in anatomy books. The earliest movable books for children, dating from the eighteenth century, were of the lift-the-flap variety, inviting children to lift a flap to reveal a picture beneath—perhaps opening the shutter to a window or a door to a cabinet. Another early device, which is still widely used, is the pull-tab, which can be used to reveal a hidden picture or operate several moving parts at once.

In the nineteenth century, movable books approached high art. Nineteenth-century artists used a technique we call scanimation, in which sliding paper gives the illusion of motion. Today, this technique can be found in the skillfully executed books of Rufus Butler Seder, including *Gallop! Star Wars*, and *ABC Animals*. The nineteenth century also perfected the elaborate pop-up book that opened to reveal dramatic three-dimensional scenes with several moving parts, including rotating paper discs called *volvelles*. German illustrator Lothar Meggendorfer (1847–1925) became famous for his pop-up creations, and the Movable Book Society annually awards the Meggendorfer Prize in his memory to honor a modern creator of pop-up and movable books. We typically associate pop-up books with the very youngest children. Dorothy Kunhardt's *Pat the Bunny* (1940) remains to this day a seemingly timeless tactile book that uses both the lift-the-flap and pull-the-tab devices. More of an activity book than story book, it contains textured surfaces (cotton to suggest the bunny's fur and sandpaper to represent Daddy's scratchy beard) and movable Parts (drawers that pull out). It is one of the best-selling picture books of all time. In the United States today, among the most celebrated of pop-up artists is Robert Sabuda. His lavish pop-up books include a dazzling version of L. Frank Baum's *The Wonderful Wizard of Oz*, Lewis Carroll's *Alice's Adventures in Wonderland*, his own *Winter's Tale* and *The White House: A Pop-up of Our Nation's Home*, and many more. Every page opens to an elaborate set piece with many movable parts (resulting in some very thick books). Equally accomplished is Matthew Reinhart, who has collaborated with Sabuda on several books, including *Encyclopedia Prehistorica: Dinosaurs*, a masterful work appealing to the fascination so many young children have with those awesome creatures. On his own, Reinhart has created works such as the intriguing concept books *Animal Popposites: A Pop-up Book of Opposites* and *Cinderella: A Pop-up Fairy Tale*. All these books have raised the bar for future pop-up and movable books.

Alphabet Books

Hornbooks, battledores, and primers (see Chapter 1) might be considered the earliest alphabet books. But it was in the late nineteenth century that carefully crafted, artistically beautiful alphabet books began to come into their own, *Kate Greenaway's Alphabet* (1885) being among the first. Since then, the concept of the alphabet book (and its sister, the counting book) has been a mainstay among books for young children. This is partly because the books can help teach children to count and recognize letters, but it's also because they provide authors and illustrators limitless creative possibilities. In alphabet and counting books, artists can concentrate on images without being constrained by a storyline. Alphabet and counting books offer their own challenges: without a story, what will maintain the reader's attention, and what will give the book a sense of artistic unity? To resolve these matters, most alphabet and counting book illustrators focus on a theme to unify their books. For example, they may be unified by a subject (such as animals in Bert Kitchen's *Animal Alphabet*), a specific design pattern (as in Suse MacDonald's *Alphabatics*, in which the letters are transformed into objects), an idea, or a theme (such as the alphabet drama in Chris Van Allsburg's *Z Was Zapped*, in which each letter appears successively on stage only to meet some bizarre fate).

Most alphabet books operate on the premise that children learn the sounds of the alphabet through words that begin with those letters. This is, in many ways, a false premise. For example, the letter *A* might be represented by a word like "apple," but "A" is pronounced in several ways. We could just as well use "aardvark," "air," "ape," or "automobile"—all of which have different "*A*" sounds. The consonants are usually much easier. The sounds of "*B*," "*D*," and "*F*," for example, are quite consistent, and Dr. Seuss' lively alphabet book, *Dr. Seuss's ABC*, can effectively demonstrate the sound of "*F*" with a mythical creature called the "Fiffer Feffer Feff." However, the consonant *C* is another matter. Does it sound like the "*C*" in "ceiling" or in "cat" or in "church" or in "czar" or in "chute"? It can even be silent, as in "ctenoid" (meaning having teeth like structures, like a comb). And what about that troublesome "*X*"? It is interesting to see how many alphabet books resort to using "xylophone," which really starts with the sound for "*Z*." We turn again to Dr. Seuss, who had a better idea, showing us that we can learn the sound of "*X*" by listening to such words as "ax" and "extra fox."

The point is, at their best, alphabet books can offer only approximate associations of sounds and letters. The quirkiness of the English language makes the alphabet book an imperfect tool. Children quickly learn that the associative sounds of letters frequently don't help them pronounce or spell words. Try pronouncing these words as they are spelled: *bough, cough, island, knot, weight, Wednesday.* In the end, we have to accept that the erratic spelling of English requires that we memorize the spellings and sounds of hundreds and hundreds of words.

So if it is designed to introduce letters and their sounds and shapes to children, the alphabet book's first goal should be clarity and simplicity. Most alphabet books place the letters and the pictures that represent them side by side on the same page, or on facing pages. An exception is Chris Van Allsburg's *Z Was Zapped*, in which readers are invited to guess what calamity is befalling each letter (*B* is "badly bitten," *K* is "kidnapped," and so on). The text for each illustration is on the reverse side of the page, where readers can confirm their guesses. It is also helpful if the letters are set in a clear and easily recognizable typeface. The artist must decide whether or not to include both upper- and lowercase letters (of course, children have to learn both eventually).

Although familiar words usually accompany the letters ("A is for apple, B is for bear"), sometimes it is fun to offer challenges. Bert Kitchen's *Animal Alphabet* includes stunning paintings of such creatures as an ibex, a dodo, and a jerboa—unfamiliar animals to many children (and adults), but what a great way to discover new and strange animals. After all, one of the important objectives of any book should be to expand our understanding of the world. How else do we learn new things? On the other hand, Joan Walsh Anglund's *A Is for Always* uses abstract concepts far beyond cognitive skills of its intended readers—very young children. For example, *D* is for "determined," *E* is for "efficient," and *Y* is for "young-in-heart." Try explaining those words to a three-year-old.

Finally, we come to those alphabet books that really have no intention of teaching the alphabet—those for advanced readers (sometimes even grownups). Many of these books are really exercises in artistic creativity. Margaret Musgrove's *Ashanti to Zulu: African Traditions* is a rather sophisticated alphabet book for much older children (those in the period of concrete operations). It presents the alphabet through descriptions of traditional African cultures. Chris Van Allsburg's *Z Was Zapped*, mentioned previously, describes a series of alphabetical disasters befalling each letter in turn, and is clearly meant for readers who already know the alphabet. Judith Viorst's *The Alphabet from Z to A (With Much Confusion on the Way)* even casts aside the traditional order of the letters. Graeme Base's *Animalia* is a lavishly illustrated book that uses, as the title suggests, animals to introduce the letters of the alphabet. The full-color, double-page spreads abound with objects that help to reinforce the letter sounds, and throughout are hidden pictures of the artist as a child. The result is a visual feast that accompanies an imaginative, tongue-twisting text—a treat for adults as well as for children. Oliver Jeffers' comical *Once*

Upon an Alphabet: Short Stories for All the Letters, is a witty take on the alphabet book, as it provides a short story for each letter. It's the sort of alphabet book that can be enjoyed by all ages. And there is Edward Gorey's *The Gashlycrumb Tinies*, which depicts the demise of 26 children in a series of morbid catastrophes (one falls down the stairs, one chokes on a peach, one is trampled in a brawl, one drinks too much gin)—gruesome, perhaps, but the hysterical illustrations will make this an immediate hit for a teenager. So, an alphabet book is not always an educational tool; it may just be an aesthetic treat for all readers.

Counting Books

Counting books or number books (both names are used) may be even less successful than alphabet books in achieving their goals. The concept of counting is something that children do not fully grasp until they reach Piaget's period of concrete operations, for they need to understand the concepts of conservation (some things remain the same even if their shape changes), reversibility (some things can be undone), and so on. Nevertheless, counting books offer opportunities for young children to practice their numbers and to count (and, like alphabet books, they offer artists opportunities to showcase their talents). Alison Jay's *1, 2, 3: A Child's First Counting Book* is an example, with imaginative and colorful illustrations drawn from familiar folk tales. Anthony Browne's *One Gorilla: A Counting Book* asks readers to count various species of primates drawn in Browne's inimitable style. Tom and Muriel Feelings' very beautiful counting book, *Moja Means One: A Swahili Counting Book*, introduces cultural information along with counting concepts; it is clearly intended for readers who can already count. Molly Bang's award-winning *Ten, Nine, Eight*, asks the readers to count backward. Pat Hutchins's *The Doorbell Rang* includes the concepts of division and addition. And S. T. Garne's *One White Sail*, illustrated by Lisa Etre, takes readers to the magic of the Caribbean with such evocative lines as "Five blue doors/in the baking hot sun/ Six wooden windows/let the cool wind run." Today, counting books have joined the ranks of the many very handsome picture books being produced for young children, and we no longer have to settle for the ordinary and the humdrum.

Concept Books

Concept books are similar to alphabet and counting books in that they are usually instructional, but introducing ideas such as colors (Bill Martin Jr.'s *Brown Bear, Brown Bear, What Do You See?* or Leo Lionni's *A Color of His Own*), shapes (Suse MacDonald's *Shape by Shape*), or opposites (Laura Vacaro Seeger's *Black? White! Day? Night!*). These books are short, and rely chiefly on illustration to get their points across. They work best when they are kept simple and direct. *Eric Carle's Opposites* is an example that identifies very basic concepts—day/night, up/

down—and additionally included tabs that young readers lift to reveal the opposite. This interactive book allows them to guess what the opposite is.

Again, we have to look to Piaget for guidance. For, as with numbers and counting, certain concepts are simply beyond the developmental stage of very young children. If the concepts can be easily classified, differentiated, and visually depicted—for example, basic colors or shapes (square, circle, triangle)—most three- and four-year-olds can grasp them. Relative size can also be explained to very young children, (For an example of an illustration providing an unusual—and dramatic— perspective, see David Aquilar's drawing of the Solar System in Chapter 10, Figure 10.3.). But many concepts are either too sophisticated for the very young or unsuited to a book format. For example, books describing sounds (such as sounds of bells, horns, drums, and so on) are seldom helpful, unless they contain, as many do now, actual recordings of the sounds being presented. Equally difficult is trying to explain movement—fast and slow, for example—in a book for a 3-year-old. Some concepts are best taught through life experiences rather in the pages of a book.

Picture Storybooks

Wordless Picture Storybooks

By far, most of the picture books young children read (or have read to them) are the picture storybooks. These include the wordless picture storybook, which is usually intended for very young children. Wordless picture books present interesting challenges for both the illustrator and the reader. (See the essays by Cianciolo [1984] and Groff [1984] for two different viewpoints on the value of wordless picture books.) The key to a successful wordless picture book is the storytelling quality of its illustrations. Indeed, some wordless picture books are quite sophisticated and intended for older readers. In Mitsumasa Anno's *Anno's Journey*, a lone traveler makes his way through Europe on horseback; moving from countryside to village to city, he travels across time as well. If we look closely, we will see, among other things, Little Red Riding Hood and the Big Bad Wolf, Don Quixote tilting at a windmill, Big Bird and Kermit the Frog from *Sesame Street*, a developing romance, an escaping prisoner, and so on. It is also a seek-and-find book in which we are invited to locate the traveler in each picture. The most famous seek-and-find books are probably the *Where's Wally* books, created by the British illustrator Martin Handford (the American editions became *Where's Waldo?*).

Other examples include Eric Rohmann's Caldecott Award–winning *My Friend Rabbit* (see Figure 5.1), a delightful story in pictures showing Rabbit's bizarre idea for retrieving Mouse's airplane from a treetop—stacking animals (including a hippo to a rhinoceros to an elephant, among others) in order to reach the high branches.

"Not to worry, Mouse,
I've got an idea."

FIGURE 5.1 ■ Eric Rohmann's Caldecott Award–winning *My Friend Rabbit* is virtually a wordless picture book, with only minimal text at the very beginning, in the middle, and at the end of the story. This illustration is the final one in the book. Rohmann has placed the characters in the upper-right corner, suggesting that they are high up in the tree. Note that he also uses artistic conventions to suggest movement.

Although not entirely wordless—it has a brief introductory and a briefer concluding sentence—the book's impact comes from the comical illustrations, including four wary ducklings who watch the whole fiasco. David Wiesner, a three-time Caldecott medalist, is a modern master of the wordless picture book. His *Tuesday* (see Figure 5.2) is a fanciful tale of what might happen if, for one night only, frogs could fly. The stunning full-color illustrations, with an unsettling surrealistic mood, depict a series of vignettes—a record of the occurrences on this magical night. And Chris Raschka's charming Caldecott Medal-winning *A Ball for Daisy* is the deceptively simple story of a dog losing her favorite toy—a red ball—and the subsequent events. It is an excellent example of how a gifted illustrator can convey both meaning and emotion with just a few lines and a splash of color.

The success of a wordless storybook depends on the narrative quality of the pictures. Are the picture details adequate to replace the words? Does the sequence of the illustrations convey the plot development? Is the style of the illustrations

FIGURE 5.2 ■ David Wiesner's *Tuesday,* a delightfully surreal story about frogs taking flight on the lily pads one evening, is superbly illustrated by these surrealistic images. Surrealism is all about startling juxtapositions—very realistic frogs engaged in very unreal behavior. Wiesner uses a color palate of blues and lavenders appropriate to the evening, and his details are exquisitely realistic—notice the patterns on the rotting log and a delicate waterlily in bloom. But he does not take himself too seriously, and thoroughly enjoys giving human expressions to the fishes gaping up from the pond and the dumbfounded turtle as they watch the smug frogs lift off on their fanciful night journey.

Source: From *Tuesday* by David Wiesner. Copyright 1991 by David Wiesner. Reprinted by permission of Clarion Books, an imprint of Houghton Mifflin Harcourt Publishing Company. All rights reserved.

suited to the tone and theme of the story? And, of course, most important of all, are the illustrations and the concept compelling?

The Picture Storybook's Appeal: An Example

To begin our examination of the makeup of the typical picture storybook, let's look at one deceptively simple example of the genre, *The Tiger Who Came to Tea,* written and illustrated by Judith Kerr (see Figure 5.3). First published in 1968, it

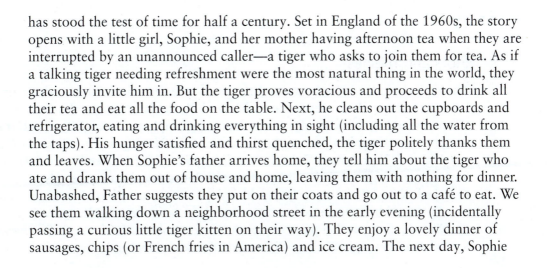

FIGURE 5.3 ■ In this illustration from Judith Kerr's *The Tiger Who Came to Tea*, the text merely tells us of the tiger's outrageous behavior, devouring all the food and drink in the house. The illustration, however, depicts Sophie's clear affection for the mysterious stranger who arrived unexpectedly for tea, removing any cause for the reader's concern.

has stood the test of time for half a century. Set in England of the 1960s, the story opens with a little girl, Sophie, and her mother having afternoon tea when they are interrupted by an unannounced caller—a tiger who asks to join them for tea. As if a talking tiger needing refreshment were the most natural thing in the world, they graciously invite him in. But the tiger proves voracious and proceeds to drink all their tea and eat all the food on the table. Next, he cleans out the cupboards and refrigerator, eating and drinking everything in sight (including all the water from the taps). His hunger satisfied and thirst quenched, the tiger politely thanks them and leaves. When Sophie's father arrives home, they tell him about the tiger who ate and drank them out of house and home, leaving them with nothing for dinner. Unabashed, Father suggests they put on their coats and go out to a café to eat. We see them walking down a neighborhood street in the early evening (incidentally passing a curious little tiger kitten on their way). They enjoy a lovely dinner of sausages, chips (or French fries in America) and ice cream. The next day, Sophie and her mother shop for more food, buying a huge tin of tiger food just in case the tiger should return—"but he never did."

The simple pencil-and-crayon drawings capture life in postwar England, when many people had limited means and dining out was a rare treat. The story has a pervasive magical quality—a famished talking tiger dropping in unexpectedly for tea is treated as an ordinary everyday occurrence. And, as in most successful picture books, the illustrations carry us beyond what the text tells us. What might have been a terrifying experience is portrayed as a mildly inconvenient disruption of the daily routine. In fact, the story depicts an exciting interlude in the ordinarily humdrum everyday life of a little girl. It is every child's dream. As readers, we want to believe in the story.

For 50 years, this has been one of the most popular picture books in England. It has been made into a play, and even enjoys a Facebook page. The book's popularity derives from its juxtaposition of mystery and familiarity, of the extraordinary and the everyday, of excitement and contentment. But we might also argue that *The Tiger Who Came to Tea* has all the elements children look for in a good picture storybook:

- an engaging and well-told story,
- interesting characters we care about,
- illustrations that both depict and extend the narrative,
- an artistic style that captures the mood of the text, and
- illustrations and text that complement each other.

Let's examine these features in a bit more depth.

The Story

Plots and Themes

The typical picture book contains 32 pages and fewer than 2,000 words (many have far fewer), which means the author and illustrator must use the space wisely. When a storyline is involved, the text has to be simple and straightforward. If there is a plot (see Chapter 4), it may be dramatic, as in *The Tiger Who Came to Tea* (see Figure 5.3) or Beatrix Potter's *The Tale of Peter Rabbit* (see Figure 5.4), which focuses on a single issue that must be resolved. Or, the plot may be episodic, as in Ezra Jack Keats' *The Snowy Day*, which depicts a series of loosely related events usually united by a theme (what can a little boy do in the snow?).

We even find parallel plots in picture books. Robert McCloskey's *Blueberries for Sal* describes a girl (Sal) and her mother picking blueberries on a hill.

Unbeknownst to them, on the other side of the hill, a mother bear and her cub are eating blueberries. Two sets of characters are engaged in their separate (or parallel) activities. In an unexpected mix-up, Sal ends up with the mother bear, and the cub ends up with Sal's mother—to the surprise of the mothers. Everything, happily, is straightened out in the end, and the proper families are reunited. The point is that a good picture-book story is engaging but not necessarily simplistic. It makes the child reader want to keep reading.

Naturally, the older the intended audience, the more sophisticated the story needs to be, or the more complicated the characters, which brings us to the next story element—the theme. Just as in books for adults, picture book stories have themes, central ideas that govern the plot. Although it is tempting to state the theme with a single word, such as "family," "courage," "perseverance," or "acceptance," you will recall from Chapter 4 that the theme of a book is an idea that is expressed in a complete sentence. For example, if we were to identify a theme in *The Tiger Who Came to Tea*, it might be something like this: "Life is an adventure to be welcomed and celebrated." Or if we were to look for a theme in Maurice Sendak's *Where the Wild Things Are*, we might find this: "Our actions have consequences." Other themes might include these: "A parent's love in unconditional" or "Our dreams can help us cope with reality." A single book may actually have several themes. Why is it important for us to identify themes in children's books? Themes express attitudes on life and on society. Recently, an apparently innocent picture book came under fire for its portrayal of American history. Ramin Ganeshram's *A Birthday Cake for George Washington*, illustrated by Vanessa Brantley-Newton and published in 2016, depicts an African-American slave and his daughter preparing the President's birthday cake and discover they are out of sugar. Although the plot seems innocent enough, the portrayal of the slaves as cheerfully working in the service of the Washington family ignores the harsher realities of slave life in early America. In other words, the theme running through the story is that Washington's slaves happily served their master, and that they saw it as an honor to be a slave of the first American President—a sentiment that is at odds with historical facts. Critics argue that apologists for slavery are out of place in twenty-first-century American picture books. We always need to be alert to social and political messages conveyed by both words and pictures.

Characters

It is not realistic to expect fully developed, dynamic characters in a short picture book, but that does not mean the characters cannot be interesting or that they do not have depth. The characters in a picture book tend to be identified by one or two dominant traits. For example, Beatrix Potter's Peter Rabbit is adventurous and impishly rebellious. Ezra Jack Keats' Peter in *The Snowy Day* is a typically curious little boy delighting in the new snow. And Sophie in *The Tiger Who Came to Tea* (see Figure 5.3) is portrayed as a gentle, loving, and accepting girl, who has nothing to fear from the strange tiger who invites himself to tea. Children tend to identify with characters like themselves, and protagonists in picture books are most often young children (or animals like Peter Rabbit, who exhibit childlike qualities). In fact, we can usually determine the age of the intended reader by establishing the age of the protagonist. Keats' Peter appears to be about 5 years old; hence, the intended reader can be assumed to be around age 4 or 5. (This is admittedly a little harder when the protagonist is a talking animal or a machine, like Mary Ann, the steam shovel in Virginia Lee Burton's *Mike Mulligan's Steam Shovel*, in which case we have to rely on the treatment of the subject and the language.)

Language

The picture-book format requires that the language be carefully chosen to accompany the pictures. The language has to be economical—it can't take up too much space. Also, very young children enjoy repetitious word patterns, which aid the memory and invite them to join in the reading. Anyone who has read Wanda Gág's classic *Millions of Cats* can attest to this. Children love to join in the refrain: "hundreds of cats, thousands of cats, millions and billions and trillions of cats."

And (this may surprise you), the language need not be simple. We should not be put off if a book includes some difficult words. In *The Tale of Peter Rabbit* (see Figure 5.4), Beatrix Potter uses "implored," "exert," "sieve," "scuttered," "fortnight," and "chamomile"—not exactly everyday words—and children have been enjoying that book for over a century. (A word to adults—if you don't know a word in a children's book, look it up!) Part of growing up is learning the language, expanding the vocabulary, and that is a good deal of what reading is all about. Children also like made-up words. Joseph Jacobs retells an old folk tale, *Master of All Masters*, in which the maid must learn odd new names for everyday items (a bed becomes a "barnacle," a cat a "white-faced simminy," and a fire a "hot cockalorum"). It is hilarious wordplay, and children love these linguistic acrobatics. It is good to keep in mind that many (perhaps most) children enjoy language and a good picture book adds to that enjoyment.

Picture-Book Art

The time was when children's picture books contained rather crude, artless illustrations, perhaps because adults did not think children would know the difference. But with the advent of more sophisticated printing techniques (including color printing) in the nineteenth century, picture-book art became real art, and talented artists began illustrating books for children. Today, we can find gorgeously illustrated books for children by first-rate artists. There is no need to settle for inferior artwork in children's books. But it is helpful to know something about book illustration and pictorial art in general to help us in selecting and evaluating picture books for children.

Picture-book art is by and large narrative art; that is, it tells a story or conveys a concept. But it often goes far beyond that. By applying lines, shapes, textures, and colors to a flat surface, and effectively using space and arrangement, an artist can create the illusion of three dimensions or evoke specific emotional responses in us, such as joy or sadness, serenity or agitation. Let's examine these artistic elements more closely to see how they are used in children's picture books.

Line, Shape and Space

When we strip everything else away, a drawing is made up of lines, shapes, and empty space. Lines convey meaning; they indicate the forms of objects—for example, an artist can use a line to draw a dog—but lines can also suggest texture, depth, and motion. Horizontal lines can suggest calm and stability (recalling firm, solid ground), whereas vertical lines can suggest height and distance. Sharp and zigzagging lines can suggest excitement and rapid movement (think of a lightning bolt). In Ludwig Bemelmans's illustration for *Madeline* (Figure 5.5), the lines direct our eyes from the middle of the page to the bottom; the uniformed girls, "in two

FIGURE 5.4 ■ Beatrix Potter's watercolor illustration for *The Tale of Peter Rabbit* shows Peter brazenly eating radishes from Mr. McGregor's garden—defying his mother's warning. The style, despite Peter's handsome coat, is largely realistic. Potter's light hand and delicate coloring give her illustrations both warmth and charm.

FIGURE 5.5 ■ *Madeline*, by Ludwig Bemelmans, is the first of several books about an irrepressible little girl in a Parisian convent school. The illustrations are interesting examples of Expressionistic art. Notice the angularity of the figures and the exaggerated height of the nun, Miss Clavel, accompanying the 12 little girls who walk, as we are told, in "two straight lines" (surely a commentary on convent school discipline). The Paris Opera in the background is loosely sketched; there is no attempt at realistic depiction. There is a carefree jocularity in these pictures that aptly characterizes the mood of the story.

straight lines," are moving toward us. The lines suggest the orderliness of the convent school, overseen by the dominating and very straight figure of Miss Clavel. Nevertheless, there are barely two straight lines in the entire sketch, and the Paris Opera House seems to be suggested rather than carefully drawn. Ultimately, the lines draw us to the kindly figure in the lower left feeding the horse. For another use of line, see Nielsen's portrayal of the ball from "The Twelve Dancing Princesses" (Chapter 7, Figure 7.7). The sweeping curve of the lines suggests an otherworldly grace and elegance appropriate to the magical story's fairy-tale setting.

Like lines, shapes such as circles, ovals, squares, rectangles and triangles can define objects, and can also elicit emotional reactions. Rounded shapes tend to suggest comfort, warmth (see Figure 5.1 and also Zelinsky's portrait of Rapunzel's family, Chapter 7, Figure 7.6), energy and harmony (see Figure 5.6). On the other hand, squares, rectangles, and triangles can convey stability and conformity, but if they are tilted in unusual ways, they become unsettling and suggest something out of kilter (see Figure 5.7).

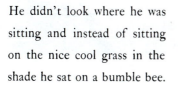

He didn't look where he was sitting and instead of sitting on the nice cool grass in the shade he sat on a bumble bee.

FIGURE 5.6 ■ This illustration by Robert Lawson for *The Story of Ferdinand* by Munro Leaf is a good example of the correlation of picture and text. (Without the text, we might not understand what is about to happen to the bee.) Notice also how the various textures are depicted—the bull's hair, the bee's body, the clover. We should not overlook the comically expressive eye of the bee as it realizes it is about to be sat upon.

FIGURE 5.7 ■ We the viewers are at a child's eye level, looking over the table and up at the menacing monkeys (made even more disturbing from this point of view) in this surrealistic pencil drawing from Chris Van Allsburg's *Jumanji*. The figures seem to crowd us, adding an almost claustrophobic feeling, and the scene appears to be a moment uncomfortably frozen in time—an appropriate mood for this story of a mysterious board game that comes to life.

We often do not think of space—literally the empty parts of the page—as an artistic element, but it is, in fact, very powerful. There is an old story about a Japanese artist who, when asked what was the most important part of a painting, replied, "The part that is left out." Space is actually what draws our attention to objects on the page. If a page contains very little empty space but is instead crowded with images, our attention is necessarily divided; we do not know exactly where to look. The lack of open space on a page may contribute to a claustrophobic or uneasy feeling (see *The Story of Ferdinand*, Figure 5.6) or perhaps confusion or chaos (see *Jumanji*, Figure 5.7). However, a lot of empty space on a page can suggest loneliness, emptiness, or isolation, or it can direct our attention to certain objects. The illustration from Rohmann's *My Friend Rabbit* (Figure 5.1) uses empty space in the bottom half of the illustration to force our eyes upward (so we feel we are looking to the treetops, where Mouse and Rabbit are stranded). The next time you look at a picture, carefully consider the effect of the lines, of the shapes, and of the open space. Try to imagine how altering these features might change your attitude or interpretation of the whole work.

Texture, Composition and Perspective

One of the illusions a graphic artist creates is to give a flat surface (such as the paper) the characteristics of three dimensions and texture—the suggestion of fur, wood grain, smooth silk, and so on. Texture is achieved through the skillful use of the medium—paint layers, brush strokes, pencil marks, and so on. Texture generally evokes a realistic quality in an illustration. Notice the illusion of animal fur Robert Lawson gives us in *The Story of Ferdinand* (Figure 5.6) and Chris Van Allsburg creates in *Jumanji* (Figure 5.7). The texture of luxurious fabric is evident in Paul Zelinsky's family portrait (see Chapter 7, Figure 7.6).

The composition refers to the arrangement of the objects in a picture, which can produce an emotional impact. For example, grouping many large shapes together may suggest stability (see Rapunzel, Chapter 7, Figure 7.6) or discomfort (see *Jumanji*, Figure 5.7). John Burningham's illustration from *Mr. Gumpy's Outing* in Figure 5.8 looks simple, even artless, at first glance. But note the arrangement. It is divided into two parts—the upper half yellow, the lower half green. The cat is placed directly in the center, its bright orange face to the left, and a host of white daisies around its (hidden) legs and feet. The composition is balanced by the cat's tail jutting up boldly on the right side, reaching the very top edge of the illustration (and beyond). The result is much more interesting, even more emotional, than if he had merely drawn a realistic cat.

Perspective, or point of view, refers to the artist's attempt to give a picture depth, an illusion of three dimensions. Perry Nodelman points out that most picture books give us the "middle shot"—that is, not too close up and not too far away. Example can be seen in Figures 5.1, 5.3, and 5.4. This places the emphasis on storytelling rather than, say, character development (as a close-up might) or landscape description (as with a panoramic view). However, close-ups and landscapes are often used to great effect. See the bird's-eye view found in *Madeline's Rescue* (see Figure 5.5). Shifting the angle of the view can provide some interesting effects, such as found in Weisner's unusual perspective in *Tuesday* (see Figure 5.2), where the viewer is looking upward. Here, the distant moon appears smaller than the frogs being lifted into air on lily pads. Indeed, the viewer is seeing the frogs from the same point of view as the awestruck fish in the pond. Similarly, Chris Van Allsburg uses unusual perspective to heighten the disturbing qualities of his

FIGURE 5.8 ■ John Burningham is noted for his striking use of color, as seen in this portrait of a cat from *Mr. Gumpy's Outing,* a comical tale for very young readers. The style of the illustration is akin to naïve art, but there is an Expressionistic quality in the unusual coloring and the cat that is entirely made of circles and rectangles, with two triangles for ears.

Source: From *Mr. Gumpy's Outing* by John Burningham. Copyright 1971 John Burningham. Reprinted by arrangement with Henry Holt and Company, LLC. *Mr. Gumpy's Outing* published by Jonathan Cape. Reprinted by permission of The Random House Group, Ltd.

surrealistic tale *Jumanji,* the story of a board game that comes to life. In Figure 5.7, we are viewing the scene from an unsettling angle, as if we were hiding behind the table. We almost seem to be intruders. Films use the same technique to create suspense.

Artistic Media

An artistic medium is simply the material or materials (media) that an artist chooses to produce an illustration—pencil, ink, oils, watercolors, acrylics, woodblocks, and so on. Media are generally grouped into four broad categories: painterly, graphic, photography and digital art, and collage.

PAINTERLY MEDIA   Painterly media (paint, chalk, ink, and so on) are applied to a surface with an instrument such as a brush, pen, or pencil. Paint itself consists of pigment mixed with some liquid or paste to make it spreadable. Many variations are possible, depending on the medium used to mix with the pigment. Among the most common are the following:

- *Watercolors*, as their name implies, are pigments mixed with water, resulting in transparent, typically delicate pictures, as in Potter's *The Tale of Peter Rabbit* (Figure 5.4).
- *Tempera* is made by mixing pigments with egg yolk or other albuminous substance. Tempera is not as transparent as watercolor, and can produce some brilliant hues. (See Maurice Sendak's *Where the Wild Things Are*.)
- *Gouache* (pronounced "gwash") is a powdered paint similar to tempera but mixed with a white base, resulting in a delicate hue. (See Margot Zemach's *Duffy and the Devil*.)
- *Oil paint* typically uses linseed oil as a base, and is among the most opaque of media. One of the best examples is found in Paul O. Zelinsky's illustrations for *Rapunzel* (see Chapter 7, Figure 7.6).
- *Acrylics* use a plastic base, a product of twentieth-century technology, and produce very brilliant colors. (See Barbara Cooney's illustrations for Donald Hall's *The Ox-Cart Man*.)
- *Pastels* differ from the rest in that they are typically applied in powdered form (often with the fingers). (See Chris Van Allsburg's *The Wreck of the Zephyr*.)
- *Chalk*, *pencil*, *ink*, and *crayon* drawings, although technically not painting, follow the same general principles as painterly techniques. Chris Van Allsburg's *Jumanji* (Figure 5.7) is illustrated with pencil drawings, and Judith Kerr's drawings for *The Tiger Who Came to Tea* (Figure 5.3) were done in pencil and crayon.

Each of these media produces differing effects, and two or more may be used in combination as well.

GRAPHIC MEDIA   We are using this as an umbrella term for the process of creating images cut on a surface (such as wood, stone or metal), which is then inked then pressed onto paper. Three methods are most commonly used in children's books:

- *Woodblocks* were the very earliest form of reproducible art, dating back to the late Middle Ages. The artist draws an image in reverse on a block of wood, then carves away all the areas that are not to be printed. Ink is spread over the finished block, which is then pressed onto paper, resulting in the transfer of the image from block to paper. (See Chapter 1, Figure 1.2 and Figure 1.3).

- *Linocuts* are similar to woodblocks, but the artist uses blocks of linoleum rather than wood. Marcia Brown used this method in *Dick Whittington and His Cat* (1950), a Caldecott Honor book, is an early example of this technique.

- *Lithography* is a complex process that involves first drawing a design on a smooth, flat stone ("lithos" means stone) or a metal plate with a waxy mixture similar to a crayon. As in woodblocks, the image must be done in reverse. The stone or plate is then treated with a chemical fixative, wetted with water, and inked. The ink sticks only to the waxed areas, and when paper is pressed onto the stone, an impression is made. Robert McCloskey's beloved Caldecott Medal-winning *Make Way for Ducklings* (1942) was done with lithography.

PHOTOGRAPHY AND DIGITAL ART   Photography may be considered an artistic style as much as a technique. A good photograph requires a sense of composition—the meaningful arrangement of objects to achieve a desired effect. In picture books, we normally expect something more creative than cell phone snapshots, and when photographs are used to tell stories, it is principally for realistic stories. Photographs are especially effective in informational books. When imaginatively used in black and white or in color, photography can be dramatic, beautiful, and highly expressive.

Since the 1990s, digital art—art generated by a computer—has become more prevalent in children's picture books. One of the first artists to make a name in this field was J. Otto Seibold, beginning with *Mr. Lunch Takes a Plane Ride* (1993) written by Vivian Walsh and, most recently, Seibold's own *Lost Sloth* (2013), a charming work for very young readers. Both are good examples of Seibold's work, which, with its emphasis on geometric shapes, bears a resemblance to cubist abstraction. Yet it is not without detail, and the illustrations fit beautifully with the convoluted and comical storyline.

COLLAGE   Collage consists of a combination of materials that are cut, torn, pasted, or otherwise assembled to create an artistic whole. "Collage" comes from the French word *coller*, meaning "to glue." The technique dates back to ancient China, but its modern use is traced to Pablo Picasso and George Braque. Artists may use paper, cloth, wood, plastic—the possibilities are limited only by the imagination. The trick is to combine the various parts into a harmonious whole. In children's books, collage has been successfully used by Ezra Jack Keats (*The Snowy Day*), Leo Lionni (*Frederick*), and Eric Carle (*The Very Hungry Caterpillar*).

COLOR   Children are especially responsive to color, and very early on, they choose "favorite" colors, which we like to imagine reflect their personalities. Color is one of the most emotionally evocative of artistic elements. Psychologists tell us that reds and yellows are warm or hot colors that suggest excitement, whereas blues and greens are cool or cold colors that suggest calm or quiet. These reactions may be embedded in our responses to the natural world—red and yellow are suggestive of warmth and happiness, and are the colors of sunlight and fire; we find blue to be soothing and melancholy, perhaps because we associate it with calm waters or the broad expanse of the sky and the lonely universe beyond. Colors also take on associative values—purple signifies royalty; green denotes envy or illness, but also life and renewal; red indicates danger, but also boldness; blue signals depression, but also loyalty and serenity; yellow suggests cowardice, but also cheerfulness; and so on. However, these responses are often cultural. In imperial China, for example, the color yellow was reserved for the emperor, and throughout Asia, brides often wear red, while white is a traditional color of mourning.

Artists use color to establish the tone of a work. Beatrix Potter uses soft earthy colors in her pastoral story *The Tale of Peter Rabbit* (Figure 5.4), whereas John Burningham, in his light-hearted story *Mr. Gumpy's Outing* (Figure 5.8) experiments with a wilder, less conventional, palette. Kay Nielsen uses sharp contrasts that focus our attention on the dancing couple in "The Twelve Dancing Princesses" (see Chapter 7, Figure 7.7), and the colors inside the palace suggest an artificial, almost otherworldly, elegance. David Wiesner turns to the deep blues and greens of the nighttime in *Tuesday* (Figure 5.2). And Paul Zelinsky uses rich primary colors in his pleasant family portrait for *Rapunzel* (see Chapter 7, Figure 7.6), in which he deliberately imitates the art of the Renaissance; the illustration is reminiscent of a portrait of the Holy Family by the great sixteenth-century Italian painter Raphael.

Some of the most-loved picture books, however, have no color at all. Wanda Gág uses simple black and white in *Millions of Cats*, as does Robert Lawson in *The Story of Ferdinand* (Figure 5.6). Chris Van Allsburg shows a strong preference for black and white (and many shades of gray) in his books, including *Jumanji* (Figure 5.7). Robert McCloskey likes to use monochrome—that is, just a single color. His *Make Way for Ducklings* is illustrated in sepia (a brown tone), and *Blueberries for Sal* is appropriately illustrated in blue. Professional photographers have long preferred black and white or monochrome for its evocative subtleties. Without color as a distraction, the viewers pay closer attention to the lines, shapes, composition, perspective, and texture. It is certainly a mistake to think that children require garish colors in their books, or that they will reject books with black-and-white illustrations.

Artistic Style

Our final consideration when it comes to art in children's picture books is the artist's style. Artistic style refers to the visual characteristics of an illustration. Children's picture books reflect many different styles of art. In the best examples, the artistic style fits the mood established by the text. The best artists develop their own personal styles drawn from their life experiences, education, individual tastes, and specific talents. However, we can make some broad generalizations about artistic styles in children's books.

REALISM Realistic or representational art portrays the world with faithful attention to detail. Zelinsky's exquisite illustrations for *Rapunzel* (see Chapter 7, Figure 7.6) are inspired by the realistic art of the Italian Renaissance, which was, in turn, influenced by the realistic art of classical Greece and Rome. The rich colors, the architectural and landscape detail, the elaborate clothing—all attest to the care with which Zelinsky is attempting to re-create the world of fifteenth- and sixteenth-century Italy. Robert Lawson aims at realism in his depiction of the bee and Ferdinand—or what we can see of him (Figure 5.6).

CARTOON ART Cartoons consist of exaggerated caricatures that are used for comic or satiric effect—it is fairly safe to say that there are no serious cartoons (although the term is also used to describe a full-scale design for a work such as a tapestry or fresco). Cartoon art is very popular in children's books, probably because of its playfulness. Cartoons are simple, straightforward, and often outrageous, making them a frequent choice for illustrating nonsense, comical satire, and political points of view. Dr. Seuss's drawings are cartoons at their most delightful and outrageous. His colors are bold, the lines are distinct, and the features are distorted, avoiding any resemblance to reality. Eric Rohmann's illustrations for *My Friend Rabbit* (Figure 5.1) is an example of cartoon art, illustrating the nonsensical adventures of a mouse and rabbit. (Incidentally, do not mistake Figures 5.4 and 5.8 for cartoons—Potter's illustration is far too realistic, and Burningham's colors are far too subtle for cartoon art.)

FOLK ART Folk art reflects a specific cultural or social group. It is often decorative, providing ornamentation for everyday utilitarian objects, such as dishes, pottery, furniture, jewelry, fabric, and so on. Because of its cultural associations, it is favored for illustrating folk tales. Gerald McDermott's *Anansi the Spider* (see Chapter 7, Figure 7.9), with its geometric designs and bold colors, suggests west

African influences. When Barbara Cooney illustrated Donald Hall's *The Ox-Cart Man*, a story set in New England in the early nineteenth century, she imitated the primitive folk art paintings of the period.

NAÏVE ART   Naïve art is made deliberately to resemble a child's drawings. The figures appear two-dimensional, and are usually disproportionate (for example, the head might be too big, the arms and legs do not bend, and so on). Sometimes, the perspective is off. It used to be said that the naïve artist was one unschooled in art, but sometimes an artist will deliberately adopt the style to achieve a childlike or simple effect. Judith Kerr's charming illustrations for *The Tiger Who Came to Tea* (Figure 5.3) contain many features of naïve art, which is perfectly suited to this both simple and fanciful tale—they lack the wild exaggeration we often find in cartoon art, and the accuracy of detail we find in realistic art.

ART NOUVEAU   Although now rare in children's books, art nouveau was a late nineteenth-century reaction to the more formal academic art. It often contains organic motifs (especially floral designs), fluid lines, and highly stylized forms. Art nouveau's most famous representative in the book world was Aubrey Beardsley, who was heavily influenced by Asian art, particularly Japanese watercolors. The result is a decorative and sophisticated style exquisitely realized in the work of Danish illustrator Kay Nielsen. Contrast Nielsen's stylized work (see Chapter 7, Figure 7.7) with the more realistic art of Paul Zelinsky (see Chapter 7, Figure 7.6).

EXPRESSIONISM   Expressionism is another product of the twentieth century, with Marc Chagall, Wassily Kandinsky, and Paul Klee being among the most famous expressionists. These artists are not interested in realistic accuracy. They use distorted, misshapen figures, unusual perspectives, and colors that establish mood rather than depict reality. Again, true expressionism is rare in children's picture books, but Bemelmans's illustrations for *Madeline* come close (Figure 5.5). Nothing is portrayed realistically—shapes and colors are distorted or exaggerated, depth of field is ignored. The effect is indeed playful. John Steptoe in *Daddy Is a Monster . . . Sometimes* exhibits expressionistic qualities using a special style called *Les Fauves* ("the beasts").

SURREALISM   Surrealism is another early twentieth-century phenomenon, although some examples can be found as far back as the Renaissance in Hieronymus Bosch's unsettling paintings. A surrealist draws with realistic details—sometimes almost photographically realistic—but the subject matter is entirely unrealistic, using jarring juxtapositions that often result in an unsettling, sometimes nightmarish, quality. This style is used frequently by Chris Van Allsburg (see *Jumanji*, Figure 5.7).

Do we need to know all about artistic styles to appreciate a good children's book? Of course not. But we should acknowledge that modern-day children's book art is frequently of the highest quality and practiced by talented and award-winning artists at the top of their profession.

Design and Meaning in Picture Books

If you have ever read a picture book in which the pictures did not correspond with the words on the page, you know how important picture-book design is. This matching up—which is called *juxtaposition*—is just one of many aspects of a successful picture book. Among the features important to the design and meaning of picture books are rhythm and movement, tension, and page layout.

RHYTHM AND MOVEMENT   John Warren Stewig defines *rhythm* as "controlled repetition in art" (76). Good picture-book design creates a sense of rhythm as we move from page to page—a rhythm that matches the narrative. In Western culture, we read books and pictures from left to right. Some argue, therefore, that we identify most closely with objects on the left; protagonists often appear on the left and antagonists on the right. For example, Nielsen's illustration from "The Twelve Dancing Princesses" depicts the princess on the left (see Chapter 7, Figure 7.7). In McDermott's illustration from *Anansi the Spider* (see Chapter 7, Figure 7.9), the protagonist, the spider Anansi, appears on the left as he is being devoured by a fish. And in Potter's illustration for *The Tale of Peter Rabbit* (Figure 5.4), Peter is on the left but he is looking toward the right (to the next page).

In Paul Zelinsky's illustrations for his *Rumpelstiltskin*, the fiendish title character is on the right side in nine of the 11 illustrations in which he appears. But in Van Allsburg's illustration from *Jumanji* (Figure 5.7), the presumed protagonist, the girl in the doorway, is on the right, with the unsettling figures of the monkeys on the left. This reversal of the normal order of things may contribute to the apprehensive, eerie feeling that this illustration evokes—appropriate for the story of an innocent game board mysteriously coming to life. Burningham's cat stares out at us from the left (Figure 5.8), causing us to look first at its face and then to the rest of its body. Rapunzel's children in Zelinksy's illustration (see Chapter 7, Figure 7.6) are also looking up to the right. Of course, these are not hard-and-fast rules, but, in general, story movement is from left to right. (We should note that the left-to-right orientation is purely conventional. Israeli picture books are designed to be read from right to left, since Hebrew texts are written in reverse of Western texts—right to left, back to front—and as a result, the movement in the pictures is also from right to left.)

This movement also suggests another anomaly in the picture book: the interrupted rhythm that occurs when we read it. The movement is not continually forward; rather, we look at the pictures, then we read, then we look at the pictures again. The pictures create a starting and stopping pattern that the text must accommodate. This is why some picture book texts sound fairly inane when read without the pictures (*Goodnight Moon* and Pat Hutchins's *Rosie's Walk*, discussed below, make very little sense without the accompanying illustrations). Effective picture books are usually designed so that a natural pause occurs at the page turns. At the same time, the book should make us want to turn the page, either to be surprised or to have our expectations confirmed.

TENSION   Good picture books create what Nodelman refers to as "directed tension," in which the pictures are at odds with or reach beyond the words, resulting in our heightened interest and excitement. We have already noted one excellent example in Kerr's *The Tiger Who Came to Tea* (Figure 5.3).

Another fine example is Pat Hutchins's *Rosie's Walk*. The text of this book contains but one sentence—a string of prepositional phrases—describing Rosie the hen's afternoon excursion "across the yard," "over the haystack," "around the pond," and so on, until she gets back "in time for dinner." But the illustrations reach beyond the text, and we see that, unbeknownst to her, Rosie is being stalked by a fox, whose attempts to capture her are met with one comical disaster after another. Rosie arrives safely home in time for dinner, never realizing the danger she was in. The effect of the book is entirely dependent on the tension between the text and the illustrations. It is this tension that makes us want to turn the page to see how Rosie will escape or how the fox is thwarted again. Books without such tension (where, for example, the pictures do no more than mimic the words or vice versa) can quickly become boring.

PAGE LAYOUT   Another element of book design is the arrangement of the pictures and text on the page. It can be very disconcerting when the words on a page do not actually refer to the illustrations we're looking at—and this does happen. A skillful picture-book designer will ensure that the words we are hearing (or reading) and the pictures we are seeing actually correspond with each other.

Dimensionally, many picture books are wider than they are high, and this makes them especially suited to narrative illustration (see *Tuesday*, Figure 5.2). This shape allows for the depiction of scenes, which are often crucial to storytelling. On the other hand, tall and narrow books tend to focus on character and diminish the setting (*The Tiger Who Came to Tea*, Figure 5.3, and *The Tale of Peter Rabbit*, Figure 5.4); a portrait in art is typically taller than it is wide (unless it is a portrait of an elephant). The size of a book also affects us. We often associate very small books and very large books with the youngest readers—small books are easy for little hands to handle, and large books are eye-catching. Medium-sized books, however, are often more complex. The point is that a book's size and shape are not randomly selected—there is usually a very good reason for the choices.

That pictures and text should be properly juxtaposed—that is, the text should correspond with the pictures—is just common sense. But other considerations in a book's layout may include the use of borders, vignettes, and panels. Borders frame the page, and can enclose either text or illustrations. Contrast the irregular, almost informal, border that Beatrix Potter uses (see Figure 5.4) with the very formal, clean-edged border used by Zelinsky and Neilsen (see Chapter 7, Figure 7.6 and Figure 7.7). In the discussion of *Where the Wild Things Are* below, we will see where borders can actually contribute to the meaning of a book.

A panel refers to the framing of two or more illustrations on the same page, allowing us to see several perspectives all at once. Mo Willems uses this to great effect in *Don't Let the Pigeon Drive the Bus* and others, in which he depicts the pigeon going through a series of moods as he argues his case. A vignette is a small, incidental picture that is appended to the principal illustration or perhaps placed around the borders, sometimes for additional information and sometimes for humor. David Macaulay uses vignettes in his *The New Way Things Work*. This large, nonfiction picture book visually describes how hundreds of machines and devices work—from toasters to computers. On each page, Macaulay places tiny figures of wooly mammoths who wisecrack their way through the book. They add comic relief to a book that might overwhelm some readers.

Another important feature in the layout of a picture book is the handling of the gutter, or the binding crease between facing pages. This is especially important when the illustrations are double-page spreads. Ideally, the two pages come together perfectly at the gutter, and a good book designer ensures that illustrations are correctly aligned and that nothing is lost.

Typography refers to the style and size of the lettering, and the placement of the words on the page. Some books use more than one typeface, often to identify varying speakers, as in Carolivia Herron's *Nappy Hair*. Sometimes, we find hand lettering (used by Wanda Gág in *Millions of Cats* and Jean de Brunhoff in *The Story of Babar*). The placement of the text can range from the very formal—the text appearing in the same place on every page—to the very informal—the text moving about from page to page. In some books, the text forms patterns on the page, as in Lloyd Moss's *Zin! Zin! Zin! A Violin*, illustrated by Marjorie Priceman, where the words undulate in waves like the musical sounds from instruments. So, the choice of typeface and placement of the text can have an important effect on our response to a picture book.

BOOK DESIGN   A brilliant text or an exquisite artwork will not guarantee a successful picture book, for the text and illustrations have to work together to form a pleasing and meaningful whole. Maurice Sendak's *Where the Wild Things Are* (1963) is an example of how the layout of pictures and a well-worded text can enrich each other. As the story opens, Max, a rather naughty boy, is causing havoc about his house. The first pictures are small, with large white borders around them. Max is then sent to his room for his misbehavior. (We never see nor hear his mother, for this is Max's story.) Gradually, his room is transformed into a forest, then an ocean tumbles by. The illustrations grow larger on each succeeding page until the border disappears altogether. Eventually, the pictures spill onto the facing page and finally become two-page spreads.

The accompanying text describes a magical event. Max steps into his private boat and sails to the land where the Wild Things are. He becomes their king and presides over a "wild rumpus" during which the creatures, led by Max, do whatever they like (the dream of every child?). During the rumpus sequence, the pictures fill the pages entirely, and there are neither words nor boundaries, which perfectly captures Max, absorbed in his dream fantasy, unfettered and animal-like. Both language (a symbol of civilization) and the border enclosing the illustrations (perhaps signifying the necessary restraints imposed by civilized life) have vanished. Finally, Max tires of being king of the Wild Things, and longs to be "where someone loved him best of all"—children really do want to have rules and order in their lives. So, he sails back to the comfort of his bedroom, where he finds his supper waiting for him, during which time the borders gradually reappear (the return of rationality?). At the end of the story, Max appears very much like a vulnerable little boy, no longer the wild thing who terrorized the household. The final words describing his supper—"and it was still hot"—appear on a page without illustration, causing us to focus entirely on their meaning alone. These simple words bring us back to reality and, more importantly, imply unconditional parental love.

Perry Nodelman suggests that words in picture books accomplish three things, and we can find examples of all three in *Where the Wild Things Are*:

- Words express the emotional and narrative content of the pictures. ("The night Max wore his wolf suit and made mischief of one kind and another, his mother called him 'wild thing' . . . and he was sent to bed without eating anything.")

- Words express cause-and-effect relationships, either within parts of a single picture or within a series of pictures—for example, the words can indicate the passage of time between two pictures. ("That very night in Max's room a forest grew and grew . . . .")

- Words express what is important and what is not. (". . . he found his supper waiting for him—and it was still hot.") (Nodelman 215)

So we see that a successful picture book requires a total collaboration of words and pictures, which is perfectly reflected in Sendak's wondrous creation.

Another inventive use of picture-book layout is found in John Burningham's *Come Away from the Water, Shirley* (1977). This book portrays a day at the beach for the imaginative Shirley and her humdrum parents (don't most children think their parents are humdrum?). The layout comprises a series of corresponding pages, with the left-hand side depicting the dull routine of the parents (reality) and the right-hand side depicting Shirley's world (childhood imagination). The parents' world is drawn in sparse colors (made by crayon) on a large white background. In contrast, on the facing page, Shirley's world is portrayed in bright painterly colors suited to her childlike imagination as she enjoys adventures on the beach (finding a stray dog, playing pirates with other children, walking the plank, heroically escaping, and digging up a buried treasure). In contrast to the childlike, naïve style of the left-hand pages, the illustrations depicting Shirley's adventures are inspired by Expressionism—lively, brightly colored, and with playful distortions. Ironically, the parents are portrayed with childlike drawings, and the child is portrayed with a sophisticated artistic style. (See Chapter 3 for a discussion of irony.) The text consists entirely of the mother's words, which are either admonitions to Shirley or empty promises (all of which Shirley ignores). Shirley's world remains outside the reach of the adults.

David Wiesner's *The Three Pigs* (2001) is an inventive takeoff on the traditional folktale. The story opens very much like the familiar tale—three pigs being threatened by a ravenous wolf who blows down their houses—until, unexpectedly, the pigs are blown (by the wolf's huffing and puffing) clean out of their own story. Now they find themselves as characters in search of a story, wandering in and out of other storybooks. Wiesner uses a variety of artistic styles throughout the book, indicating the various kinds of stories the pigs stumble upon—a cartoonish nursery rhyme, a romantic tale of a knight and a dragon, and so on. Not only do the artistic styles change between the various stories, so do the typefaces, each chosen to suit the specific tale. The wildly imaginative and comical story is a refreshing twist on a familiar folk tale, and at the same time, Wiesner invites us to explore the meaning of fiction and reality. This is an example of a postmodern picture book, in which the book seems aware of itself as a book—and in which time and place are not linear and truth is not self-evident. Wiesner's *Tuesday*, David Macaulay's *Black and White*, Anthony Browne's *Voices in the Park*, and Emily Gravett's *Wolves* are other examples of this increasingly popular sub-genre.

Of course, we do not always find such powerful symbolism in a book's layout. But books like these demonstrate the possibilities that lie in the picture book format, and remind us of the importance of elements such as the style, size, and placement of illustrations. Words and pictures work together in a good picture book, and the resulting sum is something far greater and more rewarding than the individual parts.

Graphic Novels

Before we leave picture books, we should mention the rise of new kind of picture book—one for young adults (and older). Comic books have been around for decades, but in the past 20 years, a new phenomenon has arisen—the graphic novel, which is a novel in comic-book format. Graphic novels are for older audiences—early teens and up—than are most picture books. They are longer, and the stories more sophisticated. Nevertheless, as in the picture book, the illustrations and text of a graphic novel are equally important. In Japan, people of all ages read comics called manga, and although manga technically refers to comics of Japanese origin, the term is being rapidly adapted to any book-length work in graphic or comic book format. (The term *comic* is highly problematic, since many of these works are not at all humorous, but it is helpful in describing the format.) The comic-book format places illustrations in frames, with captions or dialogue bubbles, and in sequence. The sequencing conveys a specific meaning—it can suggest the passage of time or a shift of scenes, it can create suspense or shift the reader's attention, and so on.

Proponents of the graphic novel argue that it creates a bridge between the visual media (the media in which most young people are immersed) and the written media. The graphic novel can work very well with struggling readers, in much the same way that texts with pictures help students of a foreign language. Consequently, it can be argued that the graphic novel, rather than being a distraction, is actually an enticement to reading. It is also argued that these works, in addition to developing visual literacy and getting young people to read, introduce such serious issues as philosophy, history, science, and ethics.

Certainly, reading graphic novels is more intellectually demanding than watching television or texting messages to friends and relatives, and being engrossed in graphic novels may be preferable to many other pastimes in which young people could engage. Entire books have been written on the art of the graphic novel (see McCloud's *Understanding Comics* and *Reinventing Comics*). There is even an argument for the use of graphic novels in the classroom (see Yang, "Graphic Novels in the Classroom"). In 2007, a graphic novel, Gene Luen Yang's *American Born Chinese*, was awarded the prestigious Michael Printz Award for distinguished young adult literature. In 2008, Brian Selznick won the Caldecott Medal for *The Invention of Hugo Cabret*, which, at over 500 pages, contains many characteristics of the graphic novel.

Summary

Picture books, once thought of as objects of innocent amusement for toddlers, have metamorphosed into complex and sophisticated works of art that can be enjoyed by people of any age. The modern-day picture book represents a collaboration of both storytelling and visual art, in which the text and illustrations share equally in the reading experience. This makes the picture book different from the illustrated book, where the pictures merely decorate the text or serve some instructional purpose. The successful modern picture book contains an engaging plot and characters, uses language that is both clear and evocative, is entertaining, and, at times, is thought-provoking. Modern picture-book illustrations contain the same elements we expect to find in any pictorial art—effective use of line, shape, space, texture, composition, and perspective. These are all portrayed through a variety of artistic media—oil, watercolor, pencil, woodblock prints, collage, photography, or digital graphics—and in a variety of artistic styles, from Realism to Expressionism, from Naïve art to Surrealism. Today's picture books for children are dynamic and invigorating. And adults have the enjoyable obligation to share with children the infinite variety of the modern picture book.

Works Cited

Cianciolo, Patricia. "Visual Literacy and to Study Literature." *Jump Over the Moon.* Pamela Barron and Jennifer Q. Burley, eds. New York: Holt (1984), 139–144.

Groff, Patrick. "Children's Literature Versus Wordless Books?" *Jump Over the Moon.* Pamela Barron and Jennifer Q. Burley, eds. New York: Holt (1984), 145–154.

Nodelman, Perry. *Words about Pictures: The Narrative Art of Children's Picture Books.* Athens: University of Georgia Press, 1988.

Stewig, John Warren. *Looking at Picture Books.* Fort Atkinson, WI: Highsmith Press, 1995.

Recommended Resources

Alderson, Brian. *Looking at Picture Books 1973.* New York: Children's Book Council, 1974.

Bader, Barbara. *American Picturebooks from Noah's Ark to the Beast Within.* New York: Macmillan, 1976.

Barrett, Terry, and Kenneth Marantz. "Photographs as Illustrations." *The New Advocate* 17 (Fall 1989): 103–153.

Benedict, Susan, and Leonore Carlisle, eds. *Beyond Words: Picture Books for Older Readers and Writers.* Portsmouth, NH: Heinemann, 1992.

Cianciolo, Patricia. *Picture Books for Children,* 4th ed. Chicago: American Library Association, 1997.

Cummins, Julie, ed. *Children's Book Illustration and Design.* Glen Cove, NY: PBC International, 1992.

Dooley, Patricia. "The Window in the Book: Conventions in the Illustrations of Children's Books." *Wilson Library Bulletin* (October 1980): 108–112.

Gombrich, E. H. *The Image and the Eye: Further Studies in the Psychology of Pictorial Representation.* Ithaca, NY: Cornell University Press, 1982.

Haining, Peter. *Movable Books: An Illustrated History.* London: New English Library, 1979.

Hopkins, Lee Bennett. "Pop Go the Books." *CLA Bulletin* 16 (Fall 1990): 10–12.

Kiefer, Barbara. "Critically Speaking: Literature for Children." *The Reading Teacher* (January 1985): 458–463.

_____. *The Potential of Picturebooks: From Visual Literacy to Aesthetic Understanding.* Englewood Cliffs, NJ: Prentice Hall, 1995.

Lacy, L. E. *Art and Design in Children's Books: An Analysis of Caldecott Award Winning Illustrations.* Chicago: American Library Association, 1986.

Lindauer, Shelley L. Knudson. "Wordless Books: An Approach to Visual Literacy." *Children's Literature in Education* 19, 3 (1988): 136–142.

MacCann, Donnarae, and Olga Richard. *The Child's First Books.* New York: Wilson, 1973.

Matulka, Denise I. *A Picture Book Primer.* Santa Barbara, CA: Libraries Unlimited, 2008.

McCloud, Scott. *Reinventing Comics: How Imagination and Technology Are Revolutionizing an Art Form.* New York: Harper, 2000.

——. *Understanding Comics: The Invisible Art.* New York: Harper, 1994.

Nikolajeva, Maria, and Carol Scott. *How Picture Books Work.* New York: Garland, 2000.

op de Beeck, Nathalie. *Suspended Animation: Children's Picture Books and the Fairy Tale of Modernity.* Minneapolis: University of Minnesota Press, 2010.

Pritchard, David. " 'Daddy, Talk!' Thoughts on Reading Early Picture Books." *The Lion and the Unicorn* 7/8 (1983/84): 64–69.

Roxburgh, Stephen. "A Picture Equals How Many Words? Narrative Theory and Picture Books for Children." *The Lion and the Unicorn* 7/8 (1983/84): 20–33.

Salisbury, Martin, and Morag Styles. *Children's Picture Books: The Art of Visual Storytelling.* London: Laurence King, 2012.

Schoenfield, Madalynne. "Alphabet and Counting Books." *Day Care and Early Education* 10 (Winter 1982): 44.

Shulevitz, Uri. *Writing with Pictures: How to Write and Illustrate Children's Books.* New York: Watson-Guptin, 1985.

Spitz, Ellen Handler. *Inside Picture Books.* New Haven, CT: Yale University Press, 1999.

Stewig, John Warren. "Alphabet Books: A Neglected Genre." In *Jump Over the Moon.* Pamela Barron and Jennifer Q. Burley, eds. New York: Holt, 1984, 115–120.

Thomas, Della. "Count Down on the 1–2–3's." *School Library Journal* 15 (March 1971): 95–102.

Yang, Gene. "Graphic Novels in the Classroom." *Language Arts* 85, 3 (January 2008): 185–192.

Picture Books: A Selected and Annotated Booklist

Alphabet Books

Anno, Mitsumasa. *Anno's Alphabet.* New York: Harper, 1975.
- Clever illustrations of the letters that play tricks with the eye, in the vein of M. C. Escher.

Base, Graeme. *Animalia.* New York: Abrams, 1987.
- An animal alphabet with dramatic illustrations; a feast for the eye.

Bingman, Kelly. *Z Is for Moose.* Illus. Paul O. Zelinsky. New York: Greenwillow, 2012.
- An irrepressible moose cannot wait his turn in this very funny animal alphabet.

Burningham, John. *John Burningham's ABC's.* New York: Crown, 1985.
- A charming first alphabet book with simple cartoon pictures.

Elting, Mary, and Michael Folsom. *Q Is for Duck: An Alphabet Guessing Game.* 1980. Illus. Jack Kent. Logan, IA: Perfection Learning, 2005.
- For slightly older children, the alphabet in riddles and comical illustrations. A modern classic.

Gaiman, Neil. *The Dangerous Alphabet*. New York: HarperCollins, 2008.
- A story in which two children escape a succession of dangers as a boat takes them through haunted reaches.

Gerstein, Mordecai. *The Absolutely Awful Alphabet*. New York: Harcourt, 1999.
- A book where the letters of the alphabet are ghoulish, nasty, ugly, and weird— just the sort of things some young children love.

Gorey, Edward. *The Gashlycrumb Tinies*. New York: Houghton Mifflin, 1997.
- Catastrophes visit 26 hapless children in this alphabet book for teens and older. Showcases Gorey's characteristic dark humor—ghoulishly funny.

Green, Dan. *Wild Alphabet: An A to Zoo Pop-up Book*. London: Kingfisher, 2010.
- Inventive pop-up alphabet book, including animals both familiar and unusual.

Hudes, Quiara Alegria. *Bienvenidos a Mi Barrio! (Welcomes to My Neighborhood!): A Barrio ABC*. New York: Scholastic, 2010.
- A multicultural alphabet book in which a young girl gives her friend an alphabetic tour of her neighborhood.

Isadora, Rachel. *City Seen from A to Z*. New York: Greenwillow, 1983.
- Stunning paintings (you will think they are photographs) in which letters are discovered in everyday objects.

Jeffers, Oliver. *Once Upon an Alphabet: Short Stories for All the Letters*. New York: Philomel, 2014.
- An eccentric and entertaining book featuring very short stories about the hard-working letters of the alphabet. Comical, surprising, stimulating.

Johnson, Stephen T. *Alphabet City*. New York: Viking Penguin, 1995.
- Letters of the alphabet are discovered in a cityscape. Remarkable illustrations, and very original.

Kitchen, Bert. *Animal Alphabet*. New York: Dial, 1984.
- A wordless book with dramatic illustrations of animals, including some quite unusual ones.

Kontis, Alethea. *AlphaOops! The Day Z Went First*. Illus. Bob Kolar. New York: Candlewick, 2006.
- A book in which unruly letters bicker as they introduce themselves. Digital art captures the chaos.

MacDonald, Suse. *Alphabatics*. New York: Bradbury, 1986.
- A book in which animals morph into letters.

Martin, Bill Jr., and John Archambault. *Chicka Chicka Boom Boom*. Illus. Lois Ehlert. New York: Simon & Schuster, 1989.
- A childhood classic for the very young with rollicking rhymes and comical illustrations. Don't miss this one.

McGuirk, Leslie. *If Rocks Could Sing: A Discovered Alphabet*. New York: Tricycle Press, 2011.
- Rocks in the shapes of objects are used to illustrate this imaginative alphabet book.

McLimans, David. *Gone Wild: An Endangered Animal Alphabet*. New York: Walker, 2006.
- Beautiful and clever illustrations in black and white dramatize the plight of rare animals.

Musgrove, Margaret. *Ashanti to Zulu: African Traditions*. Illus. Leo and Diane Dillon. New York: Dial, 1976.
- For older readers, an introduction to African culture in alphabet format.

Oxenbury, Helen. *Helen Oxenbury's ABC*. New York: Delacorte, 1983.
- A book with warm illustrations for very young children.

Pelletier, David. *The Graphic Alphabet*. New York: Scholastic, 1996.
- A book for older readers, in which the letters are drawn to depict the representative words. Very similar to Van Allsburg's *Z Was Zapped*.

Pinto, Sara. *The Alphabet Room*. New York: Bloomsbury, 2003.
- A book for very young children, with beautiful illustrations and a hide-and-seek alphabet game.

Rankin, Laura. *The Handmade Alphabet*. New York: Dial, 1991.
- A striking book that depicts the American Sign Language signs for each letter.

Seuss, Dr. *Dr. Seuss's ABC*. New York: Random, 1963/1988.
- For beginners, the perfect book for learning letter shapes and sounds.

Sierra, Judy. *The Sleepy Little Alphabet: A Bedtime Story from Alphabet Town*. Illus. Melissa Sweet. New York: Knopf, 2009.
- A very funny rhyming story about the letters of the alphabet trying to go to sleep, but each one needing something first.

Spieker, Diana. *Alphabetica: Odes to the Alphabets*. Illus. Krista Skehan. San Francisco, CA: Personify Press, 2009.
- A book that presents the letters through a collection of concrete poetry; beautifully illustrated.

Thurlby, Paul. *Paul Thurlby's Alphabet*. Dorking, Surrey: Templar, 2011.
- A cleverly composed and refreshing alphabet book by a graphic artist who creates retro illustrations.

Van Allsburg, Chris. *Z Was Zapped*. Boston: Houghton Mifflin, 1987.
- A book for older readers, with stunning illustrations that depict disasters befalling the letters.

Wildsmith, Brian. *Brian Wildsmith's ABC*. New York: Watts, 1962.
- A book for beginners, with striking art in bold colors.

Counting, Concept, Tactile, and Movable Books

Anno, Mitsumasa. *Anno's Counting Book*. New York: Crowell, 1977.
- Clever illustrations play tricks on our eyes.

Bang, Molly. *Ten, Nine, Eight*. New York: Greenwillow, 1983.
- A counting book that goes in reverse.

Browne, Anthony. *One Gorilla: A Counting Book*. New York: Candlewick, 2013.
- An assortment of primates, evocatively drawn, to illustrate the concept of counting.

Burningham, John. *John Burningham's 123*. New York: Crown, 1985.
- A very good beginning book.

Carle, Eric. *Eric Carle's Opposites*. New York: Grosset and Dunlap, 2007.
- A beginner's book with full-page flaps that the reader pulls to reveal opposites.

Cumpiano, Ina. *Quinito, Day and Night/Quinito, día y noche*. Illus. José Ramírez. San Francisco: Children's Book Press, 2008.
- A bilingual book about opposites found in our daily lives.

Falconer, Ian. *Olivia Counts*. New York: Atheneum, 2002.
- A book in which Olivia, the inimitable pig, learns to count.

Feelings, Muriel. *Moja Means One: A Swahili Counting Book*. Illus. Tom Feelings. New York: Dutton, 1971.
- A counting book with an introduction to a new culture.

Garne, S. T. *One White Sail*. San Marcos, CA: Green Tiger, 1992.
- A counting book with beautiful illustrations and a simple lyrical text.

Hoban, Tana. *Shapes, Shapes, Shapes*. New York: Greenwillow, 1986.
- A book of photographs that capture shapes in the real world.

Jay, Alison. *1, 2, 3: A Child's First Counting Book*. New York: Dutton, 2007.
- A book in which simple but striking illustrations make overtures to famous folk tales.

Kunhardt, Dorothy. *Pat the Bunny*. New York: Golden Books, 1940.
- An early, and still favorite, tactile book for the very, very young.

Lionni, Leo. *A Color of His Own*. New York: Knopf, 1975.
- A book of simple collage illustrations that depict animals of different colors—except for the chameleon. A long-time favorite.

MacDonald, Suse. *Shape by Shape*. New York: Little Simon, 2009.
- A book depicting basic shapes that morph into a prehistoric animal. Imaginative collage illustrations.

Marino, Gianna. *One Too Many: A Seek and Find Counting Book*. San Francisco, CA: Chronicle, 2010.
- A wordless counting book filled with a host of animals and some challenges for young children.

Murphy, Chuck. *Opposites (Slide 'n' Seek)*. New York: Little Simon, 2001.
- An interactive book of opposites, one of a series by this illustrator.

Reinhart, Matthew. *Animal Popposites: A Pop-up Book of Opposites*. New York: Little Simon, 2002.
- A clever book about animals by one of the masters of the modern pop-up book.

Sabuda, Robert. *Winter's Tale: An Original Pop-Up Journey*. New York: Little Simon, 2005.
- A stunning pop-up book about the magic of winter; this master of pop-up books has also created *Alice's Adventures in Wonderland*, *The Wonderful Wizard of Oz*, *The Night Before Christmas*, and many others.

Seder, Rufus Butler. *Gallop!* New York: Workman, 2007.
- Using a technique called scanimation, a board book that produces pictures in motion.

Seeger, Laura Vacaro. *Black? White! Day? Night! A Book of Opposites*. New York: Roaring Brook, 2006.
- With brightly colored cutouts and lift-up flaps, an interactive concept book in which things turn out to be the opposite of what they seem.

——. *Green*. New York: Roaring Brook Press, 2012.
- This book explores the many shades of green with striking die-cut illustrations.

Shannon, George. *White Is for Blueberry*. Illus. Laura Dronzek. New York: Greenwillow, 2005.
- A book of colors with stunning illustrations and surprising subjects.

Sidman, Joyce. *Red Sings from the Tree Tops: A Year in Colors*. Illus. Pamela Zagarenski. New York: Houghton Mifflin, 2009.
- Colors combined with sounds and smells of the seasons in a richly imagined book.

Tafuri, Nancy. *The Big Storm: A Very Soggy Counting Book*. New York: Simon & Schuster, 2009.
- A book in which attractive illustrations depict animals seeking shelter in a storm, increasing in number as they do.

Van Fleet, Matthew. *Monday the Bullfrog*. New York: Simon & Schuster, 2006.
- A delightful tactile book in the shape of a frog; for the very young.

Wildsmith, Brian. *Brian Wildsmith's 1,2,3's*. New York: Watts, 1965.
- A very good beginning counting book.

Wood, Audrey. *The Deep Blue Sea: A Book of Colors*. Illus. Bruce Wood. New York: Blue Sky Press, 2005.
- A cumulative rhyme and distinctly colorful pictures introduce young children to colors.

Picture Storybooks

This is a list of some outstanding children's picture storybooks, including timeless classics and more recent publications. The books are for a variety of age ranges, from toddler through about second grade.

Allard, Harry, and James Marshall. *Miss Nelson Is Missing*. Illus. James Marshall. Boston: Houghton Mifflin, 1977.
- A comical tale of a clever, crafty schoolteacher and her students, with wild cartoon illustrations.

Allen, Jeffrey. *Mary Alice, Operator Number 9*. Illus. James Marshall. Boston: Little, Brown, 1975.
- A story of a community of talking animals that has trouble replacing a telephone operator. A great read-aloud.

Ardizzone, Edward. *Little Tim and the Brave Sea Captain*. 1936. New York: Penguin, 1983.
- A long-time favorite for older readers, featuring Ardizzone's lively sketches.

Bang, Molly. *When Sophie Gets Angry—Really, Really Angry . . .* New York: Greenwillow, 2004.
- A story of a young girl who experiences the emotional roller coaster of anger and eventually comes to terms with her feelings.

Bemelmans, Ludwig. *Madeline*. New York: Viking, 1937.
- A classic about an irrepressible girl in a Paris convent school, the first of a popular series.

Brett, Jan. *The Mitten*. New York: Putnam, 1989.
- A retelling of a familiar cumulative tale in which a succession of animals seek shelter in a lost mitten.

Brooke, L. Leslie. *Johnny Crow's Garden*. 1903. London: Warne, 1978.
- A longtime favorite rhyming book in which talking animals frolic in Johnny Crow's garden.

Brown, Margaret Wise. *The Dead Bird*. Illus. Remy Charlip. New York: HarperCollins, 2005.
- A touching story of children who find a dead bird, and what they do.

——. *Goodnight Moon*. Illus. Clement Hurd. New York: Harper, 1947.
- A classic bedtime story about a bunny who doesn't want to go to sleep.

——. *The Runaway Bunny*. Illus. Clement Hurd. New York: Harper, 1942.
- A story of a bunny who comes up with inventive ideas to run away from home.

Browne, Anthony. *Voices in the Park*. New York: DK Ink, 1998.
- An outing in the park depicted from varying points of view. An unusual and complex picture book.

Bruel, Nick. *Bad Kitty*. New York: Roaring Brook Press, 2003.
- The first of several books featuring an irascible cat entangled in many misadventures. These books are hilarious.

Bryan, Jennifer. *The Different Dragon*. Illus. Danamarie Hosler. Ridley Park, PA: Two Lives, 2006.
- A touching story about a boy living with his lesbian mothers.

Burningham, John. *Come Away from the Water, Shirley*. New York: Harper, 1977.
- A clever story about a day at the beach that juxtaposes the child's imagination and her parents' dull reality.

Burton, Virginia L. *The Little House*. Boston: Houghton Mifflin, 1942.
- A classic tale portraying the effects of the passage of time on a quaint house, which is the main character.

Carle, Eric. *The Very Hungry Caterpillar*. New York: Philomel, 1986.
- A perennial favorite among very young children as they watch a caterpillar turn into a butterfly.

Cisneros, Sandra. *Hairs/Pelitos*. Illus. Terry Ybánez. New York: Knopf, 1994.
- A bilingual picture book celebrating diversity.

Clifton, Lucille. *Some of the Days of Everett Anderson*. Illus. Evaline Ness. New York: Holt, 1970.
- A small African-American boy celebrates his life in the city; the first of a series about Everett Anderson.

Cochran, Bill. *The Forever Dog*. Illus. Dan Andreasen. New York: HarperCollins, 2007.
- A sensitive and realistic treatment of the loss of a pet and, by extension, of death in general.

Cooney, Barbara. *Miss Rumphius*. New York: Viking, 1982.
- A beautifully illustrated book about the productive life of a New England woman.

Cronin, Doreen. *Click, Clack, Moo: Cows That Type*. Illus. Betsey Lewin. New York: Spotlight, 2006.
- A very funny story about some clever cows and a farmer.

——. *Diary of a Spider*. Illus. Harry Bliss. New York: HarperCollins, 2003.
- The title says it all—except that it is a very funny diary.

Daywalt, Drew. *The Day the Crayons Came Home*. Illus. Oliver Jeffers. New York: Philomel, 2015.
- Hilarious sequel to the enormously popular *The Day the Crayons Quit*.

de Brunhoff, Jean. *The Story of Babar, the Little Elephant*. 1933. Several modern editions.
- A long-time-favorite tale about the adventures of an elephant.

de la Peña, Matt. *Last Stop on Market Street*. Illus. Christian Robinson. New York: Putnam, 2015.
- Folk art illustration is perfectly suited to this deceptively simple story about a bus ride, revealing both human kindness and social inequities, particularly as experienced by people of color. One of the rare books to be awarded both the Newbery Medal and a Caldecott Honor citation; de le Peña is the first Hispanic to win a Newbery Medal.

Demas, Corinne. *Saying Goodbye to Lulu*. Illus. Ard Hoyt. New York: Little, Brown, 2009.
- A first-person narrative of a young girl who must accept the death of her beloved dog.

Demi. *Buddha*. New York: Henry Holt, 1996.
- A beautifully illustrated picture book about the life and legends of the Buddha.

——. *Muhammad*. New York: Margaret K. McElderry, 2003.
- A picture-book narrative of the prophet's life, with an explanation of Islam.

dePaolo, Tomie. *Nana Upstairs, Nana Downstairs*. New York: Putnam, 1973.
- A story featuring a boy's relationship with his grandmother and great-grandmother, and how he deals with their eventual deaths.

de Regniers, Beatrice Schenk. *May I Bring a Friend?* Illus. Beni Montressor. New York: Atheneum, 1964.
- A story of a young boy befriended by a king and queen. A wonderful rhyming tale with striking illustrations.

Duvoisin, Roger. *Petunia*. New York: Knopf, 1950.
- A modern fable about a silly goose who misunderstands the importance of books.

Emberley, Barbara. *Drummer Hoff*. Illus. Ed Emberley. New York: Prentice Hall, 1967.
- A cumulative tale with a Revolutionary War setting and striking woodcuts.

Erlbruch, Wolf. *Duck, Death and the Tulip*. Minneapolis, MN: Lerner Publishing for Gecko Press, 2011. (First published in Germany, 2007.)
- A starkly simply but profoundly moving allegory about death.

Ets, Marie Hall. *Play with Me*. New York: Penguin, 1955.
- For very young children, a quiet tale of a little girl's wondrous adventure in nature.

Falconer, Ian. *Olivia*. New York: Simon & Schuster, 2000.
- The first of many books about the irrepressible little pig Olivia, a modern-day feminist heroine.

Feelings, Tom. *The Middle Passage: White Ships/ Black Cargo*. New York: Dial, 1995.
• Powerful illustrations depict the horrific journey of the slaves from Africa to America.

Freeman, Don. *Corduroy*. New York: Viking, 1968.
• A long-time favorite about a teddy bear who wants a home.

Gág, Wanda. *Millions of Cats*. New York: Coward-McCann, 1928.
• Usually considered the first true American picture book, with charming black-and-white illustrations and a memorable refrain.

Gallaz, Christophe. *Rose Blanche*. Illus. Roberto Innocenti. Mankato, MN: Creative Education, 1985.
• A picture book of the Holocaust, as seen through the eyes of a young German girl.

Garza, Carmen Lomas. *Family Picture/Cuadros de Familia*. San Francisco: Children's Book Press, 1990.
• A celebration of the author's girlhood. A bilingual text with outstanding illustrations.

Geisert, Arthur. *Hogwash*. Boston: Houghton Mifflin, 2008.
• An intricately detailed wordless picture book about the pigs needing a bath.

Gerstein, Mordecai. *The Man Who Walked between the Towers*. New York: Roaring Brook, 2003.
• An account of an actual daredevil feat by an aerial artist in New York City in 1974.

Gramatky, Hardie. *Little Toot*. New York: Putnam, 1939.
• A classic story of an animated tugboat who comes to the rescue.

Gravett, Emily. *Dogs*. New York: Simon & Schuster, 2010.
• A book filled with enticing pictures of dogs of every shape and size.

____. *The Rabbit Problem*. New York: Simon & Schuster, 2010.
• A clever and lively book about a growing family of rabbits engaging in math.

____. *Wolves*. UK: Macmillan, 2005.
• A rabbit borrows a book about wolves from the library, with some unexpected consequences as a wolf steps out of the book.

Guojing. *The Only Child*. New York: Random/ Schwarz & Wade, 2015.
• A wordless picture book set in China about a young girl's magical journey to visit her grandmother.

Hall, Donald. *The Ox-Cart Man*. Illus. Barbara Cooney. New York: Penguin, 1983.
• Sensitive folk-art illustrations and a soothing poetic text relate this simple tale of New England in the early nineteenth century.

Henkes, Kevin. *Kitten's First Full Moon*. New York: Scholastic, 2004.
• A story of a kitten who thinks the moon is a bowl of milk.

Herron, Carolivia. *Nappy Hair*. Illus. Joe Cepeda. New York: Knopf, 1997.
• The joyful celebration of a young African-American girl's hair.

Hutchins, Pat. *Rosie's Walk*. New York: Simon & Schuster, 1968.
• In this book of colorful, stylized illustrations, Rosie the hen takes a walk through the barnyard and never realizes the imminent danger lurking there.

Innocenti, Roberto, and Christophe Gallaz. *Rose Blanche*. New York: Creative Education, 1985.
• An arresting picture book about a young German girl aiding Jews in a concentration camp.

Jain, Mahak. *Maya*. Illus. Elly MacKay.
• Arresting illustrations and an evocative text combine to tell a story of love, loss and joy in modern-day India.

Janisch, Heinz. *The King and the Sea*. Illus. Wolf Erlbruch. Gecko Press, 2015.
• A German allegory about a king's encounters with people, objects and forces provide philosophical insights on the nature of power.

Jin-Ho, Jung. *Look Up!* New York: Holiday House, 2016.
- Activity on a city sidewalk takes on new meaning from the perspective of a boy watching from a balcony high above, with strikingly original illustrations.

Johnson, Crockett. *Harold and the Purple Crayon.* 1962. New York: Harper, 2012.
- A classic tribute to a child's imagination where Harold creates his own world with his purple crayon.

Joyce, William. *Rolie Polie Olie.* New York: Scholastic, 2001.
- Adventures on a planet inhabited by friendly robots.

Juster, Norton. *The Hello, Goodbye Window.* Illus. Chris Raschka. New York: Hyperion, 2005.
- A story in which a little girl describes her magical relationship with her grandparents.

Katz, Karen. *My First Ramadan.* New York: Henry Holt, 2007.
- A picture book about a young boy observing the Muslim holy month with his family.

Keats, Ezra Jack. *The Snowy Day.* New York: Viking, 1962.
- A landmark book by a talented author/illustrator in which a little African-American boy has adventures in the snow.

Kerr, Judith. *The Tiger Who Came to Tea.* 1968. Somerville, MA: Candlewick, 2009.
- A simple tale about an unexpected guest; a favorite for nearly 50 years.

Kitamura, Satoshi. *Lily Takes a Walk.* New York: Dutton, 1987.
- A story of a little girl taking a walk with her dog, who has an overactive imagination.

Klassen, Jon. *This Is Not My Hat.* New York: Candlewick, 2012.
- A story of a brazen fish stealing a hat, but not without dire consequences.

Kraus, Robert. *Leo the Late Bloomer.* Illus. Jose and Ariane Aruego. New York: Simon & Schuster, 1987.
- The popular story of a young tiger who can't seem to do anything.

Krauss, Ruth. *The Backward Day.* Illus. Marc Simont. New York: Harper, 1950.
- The story of a boy who decides to do everything backward.

____. *The Carrot Seed.* Illus. Crockett Johnson. New York: Harper, 1945.
- A beautifully simple tale of a boy who plants and nurtures a seed with ultimate success; still popular after 60 years.

LaMarche, Jim. *Pond.* New York: Paula Wiseman/Simon & Schuster, 2016.
- Stunning illustrations help tell the story of three children who discover the joy of caring for the natural world.

Langstaff, John M. *A Frog Went A-Courtin'.* Illus. Feodor Rojankovsky. New York: Harcourt, 1955.
- Award-winning illustrations and a favorite folk rhyme.

Leaf, Munro. *The Story of Ferdinand.* Illus. Robert Lawson. New York: Viking, 1936.
- Lovely black-and-white illustrations in the story of a gentle bull in Spain.

Lionni, Leo. *Frederick.* New York: Knopf, 1967.
- A story of a mouse who spends his days in contemplation while the others work—and then repays them; one of many books by a popular author/illustrator.

____. *Inch by Inch.* New York: Knopf, 1967.
- The story of an inchworm who enjoys measuring everything, until he is asked to measure a song.

Liwska, Renata. *Little Panda.* New York: Houghton, 2008.
- A reassuring story told by a grandfather panda to his grandson.

Lobel, Arnold. *Fables.* New York: HarperCollins, 1980.
- Original fables in the spirit of Aesop.

Marshall, James. *George and Martha*. New York: Scholastic, 1972.
- A story of lovable anthropomorphic hippos with Marshall's characteristic cartoon illustrations.

Martin, Bill. *Brown Bear, Brown Bear, What Do You See?* Illus. Eric Carle. New York: Holt, 1967.
- Perfect for the very young in its combination of rhyme, rhythm, and repetition, and the introduction to colors and animals.

Mattick, Lindsay. *Finding Winnie: The True Story of the World's Most Famous Bear*. Illus. Sophie Blackall. New York: Little, Brown, 2015.
- The heart-warming story of the bear who inspired A. A. Milne's *Winnie-the-Pooh*.

McCloskey, Robert. *Blueberries for Sal*. New York: Viking, 1948.
- The story of a mix-up that occurs when a mother and her daughter and a bear and her cub go blueberry picking.

____. *Make Way for Ducklings*. New York: Viking, 1944.
- A classic tale of a family of mallard ducks in Boston.

McDermott, Gerald. *Arrow to the Sun: A Pueblo Indian Tale*. New York: Viking, 1974.
- A strikingly illustrated retelling of a cultural origins tale.

____. *Raven: A Trickster Tale from the Pacific Northwest*. New York: Harcourt, 1993.
- A beautifully illustrated tale about Raven's bringing light to the world.

Muth, Jon. *Zen Shorts*. New York: Scholastic, 2005.
- A beautiful and thought-provoking book in which a magical panda shares Buddhist stories with three children.

Novesky, Amy. *Elephant Prince: The Story of Ganesh*. Illus. Belgin K. Wedman. San Rafael, CA: Mandala, 2004.
- A picture book about one of Hinduism's most endearing gods.

Peet, Bill. *Encore for Eleanor*. Boston: Houghton Mifflin, 1985.
- One of many books by a great illustrator/storyteller—this one about an elephant who doesn't want to retire.

Pinkney, Jerry. *The Lion & the Mouse*. New York: Little, 2009.
- A familiar fable dramatically illustrated.

Polacco, Patricia. *The Keeping Quilt*. New York: Simon & Schuster, 1988.
- A picture book about an immigrant Jewish family attempting to keep Russian traditions.

Politi, Leo. *Pedro, the Angel of Olivera Street*. New York: Scribner, 1947.
- One of the earliest picture books featuring Latinos.

Portis, Antoinette. *Not a Box*. New York: HarperCollins, 2006.
- A charmingly simple book that explores the imaginative possibilities of a cardboard box.

Potter, Beatrix. *The Tale of Peter Rabbit*. London: Warne, 1901.
- The first of several talking animal tales by a celebrated illustrator.

Provensen, Alice, and Martin Provensen. *The Glorious Flight: Across the Channel with Louis Bleriot*. New York: Viking, 1983.
- A story based on an historical event, with striking full-color illustrations.

Raffi. *Baby Beluga*. New York: Crown, 1992.
- The story of a baby beluga whale discovering his independence.

Raschka, Chris. *A Ball for Daisy*. New York: Schwartz & Wade, 2011.
- A charming wordless picture book with lively drawings about a dog losing her favorite toy.

Rey, A. H. *Curious George*. Boston: Houghton Mifflin, 1941/1973.
- The first of a popular series about an inquisitive monkey.

Reynolds, Aaron. *Creepy Carrots!* Illus. Peter Brown. New York: Simon & Schuster, 2012.
- A "horror" story for the very young, with atmospheric, film noir illustrations.

Ringgold, Faith. *Tar Beach*. New York: Crown, 1991.
- A picture book with a Depression-era setting in Harlem. A magical tale with a comment on social injustice.

Rohmann, Eric. *My Friend Rabbit*. New York: Roaring Brook, 2002.
- An almost wordless picture book about a well-meaning, but hapless, rabbit.

Rosenthal, Amy Krouse. *Spoon*. Illus. Scott Magoon. New York: Hyperion, 2009.
- A clever and warmly humorous story about a little spoon examining his existence; see also Krouse and Magoon's *Chopsticks*.

Rylant, Cynthia. *Dog Heaven*. New York: Blue Sky Press, 1995.
- Speculation on a dog's afterlife that is intended for grieving pet owners.

____. *When I Was Young in the Mountains*. Illus. Diane Goode. New York: Dutton, 1982.
- A book of recollections of childhood with sensitive illustrations.

Santat, Dan. *The Adventures of Beekle: The Unimaginary Friend*. New York: Little, Brown, 2014.
- A charming fantasy about an imaginary animal who sets out to find a real friend.

Say, Allen. *Grandfather's Journey*. New York: Houghton Mifflin, 1993.
- The story of a Japanese immigrant to America pulled between two cultures.

Seibold, J. Otto, and Vivian Walsh. *Mr. Lunch Takes a Plane Ride*. Illus. J. Otto Seibold, New York: Viking, 1993.
- A book in a series of favorites about a talking dog who engages in zany adventures.

Selznick, Brian. *The Invention of Hugo Cabret*. New York: Scholastic, 2007.
- More graphic novel than picture book, a fascinating quasi-mystery set in 1930s Paris.

Sendak, Maurice. *Where the Wild Things Are*. New York: Harper, 1963.
- An irascible boy's dream adventure—a modern classic. Not to be missed are the companion books, *In the Night Kitchen* and *Outside Over There*.

Seuss, Dr. *And to Think That I Saw It on Mulberry Street*. New York: Vanguard, 1937/1973.
- The first of many books by the wildly popular children's author/illustrator.

Simont, Marc. *The Stray Dog*. New York: HarperCollins, 2003.
- The story of a stray dog finding a home, charmingly illustrated.

Smith, Lane. *Grandpa Green*. New York: Roaring Brook, 2011.
- A boy's memories of his great-grandfather, told in a walk through his garden.

Steig, William. *Sylvester and the Magic Pebble*. New York: Windmill, 1969.
- The story of a little donkey who finds a magic pebble—and the trouble that ensues.

Steptoe, John. *Mufaro's Beautiful Daughters*. New York: Lothrop, 1974.
- A beautifully illustrated picture-book version of a traditional Zimbabwean folk tale.

____. *My Daddy Is a Monster . . . Sometimes*. New York: Viking, 1980.
- Unusual illustrations capture a father's changing moods.

Stewart, Sarah. *The Gardener*. Illus. David Small. New York: Farrar, Straus & Giroux, 1997.
- The story of a girl during the Depression creating a rooftop garden to cheer up her cantankerous uncle.

Swanson, Susan. *The House in the Night*. Illus. Beth Krommes. New York: Houghton Mifflin, 2009.
- A bedtime story in the form of a cumulative tale with stunning scratchboard illustrations.

Tafolla, Carmen. *What Can You Do with a Paleta?* Illus. Magaly Morales. New York: Tricycle, 2009.
- A playful picture book illustrating life in the barrio while celebrating the Mexican popsicle.

Tonatiuh, Duncan. *The Princess and the Warrior: A Tale of Two Volcanoes.* New York: Abrams, 2016.
- The legend of two volcanoes near Mexico City, illustrated with Mixtec-inspired collages.

Van Allsburg, Chris. *The Polar Express.* Boston: Houghton Mifflin, 1985.
- A classic Christmas story by a talented author/illustrator.

Viorst, Judith. *The Tenth Good Thing about Barney.* Illus. Erik Blegvad. New York: Aladdin, 1987.
- A story in which children deal with the loss of a pet.

Waber, Bernard. *The House on East 88th Street.* Boston: Houghton Mifflin, 1962.
- An old favorite about a crocodile who makes his home with a human family. Its equally popular sequel is *Lyle, Lyle Crocodile.*

Wells, Rosemary. *Noisy Nora.* New York: Dial, 1973.
- A charming story about a disgruntled and neglected middle child in a mouse family.

Weatherford, Carole Boston. *Freedom in Congo Square.* Illus. R. Gregory Christie. Little Bee Books, 2016.
- Based on historical fact, a story of New Orleans slaves finding a brief respite in their weekly gatherings in Congo Square, illustrated with paint and collage inspired by folk art.

Wiesner, David. *Flotsam.* New York: Clarion, 2006.
- The story of a boy fascinated with science who makes an unexpected discovery while exploring the beach.

____. *Tuesday.* New York: Clarion, 1991.
- A magical tale of a night when frogs float through the air on lily pads.

Willard, Nancy. *A Visit to William Blake's Inn.* Illus. Alice and Martin Provensen. New York: Perfection Learning, 1982.
- A collection of poems describing the guests coming to an inn, inspired by the work of the eighteenth-century poet William Blake. A Newbery Medal winner and a Caldecott Honor book, the first book to be honored in both categories.

Willems, Mo. *Don't Let the Pigeon Drive the Bus!* New York: Hyperion, 2003.
- The first of a series of books about the adventures of an irrepressible pigeon, including *The Pigeon Finds a Hot Dog* and *The Pigeon Wants a Puppy.*

____. *Knuffle Bunny: A Cautionary Tale.* New York: Hyperion, 2004.
- The first of a very funny series about a young girl's attachment to her stuffed bunny.

Willhoite, Michael. *Daddy's Roommate.* Boston: Alyson, 1990.
- A young boy's description of the time spent with his gay father.

Williams, Vera B. *A Chair for My Mother.* New York: Greenwillow, 1982.
- A touching story for very young readers about a family that works together through hard times.

Yep, Laurence. *Dragon Prince: A Chinese Beauty and the Beast Tale.* Illus. Kam Mak. New York: HarperCollins, 1997.
- Lovely illustrations accompany the retelling of a traditional tale.

Yolen, Jane. *Owl Moon.* Illus. John Schoenherr. New York: Philomel, 1987.
- The story of a little girl and her father spending a magical winter evening looking for owls.

Yorinks, Arthur. *Hey, Al.* New York: Farrar, Straus & Giroux, 1986.
- A no-place-like-home tale of a poor janitor and his dog who are magically transported to a paradise.

Young, Ed. *Hook.* New York: Roaring Brook Press, 2009.
- A story of chickens hatching an eagle egg and then helping the eaglet find his true home.

_____. *Lon Po Po: A Red-Riding Hood Story from China.* New York: Philomel, 1990.
- A Chinese folk tale beautifully illustrated by an award-winning artist.

Zelinsky, Paul O. *Rapunzel.* New York: Dutton, 1997.
- A traditional retelling with stunning illustrations. One of several folk tales Zelinsky has illustrated.

Zion, Gene. *Harry, the Dirty Dog.* Illus. Margaret Bloy Graham. New York: Harper, 1956.
- The hilarious tale of a dog who will do anything to avoid taking a bath—with very funny cartoon illustrations; the first of several books about Harry.

Zolotow, Charlotte. *Mr. Rabbit and the Lovely Present.* Illus. Maurice Sendak. New York: Harper, 1962.
- A quiet book about a little girl seeking a rabbit's advice on gifts.

CHAPTER 6

Poetry

For the Love of Language

"Poetry is an echo, asking a shadow to dance."

–Carl Sandburg

Introduction

Poetry is quite often the first literary form to which children are introduced—from ancient nursery rhymes ("Rock-a-bye Baby") to playful nonsense verses ("Ring Around the Rosie"). Unfortunately, as they grow older, many children come to see poetry as something for the literary elite—something almost mysterious, not to mention stuffy. To be sure, poetry can be elusive; even defining it is difficult. Poet Samuel Taylor Coleridge defined poetry as "the best words in their best order." His good friend, poet William Wordsworth, called it "the spontaneous overflow of powerful feelings." And Robert Frost described poetry as "where an emotion has found its thought and the thought has found the words." These definitions suggest poetry's ephemeral quality—although perhaps none so much as Carl Sandburg's poetic words in the epigraph above. But most agree that it has to do with the sound of language and the way language is used to express thought and feeling. Yes, some poetry can be difficult (but the same goes for any written form). And we all do not enjoy the same poetry (which is also true of virtually all art). But to dismiss all poetry is to neglect much of the most beautiful and powerful literature.

There's a poem out there for everyone—probably lots of poems out there for everyone. We just need to be open to the challenge. In this chapter, we will consider poetry for children of all ages—from the rollicking rhymes of the nursery to the magical stanzas of poets for adolescents. With its interwoven patterns of sound and imagery, poetry is among the most complex of literary forms, and in this chapter, we will try to unravel some of the mysteries of poetry—without undoing the magic. (Which is a tough job!) Let's begin with the first poems most children come to know, the Mother Goose rhymes.

Mother Goose Rhymes

The Origins

No one knows who Mother Goose was, or even where the name came from. The term "Mother Goose" first pops up in the seventeenth century, when a Frenchman, Charles Perrault, named his collection of folktales *Tales from Mother Goose*. Some speculate that the name may have been popularly given to a woman who in earlier times kept the village geese and was the traditional community storyteller. Whatever her origins, by the end of the eighteenth century, the name Mother Goose had become associated not with folktales, but with nursery rhymes, and she has been inextricably tied to the poetry of the nursery ever since.

Mother Goose rhymes are not only a child's first introduction to literature, they are an indelible part of our cultural heritage. Who doesn't know about Humpty Dumpty's catastrophe, Little Bo Peep's loss, Little Boy Blue's laziness, and Old Mother Hubbard's poverty? They find their way into a multitude of references in our daily lives. The lilting rhythms, the comical rhymes, the unusual sounds of these verses ("Mistress Mary, quite contrary," "Hey! Diddle, diddle, the cat and the fiddle," "Hickory, dickory, dock," and so on) endear them to young children. These are often the first words they memorize, and the rhymes are often a child's first introduction to memorable fictional characters. In addition to those mentioned above, there are Jack Sprat (see Figure 6.1, Figure 6.2, and Figure 6.3), Little Miss Muffet (see Figure 6.4 and Figure 6.5), Little Jack Horner, Old King Cole, the Queen of Hearts, Georgie Porgie, Wee Willie Winkie, Simple Simon, Peter the Pumpkin Eater, and the Old Woman who lived in a shoe (to name but a few).

Nursery rhymes were always meant to be fun, and were frequently subversive (as are most things that are fun). Curiously, many of them were not originally meant for children. Instead, they were derived from war songs, romantic lyrics, proverbs, riddles, political jingles, lampoons, and the cries of street vendors (an early version of the television commercial). Most of the better-known rhymes can be traced back to the sixteenth, seventeenth, and eighteenth centuries. "Three Blind Mice" was set to music as early as 1609; "Jack Sprat" may have ridiculed a certain Archdeacon Spratt in the mid-seventeenth century; and "Little Jack Horner" may have referred to a Thomas Horner of Mells, whose "plum" was the land he acquired from the monasteries dissolved by Henry VIII in 1536. Most heroes of nursery rhymes come from the lower walks of life: Simple Simon, Tom the Piper's Son, Mother Hubbard, the Old Woman in the Shoe, the Crooked Man Who Walked a Crooked Mile, and so on. Nursery rhymes that mention kings and queens ("Sing a Song of Sixpence" and "Old King Cole," for example) are often comical and irreverent. Scarcely hidden beneath the surface of these rhymes and jingles are the jibe and the barb, and oftentimes wisdom:

FIGURE 6.1 ■ This woodcut engraving from an early American Mother Goose book depicts Jack Sprat ("who could eat no fat" and his wife ("who could eat no lean") together licking the platter clean. Intended as comic touch, the result is nearly grotesque. Contrast this with Figure 6.2 and Figure 6.3, two other pictorial interpretations of the famous nursery rhyme.

For every evil under the sun,
There is a remedy, or there is none;
If there be one, try and find it,
If there be none, never mind it.

Mother Goose and Child Development

Mother Goose rhymes are often a child's first introduction to poetry, and much of the language is actually quite lovely (even if it does not make any sense). Take this old and popular rhyme:

Ride a cock horse to Banbury Cross
To see a fine lady upon a white horse;
With rings on her fingers and bells on her toes,
She shall have music wherever she goes.

FIGURE 6.2 ■ Frederick Richardson's lively illustration from the famed Volland *Mother Goose* (1915), edited by Eulalie Osgood Grover, is far more sophisticated than the nineteenth-century portrayal seen in Figure 6.1. This is the work of a talented illustrator who is able to imbue his figures with a human touch. The addition of the hopeful cat adds yet another dimension to the simple rhyme.

No one knows where or when this rhyme came about, who the "fine lady" is (Lady Godiva? Queen Elizabeth I?), what a "cock horse" is (A high-spirited horse? A stallion? A hobby horse?), or why she has bells on her toes (A fashion statement? A sign of class?). But none of this matters to the enjoyment of the verse—in fact, the mystery only makes it more evocative.

In addition to their sheer joy, nursery rhymes can help infants and toddlers in unexpected ways. They can assist in cognitive development, such as counting— "One potato, two potato, three potato, four" and "One, two, three, four, five /

FIGURE 6.3 ■ Blanche Fisher Wright's illustration for "Jack Sprat" (from the 1916 *Real Mother Goose*) depicts a well-to-do couple (perhaps eighteenth- or early nineteenth-century), beautifully drawn, but without the playfulness or joviality we find in Richardson (published at almost the same time). Even Wright's cat is well dressed. The contrast demonstrates the power of illustration to influence our interpretation and response to the rhyme.

FIGURE 6.4 ■ Kate Greenaway could not bring herself to include unsavory elements in her illustrations; consequently, she detracts from the drama by focusing all attention on the prim and proper Miss Muffet, who "sat on a tuffet eating her curds and whey." The spider, who would eventually frighten her off, is barely noticeable off to the left.

Little Miss Muffet,
Sat on a tuffet,
Eating some curds and whey;
There came a great spider,
And sat down beside her,
And frightened Miss Muffet away.

Once I caught a fish alive." Nursery rhymes broaden vocabularies. The crooked man who "walked a crooked mile and found a crooked sixpence against a crooked stile," "Jack be nimble," and "Pease porridge hot" all include words not normally used by children. This is a great way to expand a child's language skills. And what about this famous riddle:

As I was going to St. Ives
I met a man with seven wives;
Every wife had seven sacks,
Every sack had seven cats,
Every cat had seven kits,
Kits, cats, sacks, and wives,
How many were going to St. Ives?

FIGURE 6.5 ■ Arthur Rackham, in contrast to Greenaway, portrays a truly monstrous-looking but not ungentlemanly spider in his illustration for the popular nursery rhyme. The spider's appearance completely overwhelms the picture, and there is a wonderful contrast between the sedate Miss Muffet (somewhat more mature than Greenaway's), her lips daintily pursed, and the grotesque creature about to interrupt her. Rackham's surrealistic, frequently nightmarish quality is tempered here by a bit of wry humor as the spider gallantly doffs his hat.

(One, of course—just the speaker.) And here is a riddle that has stumped many a child:

> Elizabeth, Elspeth, Betsy, and Bess,
> They all went to together to seek a bird's nest,
> They found a bird's nest with five eggs in,
> They all took one and left four in.

And how could four eggs remain? Because Elspeth, Betsy, and Bess are nicknames for Elizabeth—there is only one girl. (It may be a little unfair, but aren't all riddles?)

Nursery rhymes, with their lively meter, appeal to children's natural sense of rhythm, perhaps hearkening back to the womb and the rhythmic beat of the mother's heart. The repeated refrains and insistent rhymes provide children with the pleasures of balance and structure in language. The playful sounds of nonsense words ("Hickory dickory dock," "Diddle, diddle dumpling, my son John," "Higgledy, piggledy, my black hen," "Eeny, meeny, miny, mo") appeal to the sheer joy in the sounds of words.

Many nursery rhymes are interactive, and can contribute to a child's physical development. "Pat-a-Cake, Pat-a-Cake" and "This little piggy went to market" call for physical coordination and interpersonal contact; "Ring Around the Rosie" and "London Bridge Is Falling Down" call for the exercise of large-motor skills as well as social interaction. Jump-rope rhymes are simply nursery rhymes gone to the playground, and appear to be an almost worldwide childhood pastime (see Butler, *Skipping Around the World*). By extension, we could also argue that some of these jingles help children release aggression and hostility in acceptable ways. Take, for example, this popular jump-rope jingle:

> Fudge, fudge, tell the judge
> Mother has a newborn baby;
> It isn't a girl and it isn't a boy;
> It's just a fair young lady.
> Wrap it up in tissue paper
> And send it up the elevator:
> First floor, miss;
> Second floor, miss;
> Third floor, miss;
> Fourth floor;
> Kick it out the elevator door.

This brings us to one of the controversies surrounding many nursery rhymes—their often violent content. We find babies dropping from treetops, cradle and all; a farmer's wife chopping off the tails (or heads) of three blind mice; a beleaguered old woman living in a shoe with unruly children whom she apparently beats; a ladybug whose children (save for one) are all lost in a fire; a man who keeps his wife in a pumpkin shell; and more. Indeed, one assiduous critic, Geoffrey Handley-Taylor, discovered in a collection of some 200 familiar nursery rhymes at least 100 rhymes with "unsavory elements," including eight allusions to murder, two cases of choking to death, one case of decapitation, seven cases of severing of limbs—and the list goes on (Baring-Gould, 20).

From time to time, well-meaning adults have attempted to tidy up the familiar nursery rhymes; to make them more respectable, as it were. Sylvia Long has produced a beautifully illustrated modern collection of nursery rhymes, *Sylvia Long's Mother Goose*, that eliminates some of the more indelicate aspects of the verses. The baby who rocks in the treetop is a little bird who flies to safety when the bough breaks; the old woman who lives in a shoe is a spider who doesn't spank her children, but kisses them before putting them to bed. But such adaptations may be more for adults than children. The rhymes are certainly much less exciting, and probably less memorable. Young readers are wise enough to realize that what occurs in a nonsense rhyme is not what ought to occur in real life. And it is fairly safe to say that no child ever turned violent from reading nursery rhymes. Reading provides vicarious pleasure; this is no different for children than for adults (reading murder mysteries does not create murderers). Even very young children know when something is "just a story" or "only make-believe."

Choosing Mother Goose Books

Pity the young child who does not have a good Mother Goose book. But there are so many to choose from, it is often difficult to tell which are the good ones. Below are some points to consider when choosing from the many collections available:

- Is the book attractive and well made? These books get a lot of use. A flimsy paperback may be ultimately a waste of money.
- Are there enough rhymes to justify the cost of the book? Usually, the larger collections are the best buy—although many homes will have more than one collection.
- Is there a balance between the familiar rhymes and those that are less often anthologized? You want the old standbys, but it's good to have some fresh verses as well. In other words, try to get the most for your money.
- Are the illustrations examples of good art, both imaginative and well executed? (For more about this, see Chapter 5.) It is great if each rhyme has its own illustration; although this is not always possible in larger collections.
- Are the pages uncluttered in appearance, and are the rhymes juxtaposed with the proper pictures? Remember, children are often looking at the illustrations while the rhymes are being read to them.
- Is there an index so that specific rhymes can be easily located? This is not essential, but an index is very helpful for grown-ups trying to fill special requests.
- In newer collections, you might want to look for rhymes from other cultures—African, Asian, American Indian, and so on. Of course, don't pass

up such classic collections as the classic Volland edition of Eulalie Osgood Grover's *Mother Goose* illustrated by Frederick Richardson (see Figure 6.2), Blanche Fisher Wright's *The Real Mother Goose* (see Figure 6.3), Marguerite de Angeli's *Book of Nursery and Mother Goose Rhymes* or Raymond Briggs's *The Mother Goose Treasury* simply because they are not sufficiently multicultural. That would be a great loss.

Mother Goose rhymes are among the treasures of childhood. These rhymes need no defense; they are pure fun. Their delightful nonsense and eccentric characters remain with us long beyond childhood.

The Sounds in Poetry

As we have seen, a child's first introduction to poetry is through the sound of its language—specifically its rhyme and rhythm. Mother Goose rhymes, in fact, are so-called because they always rhyme; that is, they repeat sounds. But there is much more to poetry than rhyming "June" with "moon" and "spoon." In addition to their insistent rhymes, Mother Goose verses also rely on regular rhythm; that is, they have a predictable beat. This can be monotonous, as in "Mary had a little lamb," but sometimes it is more imaginative, as in "Hickory, dickory, dock." But our language offers us so many more possibilities for rhyme and rhythm, which we will explore now.

Rhyme

Simply put, rhyme is the repetition of similar sounds in a word, line, or stanza. End rhyme is perhaps the most widely recognized rhyme in poetry; it occurs when the last words of two or more lines repeat the same sounds. To describe a poem's end-rhyme scheme, we assign a letter of the alphabet to the ending sound of each line, beginning with "a." Any line rhyming with the first line of the poem is called the "a" rhyme, the second rhyme is the "b" rhyme, and so on. Too often, end-rhyme devolves into trite and unimaginative rhymes, as in that old jingle,

> Roses are red, violets are blue,
> Sugar is sweet, and so are you.

And these quickly devolve into parodies:

> Roses are red, violets are blue,
> Your feet stink, and so do you.

But end-rhyme is often most enjoyable when it is unexpected, as in this example from Henry Wadsworth Longfellow (the letters following each line identify the rhyme scheme so you can see the pattern):

There was a little girl (a)
Who had a little curl (a)
Right in the middle of her forehead. (b)
When she was good (c)
She was very, very good, (c)
But when she was bad she was horrid. (b)

OK, so it's not a great poem, but the rhyme of "forehead" with "horrid" makes it memorable. And, yes, the two words don't rhyme precisely, but they clearly echo each other—which is what rhyme actually does. In fact, English is not the easiest language in which to make end-rhymes. It is claimed that English has no rhyme for "orange," for instance—unless we consider "Blorenge," the name of a hill in Wales. And what about "purple"? Well, it rhymes with "curple" (a donkey's hind legs) and "hirple" (which means to limp)—at least according to one source (see Held). The problem is obvious: English end-rhymes are sometimes hard to come by.

But repeated sounds don't always occur at the end of a line, or even at the end of a word. For example, we can repeat the initial sound of a word. We call this *alliteration*—as in, "Billy Button bought a buttered biscuit." But as with most other things, alliteration is best in moderation, as in these lines from Alfred, Lord Tennyson's "The Eagle":

He clasps the crag with crooked hands;
Close to the sea in lonely lands,
Ring'd with the azure world, he stands.
The wrinkled sea beneath him crawls;
He watches from his mountain walls,
And like a thunderbolt he falls.

The end-rhyme pattern is quite simple: a, a, a, b, b, b. But notice how Tennyson sprinkles the consonant sounds *l*, *w*, and hard *c* (or k) throughout the poem—at the beginning, the end, and in the middle of words. (The repetition of consonant sounds is called *consonance*.) Also, in the first stanza, Tennyson repeats certain vowel sounds as well, such as the short *a* in *clasps*, *crag*, *hands*, *azure*, and *stands*. (The repetition of vowel sounds is called *assonance*.) Notice too that all these repeated sounds are close enough to make the repetition effective but not so close as to make it annoying (as in tongue twisters like "the sixth sick sheik's sixth sheep is sick" or "the thistle sifter sifted seven thick thistles"—try saying them 10 times fast). Tennyson's use of sound is not accidental. The poet chose these words deliberately for their musical effect.

And listen to these lines from Robert Louis Stevenson's "The Moon." The poet makes use of alliteration, consonance, and assonance throughout the poem:

> The moon has a face like the clock in the hall;
> She shines on thieves on the garden wall,
> On streets and fields and harbor quays,
> And birdies asleep in the forks of the trees.

See how many examples of sound repetition you can find. (Remember that *quays* is pronounced as if it were spelled *keys*.) As adults, we sometimes overlook the sounds of language and concentrate only on the meaning. Fortunately, children are not so narrow, and they love to play with the sounds of language, and poetry lets them enjoy those sounds.

Rhythm

Just as important as rhyme is rhythm, the pattern created by the stresses on syllables we find in spoken English. (For instance, listen to the difference in the way we pronounce "personal" and "personnel.") When these stresses are placed into a regular pattern, we have rhythm—just as in the beat to a musical tune. Rhythm results when we have a regular repetition of strong beats or stressed syllables (in boldface) accompanied by unstressed syllables. Read these lines of Shakespeare's (the bold-faced syllables are stressed):

> **Mer**rily, **mer**rily, **shall** I live **now**
> **Un**der the **blos**som that **hangs** on the **bough**

When combinations of stresses form patterns, we call them *meters*. Very simply, there are four common meters, each having either two or three syllables. Listen for the patterns in the way we pronounce the following feminine names, each one representing a different meter:

> **Mar**-y (a stressed syllable followed by an unstressed syllable—called a *trochee*)
>
> Ma-**rie** (an unstressed syllable followed by a stressed syllable—called an *iamb*)
>
> **Mar**-i-an (a stressed syllable followed by two unstressed syllables—called a *dactyl*)
>
> Mar-y-**anne** (two unstressed syllables followed by a stressed one—called an *anapest*)

Experiment with your own name—can you determine which syllables should be stressed? Sometimes this takes practice. The trick is to speak the words naturally and not put an emphasis where there isn't one.

Few poems maintain a consistent rhythm throughout—for that would be terrifically monotonous, as in this nursery rhyme. Again, the stressed syllables are in boldface:

> **Mary had** a **little lamb,**
> Its **fleece** was **white** as **snow,**
> And ev'rywhere that **Mary went**
> The **lamb** was **sure** to **go.**

Every other syllable is stressed without fail, which contributes to the rather tedious, sing-song quality of the verse. Most readers prefer poetry with a less insistent rhythm, as in these closing lines of Edward Lear's "The Owl and the Pussy Cat," describing the pair's wedding feast:

> They **dined** on **mince** and slices of **quince,**
> Which they **ate** with a **run**cible **spoon;**
> And **hand** in **hand,** on the **edge** of the **sand,**
> They **danced** by the **light** of the **moon,**
> The **moon,**
> The **moon,**
> They **danced** by the **light** of the **moon.**

Notice the changes in rhythm from line to line (alternating between iambs to anapests). The end-rhyme may seem monotonous—a, b, c, b, b, b, b—but it is relieved by interesting internal rhyme (short and long "i's in the first line and short "a's" in the third and fourth lines). The unusual rhythm and rhyme combined with evocative word pictures make for a very pleasing poem and one that is fun to read aloud.

The Pictures in Poetry

Again, the nursery rhymes taught us to look for pictures in poetry—whether it be the man in the moon, an old woman living in a shoe, a crooked man with his crooked mouse, or a cat with its fiddle. The nursery rhymes invite us to visualize things. And so it is in all good poetry. It creates pictures (or images) in our minds, and makes us see something in a new way. If the images are not new and fresh, the poem seems trite and dull (like "roses are red, violets are blue"). Good poets try to awaken our senses—all of our senses—by describing things we can see, hear, taste, feel, or smell. The poet does this in one of two ways.

First, the poet can simply describe something directly in sensory terms—make reference to sight, sound, smell, taste, and texture. A rose, for example, may look red, feel smooth, and smell sweet (I don't think we want to taste it). Second, the poet can describe something (people, objects, feelings, and so on) figuratively using similes ("she was light as a feather"), metaphors ("it is raining cats and dogs"), or personification ("the sea is angry tonight"). Let's look a little closer at each of these.

Direct or Sensory Description

SIGHT Poets use visual imagery details to give us both a picture and a feeling. So, as we read John Clare's "Autumn," we can form a specific image in our minds from the details provided:

> I love to see the cottage smoke
> Curl upward through the naked trees;
> The pigeons nestled round the cote
> On dull November days like these.

SOUND Sounds are also evocative. In these lines from "To Autumn," John Keats is describing the musical sounds of nature:

> Hedge-crickets sing; and now with treble soft
> The redbreast whistles from a garden-croft;
> And gathering swallows twitter in the skies.

Perhaps one of the most famous allusions to sound is found in Edgar Allan Poe's "The Raven," which opens with a raven rapping and tapping at the door:

> Once upon a midnight dreary, while I pondered, weak and weary,
> Over many a quaint and curious volume of forgotten lore—
> While I nodded, nearly napping, suddenly there came a tapping,
> As of some one gently rapping, rapping at my chamber door.
> "'Tis some visitor," I muttered, "tapping at my chamber door—Only this
>   and nothing more."

SMELL The sense of smell can be very suggestive and call up past memories for us. Walt Whitman, a lover of nature, frequently uses the imagery of smell to get his readers to feel what he is feeling. In these lines, he turns to warm and earthy smells of the outdoors: "The smell of apples, aromas from crush'd sage-plant, mint, birch-bark" and ". . . in the fragrant pines and the cedars dusk and dim."

TASTE Tastes can also summon up emotional responses, as in Mary O'Neill's description of the color brown: "Brown is cinnamon / and morning toast." And notice the combination of sensory images (of sight, smell and taste) in these lines from Eliza Cook's poem "The Mouse and the Cake":

A mouse found a beautiful piece of plum cake,
The richest and sweetest that mortal could make;
'Twas heavy with citron and fragrant with spice,
And covered with sugar all sparkling as ice.

(Iona and Peter Opie. *The Oxford Book of
Children's Verse*. Oxford: Oxford University
Press, 1973.)

TEXTURE   And finally there is texture—our sense of touch. Listen to Walter de laMare describe the experience of cool leaves brushing against skin: "Through the green twilight of a hedge / I peered with cheek on the cool leaves pressed." And in these lines, John Keats describes a cold St. Agnes's Eve (January 20) that almost makes us shiver, and the image of the poor hare is heart-rending:

St. Agnes' Eve—Ah, bitter chill it was!
The owl, for all his feathers, was a-cold;
The hare limp'd trembling through the frozen grass . . . .

Figurative or Comparative Description

In addition to describing the world through sight, sound, taste, touch, and smell, poets help us better understand their messages by making comparisons. All of us make comparisons every day in our speaking, it's just that poets are a bit more imaginative. The three most common types of comparison are similes, metaphors, and personification.

SIMILE   A simile is a comparison between two things that is expressed using the terms *like* or *as*. We use similes all the time—"busy as a bee," "happy as a clam," "hungry as a horse," "swimming like a fish," "running like clockwork." We use similes to make our points clearer and perhaps make our speech more colorful. Poets use similes for very much the same reasons. The first stanza of Robert Burns' "A Red, Red Rose" contains two familiar similes:

My love is like a red, red rose
        That's newly sprung in June:
My love is like the melody
        That's sweetly played in tune.

METAPHOR   A metaphor is also a comparison, but it is a little trickier than a simile, because the comparison is not stated directly—it's done without *like* or *as*. Whereas a simile is a stated comparison, a metaphor is an implied comparison. We also use metaphors every day, but often we don't recognize them, because they have become so familiar. We say "our hearts are broken" or "we get cold feet"; we use a "computer mouse" or visit a "chat room"; some people (not any of us, of course) "talk trash" or "pig out"; we may compliment a friend by saying "you're a saint"; and we've all suffered the "hard knocks" of life. All of these are metaphors—we do not mean literally what we say. When we eat a spicy chili pepper, our tongues are not really "on fire" and when we're "bored to tears" we are not usually weeping. We can't seem to live (or talk) without metaphors. Some poems are made up entirely of metaphors, as in this poem by Valerie Bloom:

> Time's a bird, which leaves its footprints
> At the corner of your eyes.
> Time's a jockey, racing horses,
> The sun and moon across the skies.
> Time's a thief, stealing your beauty,
> Leaving you with tears and sighs.
> But you waste time trying to catch him,
> Time's a bird and Time just flies.
>
>   ("Time's a Bird" copyright © Valerie Bloom,
> 2000, from *Hot Like Fire* published by Blooms-
> bury, reprinted by permission of Valerie Bloom.)

Notice how Bloom applies each metaphor to a different aspect of time, and notice how she weaves in other metaphors as well, such as comparing the sun and moon to racing horses. This is a good example of how metaphor enriches poetry.

PERSONIFICATION   Personification is really a variation of simile and metaphor, in which the poet, by way of comparison, gives human qualities to an inanimate object, an abstract idea, or a force of nature. We speak of an "angry sea" or a "calm lake," a "cheerful room" or time "marching on." When Valerie Bloom writes "Time's a thief," she is using a personification. Notice how Robert Louis Stevenson describes the winter sun as a drowsy child in his poem "Winter-Time":

> Late lies the wintry sun a-bed,
> A frosty, fiery sleepy-head;
> Blinks but an hour or two, and then,
> A blood-red orange, sets again.

The best poets give us bold, imaginative similes, metaphors and/or personification. And all these techniques help make us see things in new and sometimes unusual ways. Poetry is more than just a clever use of rhyme and rhythm. It is a way of seeing our lives and the world around us afresh.

The Kinds of Poetry

Poetry is a richly diverse genre that wears many clothes (to use a rather tired metaphor!). Two broad categories exist—narrative poetry, which tells a story, and lyric poetry, which describes a poet's feelings or emotions. There are many variations.

Narrative Poetry and Ballads

A narrative poem tells a story. It includes characters, action, and plot. Robert Browning's "The Pied Piper of Hamelin" and Henry Wadsworth Longfellow's "The Song of Hiawatha" are two nineteenth-century verse narratives still in print today. The early twentieth-century poet Alfred Noyes wrote "The Highwayman," a tragic story of love and betrayal, ending with the violent death of the highwayman and his beloved. This narrative poem remains popular in England after more than a century.

For younger children, ballads are probably more accessible than the longer narrative poems. A ballad is a short narrative poem that typically describes a single event or tells the exploits of a hero or heroine. Traditional ballads use the so-called ballad stanza, which contains four lines, each with eight syllables and with the second and fourth lines rhyming. A four-line ballad stanza usually results in this rhyming pattern: *a-b-c-b*, although many variations are found. One of the most famous ballads, "Barbara Allen," concerns tragic lovers and dates from the Middle Ages. The opening stanza sets the scene and introduces the main character (the rhyme scheme is indicated by the letters at the end of each line):

> In Scarlet town, where I was born, (a)
> There was a fair maid dwellin', (b)
> Made every youth cry Well-a-way! (c)
> Her name was Barbara Allen. (b)

We learn that a young lad, Sweet William, is on his deathbed and begs to see Barbara Allen, but the hard-hearted maiden ignores him, and he dies. Then she is overcome by remorse, and is determined to join her beloved in death with one last request:

> O mother, mother, make my bed,
> O make it soft and narrow:
> My love has died for me today,
> I'll die for him tomorrow.

It should not be surprising that both folk and country songs have been greatly influenced by the traditional ballad.

Lyric Poetry

In ancient Greece, poems were typically sung to music played on a stringed instrument called a lyre. Thus, these poems were called lyrics. Today, we use the term *lyric poem* to refer to any shorter poem that expresses the poet's personal feelings or emotions. The association between lyric poems and music remains with us, for we call the words set to music "lyrics," whether or not they are "poetic." Lyric poems themselves come in an endless variety of forms—including cinquains, elegies, haiku, pastorals, odes, rondeaux, rondels, sestinas, sonnets, triolets, villanelles, and many more, with new ones still being created. Each form has its own rules for stanza length, line length, rhyme scheme, and so on. There is also free verse, which ignores all the established rules and lets the poets do just as they please (sometimes it works, and sometimes it doesn't).

What we look for in a lyric poem are fresh and thoughtful imagery, new ways of looking at things, and inventive use of rhyme and rhythm or language patterns. Following are examples of common lyric forms found in poetry for children.

HAIKU Japanese in origin, haiku typically consists of 17 syllables (the number of words doesn't matter) divided into three lines and is usually on the subject of nature and our relationship to nature, such as this example from the sixteenth-century Japanese poet Basho, translated by Harry Behn:

> An old silent pond,
> A frog jumps into the pond
> Splash! Silence again.
>
> (from *Cricket Songs,* 1964, Harcourt Brace
> and World)

This poem captures a single moment in nature—the series of one- and two-syllable words evoke an action of utter simplicity, a moment of breathless quiet for a moment interrupted—and we are left with our thoughts. A haiku in English may have rhythm but it usually does not rhyme. Its strength lies in its evocative imagery. It is more like a whisper of a poem—a hint of a feeling. Successful haiku uses metaphor to give us a fresh and imaginative look at something we may view as quite ordinary.

CINQUAIN   The cinquain is another old form, this time going back to medieval Europe. The term once seems to have included any five-line poem (*cinq* is French for "five"). Then a poet named Adelaide Crapsey, in the early twentieth century, wrote a volume of poems titled simply *Verse*, in which she laid down very precise rules stipulating that the five lines should contain two, four, six, eight, and two syllables, respectively. No rhyming is necessary, but quite often, the first and last lines contain related ideas, are synonymous, or mirror each other. This type of cinquain presents an interesting puzzle for the poet—and can be great fun for children to attempt.

Crapsey's cinquain "November Night" plays on the double meaning of the last word (incidentally, notice the simile in the third line):

> Listen . . .
> With faint dry sound,
> Like steps of passing ghosts,
> The leaves, frost-crisp'd, break from the trees
> And fall.

LIMERICKS   The limerick is a five-line humorous poem in which the first, second, and fifth lines rhyme, and the third and fourth lines rhyme. The fun of the limerick lies in its rollicking rhythm and broad humor—a limerick is always comical. The following limerick has been attributed to President Woodrow Wilson:

> I sat next to the Duchess at tea;
> It was just as I thought it would be;
> Her rumblings abdominal
> Were simply phenomenal,
> And everyone thought it was me.

The limerick's form is easily imitated (often in subversive and off-color ways), and young children can have a great deal of fun creating their own.

FREE VERSE   Free verse, which became popular in the twentieth century, refers to poems that follow no established rules of form. Free verse comes closer to natural speech than most other poetry. Of course, it goes without saying that very young children—through the early elementary and even middle elementary grades—prefer the sounds of rhythm and rhyme. For them, poetry is still closely allied with song. But by middle school, many students are ready to experiment with something more daring—poetry that seems to break the rules. Free verse has a definite place in the curriculum of the upper grades, and many fine works of free verse are available to them.

The great American poet, Walt Whitman, who lived in the 19th century, wrote largely in free verse. The following poem, "When I Heard the Learn'd Astronomer," is an example of free verse, lacking regular rhythm and a rhyming pattern:

> When I heard the learn'd astronomer,
> When the proofs, the figures, were ranged in columns
>   before me,
> When I was shown the charts and diagrams, to add, divide,
>   and measure them,
> When I sitting heard the astronomer where he lectured
>   with much applause in the lecture-room,
> How soon unaccountable I became tired and sick,
> Till rising and gliding out I wander'd off by myself,
> In the mystical moist night-air, and from time to time,
> Look'd up in perfect silence at the stars.

In the absence of rhyme and rhythm, Whitman uses repetition of phrasing and a piling up of images to capture the tedium of the astronomer's boring lecture, which makes the speaker "tired and sick." And this tedium is sharply contrasted with the effect of the speaker's going outside, gazing into the night sky, and seeing the stars themselves in their "perfect silence." In other words, experiencing a phenomenon has more impact than merely talking about it.

VISUAL POETRY   Also called concrete poetry or shape poetry, visual poetry consists of words arranged to take a specific shape, usually of the poem's subject. Although visual poems go back at least to the seventeenth century, Lewis Carroll is credited with the first visual poem for children—"The Mouse's Tale" from *Alice's Adventures in Wonderland*. Characteristic of Carroll's love for puns, the poem is shaped, of course, like a mouse's tail (see Figure 6.6).

Today, visual poetry has become virtually a hybrid of literature and visual art. In fact, some visual poems almost defy reading aloud. One of the most famous examples of modern visual poetry is Reinhard Döhl's poem "Pattern Poem with an Elusive Intruder." It consists of multiple repetitions of the word *apple* making up the shape of an apple. The intruder is the slyly placed word *worm*, almost hidden

Fury said to
a mouse, That
he met
in the
house,
'Let us
both go
to law:
I will
prosecute
you.—
Come, I'll
take no
denial;
We must
have a
trial:
For
really
this
morning
I've
nothing
to do.'
Said the
mouse to
the cur,
'Such a
trial,
dear sir,
With no
jury or
judge,
would be
wasting
our breath.'
' I'll be
judge,
I'll be
jury,'
Said
cunning
old Fury;
' I'll try
the whole
cause,
and
condemn
you
to
death.'"

in a lower corner of the apple. The poem was originally written in German, using the terms *apfel* and *wurm*—an example of a foreign-language poem that needs no translation.

Visual poetry is often playful poetry, but it can be thoughtful as well. Visual poems present interesting challenges to readers in very much the same way that poetic imagery does in a conventional poem. A visual poem's impact relies heavily on its clever use of both language and design. Robert Froman's "A Seeing Poem" (see Figure 6.7) cleverly uses the form to define visual poetry itself.

FOUND POETRY   Poetry is all around us, just waiting for us to find it. So-called "found poetry" is created by taking words from other sources—books, newspapers, news releases, memos, signs, notices, advertisements of all sorts, restaurant menus, any place language can be found—and arranging the words lines like poetry. The purest found poem does not alter the words or the word order. Dorothy Wordsworth, sister of the poet William Wordsworth, loved to walk in the countryside and write down her feelings in a private journal. One of her prose sentences has been made into a poem merely by breaking it into lines:

> The lake was covered all over
> With bright silver waves
> That were each
> The twinkling of an eye.

FIGURE 6.7 ■ Robert Froman's "A Seeing Poem."

Source: Reprinted by permission of Mrs. Katherine Froman.

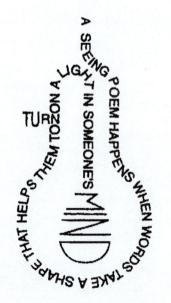

Without rhyme or regular rhythm, these lines sound poetic, giving us a lovely image of the lake.

Most found poems do not rhyme, but here is an unusual example taken from *An Elementary Treatise on Mechanics* (1819) by philosopher William Whewell: "Hence no force, however great, can stretch a cord, however fine, into a horizontal line which is accurately straight." See what happens when the words are arranged this way:

> Hence no force, however great,
> can stretch a cord, however fine,
> into a horizontal line
> which is accurately straight.

Sometimes we might wish to tweak a passage to poetic effect. Take this sentence from Jeremy Bentham, an eighteenth-century English philosopher: "Stretching his hand up to reach the stars, too often man forgets the flowers at his feet," which we might adjust to read:

> Stretching our hands up
> To reach the stars,
> Too often we forget
> The flowers at our feet.

In 2011, a new journal was launched, *Found Poetry Review*, dedicated exclusively to publishing found poems, and the entries come from people of all ages. Found poetry can help children in several ways. It makes poetry a part of their everyday lives, removes the academic stigma often associated with poetry, encourages them to seek out their own found poems, and makes them more aware of the power and possibility of language.

NONSENSE VERSE   Nonsense verse, which defies all logic as we know it, is one of the most popular kinds of poetry among young children. It usually depicts ridiculous characters in outrageous situations. Take, for example, this limerick by Edward Lear:

> There was an Old Man with a beard
> Who said, "It is just as I feared!
> Two Owls and a Hen,
> Four Larks and a Wren,
> Have built a nest in my beard!"

However, nonsense verse may include made-up words, as in these lines from one of the most famous poems in the English language, Lewis Carroll's

"The Jabberwocky," from *Through the Looking-Glass and What Alice Found There*:

Twas brillig, and the slithy toves
Did gyre and gimble in the wabe;
All mimsy were the borogoves,
And the mome raths outgrabe.

Our enjoyment comes from the playful language, the comic predicaments, the joy of the unexpected. Nonsense verse can also be subversive, going against society's conventions. And that may be its chief appeal for children; after all, childhood is about testing the waters, discovering what works, finding out how far one can go, and what the grown-ups are hiding. Writing nonsense verse can be great fun for children—it is playful, and encourages the creative use of rhythm, rhyme, and the sound of language in general, as in this popular example by Laura Richards:

Once there was an elephant,
Who tried to use the telephant—
No! No! I mean an elephone
Who tried to use the telephone—
(Dear me! I am not certain quite
That even now I've got it right.)
Howe'er it was, he got his trunk
Entangled in the telephunk;
The more he tried to get it free,
The louder buzzed the telephee—
(I fear I'd better drop the song
Of elephop and telephong!)

URCHIN POETRY Joseph T. Thomas, Jr., uses the tantalizing term *urchin poetry* to describe the work of poets who are attempting to appeal to the earthier instincts in children—those instincts that draw them to forbidden topics of childhood, especially sex, bodily functions, and excretions. Urchin poetry is identified by its subject matter and treatment, and not by any prescribed poetic pattern. It almost always rhymes and has a rhythmic beat and is, in those respects, quite conventional. However, it is characterized by its obsession with the repulsive, the outrageous, and the grotesque. Naturally, all these are fascinating to youth, perhaps largely because of the taboos associated with them.

The most famous poet in this vein is probably Shel Silverstein, whose *Where the Sidewalk Ends* and *A Light in the Attic* are filled with rollicking verses exploiting this material. With lines such as this from "Messy Room"—"And his smelly old sock has been stuck to the wall"—or his descriptions in "Sarah Cynthia Sylvia Stout"—"Gloppy glumps of cold oatmeal" and "moldy melons, dried-up mustard"—Silverstein recognizes the value of a good "gross-out." Silverstein, in fact, is almost mainstream compared to the so-called "potty poets" whose obsessions with bodily excretions—always played for a laugh—have resulted in publications of many books of poetry (we will say nothing about the quality). And the justification for all this? It may be just one more way to entice those reluctant readers into the rich (if sometimes wacky) world of books.

PLAYGROUND POETRY   As we have seen, free verse, nonsense verse, and urchin poetry all seem to relish flaunting the rules, which at times seems to be a preoccupation of children in general. It is not surprising that, when children themselves experiment with poetry, they often challenge the status quo and break down social decorum. And where does this normally occur? On the playground—either literally or figuratively. Playground poetry (see Thomas) is the original urchin poetry, for it comes from the children themselves.

We have already suggested that children seem to have a natural affinity for poetry. Perhaps it is because poetry is one of the first literary forms introduced to them—in nursery rhymes, songs, and games. And it may have something to do with the fact that our bodies are tuned to natural rhythms—our heartbeats, for instance—and nature itself is filled with myriad patterns and rhythms. All this is speculative, but it is undeniable that children, when left to their own devices, are constantly reciting and creating poetry, and it is usually a communal experience. This jump-rope rhyme was a favorite playground verse of my own daughters when they were in early elementary school:

> Cinderella dressed in yella'
> Went to town to see her fella'
> On her way her girdle busted,
> How many people were disgusted?
> 1, 2, 3, . . . [etc. until the jumper misses]

Playground poetry is very much like the traditional folktale in that it is passed along orally, often from child to child.

Playground poetry is also true living poetry—always spoken; rarely written down; and forever changing, adapting to new times, places, and circumstances. Consequently, the children themselves become poets (of sorts) as they add their individual touches to the verses. The example of "Cinderella" is popular because it mentions an "unmentionable"—a girdle. References to undergarments invariably get a rise from first- and second-graders. And earlier in the chapter, we cited the example of "Fudge, fudge, tell the judge," which is undoubtedly popular because of its fiendish violence.

But even these two poems are mild compared with what quite often is heard on the playground. I recall, for instance, this popular verse from my own childhood—and it is still in circulation—which is also urchin poetry at its most outrageous:

> Great big gobs of greasy, grimy gopher guts,
> Mutilated monkey meat,
> Dirty little birdy feet,
> Great big gobs of greasy, grimy gopher guts,
> And me without a spoon!

Playground poetry is usually recited out of earshot of adults, and is therefore the product of childhood unleashed. This poetry contains all the language and imagery that are normally taboo for children. Profanity, sex, violence, and bodily functions are all typical features of this poetry. I offer neither a defense nor castigation of these poetic offerings—only a description.

Subversive poetry, including chants, parody, and the harmless cheers recited at sporting events, has always been, and always will be, an important part of childhood. Here children can throw off the yoke of adult domination and safely release the anxiety, hostility, and pent-up frustrations that are perfectly normal aspects of growing up (although many adults like to pretend otherwise). It is also an example of the creative process at work. Taste, refinement, and judgment will come with maturity, but art itself must begin with freedom of expression.

Sharing Poetry with Children

Studies of children's poetry preferences suggest, among other things, that (1) children prefer poetry that they can understand, (2) they prefer humorous poetry, (3) they prefer new poems to older ones, and (4) they do not like serious and contemplative poems (see Terry). However, such studies can be dangerous if we rely on them entirely to determine what poetry to share with children. Doing so would result in a further narrowing of taste among children and deprive them of many fresh and imaginative poems that they just might enjoy. For most elementary school children—and perhaps even older children—an oral approach to poetry makes the most sense. Because of its rhythmical and rhyming qualities, much of poetry begs to be read aloud. Figure 6.8 lists just a few ideas for using poetry in the classroom. The suggestions move generally from simplest to most complex. Many of these exercises can be done either individually or in groups. However, before beginning any of these projects, try sharing with the students several poems by a variety of poets. This should, in fact, become a regular part of the routine in a language arts classroom. Poetry inspires poetry.

FIGURE 6.8 ■ 25 Things to Do with Poetry

1. Read one new poem every day.

2. Memorize a favorite poem (that has at least six to eight lines).

3. Write a poem with lots of alliteration—for instance, a poem about Luis, who is "lanky," "likeable," "lively," and "lucky."

4. Write a five-line poem in which every line rhymes at the end.

5. Make a list of your favorite sights, sounds, smells, tastes, and textures.

6. Drawing on the list you made in No. 5, write a poem of at least five lines about happiness.

7. Using as many sensory words as you can, write a poem about your most or least favorite food.

8. Compare two poems from different poets about your favorite season.

9. Using as many sensory words as you can, write a poem about your favorite season.

10. Make a list of *similes* that describe you, such as "happy as a clam" or "fast as lightning."

11. Make up a simile you have never heard before—and be sure you can explain it.

12. Make a list of *metaphors* that we often use, such as "a computer mouse," "putting your foot in your mouth," and "a skeleton in the closet."

13. Make up a metaphor you have never heard before—and be sure you can explain it.

14. Write a poem about your favorite color, using sights, sounds, smells, tastes, textures, and emotions you associate with the color. (See Mary O'Neill's *Hailstones and Halibut Bones*.)

15. Write a poem about yourself, using the letters of your name to begin each line.

16. Write a poem describing today's weather, using at least one simile or metaphor.

17. Write a parody of a nursery rhyme, using its rhyme scheme and rhythm, but give it a contemporary setting, something like this:

> *Mayor Flubbins sat on a wall;*
> *Mayor Flubbins had a great fall.*
> *All the townspeople—women and men—*
> *Refused to return him to office again.*

18. Write a limerick about a fictitious person, following this pattern:

> *There was an old man from Peru*
> *Who dreamt he was eating his shoe.*
> *He awoke in the night*
> *With a terrible fright*
> *And found it was perfectly true.*

(*continued*)

FIGURE 6.8 ■ 25 Things to Do with Poetry (*continued*)

19. Write a haiku about your favorite season—just 17 syllables in 3 lines.
20. Write a poem using only *one-syllable* words, but with rhyme and rhythm.
21. Write a nonsense poem about an outrageous person or animal. Try using unusual rhyme and rhythm.
22. Write a poem that uses word sounds and rhythm in an unusual way—such as a galloping rhythm in a poem about horses or soothing sounds in a poem about sleep.
23. Write a visual poem about an object, with the lines making the shape of the object.
24. Create a found poem from a newspaper item, an advertisement, a menu, a sign, or anyplace there is written language.
25. Read a collection of poems by a favorite poet.

Summary

From the rhymes of Mother Goose to the jump-rope verse and limericks on the playground, poetry is a happy part of young children's lives. Perhaps, even in those formative years, children know instinctively what eighteenth-century German philosopher Novalis said: "Poetry heals the wounds inflicted by reason." It is important that we nurture this initial love so that, as they grow older, children can appreciate the many facets of poetry—both the sound (the patterns of rhyme and rhythm) and the sense (including the exciting stories of narrative verse and the deep human emotion expressed in lyrics).

A poet is a visionary, one who sees the world in fresh and unusual ways and is capable of sharing that vision with the rest of us. It is important that we, as adults and teachers, overcome our own fears and apprehensions about poetry so we can share its bounty. And the better we come to know poetry, the richer our experience will be. Although it is helpful to have some knowledge of poetic techniques and devices—rhythm, rhyme, metaphor, simile, personification— we should not get bogged down by technical details or terminology. The best way to learn to enjoy poetry is to read and hear lots of it, in all its rich variety. Poetry presents many opportunities for creative activities through which we can explore and appreciate the richness of the art form—oral recitation, illustration, and writing, to name a few. Few literary forms offer so much in pleasure and knowledge as poetry. Lovers of poetry are not born but made through patient and careful nurturing.

Works Cited

Baring-Gould, William S., and Ceil Baring-Gould. *The Annotated Mother Goose*. New York: Potter, 1962.

Butler, Francelia. *Skipping around the World: The Ritual Nature of Folk Rhymes*. New York: Ballantine, 1989.

Held, Carl. "Orange, Silver, Now Purple (More Lexical Lunacy)." *Games*, Issue 207, 29.1 (February 2005): 4–9, 16.

Terry, Ann. *Children's Poetry Preferences: A National Survey of the Upper Elementary Grades*. Urbana, IL: National Council of Teachers of English, 1984.

Thomas, Joseph T. Jr. *Poetry's Playground: The Culture of Contemporary American Children's Poetry*. Detroit, MI: Wayne State University Press, 2007.

Recommended Resources

Ciardi, John, and Miller Williams. *How Does a Poem Mean?* 2nd ed. Boston: Houghton Mifflin, 1975.

Higginson, William J., with Penny Harter. *The Haiku Handbook: How to Write, Share and Teach Haiku*. New York: McGraw-Hill, 1985.

Hopkins, Lee Bennett. *Pass the Poetry Please*. New York: Citation Press, 1972.

Hurst, Carol. "What to Do with a Poem." *Early Years* 11 (February 1980): 28–29, 68.

Kennedy, X. J. " 'Go and Get Your Candle Lit!' An Approach to Poetry." *Horn Book Magazine* 57, 3 (June 1981): 273–279.

Livingston, Myra. *Climb into the Bell Tower: Essays on Poetry*. New York: HarperCollins, 1990.

——. *Poem-Making: Ways to Begin Writing Poetry*. New York: HarperCollins, 1991.

Oliver, Mary. *A Poetry Handbook: A Prose Guide to Understanding and Writing Poetry*. San Diego, CA: Harcourt, 1994.

Vardell, Sylvia M. *Poetry Aloud Here! Sharing Poetry with Children in the Library*. Chicago: ALA, 2006.

Poetry for Children: A Selected Booklist

The first list includes anthologies—collections that include poems by many different poets. The second list includes books by individual poets.

Mother Goose Books

Alderson, Brian, comp. *The Helen Oxenbury Nursery Rhyme Book*. Illus. Helen Oxenbury. New York: Morrow, 1986.
 • A collection for very young readers with warm illustrations.

Briggs, Raymond, illus. *The Mother Goose Treasury*. New York: Coward, McCann & Geoghegan, 1966.
 • A large collection with comic illustrations.

de Angeli, Marguerite, illus. *Book of Nursery and Mother Goose Rhymes*. Garden City, NY: Doubleday, 1953.
 • A large collection fully illustrated in both black and white and color.

dePaola, Tomie, illus. *Tomie dePaola's Mother Goose*. New York: Putnam, 1985.
 • For beginners as well as older readers, a large collection playfully illustrated.

Greenaway, Kate, illus. *Kate Greenaway's Mother Goose.* 1881. Several modern reprints.
* One of the earliest, and still a favorite. A small book with delicate illustrations.

Grover, Eulalie Osgood, ed. *Mother Goose: The Original Volland Edition.* Illus. Frederick Richardson. (1915). New York: Derrydale, 1988.
* One of the earliest classic collections, A stunning book, now reprinted. Each of the more than 100 rhymes is accompanied by a full-page color illustration.

Gustafson, Scott. *Favorite Nursery Rhymes from Mother Goose.* New York: Greenwich Workshop, 2007.
* A book for beginners, with illustrations inspired by the great classic illustrators of the nineteenth and early twentieth centuries.

Hague, Michael, illus. *Mother Goose: A Collection of Classic Nursery Rhymes.* New York: Holt, 1984.
* A short collection for the very young, with striking illustrations.

Lobel, Arnold, illus. *The Random House Book of Mother Goose.* New York: Random House, 1986.
* A large, well-illustrated collection that has been recently reissued.

Long, Sylvia, illus. *Sylvia Long's Mother Goose.* San Francisco: Chronicle, 1999.
* About 75 rhymes with very inventive illustrations, sometimes as much for the adult as for the child.

Marshall, James. *James Marshall's Mother Goose.* 1986. New York: Square Fish (Macmillan), 2009.
* Large colorful and comical illustrations.

Opie, Iona. *My Very First Mother Goose.* Illus. Rosemary Wells. New York: Candlewick, 1996.
* For beginners. Playful and colorful pictures accompany this collection of familiar rhymes.

Petersham, Maud, and Miska Petersham, illus. *The Rooster Crows: A Book of American Rhymes and Jingles.* New York: Macmillan, 1945.
* A collection of traditional American folk rhymes rather than Mother Goose rhymes.

Rackham, Arthur, illus. *Mother Goose.* 1913. New York: Marathon, 1978.
* A collection with Rackham's striking and gently humorous illustrations.

Sanderson, Ruth, illus. *Mother Goose and Friends.* Boston: Little, Brown, 2008.
* A book in which some of the traditional rhymes have been "sweetened" up.

Scarry, Richard, illus. *Richard Scarry's Best Mother Goose Ever.* New York: Golden Books, 1999.
* For beginners, with Scarry's characteristic cartoon animals.

Smith, Jessie Willcox, illus. *The Jessie Willcox Smith Mother Goose.* 1914. Several modern versions.
* The original version contains hundreds of rhymes, and is the one you should look for to get the most for your money. The board book version is drastically stripped down.

Tripp, Wallace, illus. *Granfa' Grig Had a Pig and Other Rhymes Without Reason from Mother Goose.* Boston: Little, Brown, 1976.
* Contains both familiar and lesser-known rhymes.

Withers, Carl, collector. *A Rocket in My Pocket: The Rhymes and Chants of Young America.* Illus. Susanne Suba. New York: Holt, 1946.
* American folk rhymes, as told by children.

Wright, Blanche Fisher, illus. *The Real Mother Goose.* New York: Rand McNally, 1916.
* An old classic with many rhymes. Often reprinted in abridged editions.

Poetry Anthologies for All Ages

Adoff, Arnold, ed. *I Am the Darker Brother: An Anthology of Modern Poems by African Americans*, rev. ed. New York: Simon & Schuster, 1996.

Blishen, Edward, comp. *Oxford Book of Poetry for Children*. Illus. Brian Wildsmith. New York: Watts, 1963.

Carlson, Lori M., ed. *Cool Salsa: Bilingual Poems on Growing Up Latino in the United States*. New York: Holt, 1994.

De La Mare, Walter, ed. *Come Hither*, 3rd ed. Illus. Warren Chappell. New York: Knopf, 1957.

Demi, selector and illus. *In the Eyes of the Cat: Japanese Poetry for All Seasons*. Trans. Tze-si Huang. New York: Holt, 1992.

Dunning, Stephen, Edward Lueders, and Hugh Smith, comps. *Reflections on a Gift of Watermelon Pickle*. Glenview, IL: Scott, Foresman, 1967.

Elledge, Scott, ed. *Wider Than the Sky: Poems to Grow Up With*. New York: Harper, 1990.

Esbensen, Barbara Juster, comp. *Swing around the Sun*. Illus. Khee Chee Cheng, Stephen Gammell, and Janice Lee Porter. Minneapolis, MN: Carolrhoda, 2003.

Feelings, Tom, comp. and illus. *Soul Looks Back in Wonder*. New York: Dial, 1993.

Giovanni, Nikki, ed. *Hip Hop Speaks to Children*. Naperville, IL: Sourcebooks, 2008.

Harrison, Michael, and Christopher Stuart-Clark. *One Hundred Years of Poetry: For Children*. New York: Oxford University Press, 1999.

Hopkins, Lee Bennett, ed. *Sharing the Season: A Book of Poems*. New York: McElderry, 2010.

——. *Sky Magic*. Illus. Mariusz Stawarski. New York: Dutton, 2009.

Houston, James, ed. *Songs of the Dream People*. New York: Atheneum, 1972.

Janeczko, Paul B., ed. *A Kick in the Head: An Everyday Guide to Poetic Forms*. Illus. Chris Raschka. New York: Candlewick, 2005.

——. *A Poke in the I: A Collection of Concrete Poems*. Illus. Chris Raschka. Cambridge, MA: Candlewick, 2001.

Jones, Hettie, selector. *The Trees Stand Shining: Poetry of the North American Indians*. Illus. Robert Andrew Parker. New York: Dial, 1971.

Kennedy, X. J., and Dorothy Kennedy, eds. *Knock at a Star: A Child's Introduction to Poetry*, rev. ed. Illus. Karen Lee Baker. Boston: Little, Brown, 1999.

Larrick, Nancy, ed. *Piping Down the Valleys Wild*. Illus. Ellen Raskin. 1968. New York: Dell, 1982.

Lewis, J. Patrick, comp. *National Geographic Book of Animal Poetry: 200 Poems with Photographs that Squeak, Soar, and Roar!* Washington, DC: National Geographic Children's Books, 2012.

Livingston, Myra Cohn, comp. *Dilly Dilly Piccalilli: Poems for the Very Young*. New York: McElderry, 1989.

——. *Lots of Limericks*. New York: Simon & Schuster, 1991.

Lomax, Dana Teen, ed. *Kindergarde: Avant-Garde Poems, Plays, Stories, and Songs for Children*. Illus. Cliff Hengst. Lafayette: Black Radish, 2013.

Michael, Pamela, ed. *River of Words: Young Poets and Artists on the Nature of Things*. Minneapolis, MN: Milkweed, 2008.

Moore, Lilian, ed. *Sunflakes: Poems for Children*. Illus. Jan Ormerod. New York: Clarion, 1992.

Nye, Naomi Shihab, selector. *This Same Sky: A Collection of Poems from Around the World*. New York: Macmillan, 1992.

Opie, Iona, and Peter Opie, eds. *The Oxford Book of Children's Verse*. New York: Oxford, 1973.

Orozco, José-Luis, selector-arranger. *De Colores and Other Latin-American Folk Songs for Children*. New York: Dutton, 1994.

Prelutsky, Jack, selector. *Read-Aloud Rhymes for the Very Young*. Illus. Marc Brown. New York: Knopf, 1987.

——. *The 20th Century Children's Poetry Treasury*. Illus. Meilo So. New York: Knopf, 1999.

Rampersad, Arnold, Marcellus Blount, and Karen Barbour, eds. *Poetry for Young People: African American Poetry*. New York: Sterling, 2013.

Schwartz, Alvin, selector. *And the Green Grass Grew All Around: Folk Poetry from Everyone*. Illus. Sue Truesdell. New York: Harper, 1992.

Vardell, Sylvia, and Janet Wong, comps. *The Poetry Friday Anthology: Poems for the School Year with Connections to the Common Core*. Princeton, NJ: Pomelo, 2012.
  • Primarily for teachers, includes 36 poems for each grade from K to 5—one for every week of the school year. It needs to be supplemented by many other books.

Collections by Individual Poets

Many of these poets have published several books, so look for others as well. These books are suitable for elementary and middle school readers. Some collections, of course, are more sophisticated than others.

Adoff, Arnold. *Roots and Blues: A Celebration*. Illus. Gregory Christie. New York: Clarion Books, 2011.

Agard, John. *Half-caste and Other Poems*. North Pomfret, VT: Hodder/Trafalgar Square, 2005.

Agee, Jon. *Orangutan Tongs: Poems to Tangle Your Tongue*. New York: Hyperion, 2009.

Argueta, Jorge. *Talking with Mother Earth/Hablando con Madre Tierra*. Illus. Lucía Angela Pérez. Toronto: Groundwood/House of Anansi, 2006.

Blackaby, Susan. *Nest, Nook & Cranny*. Illus. Jamie Hogan. Watertown, MA: Charlesbridge, 2010.

Bloom, Valerie. *Hot Like Fire and Other Poems*. London: Bloomsbury, 2009.

Brooks, Gwendolyn. *Bronzeville Boys and Girls*. Illus. Faith Ringgold. New York: Amistad/HarperCollins, 2007.

Brown, Calef. *Hypnotize a Tiger: Poems About Just About Everything*. New York: Henry Holt, 2015.

Chandra, Deborah. *Balloons and Other Poems*. Illus. Leslie Bowman. New York: Farrar, Straus & Giroux, 1990.

Ciardi, John. *You Read to Me, I'll Read to You*. Illus. Edward Gorey. New York: HarperCollins, 1987.

Coatsworth, Elizabeth. *Under the Green Willow*. Illus. Janina Domanska. New York: Macmillan, 1971.

Cummings, E. E. *Hist Whist*. Illus. Deborah Kogan Ray. New York: Crown, 1989.

De La Mare, Walter. *Peacock Pie*. Illus. Barbara Cooney. New York: Knopf, 1961.

Dickinson, Emily. *My Letter to the World and Other Poems*. Toronto: Kids Can Press, 2008.

Dillard, Annie. *Mornings Like This: Found Poems*. New York: Harper, 1995.

Ehlert, Lois. *Oodles of Animals*. New York: Harcourt, 2008.

Eliot, T. S. *Old Possum's Book of Practical Cats*. Illus. Edward Gorey. New York: Harcourt, Brace, Jovanovich, 1982.

Elliot, David. *In the Wild*. Illus. Holly Meade. New York: Candlewick, 2010.

Fleischman, Paul. *Big Talk: Poems for Four Voices*. Illus. Beppe Giacobbe. New York: Candlewick, 2008.

——. *A Joyful Noise: Poems for Two Voices*. New York: Harper, 1987.
(A collection of poems meant for choral reading.)

Florian, Douglas. *Lizards, Frogs, and Polliwogs*. New York: Harcourt, 2001.

Franco, Betsy. *Curious Collection of Cats*. Illus. Michael Wertz. San Francisco: Tricycle Press, 2009.

Froman, Robert. *Seeing Things: A Book of Poems*. New York: Crowell, 1974.

Frost, Helen. *Diamond Willow*. New York: Farrar, Straus & Giroux, 2008.

Frost, Robert. *Birches*. Illus. Ed Young. New York: Holt, 1988.

Giovanni, Nikki. *Spin a Soft Black Song*. Illus. George Martins. New York: Hill & Wang, 1985.

Greenberg, David T. *Bugs*. Illus. Lyn Munsinger. Boston: Little, Brown, 1997.

Greenfield, Eloise. *The Friendly Four*. Illus. Jan Spivey Gilchrist. New York: HarperColllins, 2006.

Hoberman, Mary Ann, and Linda Winston. *The Tree That Time Built: A Celebration of Nature, Science, and Imagination*. Illus. Barbara Fortin. Naperville, IL: Sourcebooks, 2009.

Holbrook, Sara. *Wham! It's a Poetry Jam: Discovering Performance Poetry*. Honesdale, PA: Boyds Mills, 2002.

Hopkins, Lee Bennett. *City I Love*. Illus. Marcus Hall. New York: Abrams, 2009.

Hughes, Langston. *The Dream Keeper and Other Poems*. New York: Knopf, 1994.

Jackson, Rob. *Weekend Mischief*. Illus. Mark Beech. Honesdale, PA: Wordsong, 2010.

Janeczko, Paul B. *Brickyard Summer*. New York: Orchard, 1989.

——. *Requiem: Poems of the Terezín Ghetto*. Cambridge, MA: Candlewick, 2011.

Jarrell, Randall. *The Bat Poet*. Illus. Maurice Sendak. New York: Macmillan, 1964.

Kennedy, X. J. *City Kids: Street & Skyscraper Rhymes*. Illus. Philippe Béha. Vancouver: Tradewind, 2010.

Kuskin, Karla. *Moon, Have You Met My Mother?* Illus. Sergio Ruzzier. New York: HarperCollins, 2003.

Lawson, JonArno. *Black Stars in a White Night Sky*. Illus. Sherwin Tjia. Toronto: Pedlar Press, 2006.

——. *Down in the Bottom of the Bottom of the Box*. Illus. Alec Dempster. Erin, Ontario: Porcupine's Quill, 2012.

——. *Enjoy It While It Hurts*. Illus. JonArno Lawson. Hamilton, Ontario: Wolsak, 2013.

Lear, Edward. *The Complete Verse and Other Nonsense*. Ed. Vivian Noakes. New York: Penguin, 2006.

Lewis, J. Patrick. *The House*. Illus. Roberto Innocenti. Minneapolis, MN: Creative Editions, 2009.

Livingston, Myra Cohn. *Calendar*. Illus. Will Hillebrand. New York: Holiday House, 2007.

Lomax, Dana Teen, ed. *Kindergarde: Avant-Garde Poems, Plays, Stories, and Songs for Children*. Illus. Cliff Hengst. Lafayette, LA: Black Radish, 2013.

Mado, Michio. *The Magic Pocket*. Trans. Empress Michiko of Japan. Illus. Mitsumasa Anno. New York: McElderry, 1998.

Mahy, Margaret. *Nonstop Nonsense*. Illus. Quentin Blake. New York: McElderry, 1989.

Marsalis, Wynton. *Jazz AZ: An A to Z Collection of Jazz Portraits*. Illus. Paul Rogers. Cambridge, MA: Candlewick, 2005.

McCord, David. *One at a Time: His Collected Poems for the Young*. Illus. Henry Kane. Boston: Little, Brown, 1977.

Moore, Lilian. *Mural on Second Avenue and Other City Poems*. Illus. Roma Karas. New York: Candlewick, 2005.

Mordhorst, Heidi. *Pumpkin Butterfly: Poems from the Other Side of Nature*. Honesdale, PA: Wordsong/Boyds Mill Press, 2009.

Myers, Walter Dean. *Blues Journey*. Illus. Christopher Myers. New York: Holiday, 2003.

——. *Street Love*. New York: Amistad/HarperTempest, 2006.

Nash, Ogden. *The Best of Ogden Nash*. Chicago: Ivan R. Dee, 2007.

Nelson, Marilyn. *Fortune's Bones: The Manumission Requiem*. Asheville, NC: Front Street Books, 2004.

——. *How I Discovered Poetry*. Illus. Hadley Hooper. New York: Penguin, 2014.

——. *A Wreath for Emmett Till*. Illus. Philippe Lardy. Boston: Houghton Mifflin, 2005.

Nye, Naomi Shihab. *A Maze Me: Poems for Girls*. Illus. Terre Maher. New York: Greenwillow, 2005.

——. *19 Varieties of Gazelle: Poems of the Middle East*. New York: Greenwillow, 2002.

O'Neill, Mary. *Hailstones and Halibut Bones.* Illus. John Wallner. New York: Doubleday, 1989.

Park, Linda Sue. *Tap Dancing on the Roof: Sijo (Poems).* Pictures by Istvan Banyai. New York: Clarion, 2007.

Paschkis, Julie. *Flutter and Hum: Animal Poems/ Aleteo y Zumbido: Poemes de Animalis.* New York: Holt, 2015.

Prelutsky, Jack. *The Frog Wore Red Suspenders.* Illus. Petra Mathers. New York: Greenwillow, 2002.

Priest, Robert. *Rosa Rose and Other Poems.* Illus. Joan Krygsman. Hamilton, Ontario: Wolsak, 2013.

——. *Ride a Purple Pelican.* New York: Greenwillow, 1986.

——. *What a Day It Was at School!* Illus. Doug Cushman. New York: Greenwillow, 2006.

Richards, Laura. *Tirra Lirra: Rhymes Old and New.* 1932. Illus. Marguerite Davis. Boston: Little, Brown, 1955.

Roethke, Theodore. *Dirty Dinky and Other Creatures.* Selectors Beatrice Roethke and Stephen Lushington. New York: Doubleday, 1973.

Rosen, Michael J. *The Cuckoo's Haiku and Other Birding Poems.* Illus. Stan Fellows. Cambridge, MA: Candlewick, 2009.

Ruddell, Deborah. *A Whiff of Pine, a Hint of Skunk.* New York: Simon & Schuster, 2009.

Schertie, Alice. *Button Up! Wrinkled Rhymes.* Illus. Petra Mathers. New York: Houghton Mifflin Harcourt, 2009.

Sendak, Maurice. *My Brother's Book.* Illus. Maurice Sendak. New York: HarperCollins, 2013.

Shannon, George. *Busy in the Garden.* Illus. Sam Williams. New York: Greenwillow, 2006.

Sidman, Joyce. *Meow Ruff.* Illus. Michelle Berg. Boston: Houghton Mifflin, 2006.

Silverstein, Shel. *A Light in the Attic.* New York: Harper, 1981.

——. *Where the Sidewalk Ends.* New York: Harper, 1974.

Singer, Marilyn. *Mirror, Mirror: A Book of Reversible Verse.* Illus. José Masse. New York: Dutton, 2010.

Snicket, Lemony. *29 Myths on the Swinster Pharmacy.* Illus. Lisa Brown. McSweeney's McMullins, 2014.

Soto, Gary. *New and Selected Poems.* San Francisco: Chronicle Books, 1995.

Starbird, Kaye. *The Covered Bridge House.* Illus. Jim Arnosky. New York: Four Winds, 1979.

Stevenson, James. *Sweet Corn: Poems.* New York: Greenwillow, 1995.

Stevenson, Robert Louis. *A Child's Garden of Verses.* Illus. Jessie Willcox Smith. 1905. New York: Scribner's, 1969.

Swenson, May. *The Complete Poems to Solve.* New York: Macmillan, 1993.

Viorst, Judith. *If I Were in Charge of the World and Other Worries.* Illus. Lyn Cherry. New York: Atheneum, 1969.

Watson, Clyde. *Father Fox's Pennyrhymes.* Illus. Wendy Watson. New York: Crowell, 1971.

Whitman, Walt. *Voyages: Poems by Walt Whitman.* Selector, Lee Bennett Hopkins. Illus. Charles Mikolaycak. New York: Harcourt, 1988.

Wilbur, Richard. *Opposites.* New York: Harcourt, 1973.

Willard, Nancy. *Household Tales of Moon and Water.* New York: Harcourt, 1982.

——. *A Visit to William Blake's Inn.* Illus. Alice and Martin Provensen. New York: Harcourt, 1981.

Williams, Vera B. *Amber Was Brave, Essie Was Smart.* New York: Greenwillow, 2001.

Wong, Janet S. *A Suitcase of Seaweed and Other Poems.* New York: Simon & Schuster, 1996.

Woodson, Jacqueline. *Brown Girl Dreaming.* New York: Puffin, 2016.

Worth, Valerie. *All the Small Poems and Fourteen More.* Illus. Natalie Babbitt. New York: Farrar, Straus & Giroux, 1994.

Folk Narratives

The Oldest Stories

"Some day you will be old enough to start reading fairytales again."

–C. S. Lewis, "Preface," *The Lion, the Witch, and the Wardrobe* (1950)

Introduction

Folktales, legends, and myths are our oldest stories—and still some of the best. They contain gripping plots, unforgettable characters, exotic settings, magic, and wonder. They reflect the essence of all literature. In "Cinderella," we find the kernel of every romance. In "Hansel and Gretel," we find the essence of the coming-of-age story. In "Jack and the Beanstalk," we find the quintessential adventure story. In "Rumpelstiltskin," we find the core of mystery. And in "Little Red Riding Hood," we find the crucible of trickery and deceit. In the folktale, human emotions, desires, fears, and hopes are stripped to their bare bones. They bring us to the very heart of humanity. The "folk" in folk narratives refers to the common people of a society, as opposed to professional writers. Folk narratives, tradition tells us, are the stories the common people passed along by word of mouth, from adult to child, from generation to generation.

The folk narratives were the products of societies in which most people could not read—societies without books, televisions, computers, and film. These are societies whose wells of knowledge depended on the spoken word. Consequently, we can never know who created the first versions of "The Frog King," "Rapunzel," or "The Three Billy Goats Gruff," or when the first "Cinderella" story was told. And we can never speak of the "author" of a folktale—only the reteller. And, since these stories have been passed along by word-of-mouth for generations, they come to us in many versions. These versions are called "variants," and no one can claim to know the original story. Most folk narratives (folktales, legends, tall tales, riddles, and so on) remained in the oral culture until fairly recently. It was only in the nineteenth century that collectors like Jacob and Wilhelm Grimm, Joseph Jacobs, Andrew Lang, Peter Asbjørnsen, Jørgen Moe, and others began to record the oral tales. And when they began looking at the tales from Africa, India, China, and the Americas, the collectors discovered striking similarities. African, Asian, and American Indian cultures all had their own versions of "Cinderella" and "Little Red Riding Hood," for example. These old stories revealed, in their marvelous ways, how very similar humans are, regardless of their cultural heritage. Whether the tales all sprang from a single source (as some argue) or simply reflect the common thread of humanity's needs, hopes, fears, and desires (as many now believe), the truth may never be known. But their power and influence on world culture cannot be denied. So the following discussion of folk narrative elements can be applied to folktales from the world over.

Elements of the Folk Narrative

Setting and Plot

"Once upon a time, in a kingdom far, far away"—so goes the traditional opening of the folk narrative. We rarely get anything more specific than this. It is true that folktale settings often suggest the place of origin—so Scandinavian folktales are set in cold, icy, and mountainous lands; German folktales are set in forests; Navajo folktales are set in the Southwestern desert; and so on. But we rarely find specific countries, cities, towns, or other places named. The setting remains distant in both time and place, and this allows it to be an enchanted place. We know from the beginning of the tale that this is a time and place where animals may talk, strange creatures may be found, and magic may occur. Folktale plots are generally of two types—dramatic or cumulative (see Chapter 4). A dramatic plot, composed of interdependent events reaching a climax and followed by a swift conclusion, is the familiar pattern of some of the most popular stories, such as "Cinderella," "Sleeping Beauty," and "Beauty and the Beast." The cumulative plot is one in which the same plot element is repeated with slight variations, leading up to the climax. This plot device is usually found in tales for very young children, who find pleasure in the repetition. Remember the story of the Gingerbread Man, a runaway cookie who, in his attempt to escape being eaten, is chased by an ever-growing parade of characters.

Character

Much like the plots, folktale characters are simple and uncomplicated. Indeed, the characters often don't even have names, just stereotypical labels (the miller, the king, the wicked witch), or their names merely describe their character traits or appearance—"Beauty," "Prince Charming," "Snow White," "Bluebeard" (see Figure 7.1 and Figure 7.2). The characters are all one-dimensional. No one ever displays any depth. No one ever faces difficult psychological choices or torments. No one ever ponders a problem very long. No one ever undergoes any deep soul searching. A character's appearance betrays his or her personality. The lovely princess will always be beautiful, good, and faithful. Prince Charming will always be handsome, brave, and generous. The witch or ogre will always be ugly, selfish, and cruel. Of course, there are occasional exceptions, such as Snow White's beautiful but vain and wicked stepmother—and whose appearance is a plot device. And, you may argue, what about the Beast in "Beauty and the Beast"? When we first see him, he is ugly and terrifying, but in the end, he is transformed into a handsome prince. However, he was always a handsome prince deep inside, his ugly appearance resulting from an evil spell that only a beautiful woman can break. A good and noble character's inner beauty cannot long be hidden, nor can a villain's ugliness. (When Snow White's stepmother attempts her murder plot, she appears as an old hag—you'd think Snow White would catch on.)

Because of the one-dimensional characters, if we have met Cinderella, then we recognize Sleeping Beauty, Snow White, Rapunzel, and dozens of other fair maidens from the folktales. Fundamentally, they are all alike, and Rumpelstiltskin is just a shorter, male version of the wicked witch who imprisoned Rapunzel, or the one who nearly ate Hansel and Gretel. Instead of being individuals, the folktale characters are types—some symbolizing goodness, humility, and generosity, others symbolizing greed, arrogance, and selfishness. We need no physical description. And perhaps it is better that way. Some critics even object to illustrating these tales, because it deprives children of imagining their own versions of the characters.

Here are some of the common character types found in folktales:

- *The beautiful maiden*—Usually helpless and at the mercy of some wicked guardian, she awaits the arrival of Prince Charming.

- *Prince Charming*—The hero is handsome, bold and deferential to beautiful maidens.

- *The wicked witch or ogre*—This villain is deformed and horrid-looking, delighting in evil for evil's sake. We never learn, for example, that the witch might have been abused as a child or was the victim of a tragic love affair. (No character ever has a backstory.) (See Figure 7.5, *Baba Yaga*.)

- *The faithful servant (or faithful companion)*—This character, whether servant or companion, serves as confidant to the hero or heroine.

- *The wise elder*—This character is generally a mysterious figure who sometimes speaks in riddles that the hero or heroine must unravel.

- *The helpful guide*—This is usually someone encountered along the way (journeys are abundant in folktales), often a talking animal who is returning

FIGURE 7.1 ■ Walter Crane's illustration for "Snow White," in his 1886 publication of *Household Stories by the Brothers Grimm*, depicts Snow White being tempted by her innocently disguised stepmother. Compare this temptress with Rackham's alarming witch from "Hansel and Gretel" (Figure 7.3).

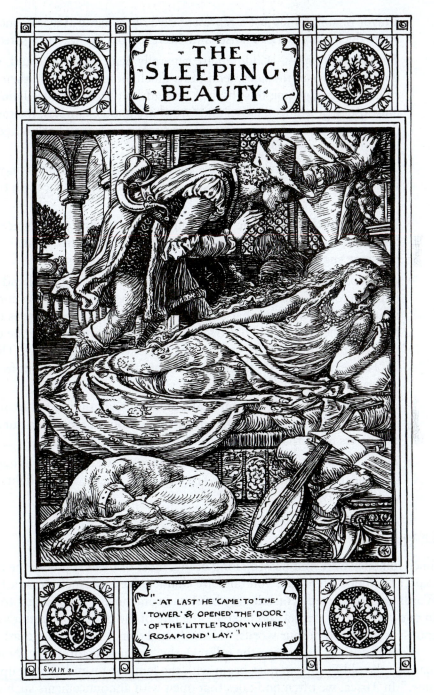

FIGURE 7.2 ■ Walter Crane's illustration for "The Sleeping Beauty" captures the moment just before the kiss that will awaken the fair princess. As in his illustration for "Snow White" (Figure 7.1), Crane depicts a scene of anticipation, capturing the moment just as a key event is about to occur.

a favor or sometimes just a representative of the natural world, such as the white duck who carries Hansel and Gretel across the water to safety.

- *The innocent babes*—Children are generally depicted as pure and, when they are heroes in the tales, tend to be much more clever than their adult counterparts. Lacking the physical strength to overcome the villains, children must use their brains. Hansel and Gretel are good examples, for they outwit the wicked witch, find her treasure, and make their way back home (with the help of the white duck).

- *The simpleton*—A usually lovable character whose foolishness may sometimes result in amazing good fortune. Who doesn't cheer on the underdog?

- *The ineffectual father*—The weak-willed father figure's prominence in folktales may suggest the prevalence of the mother in the raising of children—or it may suggest that women frequently told the stories.

- *The wicked stepmother*—This villain is an embodiment of evil and a figure found in folktales around the world. Some believe it reflects the complex relationship between mother and child: We love the care she gives us, but don't like the control she has over us; in folktales, we can love the deceased mother and hate the cruel stepmother, thus having it both ways. The witch (as in "Hansel and Gretel") is another version of this character, but freed of any maternal obligation.

- *The jealous sibling*—It does not take much imagination to figure out where this stereotype came from. The suspicion that our parents love our brothers and sisters more than they do us is a universal phenomenon.

- *The trickster*—Whether an animal or a human, we can't help liking this irascible, devilish, and endlessly fascinating character, who delights in wreaking havoc.

Language and Style

Since folktales were first passed along orally, most of them still bear the traits we expect from oral literature. Folktales are characterized by an economy of language. Words are not wasted. The tales are brief and sometimes astonishingly to the point. In one version of "Hansel and Gretel," the fate of the poor woodcutter's selfish spouse is described in four words: "His wife had died." And that is that!

Like everything else about the folktale, the language is formulaic. Notice how many of the old European tales begin with the familiar formula "once upon a time." In Africa, we often find tales that open with announcements such as "A story. A story. How does it go?" And we hardly have to mention the familiar ending "and they lived happily ever after." Then there are the magic words, such as "mirror, mirror, on the wall" or "open sesame." And we can't forget the repetitive language, such as that found in "The Three Pigs" ("little pig, little pig, let me come in") or in "The Gingerbread Man," whose annoying title character taunts everyone with "run, run, as fast as you can; you can't catch me, I'm the Gingerbread Man."

These patterns are integral to the folktale, reminding us that this is a story of the imagination, transporting us to another time and place. To eliminate the repetition or to change the pattern would destroy the magic.

Images and Symbols

Images are the pictures a storyteller (or poet) creates for us. They are the sights, sounds, tastes, textures, and smells that make a story memorable (see also the discussion "Pictures in Poetry" in Chapter 6). Because folktales are so sparsely told and were originally oral tales, the images tend to be striking and bold—easy to visualize in the mind's eye, and easy to remember. When we recall the popular tales from childhood, we find that we often associate many of them with specific, concrete objects: glass slippers, magic mirrors, poisoned apples, magic lamps, red riding hoods, and so on.

Sometimes an image becomes a symbol; that is, it stands for something greater than itself. Forests, for example, frequently represent the wild unknown—the opposite of civilization (just ask Little Red Riding Hood). Food often represents temptation or the object of desire. Think of Snow White and the apple (see Figure 7.1) or Hansel and Gretel and the gingerbread house (see Figure 7.3). Rapunzel's long hair might be interpreted as a symbol of her womanhood, allowing her to escape her captor and find her future husband (see Figure 7.4). Also, the colors we associate with folktales are the strong colors—black, red, white—and the metallic—gold, silver, bronze. There are no subtle shades of gray, no pastels—these are stories of forthright confidence and crystal clarity, without nuances, without subtleties. Of course, there is always the danger of over-reading when we begin to look for symbols. Often, the child's reading is best: Sometimes a frog is just a frog.

Motifs

A motif is a recurring thematic element, a repeated pattern—such as color or shape in painting, or a melodic phrase in music, a figure in a decorative design (a flower, animal, or geometric image). In literature, a motif is an identifiable narrative element that recurs in a tale. Folktales, in part because of their oral origins, are rich in motifs. Motifs make it easy for storytellers to enhance and alter plots, adding features from other stories they know—sometimes for convenience, sometimes to stretch out the telling, sometimes to add a new message.

FIGURE 7.3 ■ Arthur Rackham's 1909 illustration for "Hansel and Gretel" portrays the Witch greeting the lost children. Contrast Rackham's grisly witch with Crane's more deceptive temptress in Figure 7.1. Many children might delight in Rackham's more deliciously chilling interpretation of evil.

Source: Grimm, Jacob and Wilhelm. *The Fairy Tales of the Brothers Grimm.* Mrs. Edgar Lucas, translator. Arthur Rackham, illustrator. London: Constable & Company Ltd, 1909.

Some of the most commonly found folktale motifs include the following, many of which you will recognize immediately:

- Transforming humans being into beasts
- Imposing and breaking taboos (see the discussion below)
- Using magical objects (sometimes working for the hero, sometimes against)
- Casting magical spells (again, working either for or against the hero)
- Going on a journey or quest
- Meeting a magical helper
- Enduring tests or trials
- Making, breaking, or keeping bargains
- Using deception (sometimes for the good, sometimes not)

These are only a few motifs, and in their most generalized forms. Each motif may appear in hundreds of variations. As we read more and more tales, we begin to recognize these motifs and see the common traits in tales from culture to culture. In "Rumpelstiltskin," for example, we see the motifs of bargains made and broken, the intervention of an enchanted being, the use of magic, and the imposing of tests. In "Little Red Riding Hood," we find the journey, the breaking of a taboo, and the use of deception.

Taboos

A taboo, which is a type of motif, is a very common element found in folktales. It is simply a prohibition against doing,

FIGURE 7.4 ■ H. J. Ford's illustration for "Rapunzel" depicts one of the most unlikely events of the story: the prince climbing up Rapunzel's hair for their rendezvous. Of course, in the context of the folktale, we do not ask for logic, and Ford makes the scene as romantic as possible, so we never think to rationalize the event.

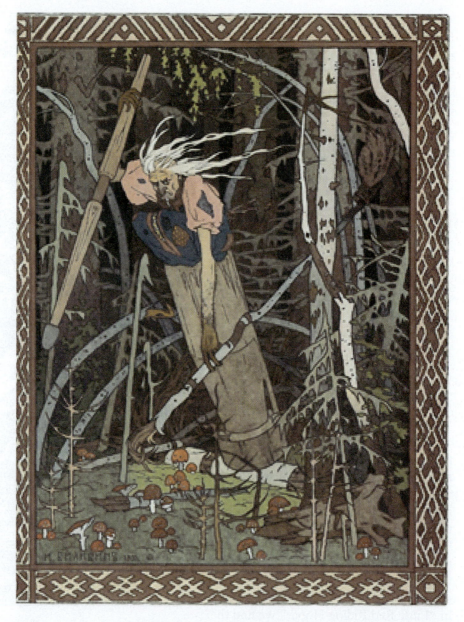

FIGURE 7.5 ■ This nineteenth-century illustration by Ivan Bilibin depicts a Russian witch called Baba Yaga, a frightful creature who flies about the forest in a mortar and carrying a pestle. But her forbidding appearance is sometimes deceptive, for she can be both villain and helper.

touching, or even saying something because it might result in some supernatural retaliation. Taboos are commonly found in pre-industrial societies, where they serve as means of placating the gods or preserving the social order. (A taboo may consist of a dietary restriction—not eating certain foods, for example; or a sexual restriction—against incest or marrying within one's clan, for example; or it could consist of forbidden words—secret names that must not be spoken aloud; and so on.) Taboos serve many purposes, but one of the most important is establishing limits and setting boundaries. Rules and taboos help make up the moral world of the folktale, just as they do in our own lives. Without rules, all would be chaos. Even little children, when they make up games at play, are insistent on having rules. And once children begin to disregard the rules, the game falls apart, and someone calls "foul." (We will explore this further when we discuss fantasy in Chapter 8.)

Just as in life, when characters in a story break the rules, they must pay. Red Riding Hood is warned not to speak to strangers in the woods, Sleeping Beauty is cautioned to stay away from spinning wheels, and Cinderella is told she must leave the ball by midnight. And what happens when taboos are inevitably broken? Characters get eaten or fall into a perpetual sleep, or magic spells are broken. As in life, most of the important lessons have to be learned the hard way. Sometimes the punishment is mitigated—perhaps a hunter will come by and rescue Red Riding Hood; a prince will come by to awaken the Sleeping Beauty (see Figure 7.2); Cinderella will be given another chance to win her prince. And that, too, is what life sometimes brings us.

Types of Folk Narratives

Folk narratives come in many forms, and few generalities will encompass all of them. Some of the most common folk narrative types are described here, but categories often overlap, and these are only suggested as general guidelines.

Talking Animal Tales

This is, admittedly, an amorphous and overlapping category, since talking animals occur in many, many tales. They appear in myths, fables, trickster tales and *pourquoi* tales. But then there are those tales that do not fit into these other patterns: they are simply good stories with talking animals for characters—"The Three Pigs," "The Three Billy Goats Gruff," "Henny Penny," "The Musicians of Bremen-Town." So, for lack of a better term, we shall call them talking animal tales. Theirs is a world where animals talk and interact with each other, sometimes living as animals, at other times living more like humans. (The three pigs, for example, do not act much like pigs, although the wolf behaves pretty much like a wolf—except for the talking.) By and large, the talking animals think and feel like humans—they have humans hopes, dreams, fears, and joys. They succumb to human weaknesses (the laziness of two of the Little Pigs or the foolishness of Henny Penny). But they can also exhibit great cleverness (see the Musicians of Bremen). The audiences for these tales are usually young children, who readily accept the anthropomorphism, and, in fact, spend much of their free time in an imaginative world where dolls, puppets, and stuffed animals take on human traits. These tales become the gateways to the great animal fantasies such as Kenneth Grahame's *The Wind in the Willows*, E. B. White's *Charlotte's Web*, and Richard Adams's *Watership Down*.

Fables

Although the term "fable" is often used to refer to any fictive tale, technically, a fable is a very brief story, usually with talking animals, and with a moral at the end—and the moral is the important distinction. The animals are typically portrayed as examples of specific human traits—greed, foolishness, pride, and so on. The best-known fables are those attributed to Aesop, a teacher who is alleged to have lived in Greece in the seventh and sixth centuries BCE. He supposedly used fables as teaching devices for his students, instructing them about human behavior and social values. Whether or not Aesop ever existed, his name will be forever associated with the fable. Here is one famous example known as the Fable of the Fox and the Grapes (see Figure 7.8):

> *A very hungry fox came upon a vineyard where hung many bunches of the most delicious, the most luscious grapes you could ever wish to see. However, the grapes were staked to a high trellis, and the fox could not reach them, no matter how hard he tried. After many vain leaps, the exhausted fox gave up, exclaiming, "Oh, those grapes look green and sour. I didn't want them anyway." And off he went.*
>
> *The moral of the story is: It is easy to find an excuse for not wanting what we cannot have.*

This, of course, is the origin of the old expression "sour grapes." We can easily recognize a fable by its brevity, its sharply defined and one-dimensional characters (usually animals), and its pointed moral lesson, which is usually announced at the end, just in case we missed it.

Wonder Tales

Also referred to by the German term *Märchen* (roughly pronounced "mér-ken"), wonder tales are some of the most famous folktales. They are popularly called "fairy tales," even though few contain "fairies," but all do include some form of magic. A wonder tale is a serious tale (if it's silly, then we called a "Merry Tale," see below) about characters who must overcome evil, usually with the aid of some magical power (which is where the "wonder" comes in). These tales are often, but not necessarily, about aristocratic or royal people—they were the movie stars and sports heroes of their day. The heroes and heroines in wonder tales are typically young, beautiful, and good. (Sometimes they are clever, but that is not a requirement, particularly if they have magical helpers on their side.) The villains are equally easy to pick out—although they can be deceitful (see the discussion on characters above). The stories are all formulaic, and they often contain the highly ritualized language and patterns as we discussed above. It is from these tales that we get the familiar expressions "once upon a time" and "they lived happily ever after." These tales are the original love stories, which makes us ask why they are so often considered reading fare for five-year-olds! In fact, we have every reason to believe that many of these stories were for much older audiences (probably adolescents), but their appeal is obviously widespread.

Although many tales were written down in the Middle Ages and Renaissance (in works such as Boccaccio's *Decameron*), the first widely known collection of wonder tales appeared in 1697 in France, when Charles Perrault published *Histoires ou Contes du Temps Passé (Stories or Tales from the Past)*, and subtitled it *Les Contes de ma Mère l'Oye (Tales of Mother Goose)*. This collection contains, among others, "Cinderella," "Sleeping Beauty," "Bluebeard," and "Little Red Riding Hood." (It does not, incidentally, contain any "Mother Goose" rhymes, and no one knows if this was the origin of that apocryphal figure.) Significantly, Perrault did not write for children, but for the aristocratic women of the court of Louis XIV. A hundred years later, when the Grimm brothers were assembling their great collection of tales (originally called *Children's and Household Tales* and first appearing in 1812), their sources (or informants, as they are called) included old women and teenage girls. Unlike Perrault, the Grimms did intend their collection for children. However, this does not mean that the tales are all for the faint of heart. Take a look at Arthur Rackham's illustration for the Grimm's version of "Hansel and Gretel" (see Figure 7.3).

Wonder tales, especially those from Perrault and Grimm (see "Rapunzel," Figure 7.4 and Figure 7.6, and "Twelve Dancing Princesses," Figure 7.7) are remarkable for their emphasis on worldliness. Living happily ever after usually means having it all. The heroes and heroines acquire both wealth and power; gold, silver, and precious jewels are frequently the rewards or objects of desire. In those tales that conclude with the hero and heroine marrying at the end and living happily ever after, we usually find that the happy couple are now a king and queen and live in a castle with servants at their beck and call. Poverty is seen as abhorrent, and wealth is an honorable goal. Of course, we should remember that many of these tales are products of an earlier time, when most people lived in dire poverty and on the brink of starvation. The tales are likely wish-fulfilling fantasies, which is why they remain so popular today.

FIGURE 7.6 ■ Paul O. Zelinsky's serene illustration for *Rapunzel* is a marked contrast from Ford's (Figure 7.4). Zelinsky evokes the elegance of fifteenth-century Renaissance Italy. Rapunzel, the Prince and their family evoke portrayals of the Holy Family, and Rapunzel herself reminds us of a Madonna looking adoringly at her twins, as she might have been painted by the great Italian painter, Raphael (1483–1520).

FIGURE 7.7 ■ Kay Nielsen, a Danish artist of the early twentieth century, was strongly influenced by the Art Nouveau movement, which was characterized by stylized figures, graceful curving lines, and decorative organic motifs (usually floral). This illustration from "The Twelve Dancing Princesses" does not attempt a realist portrayal. Instead, the figures and the setting are very theatrical, proportions are exaggerated, and we are drawn to the exquisite detail. These elegant and ethereal creatures indeed belong, appropriately, to an enchanted world.

Source: "The Twelve Dancing Princesses" in *Powder and Crinoline*, illustrated by Kay Nielsen, London, Hodder & Stoughton, 1913.

FIGURE 7.8 ■ Walter Crane was one of the earliest great children's illustrators, and among the first to make use of color. This is from his 1887 edition of *Aesop's Fables*. Aesop's pithy tales—originating in classical Greece—have been perennially popular among both children and adults. Crane's elegant illustration depicts the fable that gives us our expression "sour grapes."

Merry Tales

Also called droll, noodlehead, or simpleton tales, the merry tales are blatantly silly stories, usually with animal or peasant characters who are portrayed as foolish or gullible, presumably because of their lack of education or proper upbringing. A merry tale may include magical elements—talking animals, magic spells, enchanted creatures—but its chief trait is the foolishness of the main characters. In myths, heroic legends, and wonder tales, the characters—who are often royal or aristocratic or even divine—take themselves quite seriously; there is nothing funny about "Cinderella" or "Beauty and the Beast" (except in Disney versions, perhaps). But the characters in merry tales are always ridiculous and we are supposed to laugh either at or with them.

A merry tale allows us to let down our hair. Life requires comic relief, and merry tales provide that. They contain no lessons to be learned (except perhaps that the world has no shortage of fools). They turn the world upside down. After all, laughter is the result of an incongruous juxtaposition—the unexpected response, the out-of-place action (see the discussion of humor in Chapter 4).

Unlike in the wonder tale, where the hero usually ends up with a grand reward (the girl, the jewels, and the kingdom), the heroes of the merry tale do not always get what they want. But they seldom care. They accept life at face value, and seem quite capable of making the best of a difficult situation—even when they themselves have caused the predicament. Take this well-known example:

> A very poor couple were cutting wood for their fire one day when they heard a tiny voice cry, "Help me! Help me!" Lo and behold, it was a little imp caught beneath a great log. The couple lifted the log and released the poor imp.
>
> It turns out the imp had magical powers, and he said to them, "In gratitude for your kind assistance, I will grant you three wishes—but three only."
>
> The couple returned to their poor cottage and pondered their good fortune. The husband said, "We could wish for a great fortune or servants or a team of horses." The wife said, "Or we could wish for a fine house or new clothes or jewels."
>
> At last the husband said, "Right now I am exhausted and hungry. I just wish I had a pan full of sausages."
>
> Instantly, on the fire appeared a frying pan full of juicy sausages.
>
> The wife was furious. "You idiot! You have wasted one of our wishes on a pan of sausages! How I wish those sausages were on the end of your nose."
>
> Instantly, on the end of the husband's nose, appeared the string of sausages, straight from the frying pan.
>
> And try as they could, the couple were unable to pull the sausages from the man's nose.
>
> They now had one wish left. They could wish for money, servants, houses, jewels, but could they enjoy them if the man had to live the rest of his life with a string of sausages attached to the end of his nose? They had but one choice.
>
> They held each other's hand, closed their eyes, and together wished the sausages back in the frying pan. And so it happened.
>
> "At least," said the husband, "we got a fine supper of sausages out of it."

This tale, usually called "The Three Wishes," is a characteristic merry tale, and although we may lament the foolishness of the poor couple, something tells us they are much happier than if they had wished for riches, houses, and clothes. The magic, unlike that in the wonder tale, does the characters more harm than good, and they decide they are better off without it. And despite its obvious light-heartedness, the tale can cause us to think about what we might wish for had we the chance. Wishes reveal a great deal about human values and character.

Cumulative Tales

Cumulative tales are very brief tales that use the cumulative plot device, in which a repetitive pattern—either repeated dialogue, repeated action, or both—gradually builds up to a climax. A famous example is the story of "Henny Penny," which uses both repeated dialogue and action. Henny Penny is a foolish hen, who, when an acorn hits her on the head, thinks the sky is falling, so she runs off to tell the king. On her way, she tells her story to an equally foolish cock (Cocky Locky), a duck (Ducky Lucky), a goose (Goosey Loosey), and a turkey (Turkey Lurkey), each, in turn, joining her on her way to tell the king. At last they meet a clever fox (Foxy Loxy), who persuades them that a quicker way to the king is through his fox's den—and that is the last we ever see of the hen, the cock, the duck, the goose, and the turkey (although we are told that the fox and his family enjoyed a splendid repast that day).

We see another variation in the Russian tale often referred to as "The Turnip," about an old man who grew a turnip that was so large, he could not pull it out of the ground. His wife grabs onto him to help, then their granddaughter, their dog, their cat, all pulling together in a chain. But it not until a little mouse joins them that the turnip pops out of the ground. (The theme of this tale is expressed in that old saying about "the straw that broke the camel's back.") Similar is the tale known as "The Mitten," in which a succession of forest animals attempt to crawl into a mitten to keep warm. These might include a mouse, squirrel, fox, bear and so on, until finally a tiny ant tries to fit into the mitten, which finally explodes under the pressure. The specific animals may vary from version to version, and the sequence may be either largest to smallest or smallest to largest—but it always ends with a very tiny creature causing the final debacle.

Reading these stories aloud can be great fun. As adults, we may be tempted to rush through the repetitive phrases, but it is best to sit back and enjoy the playful language along with the children—who almost always want to join in.

Local Legends and Tall Tales

A local legend describes the feats of a local hero and sometimes has its roots in historical fact. A good example of a legend is the popular tale of William Tell that emerged from the Swiss movement for independence from Austria during the 1300s. It goes something like this:

William Tell was a man of great physical strength and the most skilled marksman in Altdorf, Switzerland. One day, the wicked Austrian governor, named Gessler, caused a hat to be propped up on a stick in the town square and ordered the people to bow to it, signifying their submission to Austrian rule. The proud William Tell refused and was arrested. Gessler ordered Tell to shoot an apple off his son's head with a crossbow from a hundred paces—or else both would be executed. The brave Tell took the bow in his hand and aimed it at the apple balanced on his young son's head. He let the arrow fly, and it split the apple in two, sparing his son and freeing Tell, who eventually killed Gessler.

Although there is no concrete evidence that Tell ever existed, the story has been told for generations, and has been the subject of a play and an opera—and his statue stands in Altdorf today. The specific local references and the mentioning of individuals' names make this a legend. Notice that, in this case, no magic is involved—only incredible skill. Legends have to have a touch of veracity.

In contrast, a tall tale might be described as a local legend on steroids. The tall tale is an outlandish tale much like the proverbial "fish story," a tale no one is going to believe, but it's still both fun to tell and hear. The tall tale is an indelible part of American culture. Americans have a long-lasting love affair with the "most extreme"—the biggest, the tallest, the richest, the fastest. One of the earliest heroes of the tall tale is Paul Bunyan, a legendary lumberjack who, with his blue ox Babe, performed astonishing feats such as leveling mountains, rerouting rivers, and digging canyons. And then there is African-American hero John Henry, a steel driver who hammered holes in rock for setting explosives to blast out tunnels. According to the legend, John Henry won a race with a steam-powered drill, only to die "with his hammer in his hand" from a burst heart. Pecos Bill, whose stories date from the early twentieth century, is a legendary cowboy of the Southwest who rides a cougar instead of a horse, uses a rattlesnake for a lasso, and eats dynamite. Sid Fleischman, a Newbery Award-winning children's author, drew on the tradition of American tall tales to write his McBroom series (*McBroom Tells the Truth*, *McBroom and the Big Wind*, and many others). The tall tales are simply pure fun.

Ghost Stories and Jump Tales

Young people revel in telling ghost stories at pajama parties and around campfires. We enjoy ghost stories because we enjoy the adrenaline rush when we are frightened—in a controlled environment. They appeal to our latent superstitious natures, our longing to believe in a world beyond the visible landscape. And they may offer us a sense of emotional achievement—a note of triumph at having heard a blood-curdling, horrifying story and coming away unruffled and unscathed. Ghost stories are especially popular among adolescents, which suggests that these stories are, indeed, part of a rite of passage. The interactive ghost story, which is common around campfires and at pajama parties, involves the audience. These are often called "jump" tales—and you will see why from this example:

There was an old woman who lived all by herself, and she was very lonely. Sitting in the kitchen one night, she said, "Oh, I wish I had some company."

No sooner had she spoken than down the chimney tumbled two feet from which the flesh had rotted. The old woman's eyes bulged with terror.

Then two legs dropped to the hearth and attached themselves to the feet.

Then a body tumbled down, then two arms and a man's head.

As the old woman watched, the parts came together into a great, gangling man. The man danced around and around the room. Faster and faster he went. Then he stopped, and he looked into her eyes.

"What do you come for?" she asked in a small voice that shivered and shook.

"What do I come for?" he said. "I come—for YOU!"

(The storyteller shouts the last words, stamps his or her feet, and jumps at someone nearby).

—(Schwartz, *Scary Stories*, 12)

Myths and Traditional Epics

Origin and Adventure Tales

In modern culture, we casually toss about the term "myth" to describe any false story or belief. But "myth" is more accurately defined as a sacred story, particularly a sacred story about the creation of the world, a culture's gods and goddesses, and the origin of certain cultural practices or traditions. Myths, in fact, form the basis of most religions. To people of Western cultures, the most familiar mythology outside the Judeo-Christian tradition (as recounted in the Old Testament) is that of ancient Greece and Rome. The popular figures of ancient Greek and Roman legend include Athena, Hercules, Achilles, Aphrodite, Odysseus, Theseus, Jason and Medea, and Perseus, among many others.

Every child should know the stories of the labors of Hercules, the Trojan Horse, the adventures of Odysseus, and of Theseus and the Minotaur or Perseus and Medusa—to name but a few. They were indeed the first superheroes, the prototypes of Superman, Batman, and Wonder Woman. Children's versions—such as Padraic Colum's *The Children's Homer* and *The Golden Fleece and the Heroes Who Lived before Achilles*—are not only thrilling tales, they are iconic. Classical mythology is imbedded in all Western culture. Even our daily lives are imbued with references to Greek and Roman gods, goddesses and heroes. We have given their names to the planets (Venus, Jupiter, Saturn) and galaxies (Andromeda, Orion), and, on a more mundane level, months of the year (January, March, May, June), body parts (Achilles tendon), cleaning agents (Ajax), synthetic fibers (Herculon), automobiles (Mercury), map books (Atlas), athletic games (Olympics), and spacecraft (Apollo,

Gemini), all of which derive from Greek or Roman mythology. These tales are not to be missed.

After the fall of ancient Greece and Rome, Europe entered the Middle Ages, which continued this heroic tradition with tales of knights in shining armor performing heroic feats. Some knights sought the Holy Grail (the cup alleged to be used by Christ at the Last Supper), and this was the subject of many medieval adventure stories that were enjoyed by children. Rosemary Sutcliff's *The Light Beyond the Forest* is a modern-day retelling of the medieval quest for the Holy Grail. Another popular hero from the Middle Ages was Beowulf, a slayer of monsters, and Michael Morpurgo's *Beowulf* is a gripping retelling of that story for children.

The Beowulf story actually derives from another important influence on the Western tradition—that of Norse mythology, which reflects the harsh way of life engendered by the severe, yet dramatically beautiful, Scandinavian lands. In Norse mythology, the gods and goddesses were defenders of humanity against the mighty forces of evil. Like the Greek and Roman gods and goddesses, the Norse deities were anthropomorphic—that is, they had human forms. But compared with the Greek deities, the Norse gods and goddesses were a much more serious lot who were engaged in a perpetual struggle with the forces of evil—a struggle that they were destined to lose. Individual codes of honor were highly esteemed in this war-conscious society. We remember the Norse gods in our days of the week: Tuesday is named for Tiw (the Norse god of war), Wednesday for Woden (the father of the gods), Thursday for Thor (the thunder god), and Friday for Fria (the goddess of fruits). This fascinating mythology still lingers with us (and hints of its influence can be seen in the popular television fantasy *Game of Thrones*).

The Greeks, Romans, and Norse, like the Hebrews, all envisioned their deities in human form—that is, the gods generally resembled people. Other cultures, however, have viewed their deities differently. For instance, the ancient Egyptian gods and goddesses were often depicted as part human and part animal. The Hindu deities took on many unusual forms, some possessing multiple heads and limbs, some blue in color, and so on. The Incas of South America had several gods, including one called Urcuchillay, who was a llama, an animal indispensable to Incan culture. And the ancient Hawaiians tell of the god Ka-moho-ali'i, who was a shark (actually, he could take the form of any fish), appropriate for an island culture in the middle of the Pacific Ocean. A culture's gods reveal much about its physical environment, lifestyle, and view of the universe, and of humanity's role in that universe.

Throughout the world, we find cultures with compelling myths to tell—from the wondrous stories of the American Indians, celebrating their belief in humanity's oneness with the natural world, to the deep well of tales from Africa and Asia, with their special brand of enchantment. Today, these myths are becoming widely available in children's versions, and are excellent methods of introducing world cultures. Many of the collections of folktales listed in the bibliography at the end of this chapter are retellings of mythological tales from around the world.

The lasting influence of the great epics is evident in our modern-day fantasy fiction, which is the subject of Chapter 8. Anyone who has seen such popular films as George Lucas's *Star Wars* series, Peter Jackson's *The Lord of the Rings* series, or James Cameron's *Avatar* is well aware of this influence.

Trickster Tales

Although tricksters have found their way into popular culture (Br'er Rabbit, Bugs Bunny, Woody Woodpecker, Felix the Cat, and the Joker in *Batman*), the traditional trickster is a mythological figure—sometimes a demi-god (half-god, half-human), whose role is to challenge society's norms and rules—to keep us on our toes, as it were. The trickster is often a shape-shifter, a creature who can morph into any form, which is part of the trickster's deceptive qualities. Among the American Indians we find Coyote, Raven, and the little humpback figure of Kokopelli; in Europe, the fox was often a trickster. The trickster often sets out to break the rules—and when he does, sometimes good things happen, and sometimes bad things happen. The natives of the Pacific Northwest tell about the time when the world was in darkness. All the light was concealed in a box and jealously guarded by Old Man (a sort of ancestral god). Raven came along and outwitted Old Man to get the light for himself. However, once light escaped from the box, there was no controlling it, and that is how we have light today (see Gerald McDermott's *Raven*).

A favorite African trickster is Anansi the Spider (see Figure 7.9). In one tale, Anansi asks the Sky God for all the world's stories. The Sky God agrees, but only if Anansi can complete three tasks: Bring the Sky God a python, hornets, and a leopard. Through his cunning, he outwits the animals, and that is why Anansi today is the keeper of the world's stories. There is something appropriate about the trickster being the source of story—for at the root of story is the storyteller's ability to make us believe falsehoods (isn't every made-up story really a lie of sorts?). Everyone enjoys the trickster for his incorrigibility, his talent for survival, his unpredictability, his brazenness. Often, the trickster does what we wish we could do if we had the courage. The trickster is a necessary part of society, the one who always keeps the rest of us on our toes. It is easy to see why children love these figures.

Pourquoi Tales

The *pourquoi* tale is one that explains the origin of something (*pourquoi* is French for "why"). Unlike the trickster tale, which focuses on a specific character type, the *pourquoi* tale is defined by its purpose—to explain how something in our world came about. In fact, sometimes a trickster tale is also a *pourquoi* tale. The story

FIGURE 7.9 ■ This illustration from Gerald McDermott's *Anansi the Spider* depicts the trickster spider being devoured by a fish. However, the incorrigible Anansi is ultimately saved by the combined efforts of his six sons, each of whom is imbued with a unique magical talent. The bold colors and geometric shapes chosen by McDermott capture the spirit of African folk art, and note Anansi's face, which recalls an African tribal mask.

of Raven bringing light to the world, described above, is a very good example. A touching, and very popular, example comes from the Ojibwe people of western Michigan and explains the origin of the Sleeping Bear Dune, a large sand dune on the northwestern shore of Michigan's Lower Peninsula. The story goes like this:

> *A mother bear and her two cubs were swimming east across Lake Michigan when, in the midst of a great storm, the cubs tired and could go no longer. Their mother, who had reached the shore, watched helplessly as her cubs drowned in the lake. Unable to take her eyes from the water where her cubs perished, she died of grief. The mother bear's body was transformed by the Great Spirit Manitou into the mighty sand dune, and her cubs became the two islands known today as North and South Manitou Islands.*

Traditional cultures worldwide enjoy many *pourquoi* tales explaining the origins of animals, land features, and customs. For example, the Old Testament tells us that God placed a rainbow in the sky following the great flood as sign of his promise never to destroy to the Earth by water—hence, we see rainbows in the sky. The *pourquoi* tale is among the most popular of stories for young children. It may be in part because they are so outrageous—in fact, they often take on the characteristics of the tall tale (which, as we have seen, can also explain origins). Verna Aardema's *Why Mosquitos Buzz in People's Ears*, which won the 1976 Caldecott Medal for its illustrators, Leo and Diane Dillon, remains beloved to this day. A popular British/Kenyan television series aimed at preschoolers, *Tinga Tinga Tales*, is devoted entirely to the telling of folktales (many from Africa, but also from other parts of the world). The great majority of these are *pourquoi* tales explaining why, for example, the giraffe has a long neck, the zebra has stripes, the skunk smells, the snake has no legs, and so on.

Folktales in the Classroom

Because of their brevity, straightforward narratives, sharply defined characters, and inventive qualities, folktales are a rich source of educational activities. For the youngest readers, the stories spark an interest in reading and storytelling. They also help develop the imagination, and can serve as a springboard to art projects (see Chapter 4). However, folktales offer a multitude of opportunities for older readers as well. (We never really outgrow them, as proven by their constant re-emergence in new dress on today's movie screens.) *Twenty Things to Do with Folk Narratives* (Figure 7.10) provides just a few suggestions. Only our imaginations limit the possibilities.

FIGURE 7.10 ■ Twenty Things to Do with Folk Narratives

1. Share a favorite folktale from memory—and make your retelling as dramatic as possible. (If you can find a written version of the tale, compare it with your memory of the tale.)
2. Join a group and prepare a story theater presentation of a favorite folktale.
3. Read a folktale (new or familiar) and make a list of the characters, along with the character traits each possesses. Identify the hero(ine), the villain, the faithful helpers, the jealous sibling, the wise elder and any other types the tale might include.
4. Create a collage for your favorite folktale. Make sure it includes all the important elements of the story.

5. Compare two or more versions of the same tale, and consider how the differences change the meaning. (Multiple versions are easy to find, especially of tales like "Little Red Riding Hood," "Hansel and Gretel," "Cinderella," and "The Three Pigs." Try to select vastly different versions.)

6. Make up a new ending for an old folktale—and explain how it changes the story's meaning.

7. Make up a folktale that includes each of the following objects in its plot—a rope, a bell, a mouse, an old oak tree, and a silk scarf (or any set of objects provided by your teacher).

8. Join a group and prepare a reader's theater performance of a folktale. (Excellent free reader's theater scripts from *Reader's Theater Edition* at www.aaronshep.com are designed to include a large number of readers, and are perfect for class use.)

9. Read several parodies of folktales. (David Wiesner's *The Three Pigs*, John Scieszka's *The True Story of the Three Little Pigs*, and Eugene Trivizas's *The Three Little Wolves and the Big Bad Pig*, for example). Join a group and prepare your own parody.

10. Use a folktale to demonstrate what a motif is (or a symbol, a protagonist, an antagonist, or some other literary device).

11. Retell an old folktale in modern dress. It may or may not be a parody, for serious retellings occur all the time.

12. On your own or with a group, create an illustrated version of a favorite folktale. You are free to adapt it in any way you wish—but you will have to explain it.

13. Compose your own tall tale. Make it as outrageous as you wish, but make sure it has a point—that it explains something in nature or human behavior, or illustrates some other purpose. (For inspiration, read some tall tales before you get started.)

14. Create and describe your own mythic super-hero or super-heroine. Consider the character's origins (did he or she have parents?), physical appearance, character traits, and special abilities.

15. Write a story that describes in detail your super-hero's or super-heroine's beginnings—perhaps a miraculous birth and/or childhood, early heroic feats, or overcoming tremendous obstacles. Make sure you give your hero or heroine some identifiable character traits.

16. Compose your own creation myth. Who or what brought about the beginning of the world? Who are the important characters in your creation myth? What were those early days like? How did humans and animals come about?

17. Create a trickster figure—choose any form you like (animal, human, otherworldly). Give your figure some specific, identifiable character traits, and describe some of his or her actions befitting of a trickster.

18. Write a script for a reader's theater or story theater (see Chapter 4) that dramatizes an episode featuring your trickster figure as the central character. Prepare a performance.

19. Create and compose your own *pourquoi* tale that explains the origins of some natural feature near your home.

20. Create and compose a *pourquoi* tale that explains the origin of some animal, or perhaps an animal's appearance or behavior.

Summary

Folktales and myths are our oldest stories, and remain some of the best. Whether they are high-minded tales of good triumphing over evil, the delightful absurdity of the merry tale, or the inventiveness of myths and legends, these tales have left an indelible mark on world culture. Folktales, legends, and myths continue to be popular because, as one scholar puts it, "they are survival tales with hope" (Zipes, *Why Fairy Tales Stick*, 27). And survival often requires opportunism, exploitation, and selfishness, which explains the harsh edge we find in many of the tales. These tales go right to the core of the eternal struggle between good and evil. They show us the dangers in greed, extravagance, and lack of self-control, and the good in generosity, faithfulness, strength of character, and humility. Over and over again, we will find these messages woven into the fabric of these tales. In addition, the tales can be excellent introductions to the study of literature and culture—and as we read tales from other lands and cultures, we come to realize that far more important than our differences are the ways we are all very much alike.

Works Cited

Schwartz, Alvin, reteller. *Scary Stories to Tell in the Dark*. New York: HarperCollins, 1981.

Zipes, Jack. *Why Fairy Tales Stick: The Evolution and Relevance of a Genre*. New York: Routledge, 2006.

Recommended Resources

Armstrong, Karen. *A Short History of Myth*. Edinburgh: Cannongate, 2005.

Barber, Paul. *Vampires, Burial, and Death: Folklore and Reality*. New Haven, CT: Yale UP, 2010.

Bernheimer, Kate, ed. *Mirror, Mirror on the Wall: Women Writers Explore Their Favorite Fairy Tales*. New York: Doubleday, 1998.

Bettelheim, Bruno. *The Uses of Enchantment: The Meaning and Importance of Fairy Tales*. New York: Knopf, 1976.

Bosma, Betty. *Fairy Tales, Fables, Legends, and Myths: Using Folk Literature in Your Classroom*, 2nd ed. New York: Teachers College Press, 1993.

Bottigheimer, Ruth, ed. *Fairy Tales and Society: Illusion, Allusion, and Paradigm*. Philadelphia: University of Pennsylvania Press, 1986.

_____. *Grimms' Bad Girls and Bold Boys: The Moral and Social Vision of the Tales*. New Haven, CT: Yale UP, 1987.

Brunvand, Jan Harold. *Folklore: A Study and Research Guide*. New York: St. Martin's, 1976.

Campbell, Joseph. *The Hero with a Thousand Faces*, 2nd ed. Princeton, NJ: Princeton UP, 1968.

Chase, Richard. *American Folk Tales and Songs*. New York: Dover, 1971.

Cook, Elizabeth. *The Ordinary and the Fabulous.* Cambridge, MA: Cambridge UP, 1969.

Eliade, Mircea. *Images and Symbols.* Princeton: Princeton UP, 1991.

Frazer, James George. *The Golden Bough: A Study in Magic and Religion. (A New Abridgement from the Second and Third Editions)* Ed. Robert Frazer. Oxford: Oxford UP, 2009.

Hettinga, Donald R. *The Brothers Grimm: Two Lives, One Legacy.* New York: Clarion, 2001.

James, Ronald M. *Introduction to Folklore: Traditional Studies in Europe and Elsewhere.* James and James, 2014.

Lecouteux, Claude. *Encyclopedia of Norse and Germanic Folklore, Mythology and Magic.* Inner Traditions, 2016.

Levorato, Alessandra. *Language and Gender in the Fairy Tale Tradition: A Linguistic Analysis of Old and New Story Telling.* Houndmills, UK: Palgrave Macmillan, 2003.

Lieberman, Marcia R. " 'Some Day My Prince Will Come': Female Acculturation through the Fairy Tale." *College English* 34, 3 (1972): 383–395.

Lüthi, Max. *The European Folktale: Form and Nature.* Bloomington: Indiana UP, 1982.

_____. *The Fairytale as Art Form and Portrait of Man.* Bloomington: Indiana UP, 1984.

_____. *Once Upon a Time: On the Nature of Fairy Tales.* 1970. Bloomington: Indiana UP, 1976.

Pelton, Robert D. *The Trickster in West Africa: A Study in Mythic Irony and Sacred Delight.* U of California P, 1989.

Petrone, Penny. *Native Literature in Canada: From the Oral Tradition to the Present.* Oxford: Oxford UP, 1990.

Stone, Kay. "Fairy Tales for Adults: Walt Disney's Americanization of the Märchen." *Folklore on Two Continents.* Eds. N. Burlakoff and C. Lindahl. Bloomington: Indiana UP, 1980.

_____. "The Misuses of Enchantment: Controversies on the Significance of Fairy Tales." *Women's Folklore, Women's Culture.* Ed. Rosan, A. Jordan, and Susan J. Kalicik. Philadelphia: University of Pennsylvania Press, 1985.

Storr, Catherine. "Folk and Fairy Tales." *Children's Literature in Education* 17 (Spring 1986): 63–70.

SurLaLuneFairytales.com
• A useful and accessible website that provides information and discussion opportunities on the topic of folktales.

Tatar, Maria. *Off with Their Heads: Fairy Tales and the Culture of Childhood.* Princeton, NJ: Princeton UP, 1992.

Thompson, Stith. *The Folktale.* New York: Holt, Rinehart and Winston, 1951.

Warner, Marina. *From the Beast to the Blonde: On Fairy Tales and Their Tellers.* New York: Farrar, Straus & Giroux, 1995.

Weber, Sabra J. *Folklore Unbound: A Concise Introduction.* Waveland Press, 2014.

Yolen, Jane. *Touch Magic.* New York: Philomel, 1981.

Zipes, Jack. *Breaking the Magic Spell: Radical Theories of Folk and Fairy Tales.* Austin: University of Texas Press, 1979.

_____. *Don't Bet on the Prince: Contemporary Feminist Fairy Tales in North America and England.* London: Methuen, 1986.

_____. *Fairy Tales and the Art of Subversion: The Classical Genre for Children and the Process of Civilization.* London: Heinemann, 1983.

_____. *When Dreams Came True: Classical Fairy Tales and Their Tradition.* New York: Routledge, 1999.

Folk Narratives: A Selected and Annotated Booklist

Picture-Book Versions

Annotations have been included only if the title does not provide an adequate description.

Aardema, Verna. *Bringing the Rain to Kapiti Plain.* Illus. Beatriz Vidal. New York: Dial, 1981.
- A cumulative tale from Africa.

_____. *Why Mosquitoes Buzz in People's Ears.* Illus. Leo and Diane Dillon. New York: Dial, 1975.
- A strikingly illustrated African *pourquoi* tale.

Addo-Nkum, Kofi. *The Hunter and the Eaglet: A Ghanaian Folktale Retold.* Aurora, CO: WaveCloud, 2016.

Brown, Marcia. *Cinderella.* New York: Scribner's, 1954.

Cendrars, Blaise. *Shadows.* Illus. Marcia Brown. New York: Scribner's, 1982.
- An African story.

Climo, Shirley. *The Egyptian Cinderella.* Illus. Ruth Heller. New York: Crowell, 1989.

Cooney, Barbara. *Chanticleer and the Fox.* New York: Crowell, 1958.
- A European trickster tale.

Demi. *The Firebird.* New York: Holt, 1994.
- Based on a favorite Russian folktale.

dePaola, Tomie. *Strega Nona.* New York: Prentice Hall, 1975.
- A comic Italian folktale.

Domanska, Janina. *Little Red Hen.* New York: Macmillan, 1973.

Galdone, Paul. *Hansel and Gretel.* New York: McGraw-Hill, 1982.

_____. *Henny Penny.* New York: Clarion, 1979.
- A cumulative tale about a gullible hen who thinks the sky is falling.

Guillain, Charlotte. *The Tree of Life: An Amazon Folktale.* Illus. Steve Dorado. Chicago: Raintree, 2014.

Haley, Gale. *A Story, a Story.* New York: Atheneum, 1970.
- An African tale about the origin of all the stories.

Hyman, Trina Schart. *Little Red Riding Hood.* New York: Holiday House, 1983.

Jarrell, Randall, reteller. *Snow White and the Seven Dwarfs.* Illus. Nancy Ekholm Burkert. New York: Farrar, Straus & Giroux, 1972.

Johari, Harish. *Little Krishna.* Illus. Pieter Weltevrede. New York: Bear Cub, 2002.
- A Hindu tale about a favorite Hindu god.

Johnston, Tony. *The Cowboy and the Black-eyed Pea.* Illus. Warren Ludwig. New York: Putnam, 1992.
- A parody of "The Princess and the Pea."

Kellogg, Steven. *Paul Bunyan: A Tall Tale.* New York: Morrow, 1984.

Lester, Julius. *John Henry.* Illus. Jerry Pinkney. New York: Dial, 1994.
- An American tall tale about a man of great strength.

Lorbiecki, Marybeth. *Paul Bunyan's Sweetheart.* Illus. Reneé Graef. Ann Arbor, MI: Sleeping Bear Press, 2014.

Louie, Ai-Ling. *Yeh-Shen: A Cinderella Story from China.* Illus. Ed Young. New York: Philomel, 1982.

Marshall, James. *Red Riding Hood.* New York: Dial, 1987.

McDermott, Gerald. *Anansi the Spider.* New York: Holt, 1972.
- An African tale about an irrepressible trickster.

_____. *Arrow to the Sun.* New York: Viking, 1974.
- A creation tale from the Pueblo of the Southwest.

_____. *Raven: A Trickster Tale from the Pacific Northwest.* New York: Harcourt, 1993.
- A trickster tale about the bringing of light to humankind.

Moser, Barry, reteller. *The Three Little Pigs.* Boston: Little, Brown, 2001.

Novesky, Amy. *Elephant Prince: The Story of Ganesh*. Illus. Belgin K. Wedman. San Rafael, CA: Mandala, 2004.
- A Hindu tale about the origin of all the stories.

Orgel, Doris, reteller. *The Bremen Town Musicians: And Other Animal Tales from Grimm*. Illus. Bert Kitchen. New Milford, CT: Roaring Brook, 2004.

Pinkney, Jerry, reteller. *Aesop's Fables*. New York: SeaStar/North-South, 2000.
- The famous talking animal moral tales from ancient Greece.

_____. *Little Red Riding Hood*. New York: Little, Brown, 2007.

Polacco, Patricia. *Babushka Baba Yaga*. New York: Philomel, 1993.
- A Russian tale featuring the famous witch.

San Souci, Robert D., adapter. *Cendrillon: A Caribbean Cinderella*. Illus. Brian Pinkney. New York: Simon & Schuster, 1998.

_____, reteller. *Little Gold Star: A Spanish-American Cinderella*. Illus. Sergio Martinez. New York: HarperCollins, 2000.

Scieszka, John. *The Stinky Cheese Man and Other Fairly Stupid Tales*. Illus. Lane Smith. New York: Viking, 1992.

_____. *The True Story of the Three Little Pigs*. Illus. Lane Smith. New York: Viking, 1989.
- Both of these books by Scieszka are parodies of traditional tales.

Steptoe, John. *Mufaro's Beautiful Daughters: An African Tale*. New York: Lothrop, 1987.

Trivizas, Eugene. *The Three Little Wolves and the Big Bad Pig*. (1993) Illus. Helen Oxenbury. New York: Margaret McElderry, 1997.
- A parody with role reversal.

Wardlaw, Lee. *Punia and the King of the Sharks: A Hawaiian Folktale*. Illus. Felipe Davalos. StarWalk Kids, 2014.

Weisner, David. *The Three Pigs*. Boston: Houghton Mifflin, 2001.
- A postmodern parody.

Young, Ed. *Lon Po Po: A Red Riding Hood Story from China*. New York: Philomel, 1989.

Zelinsky, Paul O. *Rumpelstiltskin*. New York: Dutton, 1986.
- One of several strikingly illustrated European folktales by a talented illustrator.

Zemach, Harve, reteller. *Duffy and the Devil*. Illus. Margot Zemach. New York: Farrar, Straus & Giroux, 1973.

Zemach, Margot, reteller. *The Little Red Hen*. New York: Farrar, Straus & Giroux, 1983.

_____. *The Three Little Pigs*. New York: Farrar, Straus & Giroux, 1988.

Folktale Collections

Asbjørnsen, Peter, and Jørgen Moe. *East O' the Sun and West O' the Moon*. New York: Dover, 1970.
- Scandinavian folktales.

Bedell, J. M. *Hildur, Queen of the Elves, and Other Icelandic Folktales*. Interlink Publishing Group, 2015.

Bierhorst, John, ed. *The Dancing Fox: Arctic Folktales*. New York: Morrow, 1997.

_____. *Lightning Inside You: And Other Native American Riddles*. New York: Morrow, 1992.

Bloch, Marie Halun. *Ukrainian Folk Tales*. New York: Coward, McCann, 1964.

Briggs, Katharine. *British Folk Tales*. New York: Pantheon, 1977.

Bushnaq, Inea, trans. *Arab Folktales*. New York: Pantheon, 1986.

Calvino, Italo, ed. *Italian Folktales*. New York: Pantheon, 1980.

Chandler, Robert, trans. *Russian Folk Tales*. New York: Shambhala/Random House, 1980.

Chase, Richard. *The Jack Tales*. Boston: Houghton Mifflin, 1971.
- American tall tales.

Chin, Yen-Lien C., Yetta S. Center, and Mildred Ross. *Chinese Folktales: An Anthology*. UK: Routledge, 2015.

Cole, Joanna. *Best-Loved Folktales of the World*. Garden City, NY: Doubleday, 1982.

Conger, David, Marian Davies Toth, and Kay Lyons, *Asian Children's Favorite Stories: A Treasury of Folktales from China, Japan, Korea, India, the Philippines, Thailand, Indonesia and Malaysia*. Illus. Patrick Yee. Tuttle, 2006.

Daniel, Noel, ed. *The Fairy Tales of the Brothers Grimm*. Taschen, 2017.

Day, Lal Behari. *Bengali Folk Tales*. Illus. Warwick Goble. The Planet, 2016.

Demi, adapter. *A Chinese Zoo: Fables and Proverbs*. New York: Harcourt, 1987.

de Wit, Dorothy. *The Talking Stone: An Anthology of Native American Tales and Legends*. New York: Greenwillow, 1979.

Dickinson, Peter, reteller. *City of Gold and Other Stories from the Old Testament*. Illus. Michael Foreman. London: Gollancz, 1992.

Fang, Linda, reteller. *The Ch'i-lin Purse: A Collection of Ancient Chinese Stories*. New York: Farrar, Straus & Giroux, 1995.

Fredericks, Anthony D. *African Legends, Myths, and Folktales for Readers Theatre*. Westport, CT: Libraries Unlimited, 2008.

Glassie, Henry. *Irish Folk Tales*. New York: Pantheon, 1985.

Grimm, Jacob, and Wilhelm Grimm. *Household Stories*. Trans. Lucy Crane. New York: Dover, 1963.
  • One of many editions dating from 1812 and onward.

Gross, Ila Land. *Cinderella around the World*. New York: L.E.A.P., 2001.

Haley, Gail E., reteller and illus. *Mountain Jack Tales*. New York: Penguin, 1992.

Hamilton, Virginia. *The People Could Fly: American Black Folktales*. Illus. Leo and Diane Dillon. New York: Knopf, 1993.

Hausman, Gerald, collector and reteller. *How Chipmunk Got Tiny Feet: Native American Origin Stories*. New York: HarperCollins, 1995.

Haviland, Virginia. *Favorite Tales Told in India*. Boston: Little, Brown, 1973.

Hodges, Margaret, reteller. *Hauntings: Ghosts and Ghouls from Around the World*. Boston: Little, Brown, 1991.

Hurston, Zora Neale, collector. *Lies and Other Tall Tales*. Adapted and illus. Christopher Myers. New York: HarperCollins, 2005.

Jacobs, Joseph. *Celtic Fairy Tales*. 1891. New York: Dover, 1968.

_____. *English Fairy Tales*. 1890. New York: Dover, 1967.

Jaffe, Nina, and Steve Zeitlin. *While Standing on One Foot: Puzzle Stories and Wisdom Tales from the Jewish Tradition*. Illus. John Segal. New York: Holt, 1993.

Jaffrey, Madhur. *Seasons of Splendour: Tales, Myths & Legends of India*. Illus. Michael Foreman. Harmondsworth, UK: Puffin, 1987.

James, Grace, reteller. *Green Willow and Other Japanese Fairy Tales*. New York: Avenel, 1987.

Joseph, Lynn. *The Mermaid's Twin Sister: More Stories from Trinidad*. New York: Clarion, 1994.

Kherdian, David, reteller. *Feathers and Tails: Animal Fables from Around the World*. New York: Putnam, 1992.

Lang, Andrew. *The Blue Fairy Book*. 1889. New York: Dover, 1965.
  • The first of a famous series of folktales from around the world, collected in the nineteenth century.

Leavy, Una. *Magical Celtic Tales*. Illus. Fergal O'Connor. O'Brien Press, 2017.

Leeming, David, and Jack Page. *Myths, Legends, and Folktales of America: An Anthology*. Oxford: Oxford UP, 2000.

Lester, Julius. *Black Folktales*. New York: Richard W. Baron, 1969.

Lyons, Mary E., selector. *Raw Head, Bloody Bones: African-American Tales of the Supernatural*. New York: Scribners, 1991.

Mandela, Nelson. *Favorite African Folktales*. New York: Norton, 2004.

Manitonquat (Medicine Story), reteller. *The Children of the Morning Light: Wampanoag Tales.* Illus. Mary F. Arquette. New York: Macmillan, 1994.

Minford, John, trans. *Favourite Folktales of China.* Beijing, China: New World Press, 1983.

Neil, Philip, reteller. *Fairy Tales of Eastern Europe.* Boston: Houghton Mifflin, 1991.

Nic Leodhas, Sorche. *Thistle and Thyme: Tales and Legends from Scotland.* New York: Holt, Rinehart and Winston, 1962.

Opie, Iona, and Peter Opie. *The Classic Fairy Tales.* New York: Oxford University Press, 1974.

Perrault, Charles. *Perrault's Fairy Tales.* Illus. Gustave Doré. 1867. New York: Dover, 1969.

Phelps, Ethel Johnston, ed. *Kamala: Feminist Folktales from Around the World.* Illus. Suki Boynton. New York: The Feminist Press at CUNY, 2016.

_____. *Tatterhood: Feminist Folk Tales from Around the World.* Illus. Suki Boynton. New York: New York: The Feminist Press at CUNY, 2016.

Ross, Gayle. *How Rabbit Tricked Otter and Other Cherokee Trickster Stories.* Illus. Murv Jacob. New York: HarperCollins, 1994.

Rounds, Glen. *Ol' Paul, the Mighty Logger.* New York: Holiday House, 1936.

Schwartz, Alvin, reteller. *Ghosts! Ghostly Tales from Folklore.* New York: HarperCollins, 1991.

Schwarz, Howard, and Barbara Rush, retellers. *The Diamond Tree: Jewish Tales from Around the World.* New York: HarperCollins, 1991.

Singer, Isaac Bashevis. *Zlateh the Goat and Other Stories.* New York: Harper, 1966.
• Yiddish folktales.

Tatar, Maria, trans. and ed. *The Grimm Reader: The Classic Tales of the Brothers Grimm.* (Revised) New York: Norton, 2016.

Tehranchian, Hassan, adapter. *Kalilah and Dimnah: Fables from the Middle East.* New York: Harmony, 1985.

Thompson, Vivian L. *Hawaiian Tales of Heroes and Champions.* New York: Holiday House, 1971.

Vuong, Lynette Dyer. *The Golden Carp and Other Tales from Vietnam.* Illus. Manabu Saito. New York: Lothrop, 1993.

Yeats, W. B., and Lady Gregory. *A Treasury of Irish Myth, Legend, and Folklore.* New York: Avenel, 1986.

Yep, Laurence, reteller. *Tongues of Jade.* New York: HarperCollins, 1991.
• Chinese tales.

Yolen, Jane, ed. *Favorite Folktales from Around the World.* New York: Pantheon, 1986.

Epics and Myths

Alexander, Heather. *Child's Introduction to Greek Mythology: The Stories of the Gods, Goddesses, Heroes, Monsters, and Other Mythical Creatures.* Black Dog and Leventhal, 2011.

Colum, Padraic. *The Children's Homer: The Adventures of Odysseus and the Tale of Troy.* 1919. New York: Macmillan, 1982.

_____. *The Children of Odin: The Book of Northern Myths.* 1920. New York: Macmillan, 1984.

_____. *The Golden Fleece and the Heroes Who Lived before Achilles.* 1921. New York: Macmillan, 1983.

Green, Roger Lancelyn. *Heroes of Greece and Troy: Retold from the Ancient Authors.* New York: Walck, 1961.

Hamilton, Virginia. *In the Beginning: Creation Stories from Around the World.* New York: Harcourt Brace Jovanovich, 1988.

Hastings, Selina, reteller. *Sir Gawain and the Loathly Lady*. Illus. Juan Wijngaard. London: Walker Books, 1985.
- An Arthurian tale.

Heany, Seamus, trans. *Beowulf*. New York: Farrar, Straus & Giroux, 2000.

Henderson, Kathy. *Lugalbanda: The Boy Who Got Caught Up in a War*. New York: Candlewick, 2006.
- A tale from ancient Sumeria.

Hieatt, Constance, reteller. *Sir Gawain and the Green Knight*. New York: Crowell, 1967.

Jendresen, Erik, reteller. *Hanuman: Based on Valmiki's Ramayana*. Illus. Ming Li. Berkeley, CA: Tricycle Press, 1998.
- Tales from a classic Hindu epic.

Kimmel, Eric A. *The Hero Beowulf*. New York: Farrar, Straus & Giroux, 2005.

McCaughrean, Geraldine. *The Bronze Cauldron: Myths and Legends of the World*. New York: Margaret K. McElderry, 1998.

_____. *The Crystal Pool: Myths and Legends of the World*. New York: Margaret K. McElderry, 1999.

_____. *The Golden Hoard: Myths and Legends of the World*. New York: Margaret K. McElderry, 1996.

_____. *The Silver Treasure: Myths and Legends of the World*. New York: Margaret K. McElderry, 1997.

Morpurgo, Michael. *Beowulf*. Cambridge, MA: Candlewick, 2006.

Napoli, Donna Jo. *Treasury of Greek Mythology: Classic Stories of Gods, Goddesses, Heroes & Monsters*. Illus. Christina Balit. National Geographic, 2011.

Philip, Neil. *The Tale of Sir Gawain*. Illus. Charles Keeping. New York: Philomel, 1987.

Sherwood, Merriam, trans. *The Song of Roland*. New York: McKay, 1938.

Steig, Jeanne. *A Gift from Zeus: Sixteen Favorite Myths*. Illus. William Steig. New York: HarperCollins, 2001.
- A modernized and occasionally racy retelling.

Sutcliff, Rosemary. *Beowulf*. London: Bodley Head, 1961. (Published in the United States as *Dragon Slayer*.)

_____. *Black Ships before Troy: The Story of the Iliad*. New York: Delacorte, 1993.

_____. *The Light beyond the Forest: The Quest for the Holy Grail*. New York: Dutton, 1980.

_____. *The Road to Camlann*. New York: Dutton, 1982.

_____. *The Sword and the Circle: King Arthur and the Knights of the Round Table*. New York: Dutton, 1981.

_____. *The Wanderings of Odysseus*. New York: Delacorte, 1995.

Szac, Murielle. *The Adventures of Hermes, God of Thieves: 100 Journeys Through Greek Mythology*. Tr. Mike Provata-Carlone. UK: Pushkin Children's Books, 2017.

Tchana, Katrin Hyman, reteller. *Changing Woman and Her Sisters: Stories of Goddesses from Around the World*. Illus. Trina Schart Hyman. New York: Holiday House, 2006.

Westwood, Jennifer, reteller. *Gilgamesh and Other Babylonian Tales*. New York: Coward McCann, 1970.

Williams, Marcia. *Greek Myths*. New York: Walker, 2006.

Zeitlin, Steve. *The Four Corners of the Sky: Creation Stories and Cosmologies from around the World*. New York: Holt, 2000.

Fantasy

The World of Make-Believe

"Fantasy is not an escape from reality. It is a way of understanding it."

–Lloyd Alexander, "A Visit with Lloyd Alexander," video interview, Penguin (1994)

Introduction

Traditionally, children's fiction has been divided into two broad categories: realistic fiction, which portrays the possible, and fantasy fiction, which portrays the impossible. The distinction is sometimes blurred, but, at the end of the day, it does not matter. Fantasy and realism deal with the same issues. Realistic novels such as Robert Cormier's *I Am the Cheese* (a chilling tale of government corruption), Mildred Taylor's *Roll of Thunder, Hear My Cry* (about racism in the 1930s), and Katherine Paterson's *Bridge to Terabithia* (about the acceptance of death) depict the same social, psychological, and philosophical issues as fantasies like C. S. Lewis's *Chronicles of Narnia*, Phillip Pullman's *His Dark Materials* trilogy, and Patrick Ness's *A Monster Calls*. Yet, fantasy and realism have very different premises.

The unforgettable figures of Alice, Dorothy and her motley companions, the irrepressible Mr. Toad of Toad Hall, Peter Pan, Wilbur the pig, and Charlotte the spider attest to the power of fantasy in the lives of children. But this fascination with imaginative worlds reaches beyond childhood. The wild popularity of dramas such as *Star Wars*, *The Lord of the Rings* and *Game of Thrones* is evidence of the abiding appeal of these imaginative flights. However, many are under the misconception that fantasy literature is escapist literature, providing us with a respite from our humdrum existence or from the stress of everyday living. Yes, fantasy does allow us to escape our everyday lives and surroundings and experience adventures that would be otherwise impossible—but the escape is illusory for all of fantasy is rooted in our common humanity. The fact is that at the heart of most literary fantasies are the joys, the sorrows, the loves, the losses that we all experience every day. And, in a curious way, fantasy often makes us see reality much more clearly than any realistic story, because it is showing us reality in a fresh, new way. This is what Lloyd Alexander's epigraph at the beginning of this chapter is trying to tell us. When we read fantasy, we may think we're escaping, but we're not.

Despite the similarities between fantasy and realistic fiction, there is justification for observing the distinction between the two, since they do observe a different set of rules, and they often appeal to very different readers. Some people are fanatical devotees of fantasy, often of specific kinds of fantasy—science fiction, horror, or epic fantasy, for example. Still other readers insist on only true-to-life stories. The lucky ones are those readers who enjoy both kinds of literature.

Defining Fantasy

As we have noted, fantasies are stories of the impossible. In every fantasy, there is some violation of the world's natural order as we understand it. A fantasy may contain ghosts, monsters or talking animals; it may involve time travel or magic; it may be set in the distant future, on a faraway planet, in some make-believe land, in our own world, or in an alternate version of our world. But wherever the setting and whatever the fantasy elements, we will still find familiar human emotions and values—sadness, joy, fear, jealousy, courage, hate, love.

Fantasy has always been popular with children. One of the earliest classics of children's literature is Lewis Carroll's magical fantasy *Alice's Adventures in Wonderland* (see Figures 8.1 and 8.3). And, in the first decade of the twenty-first century, J. K. Rowling's fantasy series about Harry Potter was nothing less than a publishing phenomenon. So, we ask, what is this fascination? Fantasy both challenges us and appeals to our imagination. Fantasy requires an investment that we don't usually find in realistic fiction, for fantasy forces us out of our comfortable world and introduces new possibilities, new challenges, and sometimes new threats. It stretches us, taking us far away from our everyday world, to times and places that never were. Because it defies the rules and limitations we know, fantasy invites us to think about things in different ways; it gives us worlds and beings we may never have dreamed of before. It compels us to examine our values and provides us with fresh insights into our own world, into our own lives. Readers who claim not to like fantasy may just not have found the right kind of fantasy for them. For fantasy comes in many varieties, shapes, and forms—from the sober epic or high fantasies and absurd comic fantasies to creepy ghost stories, clever science fiction and futuristic fantasies, and charming talking animal fantasies. There truly is something for everyone.

FIGURE 8.1 ■ Sir John Tenniel's illustration for Lewis Carroll's *Alice's Adventures in Wonderland*, showing Alice discovering a passage into Wonderland.

Fantasy Elements

Embracing the fantasy world requires what poet Samuel Taylor Coleridge called our "willing suspension of disbelief"—that is, we have to accept the premises of the fantasy world (magic spells, enchanted objects, time travel, talking animals, dragons, wizards and witches, and so on). Now this does not mean that the entire burden rests with the reader. The writer has to get us to believe in the magic. To do this, the fantasy writer:

1. creates a memorable fantasy world, either within our primary world (that is, the world we know and live in) or in a secondary world (one that is made up by the author);
2. creates a set of consistent fantasy rules that are believable within the context of the fantasy world; and
3. creates interesting characters, preferably with depth.

Let's take a closer look at each of these.

The Fantasy World

In some fantasies, the magic actually intrudes on the primary world; that is, the magic is part of the everyday world we live in. In Natalie Babbitt's *Tuck Everlasting*, Winnie Foster, a young girl in nineteenth-century America, accidentally stumbles across a magical spring that bestows immortality on those who drink from it. The story is about how Winnie handles her knowledge of this secret magic. Mary Norton's *The Borrowers*, about the little people who live in our walls and floorboards, is another example of fantasy entering into the world we inhabit. And all ghost, vampire and zombie stories are set in our world—they don't really make sense anyplace else.

Then there are those fantasies that begin in our world—the primary world—but one or more characters are transported into a secondary world where the magical elements occur. For example, in L. Frank Baum's *The Wonderful Wizard of Oz* (Fig. 8.2), a cyclone carries Dorothy from Kansas (the primary world) to Oz (the secondary world). The story's magical characters and events are found only in Oz. So, the author does not have to explain or justify the fantasy—it simply becomes a feature of another world. C. S. Lewis's Narnia series (including *The Lion, the Witch, and the Wardrobe* and others) is another example. The stories open in England of the mid-twentieth century, but the protagonists (the Pevensie children) find a magical passage through the wardrobe into Narnia, a world apart from ours that operates under a different set of rules—the fantasy rules. We find the same concept in the Harry Potter books—Harry must go to Platform $9^3/_4$ at King's Cross Station to get to Hogwarts.

There is a third type of fantasy in which the action takes place entirely in a secondary world, a world apart from the one we know—in other words, our world does not enter the picture. Take, for example, J. R. R. Tolkien's *Lord of the Rings* cycle, including its prequel, *The Hobbit*. These tales take place entirely in Middle Earth, a self-contained secondary world. No part of this story is set in our world (in fact, our world, so far as the story is concerned, does not exist). Many epic fantasies (such as Lloyd Alexander's *Chronicles of Prydain* or Ursula Le Guin's *Earthsea* cycle) are examples, as are all the films in the *Star Wars* series. From the very beginning, the readers are absorbed in the fantasy world.

The Fantasy Characters

When we recall the great fantasies, it is often the characters we remember best—Alice and all the odd creatures in Wonderland; the irascible puppet Pinocchio; the irrepressible Peter Pan; the independent Pippi Longstocking; the humble hobbit Bilbo Baggins; the lovable pig Wilbur and the wise spider Charlotte; the determined orphan Harry Potter; and so on. Every fantasy contains a character or characters whom we will never meet in real life, from talking animals and ghosts from times past to creatures from outer space. Ask most children who their favorite fictional character is, and chances are that most will name fantasy characters.

However, despite their unusual appearance, extraordinary powers, or bizarre behavior, we are always able to connect with fantasy characters. And why is that? All fantasy characters reflect essentially human traits. So the Scarecrow, the Tin Woodsman, and the Cowardly Lion from *The Wonderful Wizard of Oz* all possess specific human qualities that we recognize (see Figure 8.2). One of the most appealing qualities about *Charlotte's Web* is how White turns a potentially frightening creepy-crawly spider into one of children's literature's most beloved characters. He portrays Charlotte as wise, compassionate, and determined. We like her because of her human qualities. For similar reasons, the selfish, gluttonous Templeton gets on our nerves. As for the vile, power-hungry Wicked Witch of the West, we don't like her because she betrays the worst in humanity. And in the *Star Wars* films, the robots C-3PO and R2-D2 are favorites because, even as machines, they betray the human traits of compassion and loyalty. In other words, fantasies are, in the end, about real life. They are just clothed in outlandish garb—and that makes them more fun. Even the youngest readers know that beneath the veneer, the costumes, and the magical powers, these are characters not that different from us.

The Fantasy Premise

All fantasies operate on premises—these are notions that readers simply have to accept if they are to enjoy the story. A premise might be accepting that animals can talk, that ghosts or vampires exist, that time travel is a reality, that other worlds with strange and wondrous creatures exist, and so on. Fantasy author Zilpha Snyder suggests that, regardless of the type, children demand two things from fantasy—that it contain *no nonsense* and that it contain *no treachery* (230). These at first may appear to be curious requirements: After all, isn't much of fantasy "nonsense"? And what does "treachery" have to do with fantasy? But these elements are quite important.

Most fantasies, even the most bizarre and outlandish, actually contain nothing that is nonsense (at least in the context of the fantasy). The facts in the fantasy story are not presented as silly or fanciful—they are, instead, presented as an alternate reality. Most successful fantasies are governed by a set of rules or premises (invented by the author). For example, in *Charlotte's Web*, the animals may talk to each other, but they do not speak to humans. Fern is an exception; presumably her youth and innocence allow her to communicate with the animals—but note that as she matures (and becomes more interested in Henry Fussy), she loses her ability (or her desire) to talk with them. In Natalie Babbit's *Tuck Everlasting*, the premise is that anyone who drinks water from a special spring will never die. Stepping through a magical wardrobe will allow the Pevensie children to enter the magical land of Narnia (the passages to Narnia vary from book to book in the series, but

FIGURE 8.2 ■ Dorothy scolds the Cowardly Lion as the Scarecrow, the Tin Woodman, and Toto look on in this depiction by W. W. Denslow, the first illustrator of *The Wonderful Wizard of Oz* (1900).

the land can only be reached through some pre-ordained method). Many fantasy writers are addicted to enchanted passageways, for they help explain and justify the magical world. In other words, the writer has to establish a set of rules or premises that help explain the fantasy world. Snyder argues that a fantasy writer should not violate the rules once they have been established. This is very much like a game invented by children on the playground. They first make up the rules, and as long as everyone follows the rules, the game is fun. But when the players begin to ignore the rules, the game soon falls apart. Fantasy readers don't mind surprises, but they insist that any surprises make sense in the context of the invented fantasy world.

This brings us to Snyder's second point—"no treachery." You will recall that, at the end of the 1939 MGM movie *The Wizard of Oz*, Dorothy is depicted awaking from a dream, which she describes to the grown-ups around her bed. These adults (all characters in the dream) smile patronizingly at her as she insists, futilely, that her experiences were real. This, for many viewers, is the one flaw in an otherwise perfectly executed film. Some viewers may feel cheated, or perhaps betrayed, by this. Viewers want to believe in Oz—in both its good and evil characters. It doesn't seem fair that we have invested our time and emotions in these characters and their adventures only to discover nothing was real. L. Frank Baum's original story, on the other hand, describes a very real adventure. Dorothy *does* go to Oz, and her adventures and the characters are real. I suspect this is what most children want to believe. (It's a little like wanting to believe in Santa Claus.) Once having made the commitment to believe, most readers do not like to find out that they have been deceived, that everything has been an elaborate hoax. Or, as a child might rightly complain, it's not fair. This is the "treachery" to which Snyder refers. You will find that most childhood fantasies—the memorable ones at least—allow us to believe in the stories and characters.

Types of Fantasy Fiction

Like folk literature, modern fantasy comes in many varieties. And not everyone likes the same types of fantasy. So it is helpful to recognize some of the differences that we may better understand how the fantasy works—and that we might help children find fantasies that suit their tastes. Some fantasies are comical, some are tragic, some frivolous, some serious. Some take place in our world, and others are set in some alternative, imaginary world. Some include talking animals, fire-breathing dragons, friendly ghosts, or other outlandish creatures. Others may have very ordinary characters (with perhaps one or two extraordinary powers). Any effort to classify modern fantasy is thwarted by this rich variety; nevertheless, it is helpful to make some tentative generalizations about common fantasy types. Keep in mind that some fantasies simply refuse to fit tidily into categories.

Animal Fantasy

Animal fantasies are those in which animals talk and behave like humans—this is called anthropomorphism. Anthropomorphic animals have long been a staple in folk narratives (see Chapter 7). Fables, of course, rely almost exclusively on talking animals, who are stand-ins for humans. Most children are fascinated with animals and are quick to ascribe human traits to them. Curiously, when the marketing of children's books first began in the eighteenth century, few of the early books featured talking animals outside folktales, since to many people, the idea of a talking animal was sacrilegious—that is, it went against biblical teachings. There was even much skepticism about the folktales and their talking animals. Dorothy Kilner's *The Life and Perambulations of a Mouse* (1783) and Mrs. Trimmer's *The Story of the Robins* (1786), are rare examples of talking animal stories in the eighteenth century. In the 1860s, Lewis Carroll included several talking animals in the Alice books (See Figure 8.3). Joel Chandler Harris's now controversial "Uncle Remis" stories (the inspiration for Disney's also controversial animated film *Song of the South* and popularized at Disney World's Splash Mountain ride) were largely borrowed from the oral narratives of African Americans in the nineteenth-century South. Beatrix Potter's beloved picture-book fantasies—*The Tale of Peter Rabbit*, *The Tale of Benjamin Bunny*, and many others—did not appear until the early twentieth century. But all of these are the precursors of the multitude of talking animal stories

FIGURE 8.3 ■ This illustration by Sir John Tenniel depicts the neurotic White Rabbit from Lewis Carroll's *Alice's Adventures in Wonderland*. Only in a bold fantasy would a rabbit, dressed in a fashionable waistcoat and carrying a pocket watch and umbrella, be seen walking upright.

Source: From *The Tale of Peter Rabbit* by Beatrix Potter. London: Warne, 1901.

in today's children's picture books—see the works of Jean de Brunhoff (*The Story of Babar* and its sequels), William Steig (*Sylvester and the Magic Pebble, Abel's Island,* and others), Ian Falconer (*Olivia* and its sequels), and Mo Willems (*Don't Let the Pigeon Drive the Bus* and its sequels), to name just a few.

Talking animals are not just picture-book fare. Kenneth Grahame's classic *The Wind in the Willows,* first published in 1908 (see Figure 8.4), is a charming episodic tale set in the peaceful countryside of Edwardian England. It features a water rat, a mole, a badger, and a toad, all leading comfortable lives in well-furnished homes with good food, hearty male companionship (the story virtually excludes women), and a few wild adventures—the most famous involving Mr. Toad and his fascination with fast motor cars.

In the 1920s, Hugh Lofting wrote the *Doctor Dolittle* books, tales of a talented veterinarian who is able to speak the languages of animals. In the 1930s and 1940s, Walter R. Brooks wrote of the comical adventures of a pig named Freddy and his talking animal friends on a farm in upstate New York. Over the course of the series, beginning with *Freddy Goes to Florida* (1927), Freddy becomes a detective, a politician, a pilot, and a magician, and the books reflect the changing times during the Depression and World War II into the 1950s. (He lives quite a long and exciting life for a pig.)

FIGURE 8.4 ■ Ernest H. Shepard's illustration for Kenneth Grahame's *The Wind in the Willows,* showing Mole and Water Rat boating on the river. We never question the peculiarity of a water rat having to take a boat—that is the prerogative of fantasy.

One of the most famous of all animal fantasies is E. B. White's *Charlotte's Web*, about Wilbur the pig and his friend, a spider named Charlotte. The plot revolves around a clever scheme to save Wilbur from being served up for Christmas dinner. In a similar vein is Dick King-Smith's comical *Babe, the Gallant Pig*, in which Babe is spared from the roasting pan by developing his skills as a sheepherder.

Among animal fantasies intended for older readers is Brian Jacques' very popular Redwall series, an example of heroic animal fantasy that draws its inspiration from medieval legends and romance. Richard Adams's *Watership Down* describes the plight of a society of rabbits forced from their homes by human encroachment. Similarly, Robert O'Brien's *Mrs. Frisby and the Rats of NIMH* is about a rat whose home, also threatened by humans, is saved by other rats who acquired advanced intelligence when they were subjects of scientific experiments. (Note the negative commentary on human society in both of these books.)

On the other hand, we should never expect to learn much about real animals from these fantasies. In all animal fantasy, the animals are anthropomorphized—they are given human feelings and human speech. This allows us to empathize with them, and from their experiences, we learn something about ourselves and humanity in general. One animal rights organization, RedRover, has urged caution in the use of anthropomorphic picture books with children, arguing that these books give children a distorted view of animal behavior. A 2014 study by Ganea et al. pointed out that "anthropomorphized animals in books may not only lead to less learning but also influence children's conceptual knowledge of animals." However, the study goes on to note that

> . . . *if the goal of the picture book interaction is to teach children information about the world, it is best to use books that depict the world in a realistic rather than fantastical manner. More specifically, if we want children to learn new things about animals, we need to expose them to stories that present the animals and their environments in a biologically realistic manner, both in the way that they are depicted and the way they are described.* (Ganea)

In other words, children, like adults, should get their facts and fiction from different books. In fact, we could argue that anthropomorphic stories instill in children an empathy for animals they might not otherwise have, and might actually encourage them to turn to nonfiction books for factual information (see Chapter 10).

Toy Fantasy

In 1883, an Italian author named Carlo Collodi (a pen name for Carlo Lorenzini) wrote *The Adventures of Pinocchio*, the story of a wooden puppet's quest to become a real boy (see Figure 8.5). This was one of the first examples of a toy fantasy—stories in which toys come to life—and in many of these tales, the

FIGURE 8.5 ■ This
illustration of Carlo Collidi's
puppet Pinocchio come to life
appeared in the first edition in
1883, and was done by Enrico
Mazzanti. It shows a more
irascible (and less sentimental)
figure than the adorable figure
created for Walt Disney's 1940
animated musical film.

animated toys wish to become human. Toy fantasies enjoyed popularity in the 1920s and 1930s with such works as Margery Williams Bianco's *The Velveteen Rabbit*, which remains a perennial favorite. It is not true, however, that all toys in these fantasies aspire to be humans. Rachel Field's *Hitty, Her First Hundred Years* is the first-person narrative of a doll reminiscing about her experiences over an entire century. This story reveals the peculiar advantages of toy protagonists over humans—toys may wear out, but they never die.

A. A. Milne's *Winnie-the-Pooh* and *The House at Pooh Corner*, first published in the 1920s, are among the best known of toy fantasies; however, many readers are apt to see these as animal fantasies (a perfect example of how shaky classification schemes can be). Winnie and his friends are technically toys, although they have many of the characteristics of animals: The owl lives in a tree, the bear lives in a den and loves honey (or "hunny," as he says). The characters behave like a large, dysfunctional family, each member with a different physical or psychological hang-up—a hyperactive tiger, a manic-depressive donkey, a paranoid pig, a dyslexic owl, a feeble-minded bear (see Manlove, 62). The allure of the stories, aside from their cuddly characters, is seeing how the toys navigate their world through love and loyalty.

Modern toy fantasies are found most frequently in picture-book format (for example, Leo Lionni's *Alexander and the Wind-up Mouse* and Don Freeman's *Corduroy*), but Russell Hoban's *The Mouse and His Child* is a serious work of toy fantasy for older readers, and is filled with sharp social satire. And we should not forget Lynn Reid Banks' *The Indian in the Cupboard* series and Disney's popular *Toy Story* films.

Eccentric Characters

Some of the most delightful fantasies are those relating the adventures of eccentric characters. These are often closely related to the tall tale, which was discussed as part of the folk narrative tradition (see Chapter 7).

An early example is Lucretia Hale's *The Peterkin Papers*, written in the nineteenth century, which describes the misadventures of a completely inept family. For example, when they purchase a Christmas tree that is too tall for the room, they decide they have to raise the ceiling. They try all manner of things to get their horse to take them on a carriage ride in the country—lightening the load, whipping the horse, tempting the horse with food—but he will not budge. It takes their wise neighbor, the Lady from Philadelphia, to point out that their horse cannot move; it's chained to the hitching post. They are usually rescued from their dilemmas by the Lady from Philadelphia, who displays infinite patience.

In the twentieth century, Harry Allard's picture books (illustrated by James Marshall) about the Stupids (Stupid being their family name) follow this tradition (*The Stupids Have a Ball*, *The Stupids Die*, and others). These books, although outrageously funny, sometimes trouble adults who dislike the use of the word "stupid," which, both as the family name and as an adjective, appears on virtually every page of these books. They fear children will be running about calling everyone "stupid." It might be argued, however, that just the opposite will occur, for through constant repetition, the term becomes "worn out," unoriginal. (It may be that was exactly what Allard had in mind.)

One of the most popular children's books of the twentieth century is Astrid Lindgren's *Pippi Longstocking*, a story set in Sweden, perhaps in the 1940s (when it was written), and peopled with very ordinary human beings except Pippi herself. Pippi is a young girl who lives by herself in her own house (with a pet monkey and a horse), and does exactly as she pleases. Her behavior is often quite outrageous—which is why children love her—but just as often, she turns out to be more sensible than many adults. We do not worry about her being alone, because she possesses superhuman strength (this is one of the premises of the fantasy). Her magical strength makes her impervious to any danger, and puts her on a superior footing to the adults in the story. Although most readers may identify with Pippi's more conventional friends, her neighbors Tommy and Annika—we all wish Pippi lived next door to us.

Another example of the eccentric character is P. L. Travers's *Mary Poppins*, the story of an unconventional nanny with magical powers. She moves in with the Banks family—a rather stiff bunch of Londoners—and brings wonder into their lives, enabling them to finally find happiness. In both *Pippi Longstocking* and *Mary Poppins*, there is a modicum of magic—Pippi's unexplained strength and Mary Poppins's uncanny magical tricks. But the real interest is in the characters and their behavior, not in their magic.

Enchanted Journeys

Remember our discussion of plot in Chapter 3, where we categorized stories into two main kinds—a stranger comes to town or someone goes on a journey. The enchanted journey is simply one that takes the hero/ine through a fantasy land, a land inhabited by fanciful creatures and where unreal things can happen. In the early eighteenth century, the English satirist Jonathan Swift wrote *Gulliver's Travels*, recounting the adventures of a stranded Englishman, Lemuel Gulliver, in Lilliput (a land populated by miniature people), in Brobdinag (peopled by giants), and in the land of the Houyhnhnms (sophisticated talking horses who deplore the deformed, savage humans, whom they call "Yahoos"). Although not originally for children, the story has been adapted for children, animated, imitated, and made into film. It is an example of the enchanted journey, one of the most common of fantasy forms (although perhaps "enchantment" is not exactly the word Swift would use to describe his satiric work).

Among the famous journey fantasies for children are Lewis Carroll's *Alice's Adventures in Wonderland* and L. Frank Baum's *The Wonderful Wizard of Oz*. Both of these describe protagonists on journeys through strange lands. It's interesting that in both cases, the heroine finds herself in the strange land by accident—it was not a choice. Swedish author Selma Lagerlöf wrote *The Wonderful Adventures of Nils*, describing a young boy's exciting travels across Sweden on the back of a goose, during which he learns about his homeland and himself. As we see, journeys are also metaphors for character growth and development: Life itself is often referred to as a journey. This brings us to a related form, the epic fantasy.

Epic Fantasy

Inspired by the heroes' journeys from mythology and folklore, the epic fantasy is an elaborate adventure story in which a kingdom or society is threatened by some powerful evil force (a vile monster, a wicked sorcerer or witch, a bloodthirsty conqueror). Coming to the rescue is a brave and mighty hero or heroine, who, often with a band of worthy and stalwart companions, vanquishes the evil forces and restores peace and contentment to the people. Epic fantasies are usually quite serious, and the hero or heroine is fighting against enormous odds for lofty ideals—which is why the epic fantasy is often referred to as "high fantasy," and this is what makes it different from the enchanted journey of Alice, for example. (Although the term "low fantasy" is often applied fantasies that take place in our world—or partly in our world—it is, perhaps, a misleading and unfortunate term.)

The stories of epic fantasies, which have been wildly popular with children since the mid-twentieth century, often involve large numbers of characters and intricately woven plots, and it is not unusual for an epic fantasy to be published in a series of several books—three each in J. R. R. Tolkien's *Lord of the Rings* and Philip Pullman's *His Dark Materials*, five in Lloyd Alexander's *Chronicles of Prydain*, and seven each in C. S. Lewis' *Chronicles of Narnia* and J. K. Rowling's Harry Potter series. Many of these stories have as their models the great epics of the classical world—Homer's *Iliad* and *Odyssey*, and Virgil's *Aeneid*—and the medieval tales of King Arthur and his gallant knights. The settings tend to be vast; that is, they deal with realms and empires, not households or cities. The hero/ine is often called to the task—and typically, in the beginning, feels unequal to the challenge. Also the hero/ine is an outsider, an orphan, or someone who is dispossessed (Harry Potter, for example, or Lyra in *His Dark Materials*). The villain represents ultimate evil, possesses unimaginable (but not invincible) powers, and commands the loyalty of a great force. The odds seem overwhelming. A journey is almost always involved, in which the hero/ine encounters many dangerous adventures that are intended to prepare him or her for the ultimate battle. Invariably, a mysterious helper shows up just at the right time, or a gift has been given the hero/ine that will later prove invaluable. (Lyra's golden compass in *His Dark Materials* is a perfect example.) Almost always, near the conclusion, a great battle occurs—often a battle between the massed forces of good and evil. These fantasies take the reader into strange new worlds, and operate on the outer fringes of the imagination.

Epic fantasy cycles have become something of a modern phenomenon, the book market being flooded by series books for both young adult and adult readers—many are, indeed, what is termed crossover literature, appealing to readers of all ages. Of course, a popular series means handsome profits for both authors and publishers, and many find their way into films—even more profitable! Unfortunately, many are derivative—often harkening back to Tolkien in particular. But if they make reading popular in a world driven by visual media and digitization, perhaps that is an accomplishment in itself.

Miniature Fantasy

At nearly the opposite end of the spectrum from the epic fantasy is the miniature fantasy, the tale of miniaturized characters living their lives in diminutive circumstances. Children are captivated by the concept of smallness—they play with dollhouses and miniature railroads, keep little treasures in tiny boxes, and hide in small places. (See Griswold, 51–73.) Their own world is in many ways a miniature world of small dishes, clothes, and furniture. It is also interesting how many children's stories include small creatures—Snow White's seven dwarfs, Dorothy's Munchkins, Tolkien's hobbits, Stuart Little, and virtually all of Beatrix Potter's characters.

We turn again to Jonathan Swift's *Gulliver's Travels*, which was one of the first works to portray a miniature society. In the first adventure of this book, Gulliver finds himself shipwrecked and inadvertently embroiled in a war between Lilliput and Blefuscu, two nations of tiny people. In the second adventure, Gulliver finds himself in Brobdingnag, a land of giants where he is now the miniature figure. Swift's purpose throughout *Gulliver's Travels* is satirical, poking fun at petty human foibles.

As with many fantasy types, miniature fantasy has proven a vehicle for promoting a variety of serious ideas. In modern children's literature, we can point to Carol Kendall's *The Gammage Cup*, a tale about the struggles of the tiny people of the Minnipin society against their ancient enemies, the Mushroom People. As with the war between Lilliput and Blefuscu, this contains many features of the heroic fantasy, but on a small scale. As in Gulliver, some readers see strong social messages in *The Gammage Cup*—either a warning against the dangers of conformity or a defense of individualism.

But, for the most part, the miniature fantasy is simply an opportunity for children to indulge their fascination with tiny worlds. Mary Norton's beloved series beginning with *The Borrowers* portrays tiny people who live in the walls of houses and steal all those things that inexplicably go missing. In general, the miniature fantasy presents, as Griswold suggests, "alternatives to consensual notions of dimension and, consequently, adult notions of importance" (73). In other words, smallness in children's books is not mere "cuteness." It provides young readers with a provocative way of looking at reality, and one with which they may readily identify.

Time Slip Fantasy

In Charles Dickens' still popular *A Christmas Carol*, Ebenezer Scrooge is allowed to see Christmas past and Christmas future, experiences that cause him to give up his miserly ways. The time slip fantasy allows a character or characters (usually by some mysterious means) to travel backward (or forward) in time. However, unlike Scrooge, most time slip travelers become players, not simply observers, in the new world they inhabit. Mark Twain's *A Connecticut Yankee in King Arthur's Court* is an early example of time slip fantasy in which, as the title implies, a nineteenth-century American finds himself in ancient Britain at the time of King Arthur. The means of transport is seldom important (and would not make any sense anyway). And often a concern is that the intrusion by a character from another time period not be allowed to alter history (although this is rarely explained). Twain uses the device for comic effect. Modern examples of the time-slip fantasy include Philippa Pearce's *Tom's Midnight Garden,* which relates a very serious story of a boy who is nightly being transported back a half century, where he befriends children who once lived in the house where he is staying. Penelope Farmer's *Charlotte Sometimes* is another modern example, but this time two characters, each from a different time period forty years apart, change places each night, their complete story and connection being revealed at the novel's end, making a wonderful mystery. Both Pearce and Farmer use the time slip device to explore human relationships and comment on the human condition from varying points of view.

Supernatural and Horror Fantasy

The supernatural in fantasy generally comes in the form of ghosts, vampires, zombies, and other supernatural apparitions when they intersect with our world. Although uncommon in earlier children's literature, ghost stories have become perennial favorites since the mid-twentieth century. Robert Bright's *Georgie and the Robbers* is a picture book about a shy ghost, and the cartoon figure Casper the Friendly Ghost (also a popular film) has a long history. But older children generally prefer more threatening ghosts; indeed, the more horrifying and gruesome the story, the better some children seem to like it. Many people have deep within them something of the ambulance chaser. Nevertheless, the most thrilling tales of the supernatural are not those that dramatize and glamorize the blood and horror, but those that leave something for our imaginations. Penelope Lively's *The Ghost of Thomas Kempe* is a popular, well-told example of a modern ghost story. Devoid of any grisly horror, Lively's novel explores the potential problems that a ghost from an earlier time might have in the modern world. The second volume of Terry Pratchett's Johnny Maxwell trilogy, *Johnny and the Dead*, is about a boy who communicates with dead spirits in a cemetery. Neil Gaimon's popular *Coraline*, in which a young girl accidentally discovers an alternate universe where she has a creepy "other mother" and "other father," is both haunting and funny.

Vampires have been a staple of modern adult literature since the nineteenth century, Bram Stoker's *Dracula* being the most famous of the early examples of this genre (although stories of the undead have been circulating since ancient times). Aside from some cartoon depictions, vampires have been relatively rare in children's literature until fairly recently. Stephanie Meyer's incredibly successful vampire series, beginning with *Twilight* in 2005, demonstrates the power of this type of fantasy among teenagers. In 2009, Meyer broke J. K. Rowling's record on the bestseller list. As often happens with writers who achieve enormous popularity, she has also received much criticism. Among the most frequent complaints is that the books are badly written, and that the author is anti-feminist. However, their appeal is undeniable and relates, according to some, to the natural human desire for immortality. Additionally, the vampire has always been associated with sexuality and seduction, which, whether we like to admit it or not, are preoccupations of the teenage psyche—and this may help account for the vampire's enduring popularity.

One of the latest crazes in children's books is the zombie book. The zombie, a corpse who has risen from the grave, is believed to be a New World phenomenon— the term "zombie" actually comes from Haiti, and some zombie tales are traced to South America. Mary Shelley's *Frankenstein* (1818) is not technically about a zombie, but the idea is the same—she simply provides a scientific explanation for a corpse coming to life, whereas the zombie is a corpse brought to life through magic. Zombies play into the bizarre human fascination with terror. We like to be scared—it's a rite of passage. And since George Romero's 1968 horror film *Night of the Living Dead*, zombies have become one of our most compelling media monsters. So we should not be surprised to see that zombies have at last reached the middle-school reader. In 2010, John Kloepfer's *The Zombie Chasers* appeared, and sequels have emerged at regular intervals ever since. Like all good zombie stories, these books are not for the faint of heart or queasy of stomach.

Science Fiction

Mary Shelley's *Frankenstein* is often credited with being the first true work of science fiction, although, it can just as easily be classified as horror fiction. *Frankenstein* is set in the real world, and the fantasy element is not presented as supernatural, but as a scientific achievement. This is the distinction between science fiction and all other fantasy. Science fiction presents the extraordinary as the result of science—not magic. This thinking became possible with the emergence of scientific inquiry, particularly in the seventeenth century, opening the way for the Industrial Revolution and the rise of the machine.

Jules Verne, famous for his books such as *From the Earth to the Moon* (1865) (see Figure 8.6) and *Twenty Thousand Leagues Under the Sea* (1870), is often called the "Father of Science Fiction." He is certainly the most widely known author of science fiction, and is the second most-translated author in the world, after mystery writer Agatha Christie. Science fiction is often termed speculative

FIGURE 8.6 ■ This famous image of the Man in the Moon being struck in the eye by a rocket ship from Earth is a still taken from the 1902 movie "A Trip to the Moon," based on Jules Verne's popular *From the Earth to the Moon*.

fiction, since writers speculate on what would happen if . . . if we could travel in outer space, if were invaded by extraterrestrial beings, if we could travel to the past or to the future. The first great English author of science fiction was H. G. Wells, and his science fictions were quite versatile. Wells's *The Time Machine* (1895) explores the possibility of travel through time, and *The Invisible Man* (1897) treats the intriguing possibilities of what would happen if we could make ourselves invisible. *The War of the Worlds* (1897) describes an invasion from outer space (from Mars, specifically). Although these are all for adults, their appeal reaches to the young adult reader as well. All of them have been made into films.

In children's books, one of the most popular science fiction themes is space travel. Eleanor Cameron's much-loved *The Wonderful Flight to the Mushroom Planet*, published in 1954, is a charming example of science fiction for middle-school readers, depicting two boys building a space ship and ultimately saving a planet (inhabited by little green people) in distress. Robert Heinlein, one of the most notable science-fiction writers of the twentieth century, also wrote books for young readers. His *Have Space Suit—Will Travel* is about a teenager who embarks on a series of adventures in outer space. Terry Pratchett's *Only You Can Save Mankind*, the first in his Johnny Maxwell series, describes the adventures of a boy who suddenly finds himself inside the computer game he was playing. Orson Scott Card's *Ender's Game*, about an alien invasion of Earth, is enormously popular despite (or because of) its violence (it's on the U.S. Marine Corps Professional Reading List).

Many works of science fiction deal with ethical problems facing humanity as science and technology outpace our development as human beings. Whether technological discoveries will be used for humanity's benefit or its destruction frequently becomes a theme of science fiction. Madeleine L'Engle, best known for *A Wrinkle in Time*, addresses such issues in her science fiction. One writer of science fiction for young people, Sylvia Engdahl, prefers to call her work "space fantasy" because she is little concerned with technology or science. Her stories (*Enchantress from the Stars*, *The Far Side of Evil*, and others) are set in the distant future and on distant planets. The settings become merely the backdrop for her tales about the development of civilization and its sociological and psychological implications. It is even worth considering whether those epic works set in "galaxies far, far away" or in alternative universes are really science fiction at all. The *Star Wars* film epics come to mind. To what extent are these science fiction, and to what extent are they epic fantasy? With heroic figures facing tremendous odds and civilizations at stake, aren't these simply modern-day versions of Homer's *Iliad* or Virgil's *Aeneid*? When it comes down to it, science fiction is simply fantasy that replaces magic with technology. As one critic notes: "How different, after all, is a wizard with a magic wand from a scientist with a microminiaturized matter-transformer? The reader does not know how either gadget works" (Roberts, 90). In the end, science fiction, whether it's set on distant planets in some unknown time or on our own Earth today, presents us with new paradigms, and forces us to adopt new ways of thinking. Because of this, science fiction is also termed, quite appropriately, speculative fiction.

Dystopias

Lois Lowry's *The Giver* offers a bleak picture of a future civilization that has attempted to curb all emotions (interestingly, the ancient Greek philosopher Plato recommended something like this in his treatise, *Republic*). Lowry's story portrays a chilling society through the eyes of its inhabitants—and we, the readers, must become the judges. The result can be unsettling, but it is also intensely thought provoking. *The Giver* is an example of an increasingly popular trend in fantasy fiction—the dystopia. Whereas a utopia portrays an ideal world, a dystopia depicts the opposite—a world where evil, corruption, injustice, poverty, and inhumanity prevail. Lowry shows a world where feelings, emotions, and sentiments are suppressed and human beings become little more than automatons unable to feel love, hate, joy, or sorrow.

Once again we turn to Jonathan Swift as a literary forebear—*Gulliver's Travels*, its wild fantasy and humor aside, is fundamentally a dystopia. Swift's story is, in fact, a thinly disguised condemnation of the world he lived in—its foolishness, pettiness, cruelty, and hypocrisy (see Figure 8.7). Perhaps all societies should have a Swift to remind us when we are being foolish, lazy, careless, or cruel. Holding a mirror up to ourselves is perhaps the great purpose of dystopian literature.

FIGURE 8.7 ■ This illustration is from an early twentieth-century edition of Swift's *Gulliver's Travels*. It depicts Gulliver awaking in the land of Lilliput, where he appears a giant among the tiny (and terrified) inhabitants.

Several popular modern writers have taken to dystopian fiction. Suzanne Collins (the *Hunger Games* trilogy) depicts a society dominated by crass commercialism, Meg Rosoff describes the horrors of a future world war (*How I Live Now*), and James Dashner presents an unsettling view of the near-distant future (*The Maze Runner*). All dystopias are thinly veiled versions of our own world or dire predictions of our world's future if we don't change our ways. In other words, they are wake-up calls.

Summary

Fantasy, like all other literature, changes with the tastes of a culture. Victorian fantasy—Lewis Carroll's *Alice* books excepted—typically described some magical element intruding on the real world resulting in some heavy-handed moral message. The early twentieth century saw the rise of escapist fantasy—animal fantasies, toy and doll fantasies, and magical stories for younger readers—all perhaps in reaction to the upheaval caused by two world wars and the Great Depression. And the fantasies of J. R. R. Tolkien and C. S. Lewis celebrated the triumph of good over evil in dramatic confrontations. Perhaps the most significant change in fantasy fiction is found in its growing audience. From very young children to YA and adult audiences, fantasy has become wildly popular. We need only mention such film series as *Star Wars, The Lord of the Rings,* or *Harry Potter* as evidence. A recent fantasy website listed over fifty categories of fantasy fiction—including Weird West Fantasy, Magical Girl Fantasy, Prehistoric Fantasy, and Steampunk Fantasy. It is safe to say that, as a genre, fantasy is certainly alive—it remains to be seen how well it is.

At its best, fantasy encourages us to examine complex ideas on a symbolic level. Fantasy is perfectly suited to the thoughtful exploration of philosophical issues at a level that can be understood and appreciated by young readers. Also, it deliberately challenges our perceptions of reality, and forces us to explore new, uncharted realms of thought. Unburdened by the conventions and prejudices of our own world, fantasy is ideally suited to present difficult social, political, and philosophical issues in an entirely new light. Many fantasies require that readers exercise patience and concentration to enter and embrace the writer's world. It is, after all, easier to read about the familiar and the everyday. But the readers who accept the challenge find great riches awaiting them.

The great psychologist Carl Gustav Jung wrote this of the importance of fantasy and its impact on the imagination and our lives:

> *The dynamic principle of fantasy is play, which belongs also to the child, and as such it appears to be inconsistent with the principle of serious work. But without this playing with fantasy no creative work has ever yet come to birth. The debt we owe to the play of the imagination is incalculable.* (82)

One critic has noted that "reading fantasy is not so much an escape *from* something as a liberation *into* something, into openness and possibility and coherence" and that we as readers get perspective on our world "by exploring a strange fictional place and learning how its pieces fit together" (O'Keefe, 11–12). At its best, fantasy is a thought-provoking genre that, in a wondrous way, can help us see our own world more clearly.

Works Cited

Ganea, Patricia A., Caitlin F. Canfield, Kadria Simons-Ghafaril, and Tommy Chou. "Do Cavies Talk? The Effect of Anthropomorphic Picture Books on Children's Knowledge about Animals." *Frontiers in Psychology* (10 April 2014). journalfrontiersin doi10.3389/fpsyg.2014.00283.

Griswold, Jerry. *Feeling Like a Kid: Childhood and Children's Literature*. Baltimore: Johns Hopkins University Press, 2006.

Jung, Carl Gustav, *Psychological Types*. New York: Harcourt, Brace, 1923.

Manlove, Colin. *From Alice to Harry Potter: Children's Fantasy in England*. Christchurch, New Zealand: Cyber editions, 2003.

O'Keefe, Deborah. *Readers in Wonderland: The Liberating Worlds of Fantasy Fiction*. New York: Continuum, 2003.

Roberts, Thomas J. "Science Fiction and the Adolescent." *Children's Literature: The Great Excluded* 2 (1973): 87–91.

Snyder, Zilpha Keatley. "Afterword." *Tom's Midnight Garden* by Philippa Pearce. New York: Dell, 1986: 230–232.

Recommended Resources

Aiken, Joan. "On Imagination." *The Horn Book* (November/December 1984): 735–741.

Alexander, Lloyd. "High Fantasy and Heroic Romance." *Horn Book Magazine* 47, 6 (December 1971): 577–584.

Attebery, Brian. *The Fantasy Tradition in American Literature: From Irving to Le Guin*. Bloomington: Indiana University Press, 1980.

Babbitt, Natalie. "Fantasy and the Classic Hero." *School Library Journal* (October 1987): 25–29.

Brennan, Geráldine, Kevin McCarron, and Kimberly Reynolds. *Frightening Fiction*. New York: Continuum, 2001.

Cameron, Eleanor. *The Green and Burning Tree*. Boston: Little, Brown, 1969.

Cooper, Susan. *Dreams and Wishes: Essays on Writing for Children*. New York: McElderry, 1996.

Dickinson, Peter. "Fantasy: The Need for Realism." *Children's Literature in Education* 17, 1 (1986): 39–51.

Egoff, Sheila. *Worlds Within: Children's Fantasy from the Middle Ages to Today*. Chicago: American Library Association, 1988.

Engdahl, Sylvia. "The Changing Role of Science Fiction in Children's Literature." *Horn Book Magazine* 47, 5 (October 1971): 449–455.

Hume, Kathryn. *Fantasy and Mimesis*. New York and London: Methuen, 1984.

Kuznets, Lois. *When Toys Come Alive: Narratives of Animations, Metamorphosis and Development*. New Haven, CT: Yale University Press, 1994.

Le Guin, Ursula. *The Language of the Night*. Ed. Susan Wood. New York: G. P. Putnam's Sons, 1979.

Lewis, C. S. "Three Ways of Writing for Children." *Horn Book Magazine* 39, 5 (October 1963): 459–469.

Marcus, Leonard E., ed. *The Wand in the Word: Conversations with Writers of Fantasy*. New York: Candlewick, 2006.

Marcus, Leonard S. "Picture Book Animals: How Natural a History?" *The Lion and the Unicorn* 7/8 (1983/1984): 127–139.

Martin, Philip. *A Guide to Fantasy Literature: Thoughts on Stories of Wonder and Enchantment*. Milwaukee, WI: Crickhollow Books, 2009.

Mendlesohn, Farah. *Rhetorics of Fantasy*. Middletown, CT: Wesleyan University Press, 2008.

Raynor, Mary. "Some Thoughts on Animals in Children's Books." *Signal* 29 (May 1979): 81–87.

Sale, Roger. *Fairy Tales and After: From Snow White to E. B. White*. Cambridge, MA: Harvard University Press, 1978.

Singer, Jerome. "Fantasy: The Foundation of Serenity." *Psychology Today* (July 1976): 33–37.

Smith, Karen Patricia. *The Fabulous Realm*. Lanham, MD: Scarecrow, 1993.

Sullivan, C. W. *Science Fiction for Young Readers*. New York: Greenwood, 1993.

Tolkien, J. R. R. *Tree and Leaf*. Boston: Houghton Mifflin, 1965.

Ende, Michael. *The Neverending Story*. 1979. Trans. Ralph Mannheim. New York: Doubleday, 1983.
- A fantasy story within a story, originally in German, about saving the world and winning a princess.

Field, Rachel. *Hitty, Her First Hundred Years*. New York: Macmillan, 1929.
- A doll's account of her adventures through an existence spanning a century.

Fleischman, Sid. *The Whipping Boy*. New York: Morrow, 1986.
- The adventures of a prince and his "whipping boy," who decide to run off together and grow up along the way.

Gaiman, Neil. *Coraline*. London: Bloomsbury, 2002.
- A horror story about a girl who finds herself trapped in a sinister alternate world.

Garner, Alan. *The Weirdstone of Brisingham*. London: Collins, 1960.
- A heroic fantasy that draws on Norse and Celtic lore, complete with wizards, elves, goblins, and more.

Gidwitz, Adam. *The Inquisitor's Tale, or, The Three Magical Children and Their Holy Dog*. New York: Dutton, 2016.
- Set in medieval France and told through multiple narrators, this tale of the struggle between good and evil is both comical and thrilling.

—. *A Tale Dark and Grimm*. New York: Dutton, 2010. A sometimes grisly, but always hilarious, retelling of the tales of the Brothers Grimm; the first of a trilogy, including *In a Glass Grimmly* (2012), and *The Grimm Conclusion* (2013).

Goldman, William. *The Princess Bride*. New York: Harcourt, 1973.
- A fairy tale spoof with all the usual suspects.

Grahame, Kenneth. *The Wind in the Willows*. 1908. Several modern editions.
- The leisurely story of several animals living the good life in the Edwardian English countryside.

Heinlein, Robert. *Have Space Suit—Will Travel*. New York: Scribner's, 1958.
- Adventures in outer space from a celebrated science-fiction author.

Hoban, Russell. *The Mouse and His Child*. New York: Harper, 1967.
- The story of two toy mice joined at the hands who eventually are discarded, pursued by a villainous rat, and long to become self-winding.

Jacques, Brian. *Redwall*. New York: Philomel, 1987.
- The first of a popular series of heroic fantasies (22 in all) featuring animals in the world of Redwall, which resembles a mythical England.

Jansson, Tove. *Comet in Moominland*. 1946. Trans. Elizabeth Portch. New York: Farrar, Straus & Giroux, 1990.
- The first of a series of magical tales about the wondrous Moomins and their eccentric friends, along with *Finn Family Moomintroll* (1948), *The Exploits of Moominpappa* (1950), *Moominsummer Madness* (1954), *Moominland Midwinter* (1957), *Moominpappa at Sea* (1965), and *Moominvalley in November* (1970).

Jarrell, Randall. *The Bat-Poet*. New York: Macmillan, 1964.
- The fable of a bat who can't sleep during the day and struggles to come to terms with his own individuality with the help of poetry.

Jones, Diana Wynne. *Howl's Moving Castle*. London: Metheun, 1986.
- A spoof on fairy tales in which a young girl boards a strange moving castle to find a way to remove a curse from herself.

Juster, Norton. *The Phantom Tollbooth*. New York: Random, 1961.
- The story of a boy whose magic toll booth transports him to the Kingdom of Wisdom.

Kendall, Carol. *The Gammage Cup*. New York: Harcourt, 1959.
- The tale of a heroic battle waged in a land of miniature peoples.

King-Smith, Dick. *Babe, the Gallant Pig*. New York: Random House, 1983.
- The charming story of a pig who learns to herd sheep. Made into a popular film.

Kipling, Rudyard. *The Jungle Book*. 1894. Several modern editions.
- Talking animal fables set in India, followed by *The Second Jungle Book*.

_____. *Just So Stories*. 1902. Illus. Barry Moser. New York: Morrow, 1996.
- Classic animal fables set in India.

Kloepfer, John. *The Zombie Chasers*. Illus. Steve Wolfhard. New York: HarperCollins, 2010.
- The first of a popular series for middle-school readers.

Lagerlöf, Selma. *The Wonderful Adventures of Nils*. 1906/1907. Various modern editions.
- A classic Swedish story of a boy journeying across Sweden on the back of a goose.

Lawson, Robert. *Rabbit Hill*. New York: Viking, 1944.
- A fable about the necessity of humans and animals living together.

L'Engle, Madeleine. *A Wrinkle in Time*. New York: Farrar, Straus & Giroux, 1962.
- A science-fiction tale of children traveling through time and space. The first of a series of five books, including *A Wind in the Door* (1973), *A Swiftly Tilting Planet* (1978), *Many Waters* (1986), and *An Acceptable Time* (1989).

Le Guin, Ursula. *A Wizard of Earthsea*. Boston: Houghton Mifflin, 1968.
- Adventures in a far-off world governed by wizards. The first of the Earthsea series, including *The Tombs of Atuan* (1971), *The Farthest Shore* (1972), *Tehanu* (1990), and *Other Wind* (2001).

Levine, Gail Carson. *Ella Enchanted*. New York: Harper Trophy, 1997.
- A retelling of the "Cinderella" story, with the addition of a multitude of fantasy characters.

Lewis, C. S. *The Lion, the Witch, and the Wardrobe*. New York: HarperCollins, 1950.
- The adventures of English children who find themselves in the magical world of Narnia. The first of the Chronicles of Narnia series, including *Prince Caspian* (1951), *The Voyage of the Dawn Treader* (1952), *The Silver Chair* (1953), *The Horse and His Boy* (1954), *The Magician's Nephew* (1955), and *The Last Battle* (1956).

Lin, Grace. *The Starry River of the Sky*. New York: Little, Brown, 2012.
- The equally enchanting companion to *Where the Mountain Meets the Moon*, but with an earlier setting. The protagonist is a young boy who longs to find a way to restore the missing moon to the sky.

Lindgren, Astrid. *Pippi Longstocking*. New York: Viking, 1950.
- The story of an extraordinary girl living in a very ordinary town—which she soon changes.

_____. *Where the Mountain Meets the Moon*. New York: Little, Brown, 2009.
- A magical tale set in China about a young girl who sets off on a journey to find happiness for her parents, beautifully interwoven with traditional Chinese folktales.

Lively, Penelope. *The Ghost of Thomas Kempe*. Illus. Antony Maitland. New York: Dutton, 1973.
- The story of an English house haunted by a seventeenth-century poltergeist.

Lobel, Arnold. *Frog and Toad Are Friends*. New York: Harper, 1970.
- A series of short stories about inseparable friends, followed by a sequel, *Frog and Toad Together* (1972). Great for early readers.

Lofting, Hugh. *The Story of Dr. Dolittle*. New York: Stokes, 1920.
- A popular magical story of a doctor who learns to speak the languages of the animals. The first of a series of 12 books.

Lowry, Lois. *The Giver*. Boston: Houghton Mifflin, 1993.
- A chilling tale of life in the future. The first in a series, including *Gathering Blue* (2000), *The Messenger* (2004), and *Son* (2012).

McCaffrey, Anne. *Dragonflight*. New York: Ballantyne, 1968.
- Adventures set in the mythical pre-industrial world. The first of the series The Dragonriders of Pern, continued by McCaffrey's son, Todd McCaffrey.

McKinley, Robin. *The Hero and the Crown*. New York: Greenwillow, 1985.
- A heroic fantasy, one of the earliest to feature a female protagonist.

Miéville, China. *Un Lun Dun*. New York: Macmillan, 2007.
- An unusual tale of heroines overcoming evil in a wacky alternate world.

Milne, A. A. *Winnie-the-Pooh*. 1926. Illus. Ernest Shepard. New York: Dutton, 1961.
- A story of several endearing toy animals encountering comical adventures.

Nesbit, E. *Five Children and It*. London: Unwin, 1902.
- The story of five children who discover an ancient fairy, the Psammead, who can grant wishes. The first of the Psammead trilogy, including *The Phoenix and the Carpet* (1904) and *The Story of the Amulet* (1906).

Ness, Patrick. *The Knife of Never Letting Go*. New York: Candlewick, 2009.
- The first of the Chaos Walking dystopian trilogy, including *The Ask and the Answer* (2010) and *Monsters of Men* (2011).

_____. *A Monster Calls (Inspired by an Idea by Siobhan Dowd)*. Illus. Jim Kay. New York: Candlewick, 2011.
- A powerfully told and dramatically illustrated story of a boy dealing with his mother's terminal illness and a monster that comes at night to tell him stories.

Nicholson, William. *The Wind Singer*. New York: Hyperion, 2000.
- A heroic adventure set in an alternate world. The first of the Windon Fire trilogy, along with *Slaves of the Mastery* (2001) and *Firesong* (2002).

Nix, Garth. *Mister Monday*. New York: Scholastic, 2003.
- The story of a young boy who finds himself master of the universe in this first of seven books in the Keys to the Kingdom series, each of which focuses on one of the seven deadly sins.

Norton, Mary. *The Borrowers*. New York: Harcourt, 1953.
- The first book in a series about tiny people who live in the walls and floorboards of our houses.

O'Brien, Robert. *Mrs. Frisby and the Rats of NIMH*. New York: Atheneum, 1971.
- The story of escaped laboratory rats helping a widowed field mouse relocate her home, where we learn about the rats' lab experiences.

Parish, Peggy. *Amelia Bedelia*. New York: Harper, 1963.
- The first of a series about a hapless housemaid who takes everything too literally.

Pearce, Philippa. *Tom's Midnight Garden*. New York: Dell, 1986.
- The story of a boy who accidentally finds a way to travel back in time.

Pratchett, Terry. *Only You Can Save Mankind.* London: Doubleday, 1992.
- The story of a boy who finds himself inside a computer game, and the adventures that ensue. The first of the Johnny Maxwell trilogy, along with *Johnny and the Dead* (1993) and *Johnny and the Bomb* (1996).

Pullman, Philip. *The Golden Compass.* New York: Knopf, 1996.
- Originally published as *Northern Lights* in the United Kingdom, the epic adventures of a young girl and boy in a parallel world. The first of the His Dark Materials trilogy, along with *The Subtle Knife* (1997) and *The Amber Spyglass* (2000).

Reid Banks, Lynn. *The Indian in the Cupboard.* New York: Doubleday, 1981.
- The story of a magic cupboard that brings to life tiny toy creatures who become involved in a variety of adventures.

Riordan, Rick. *The Lightning Thief.* New York: Miramax, 2005.
- The first book of his popular *Percy Jackson & the Olympians* series, which has rekindled an interest in classical mythology among young readers.

____. *The Lost Hero.* New York: Disney Hyperion, 2010.
- The first book of Riordan's second series, *Heroes of Olympus,* which embraces both Greek and Roman mythology.

Rosoff, Meg. *How I Live Now.* New York: Penguin, 2004.
- A book about a third world war and its aftermath in the near future.

Rowling, J. K. *Harry Potter and the Philosopher's Stone.* London: Bloomsbury, 1997.
- The wildly popular adventures of an English orphan studying to become a wizard, titled *Harry Potter and the Sorcerer's Stone* in the U.S. The first of a series, along with *Harry Potter and the Chamber of Secrets* (1998), *Harry Potter and the Prisoner of Azkaban* (1999), *Harry Potter and the Goblet of Fire* (2000), *Harry Potter and the Order of the Phoenix* (2003), *Harry Potter and the Half-Blood Prince* (2005), and *Harry Potter and the Deathly Hallows* (2007).

Selden, George. *The Cricket in Times Square.* Illus. Garth Williams. New York: Farrar, Straus & Giroux, 1960.
- The adventures of a cricket from Connecticut attempting to make a go of it in New York City.

Sharp, Margery. *The Rescuers.* Boston: Little, Brown, 1959.
- A book about a beautiful and pampered mouse, Miss Bianca, who leads a daring rescue of an imprisoned poet. Also an animated film.

Snow, Alan. *Here Be Monsters!* New York: Atheneum, 2006.
- A darkly humorous fantasy in the vein of Roald Dahl in which a young boy has run afoul of some dastardly characters who want to destroy him and the entire town.

Steig, William. *Abel's Island.* New York: Farrar, Straus & Giroux, 1976.
- A story of a mouse stranded on a deserted island who must learn to survive.

____. *Dominic.* New York: Farrar, Straus & Giroux, 1972.
- A story about a canine free spirit who sets off for a life of adventure—and finds it.

Thomas, Shelley Moore. *Good Night, Good Knight.* Illus. Jennifer Plecar. New York: Dutton, 2000.
- The first of a series of enchanting tales about a knight and his dragon friends.

Tolkien, J. R. R. *The Hobbit.* 1937. New York: Houghton Mifflin, Various editions.
- The prequel to the Lord of the Rings series is accessible to younger readers, whereas the series itself, which includes *The Fellowship of the Ring* (1954), *The Two Towers* (1955), and *The Return of the King* (1955), is for older readers.

Travers, P. L. *Mary Poppins*. New York: Harcourt, 1934.
  • The tale of an acerbic nanny who brings order and joy to a stuffy London family.

Verne, Jules. *Twenty Thousand Leagues Under the Sea*. 1864. New York: Penguin, 1987.
  • A classic story of undersea adventures from the father of science fiction.

Wells, H. G. *The Time Machine*. 1895. New York: Bantam, 1982.
  • One of the earliest and best time-travel stories.

_____. *The War of the Worlds*. 1898. New York: Putnam, 1978.
  • One of the first novels about an invasion of Earth from outer space.

White, E. B. *Charlotte's Web*. New York: Harper, 1952.
  • A classic tale of the friendship between a pig and a spider. Everyone should read this.

Williams, Margery. *The Velveteen Rabbit*. 1922. Illus. Michael Hague. New York: Holt, Rinehart & Winston, 1983.
  • The story of a stuffed rabbit who longs to become a real animal—and, of course, does.

Yolen, Jane. *Dragon's Blood*. New York: Delacorte, 1982.
  • A futuristic story featuring a species of dragons. The first in the Pit Dragon Chronicles, along with *Heart's Blood* (1984), *A Sending of Dragons* (1987), and *Dragon's Heart* (2009).

Realistic Fiction

The Days of Our Lives

> *"Truth is stranger than fiction, but it is because Fiction is obliged to stick to possibilities; Truth isn't."*
>
> –Mark Twain, *Following the Equator: A Journey Around the World* (1897)

Introduction

Realistic fiction attempts to portray society as it is (or as it was in the case of historical realism). A realistic novelist's goal is to make the characters and situations true to life—everything is described in the realm of possibility. Of course, some writers portray the world as a bit rosier than it probably is, whereas other writers portray it as far darker than we hope it is. In any case, the writer of realistic fiction attempts to recreate real-life situations, with real-life characters living in our world. When a writer re-creates an earlier time period, we call it *historical realism*, and when a writer describes his or her own time period, we call it *contemporary realism*.

But, as Mark Twain's comment in the epigraph suggests, realistic fiction, unlike life, is constrained by an obligation to seem plausible. Life is full of coincidences, such as Presidents John Adams and Thomas Jefferson both dying on July 4, 1826, exactly 50 years after they signed the Declaration of Independence. Or what about the scientific coincidence that the sun is 400 times larger than our moon, and 400 times farther away from the Earth than the moon is (which makes a total eclipse possible)? If we made up stuff like this in a novel, readers might scoff, claiming it was far-fetched. In fiction, coincidences are usually seen as too convenient, too silly, or too ridiculous. The goal of the realistic novelist is to create a story that seems real, to avoid any suggestion of artificiality.

In this chapter, we will examine the wide range found in realistic stories. For example, some fictional stories are set in the past (that is, in a time distinctly earlier than when the novel was written). Other fictional stories are set in a time contemporary with its writing (that is, in the writer's present). Of necessity, these two types of fiction have different needs—and we will be looking at them. We will then consider the many subjects we find in realistic fiction—regardless of whether it is historical or contemporary. These include everything from family relationships to friendships to social and cultural issues—the possibilities are overwhelming.

Historical Realism

Definition

In the mid-nineteenth century, Alessandro Manzoni pointed out that the difference between a historian and a historical novelist is that the historian must deal with the "bare bones of history," whereas a historical novelist's job is "to put the flesh back on the skeleton that is history" (67–68). The "flesh" he is referring to is the fictional story that provides the intimate focus framed by the wider historical events in the novel. Think of Margaret Mitchell's story of Scarlett O'Hara and Rhett Butler against the background of the Civil War in *Gone with the Wind*. The historical novel has two faces: It is part history and part fabrication. Most readers of historical fiction like to feel that the history they are reading about is accurate, even if the story is fiction (in other words, in *Gone with the Wind*, the South is still going to lose the war). At the same time, the writer's imagination has to give us an interesting story with engaging characters we want to get to know.

Although historical fiction has been around as long as there have been people to tell about the past, it was the Scottish novelist Sir Walter Scott (1771–1832) who brought it to prominence in English. His *Waverley* (published in 1814), about the Scottish rebellion against the English in 1745, and *Ivanhoe* (1819), a romantic tale of the Middle Ages, were wildly popular. Scott's books are for adults, but very quickly historical realism became popular with young readers, who were drawn by the exotic settings, colorful adventures, and heroic figures of the past. The later nineteenth century produced writers such as Robert Louis Stevenson (*The Black Arrow*, 1888) and Howard Pyle (*Otto of the Silver Hand*, 1888, see Figure 9.1), who specialized in historical fiction for young readers.

But, you might ask, don't all realistic novels eventually become historical fiction as they age? What about Louisa May Alcott's *Little Women*, for example, which is set in the 1860s? Is it historical fiction now? Actually, no. Alcott published the book in two volumes in 1868 and 1869—so it was set in what were then contemporary times. Alcott has no need to explain the social customs and mores of nineteenth-century New England; her readers would already have known about them. Nor is her interest in historical personages or events. Here is where historical

FIGURE 9.1 ■ This illustration is by Howard Pyle for his historical novel *Otto of the Silver Hand*, an adventure romance set in the European Middle Ages.

realism differs from contemporary realism. In historical realism, the writer tries to reconstruct an accurate picture of a bygone era, usually an era at least one generation (or about 25 to 30 years) prior to its writing. And a central feature of the historical novel is that it conveys a portrait of an earlier time—its politics, customs, and beliefs. The best historical novel is one that immerses us into the historical period and lets us feel what it was like to live back then.

Historical Accuracy

The term "costume drama" is often used to describe the visual media productions—movies and television dramas, particularly—that have historical settings, but little else that is authentic. In other words, the characters seem to be modern people wearing the garb of ancient Rome, the Middle Ages or colonial America. The stories themselves may be interesting, exciting, moving—and all that is good. But the problem arises when audiences are given a distorted idea of the historical period. If our purpose for reading a piece of historical fiction is to find out something about the historical period, then we ought to insist on reasonable historical accuracy.

In the award-winning film *Braveheart* (1995), the Scottish hero, William Wallace (played by Mel Gibson), is depicted in a sexual liaison with Isabella, Princess of Wales, daughter-in-law of his nemesis, King Edward I (this is admittedly not a film for young children!). As a result, Isabella becomes pregnant and their child eventually becomes king of England. This makes for excellent dramatic irony, but it is all pure nonsense. The real Isabella would have been about 10 years old at the time of Wallace's death, and she never met him. So, the question is, when working with historical fiction, how much should a storyteller bend the facts for dramatic purposes?

There are ways to present historical incidents in fiction without compromising either history or good storytelling. Christopher Paul Curtis's *The Watsons Go to Birmingham—1963*, which was published in 1995, creates a fictional African-American family who takes a family vacation to Alabama at the same time as the bombing of the 16th Street Baptist Church, which killed four innocent children who were preparing for Sunday school, a tragedy that fueled the Civil Rights movement of the 1960s. The fictional characters become observers and through their eyes we witness this heinous event. Or take Lois Lowry's *Number the Stars* (1989), a story set during the Nazi occupation of Denmark in World War II. The Nazi soldiers are rounding up the Danish Jews to send them off to the concentration camps, which would almost certainly lead to their deaths. With fictional characters, we are given a fact-based account of how the Danish people, risking great personal peril, secretly managed to get some 8,000 Danish Jews (virtually all the Jews in the kingdom) safely away to neutral Sweden. So, although the characters are fictional, the story itself is solidly based on fact. The truth can be conveyed quite effectively through fictional characters without the need to fabricate history—it is usually interesting enough in its own right.

Historical Authenticity

Authenticity refers to the sense of reality we feel when reading fiction—whether contemporary or historical. One way to capture the authenticity of a historical period is through the accumulation of specific details. Karen Hesse's *Out of the Dust* is written as the journal of a young girl struggling in the Oklahoma Dust Bowl during the worst of the Depression in the mid-1930s. The journal describes the relentless sandstorms and hardships the people had to endure—wetting sheets and blankets to place over windows and doors to absorb the blowing sand or stringing up ropes so people could find their way from house to barn in the blinding storms. That the diary is actually written in free verse might seem odd at first, but it works because it effectively conveys the unsettling emotional state of the protagonist. And her feelings reveal both the courage and the desperation of the people struggling to survive under these dreadful conditions.

Another way a writer can evoke the feeling of the past is through authentic dialogue. We know that nineteenth-century Americans did not speak the same way that Americans of today speak. (For instance, teenagers of the 1980s did not "text" anybody, no one knew what Twitter or Facebook was, and no one got "unfriended.") The following brief passage from Irene Hunt's Civil War story *Across Five Aprils* shows how the author uses the language of the period to make the setting and characters more authentic:

> *The young man got to his feet grinning. "Sure, Red, glad to oblige. Hear you been blowin' off at the mouth at some of the cracker-barrel heroes agin."*
>
> *Milton shrugged. "Word gets around fast."*
>
> *"Ben Harris was in fer a minute." The young man shook his head. "You jest ain't goin' to be happy till you git dressed up in tar and feathers, are you, Red?"* (78)

The dialect is that of uneducated rural Americans in the 1860s. The passage refers, of course, to the nineteenth-century practice of literally covering victims with tar and feathers as a form of public chastisement. Some readers find dialect difficult to read, at least at first. But if we are content to relax and enjoy its oddities, we may discover the true flavor of a time and place.

Occasionally, historical fiction is guilty of using an *anachronism*—that is, something that is out of place in the time period—a silly example would be George Washington talking on a cell phone with his officers. This might make good comedy, but it is poor historical fiction. A good historical novelist is also a good historical researcher. Along with material goods, attitudes can be anachronistic. A possible example of an anachronism is found in Avi's *True Confessions of Charlotte Doyle*, a Newbery Honor book. It is the story of a 13-year-old girl sailing to America in 1832. On the voyage, she outmaneuvers the ship's wicked captain and ultimately replaces him at the helm. Anne Scott MacLeod, although admitting the story is a "fine vicarious adventure story," calls it also "preposterous," objecting not only to the age of the protagonist but to her gender in the context of nineteenth-century chauvinism (see MacLeod 29–31).

Historical fiction can interest young readers in a historical period and encourage them to read nonfiction works about the history itself. And a fine historical novel, one that treats the history seriously and carefully recreates the time period, can also be a good supplement to a history class. Reading one of the many novels about the Holocaust and World War II (such as Lowry's *Number the Stars*, Hans Richter's

Friedrich, or John Boyne's *The Boy in the Striped Pajamas*) can give young readers a compelling sense of what it was like to live through the period. But perhaps most importantly, the individual human story can help young readers connect with historical issues, conflicts, triumphs, and tragedies. History comes alive once it is personalized—and that is what the good historical novel can do best. Of course, it goes without saying, historical fiction should never be allowed to substitute for actual history.

Contemporary Realism

Definition

Contemporary realism is set during or very near the time of its writing. Consequently, writers of contemporary fiction, unlike historical novelists, can take many things for granted. For instance, no writer of contemporary fiction today would have to define a mall, a cell phone, an iPad, or digital downloads. In other words, a contemporary novelist already shares a common body of knowledge with the readers. So we can expect less background information about the time and place in contemporary fiction than in historical fiction. An exception occurs when the story is set outside the culture of the general reader. For example, if a contemporary novel is set in foreign lands, which is very common among current YA realism, the author may need to include some social and cultural background. Aisha Saeed's *Written in the Stars,* published in 2016, is a mature YA story set in the United States and Pakistan, and treats the custom, in certain Mideastern societies, of arranged marriages. Margaret Craven's moving novel, *I Heard the Owl Call My Name,* has a setting contemporary with its publication date, 1973. However, the story takes place in the remote Indian village of Kingcome on the coast of British Columbia, where many of the native Kwakiutl (today known as Dzawada'enuxw) still cling to their ancient customs. So, of necessity, Craven provides her readers with the essential cultural and social background information to impart this tale of personal courage and dignity in the face of life and death.

Contemporary realism for children dates to the nineteenth century, with works such as Alcott's *Little Women* (1868 and 1869*),* the story of four sisters in New England growing up in the 1860s, and Charlotte Yonge's *The Daisy Chain* (1856), the story of a large English family dealing with the death of their mother. And there is that granddaddy of school stories, Thomas Hughes's *Tom Brown's School-Days* (1857). The school story (almost always about boys) is usually set in a boarding school, where the youthful characters enjoy a degree of freedom away from their parents' watchful eyes. It is common for children's and YA stories to separate parents and child protagonists, who are often orphaned or runaways, away at boarding school or summer camp, or sometimes simply lost. The point is that independent youthful protagonists can be much more interesting to read about than those who are under the watchful eyes of their parents. So we find adventure stories (like Mark Twain's the story of an orphan, *The Adventures of Tom Sawyer* [1876], or of a runaway, *The Adventures of Huckleberry Finn* [1884]), and survival stories (in the vein of Daniel Defoe's classic *Robinson Crusoe* [1719]) have always been popular with young readers. Defoe's book inspired R. M. Ballantyne's *The Coral Island* (1857), the story of three young boys stranded on a remote Pacific island who survive because of their perseverance and ingenuity—very much the same theme as Scott O'Dell's modern classic, *Island of the Blue Dolphins* (1960).

New Realism and the Problem Novel

Up until the mid-twentieth century, most contemporary stories for young readers tended toward sentimentalism (see Chapter 4) or at least romanticism—painting life as generally rosy even if there were occasional rough patches. But this began to change in the mid-twentieth century, when romanticism and sentimentalism were replaced by honest, sometimes harsh, realism—at least this was true of many books for older readers. Beginning in the 1960s, the so-called New Realism surfaced. New Realism introduced several new features to YA literature particularly, including raw emotion (lots of shouting and crying), franker language (gritty street talk), and bolder ideas (sex, drugs, and gangs). In fact, with the coming of New Realism, little remained that was taboo for the YA novel.

With the coming of New Realism, books for YA readers began to address a wide variety of issues that were formerly avoided: racial prejudice (works by Mildred Taylor and Virginia Hamilton), teenage gangs (Walter Dean Myers's *Scorpions*), drug abuse (Alice Childress's *A Hero Ain't Nothin' but a Sandwich*), LGBTQ issues (M. E. Kerr's *"Hello," I Lied*), child abuse (Mirjam Pressler's *Halinka*), mental illness (James Bennett's *I Can Hear the Mourning Dove*), sexual abuse (Cynthia Voigt's *When She Hollers*), and many others.

Many of these books also fit into a subcategory often called the problem novel, which is really a variation on the so-called social novel for adults (which goes back as far as Charles Dickens in the nineteenth century). The problem novel tends to be narrowly focused on a single hot-button issue—sex, drugs, violence—and depicts the teenage protagonist's initiation into the adult world. As a consequence, these are often coming-of-age stories, leaving the protagonist "sadder but wiser" at the end. One of the earliest of these problem novels is S. E. Hinton's *The Outsiders*, published in 1967. Hinton's starkly realistic portrayal of teenage street gangs does not shy away from either violence or death. This brutally frank book remains controversial to this day, but is part of the curriculum for many American middle and high schools.

Paul Zindel's *The Pigman* (1968) is another early example of a YA book dealing with very sensitive issues. The story is a dual narrative (that is, told from the points of view of two characters) about two teenagers, from unhappy—even abusive—homes, who befriend a lonely and neglected old man. In the course of their relationship they discover not only a great deal about the old man but about themselves as well. The frank language and sexual references have made this a controversial book, but the authenticity of its teenage narrators and its sensitive treatment of deep themes continue to ensure its place on many school reading lists.

Judy Blume's name has long been associated with the problem novel. Her *Forever*, published in 1975, was one of the first books for young readers to deal frankly with sex (which also got it banned in many places), and her *Blubber* describes the cruelty inflicted by children on an overweight girl. Blume's *Tiger Eyes* is a good example of the finely crafted problem novel, examining a teenager's coping with her father's senseless murder and the changes it brought to her life.

As with all literature, some problem novels are better than others. The mediocre problem novels contain predictable plots, shallow characters, and trite dialogue. Sometimes they are sensationalized and devolve into melodrama—they are the soap operas of YA literature. Perhaps most seriously, many of them imply that teenage problems have simplistic solutions. Of course, their predictability and easy answers make them very popular with young readers, as evidenced by the success of the *Sweet Valley High* series and the *Baby-Sitters Club* series, and, more recently, Jeff Kinney's wildly popular *Diary of a Wimpy Kid* series. At their best, problem novels explore significant psychological and sociological issues with sensitivity, and they give us vivid, complex characters. The best books always challenge us.

Some critics have raised concerns over problem novels and their use in the classroom, largely because of their frank language and sensitive subject matter. Although we usually think it is important for young people not to be sheltered from reality—that the more we know the better off we are—some argue that young people are also entitled to their innocence. Some worry that too much exposure to the dark side of teenage life—drugs, violence, emotional abuse—can be oppressive itself or, at the very least, discouraging. On the other hand, reading can be therapeutic, showing pre-teens and teenagers that they are not alone in their feelings. And a good problem novel presents us with realistic characters confronting real-life problems. Might it not be better for teenagers to get their information from a well-informed, sensitive, and articulate writer than from their confused and troubled peers? (See Reid and Stringer for a discussion of this problem.)

Topics in Realistic Fiction

Both historical and contemporary realistic novels deal with similar topics, so the following discussion of topics relates to all realistic fiction. Perhaps the most common subject in books for readers in the middle grades and older is coming of age—moving from childhood into puberty and adolescence. Many books for younger readers, although not technically coming-of-age stories, are about children coping with life's inevitable changes. Good examples are Beverly Cleary's *Ramona* books, Patricia MacLachlan's *Arthur, for the Very First Time*, Katherine Paterson's *The Great Gilly Hopkins*, and Grace Lin's *The Year of the Dog*, all of which feature young protagonists struggling with the trials of growing up.

For older readers, the issues often become more complicated. They face dramatic and often perplexing changes in their physical bodies, in their social encounters, and in their intellectual grasp of things. Most readers are drawn to stories about people like themselves facing extraordinary situations. If you want a fancy term for these coming-of-age books, it is the German word *Bildungsroman*, which means roughly "a formation or building story." Many of the great classic novels of youth and adolescence are coming-of-age stories—from Charlotte Brontë's romantic love story *Jane Eyre* to Charles Dickens's *Great Expectations* to Mark Twain's *Huckleberry Finn*, all written in the nineteenth century. And in the twentieth century, we have John Knowles's *A Separate Peace* (about a terrible secret among young schoolboys), J. D. Salinger's brutally frank (but very funny) *Catcher in the Rye* (about a troubled youth), Harper Lee's powerful *To Kill a Mockingbird* (about social injustice), and William Golding's chilling *Lord of the Flies* (about the dark side of human nature), all of which have acquired the status of classics. And all of which still deserve to be on school reading lists.

Coming of age necessarily involves gaining wisdom—but, of course, this is always at the expense of innocence. Paradoxically, growing up means giving up one kind of freedom (freedom from care) in exchange for another kind (freedom of choice). At the end of a coming-of-age story, the protagonist has learned something about him- or herself, about people, and about the world. Invariably, the protagonist is a sensitive and curious individual who is looking for answers, trying to understand his or her own physical and emotional changes, and learning about the ways of the world. Incidentally, we should note that coming-of-age stories do not have to be realistic fiction. In fact, many of the greatest fantasies are also about growing up—from Ursula Le Guin's *Earthsea* cycle to Philip Pullman's *His Dark Materials* trilogy to Suzanne Collins's *Hunger Games* trilogy. These are all about characters who mature physically, psychologically, emotionally, and socially—sometimes against their will but always of necessity. Every hero's quest—from the great folk narratives to the great fantasies to the gritty realistic novels—is a form of the Bildungsroman. This is one of the great themes of literature.

Most good novels weave together several themes, so any attempt to classify novels in this way is flawed. With that disclaimer, the following discussion attempts to highlight some of the more important themes in realistic fiction—whether historical or contemporary.

Family Relationships

The great Russian writer Tolstoy opened his novel *Anna Karenina* with the famous line: "All happy families are alike; each unhappy family is unhappy in its own way" (1). Certainly from a writer's point of view, a family without conflict would make a dull story indeed. But, in fact, a great many family stories for young readers depict happy families—although they are not without their troubles. We have already mentioned Louisa May Alcott's *Little Women* (Figure 9.2), which portrays the lives and adventures of the March family—four sisters and their mother (Father is off fighting in the Civil War). The family faces hardship, sibling rivalry, and failed romances, and tragedy even strikes as one of the sisters falls ill and dies. But the Marches triumph with their general spirit of optimism and genuine love for each other. In the early twentieth century, Eleanor Estes wrote a series of books about the Moffat family (beginning with *The Moffats*, first published in 1941), an impoverished family living in Connecticut just after World War I. They, too, are a family of four siblings—this time two boys and two girls—and their widowed mother. The family's poverty is a constant source of conflict in their lives, but they always manage, everyone helps out, and no one grumbles. Their source of strength, as with the Marches, is the family unit.

These books are fairly typical of the family stories of the nineteenth and early twentieth centuries (and it is curious how many of these early "family" stories depict single-parent families). As the twentieth century progressed, the family story transformed. More and more, in the place of happy families overcoming poverty and occasional hardship, we find families torn by internal dissension and fractured by tragic circumstances. Cynthia Voigt's *Homecoming* and its sequels are the stories of the four Tillerman children, two boys and two girls, who have been abandoned by their mother in a Connecticut parking lot. Under the leadership of Dicey, the elder sister, they set off to find their grandmother, a woman they've never met, in far-off Maryland. When they finally reach their grandmother, she turns out to be cold, distant, and cantankerous. This is hardly the happy family circle depicted by Alcott and Estes. However, in the end, through all its tribulations, the family manages to pull together. The theme is essentially the same as it has always been in the family story (the need for mutual sacrifice, understanding, forgiveness, and unconditional love), but the romantic vision is replaced by something more starkly realistic. There is, for instance, no happy reunion with their mother, who dies from a drug overdose. The reconstructed Tillerman family is representative of current trends in family stories for children, focusing on fractured, blended, and dysfunctional families or families in crisis. Single-parent homes are commonplace—which is not new, as we see from the stories of Alcott and Estes. However, today, single-parent families are usually the result of divorce rather than widowhood, as in the past.

FIGURE 9.2 ■ Jesse Willcox Smith's frontispiece illustration (1915) for Louis May Alcott's *Little Women* depicts the four March sisters listening to their mother read a letter from Father, who is off serving the Union during the Civil War.

Beverly Cleary, famous for her humorous stories of Ramona Quimby and Henry Huggins, all depicting happy families, herself became part of the general trend in 1983 with *Dear Mr. Henshaw*. This Newbery Medal–winning novel is written as a series of letters and journal entries by a young boy coming to terms with his parents' divorce. But some families are in even more dire straits. Bill and Vera Cleaver's *Where the Lilies Bloom* portrays a family of orphaned siblings trying to make it on their own in their impoverished Appalachian home; the children even have to bury their deceased father themselves. In still a different vein is Patricia MacLachlan's *Baby*, the story of a family, recently bereaved from the death of an infant, who find, on their doorstep, an abandoned baby. This poetic tale is one of healing and redemption.

If the message about the modern family story remains positive, it does suggest that the family is a diverse organism—intricately complicated, sometimes tragic, but ultimately worth fighting for.

Friendship

Very few books for young readers do not involve the forming of friendships. Many of the most popular children's fantasies are about friendship, from Kenneth Grahame's *Wind in the Willows* to A. A. Milne's *Winnie-the-Pooh* to Arnold Lobel's *Frog and Toad Are Friends*. As children grow older, friendships often become as important as family ties, and in some cases they are more important, and young readers begin turning toward realistic stories. An early example is Lucy Maud Montgomery's popular *Anne of Green Gables* (1908), which shows an orphan adapting to an unconventional family (a middle-aged brother and sister) and forming friendships in a new environment. Equally beloved is Frances Hodgson Burnett's *The Secret Garden* (1911), which describes the forming of a friendship between two children, one orphaned and one neglected (Figure 9.3). More recently, Susan Patron's *The Higher Power of Lucky*, which won the 2007 Newbery Medal, bridges the narrow gap between stories of family and stories of friends. It actually treats the disintegration of one family—Lucky's mother is dead and her father has deserted her—and the creation of a new family that includes, of all people, her father's second wife (now divorced). Stories about friendships include making new friends, keeping (and losing) old ones, disagreements among friends, and discovering unusual or unlikely friends. In many modern novels, it is with the support of good friends that young people cope with difficult home lives. One of the most popular modern children's stories on the subject of making new and unlikely friends is Kate DiCamillo's *Because of Winn-Dixie*, about a girl being raised by her father and adjusting to a new home in Florida, where she makes friends with an assortment of quirky characters and a dog.

But friendships have their rocky spots, and books dealing with friendship usually reveal relationships being put to the test and emerging stronger. Louise Fitzhugh's *Harriet the Spy* is a good example. It is the story of a fiercely

FIGURE 9.3 ■ Charles Robinson's illustration from Frances Hodgson Burnett's popular classic, *The Secret Garden*, originally published in 1910, about the redemption of a sullen orphan girl living on the moors of northern England.

Source: "There were Trees . . . and a Large Pool with an Old Grey Fountain in its Midst," Charles Robinson (1870–1937). Colour lithograph. Private Collection/ © Look and Learn/The Bridgeman Art Library.

independent only child who has to learn the value of friendship the hard way—after she has done her best to drive all her friends away. E. L. Konigsburg's *The View from Saturday* describes a motley crew of youthful intellectuals who come from a wide variety of religious and ethnic backgrounds (and supported, incidentally, by a wheelchair-bound teacher). In all these stories, the message is that friendships do not just happen, they are forged with considerable effort and sacrifice—and they come with inestimable rewards. In other words, friendships are an extension of (and sometimes a replacement for) family relationships.

Personal Growth and Development

An almost unavoidable theme in YA books, growing up or coming of age is often the elephant in the room. Indeed, there was a time when the subject was either ignored or glossed over. This is largely because coming of age means awareness of one's sexuality, which is now an important subject in YA literature. One of the earliest books dealing frankly with this subject was Judy Blume's *Are You There, God? It's Me, Margaret* (appearing in 1970), which is, among other things, the story of a young girl coping with the onset of menses. And in 1969, Paul Zindel helped to open up the discussion of premarital sex, rape, and teenage pregnancy in *My Darling, My Hamburger.* With these groundbreaking books, the floodgates were opened and few topics remained taboo for older readers. The true dark side of sexuality is sexual abuse. This issue is at the heart of Laurie Halse Anderson's *Speak*, the story of a young girl's difficult recovery from rape and how she once again finds her voice and her identity. Even more chilling is Elizabeth Scott's *Living Dead Girl*, about a pedophile abducting a 10-year-old girl and holding her for five years. Again, the purpose of books such as these is to bring to light certain unpleasant truths—nothing is to be gained from burying our heads in the sand. And, in fact, much may be lost if we do.

Of course, any book on sexuality for young people is going to face some controversy, but we need to recognize the distinction between serious books about sexuality and books that exploit sex (or pornography). The best books are honest and forthright while avoiding the lascivious. Without responsible writers creating sensitive and intelligent stories, many young people would learn about sexuality from ill-informed friends and neighbors—or worse. Sir Francis Bacon, in the sixteenth century, is first credited with saying, "Knowledge is power." And, contrary to the old saw, what we don't know *can* hurt us.

But sexuality is not the only personal issue that young people have to deal with, for they are not immune from the physical and emotional problems that adults face. Mark Haddon's *The Curious Incident of the Dog in the Night-time*, the moving exploration of a teenager's struggle with an unnamed dissociative disorder resembling Asperger's syndrome or a form of autism, has brought a much-needed public awareness to these little understood subjects. This YA book has been adapted to the stage, its important message now reaching adult audiences.

Social Issues

You may be asking why, in the discussion about sexuality, the subjects of lesbian, gay, bisexual, transgendered, and questioning (LGBTQ) individuals were not addressed. Indeed, the question of sexual identity is both a deeply personal one and, particularly in this day and age, an issue with great social consequences. When sexual orientation emerged from the closet—to use the old metaphor—it became no longer just a matter of personal growth and development. For better or worse, it became a social issue. John Donovan's pioneering novel, *I'll Get There. It Better Be Worth the Trip*, which appeared in 1969, was a groundbreaking work about a teenager's coming to terms with his homosexuality. Other significant contributions include Marion Dane Bauer's *Am I Blue?: Coming Out from the Silence* (a selection of short stories on gay and lesbian themes by various writers) and M. E. Kerr's *Deliver Us from Evie* (about a teenage lesbian). And more recently we have Alex Sánchez, who is best known for his Rainbow Boys trilogy (*Rainbow Boys, Rainbow High, Rainbow Road*), coming-of-age stories about three gay and bisexual friends. The trend we have seen since Donovan's book in 1969 is that the issue of gender identity has become less of a personal or self-awareness issue than one of social acceptance and integration.

As we might expect, these books are frequently challenged and occasionally banned. But fortunately, with more enlightened attitudes, they are gradually becoming standard reading fare and are showing up on more and more reading lists. Indeed, Sánchez's books have won numerous awards and he is a sought-after speaker, delivering a message that all of us, particularly parents, need to hear. The tolerance and sensitivity displayed by today's youth mark a refreshing change from the stifling, judgmental, and hypocritical world of the past.

We have already mentioned S. E. Hinton's groundbreaking novel *The Outsiders*, which portrays the trials of characters out of the mainstream—the title says it all. Stories of social outcasts deal with individuals who must struggle to become part of society or, as often as not, reject society for a variety of reasons (inability to fit in, perhaps, but also an unwillingness to accept hypocritical social values and mores). Mark Twain's irrepressible hero, Huckleberry Finn, is perhaps the original outsider. Scorned by society and with only one true friend, Jim, an escaped slave, he faces a rough-and-tumble world with tenacity and bravery, ultimately achieving acceptance (although by that time he is not sure he wants it).

A great many modern fictional stories today are, to one degree or another, about "outsiders," including books such as Fitzhugh's *Harriet the Spy*, Burnett's The *Secret Garden*, DiCamillo's *Because of Winn-Dixie*, Patron's *Higher Power of Lucky*, all previously mentioned. (The good books seldom fit neatly into a single category.) That they are outsiders is what makes the characters compelling. In recent years, authors have become increasingly interested in those "outsiders" who have long been neglected in children's literature—people shunned by society because they are troubled emotionally, disadvantaged physically, or challenged mentally. Katherine Paterson, in *The Great Gilly Hopkins*, portrays an emotionally troubled child placed in a foster home. *The Language of Goldfish* by Zibby Oneal describes a young girl plagued with mental illness and suicidal tendencies. *The Pigman* by Paul Zindel is about a developing relationship between two teenagers and a lonely elderly man. Robert Cormier's *Tenderness* is a chilling portrait of a teenage serial killer; you can't get much further outside than that. Gary Schmidt's *Orbiting Jupiter* is the powerful and tragic story of a troubled foster child, a teenager, who is determined to find his baby daughter. It is a tale of love and sacrifice made more moving by its sparse and elegant prose.

Adventure and Survival

Suzanne Collins's *Hunger Games* series is a popular example of the survival story in modern fantasy, but realistic fiction has its share of excellent adventure/survival stories. Modern realistic adventure and survival stories are the heirs of Daniel Defoe's *Robinson Crusoe* (1719), which many claim was the first realistic adventure story (most of its predecessors having been unabashed fantasies). It is the story of a man shipwrecked for 27 years on a desert island off the coast of South America. While there he encounters a number of adventures, including cannibals and mutineers, and even makes a servant (whom he calls Friday) of one of the natives he rescued from the cannibals (Figure 9.4). The book was immensely popular and has been retold for children several times. However, the first adventure stories written specifically for younger readers (usually boys at first) appeared in the nineteenth

FIGURE 9.4 ■ This nineteenth-century Currier & Ives print depicts Daniel Defoe's eponymous hero from *Robinson Crusoe* with his "man," Friday, and an assortment of animal companions. Crusoe, one of literature's first realistic survivalists (the book first appeared in 1719), was obviously deprived of few creature comforts during his 27-year adventure on a desert isle.

century. Robert Louis Stevenson was among the most famous authors of adventure stories, with such classics as *Kidnapped* and *Treasure Island* (an inspiration for *Pirates of the Caribbean*, and every other pirate story since, see Figure 9.5). Stevenson's characterization of Long John Silver (possibly inspired by real pirates, such as the notorious Blackbeard from the eighteenth century) is the quintessential one-legged pirate with a parrot perched on his shoulder.

A popular variation of the adventure story is the survival story—also descended from *Robinson Crusoe*—in which the protagonist is stranded (alone or with just a few friends or family members) in an unfamiliar and often dangerous place and must figure out how to remain alive and be rescued. However, few modern survival stories subscribe to Defoe's optimistic portrayal of a wild tropical paradise where the hero carves out a life of relative luxury (complete with a servant). Instead, modern survival stories portray the hardships and isolation that face the

FIGURE 9.5 ■ N. C. Wyeth's chilling and dramatic illustration for Robert Louis Stevenson's *Treasure Island* depicting Blind Pew, an evil beggar, before being trampled to death.

protagonists, who are usually humbled before the forces of nature. They adapt their lifestyles to their surroundings. Scott O'Dell's *Island of the Blue Dolphins*, which first appeared in 1960, is a work of historical fiction based on an actual incident from the early nineteenth century. This was one of the first modern survival stories to adopt this new and far more realistic approach to survival narratives. O'Dell conveys the message that, in real life, survival means sacrifice, suffering, adaptation, and often loneliness. Jean Craighead George (*Julie of the Wolves* and *My Side of the Mountain*), Harry Mazer (*Snowbound* and *The Island Keeper*), and Gary Paulsen (*Hatchet*) have followed O'Dell's example, portraying heroes and heroines who learn to live in harmony with the natural world and who often come to respect nature above the civilizing forces of humanity. In other words, they become aware of the ecosystem (see the discussion of ecocriticism in Chapter 4). We should note that survival is also a popular theme in fantasy stories—the popular 2015 film *The Martian,* starring Matt Damon, is an example, although, unlike most fantasies, this one goes to great pains to make the story feel "realistic." This is another example of the blurring lines that separate fantasy and realistic fiction.

Perhaps the most chilling, but among the most important, survival stories of modern times are those about children surviving the Holocaust. Some of these are actual memoirs and are, therefore, nonfiction—*The Diary of Anne Frank* being the most famous (although, of course, Anne Frank herself did not survive). Judith Kerr's *When Hitler Stole Pink Rabbit* is a novel inspired by the author's own harrowing experience escaping Hitler's Germany. And John Boyne's exceedingly popular *The Boy in the Striped Pajamas* is a purely fictional, but powerfully authentic, account of life in Auschwitz as seen through the eyes of a 9-year-old boy.

A key element in any survival story is its detailing of the means of survival. We see the protagonist gathering food, finding shelter from the elements, securing protection from threatening forces, and learning how to combat loneliness. Survival stories depict the individual overcoming adversity and, in the process, achieving self-awareness, which includes recognizing one's strengths and shortcomings and understanding one's innermost needs and desires.

Death and Dying

Death, surprisingly, is one of the oldest subjects we find in children's literature. In eighteenth-century children's books, characters were always dying—the virtuous winging their way to heaven and the wicked consigned to the pits of hell. In the nineteenth century, the fire and brimstone were usually omitted, and death became an object of sentimentalism, cleverly parodied by Mark Twain in *Huckleberry Finn*. (See the discussion of parody in Chapter 4.)

It may be that earlier generations were emotionally better equipped to handle death than we are today—not because they had any answers, but because death was perceived not as an anomaly but as part of the normal cycle of life. Most people died in their homes, surrounded by their family and friends. Today, we confine death to institutions—people die in hospitals and nursing homes, surrounding by medical personnel who are usually strangers. And, to exacerbate the issue, modern science has led us to believe in miracles, lulling us into a false sense of our own invulnerability. So when death does come, it seems an anomaly—an unwelcome intruder in our daily lives. We deny it, bargain with it, rage against it—we can't even utter its name. (Euphemisms for dying have been around a long time. Instead of dying, someone "passes away" or, perhaps, simply "passes.") Consequently, the difficulty in accepting death is the subject of many children's books. What we look for is a sensible and sensitive treatment of death.

We saw in Chapter 2 that for the very youngest children, the subject of death is often broached by portraying the death of an animal. In Margaret Wise Brown's classic picture book, *The Dead Bird*, some children find a dead bird, which they proceed to bury with some ceremony, and then resume their afternoon play. Very young children are usually quite resilient regarding death, and not particularly sentimental. When her mother discussed the possibility of getting a goldfish, my 5-year-old granddaughter asked, with anticipatory enthusiasm, "When the fish dies, can I dig the hole?" But, by the elementary school years, children come to realize the greater significance, the finality, of death. Consequently, books for older readers about the deaths of animals, such as Marjorie Kinnan Rawlings's *The Yearling* and Wilson Rawls's *Where the Red Fern Grows,* are means of illustrating our common humanity in the face of devastating loss.

If books for the younger readers tend to focus on the loss of animals and pets, books for older readers broach the inevitable loss of family members and even friends. Many picture books deal with the death of a grandparent, as in Tomie dePaola's touching *Nana Upstairs, Nana Downstairs*, which recounts the loss of a great-grandmother and, eventually, a grandmother. Writing about death is often quite personal for the author. Mollie Hunter's *A Sound of Chariots* reflects the author's own deep grief following the death of her father. Lois Lowry's *A Summer to Die* recalls the death of Lowry's sister. Katherine Paterson wrote *Bridge to Terabithia* as an assuagement for her young son, who had lost his best friend in a tragic accident. It is, of course, the unexpected and premature death that is most difficult to accept. James Lincoln Collier and Christopher Collier's *My Brother Sam Is Dead*, a historical novel about two brothers fighting on opposites sides during the American Revolution, is among the earliest books for young people depicting a wartime casualty. The once-unspeakable subject of teen suicide is the subject of Richard Peck's *Remembering the Good Times* and John Green's *Looking for Alaska*. As in other human arenas, children's literature about death has edged toward greater realism, more frankness and honesty, and greater intensity. Unlike the writers of the eighteenth century, who found their comfort in religious salvation, many writers today present death as the natural completion of the great circle of life or a tragic consequence over which we have little control and to which we must acquiesce. These writers present death without sentimentality, but not without sensitivity. And today, we perhaps understand the psychology of grief better than in the past (not that that makes it any easier). In *Bridge to Terabithia*, for example, we can observe the protagonist, Jesse, move through the stages of grief as he attempts to come to terms with loss—denial, anger, bargaining, depression, acceptance—and, as always, there are no answers, only reconciliation and memory. And these, as we know, have to be enough.

Mysteries and Puzzlers

Mysteries and puzzlers are often escapist fiction, creating a world somehow more exciting, more dangerous, and more interesting than we imagine our own to be. The mystery, first popularized in the early nineteenth century by Edgar Allan Poe and later refined by Arthur Conan Doyle, the creator of Sherlock Holmes, has long been a favorite of young readers. Detective mysteries lend themselves to serialization, and we even find series for beginning readers. Among the earliest are the Hardy Boys (from 1927 on) and the Nancy Drew (from 1930 on) series. These formulaic stories, written by various ghostwriters over the years, made their way in film and television as well as to foreign countries, and new incarnations keep popping up.

For younger readers is Donald Sobol's Encyclopedia Brown series (twenty-nine books in all), featuring a boy detective who succeeds because of his keen and wide-ranging intelligence. He is often assisted by his close friend, Sally, who sometimes beats Encyclopedia to the solution of the puzzle. We find another female detective in Betsy Byars's Herculeah Jones series, which relates the adventures of the young daughter of a police officer and a private detective.

The mystery, of course, always involves the solving of a puzzle. E. L. Konigsburg's Newbery-Award winning *The Mixed-Up Files of Mrs. Basil E. Frankweiler* describes an intriguing puzzle that two runaways (who hide out in the Metropolitan Museum of Art) must solve. More recently, Jack Gantos's *Dead End in Norvelt* (another Newbery Medalist) gives us a comical mystery involving a young boy sentenced to help the town's eccentric write obituaries—and a whole lot more. Interestingly, the book is partly autobiographical. As the cliché goes, everybody loves a mystery, but a successful mystery relies on cleverly planted clues and an ingenious puzzle. The puzzle must not be too easily solved, or the reader will lose interest. And the solution to the mystery must seem logical once all the pieces are put together, or the reader will feel cheated or deceived. Mysteries can become addictive and they can be a terrific choice for reluctant readers.

Sports

Very popular among an important group of readers is the sports story, which actually has its origin in the boys' magazines of the nineteenth century. As full-blown books, however, they are a twentieth-century phenomenon. One of the most popular of the early sports writers was Clair Bee, whose books, beginning with *Touchdown Pass* in 1948, are all about a high school athlete, Chip Hilton. The stories promote high moral character and good sportsmanship. Consequently, sports tales are quite often coming-of-age stories, particularly when the protagonist gains self-knowledge through participation in sports. We see this in the works of Matt Christopher (*The Fox Steals Home*) and Chris Crutcher (*Athletic Shorts*). Sherman Alexie's 2007 novel, *The Absolutely True Diary of a Part-Time Indian*, is often billed as a sports novel, because the protagonist, "Junior," plays basketball. But it is also a powerful coming-of-age story about a 14-year-old boy from the Spokane Indian Reservation in Washington who experiences a series a tragic events in his personal life while he struggles with the racial slurs and bullying in school. It is a book of great emotional depth, demonstrating that, in the hands of a talented writer, a sports story can be a compelling study of human nature.

Animals

When we think of animal stories for children, we usually think of the fantasies—stories of talking animals who share human sentiments (and often live the life of typical human beings). By contrast, animal stories in realistic fiction usually describe relationships between humans and animals, although we can find a few in which the animals themselves become the central figures (but, of course, they remain animals). Realistic animal stories first appeared in the late nineteenth and early twentieth centuries, and they seem to have been most popular in North America. Jack London's animal story, *The Call of the Wild*, is a long-time favorite realistic adventure story, in which the main character is a dog who is taken from his California home by a cruel man who forces him to pull dogsleds in Alaska. Eventually, the dog escapes and seeks his ancestral roots with the wolves (hence the title). Canadians Ernest Thompson Seton (*Wild Animals I Have Known*) and Charles G. D. Roberts (*Red Fox*) wrote stories depicting animals realistically (that is, they don't talk or wear clothes) but giving them personalities (some human connection is necessary).

The most common realistic animal stories involve humans who have developed attachments to animals. We have already mentioned two of the most beloved animal stories—Rawlings's *The Yearling* and Rawls's *Where the Red Fern Grows*—both about humans coping with an animal's death. Not surprisingly, dog stories are great favorites, some of the best-known including Eric Knight's *Lassie Come-Home* (about a heroic collie), Fred Gipson's *Old Yeller*, William H. Armstrong's *Sounder*, and Kate DiCamillo's *Because of Winn-Dixie*—some of which, we must add, include heart-wrenching endings. Sheila Burnford's *The Incredible Journey* is the story of two dogs and a cat who make a 300-mile journey across Canada in search of their owners. The book has been criticized for giving the animals a few too many human traits. Phyllis Reynolds Naylor's Newbery Award–winning *Shiloh* is a moving dog story about animal abuse. And horse stories have traditionally been wildly popular. Mary O'Hara's *My Friend Flicka*, set in the American West, is the first of a trilogy. Marguerite Henry's *Misty of Chincoteague* is the first of six books about the famous wild horses of Assateague and Chincoteague islands of the coast of Virginia. Walter Farley's The *Black Stallion*, the first of a long series, is a survival story featuring a boy and a horse. More recent developments are animal stories that address humanitarian and ecological issues. One of the earliest of these books is Farley Mowat's *Owls in the Family*, an autobiographical account about the adoption of two great horned owls who were unable to survive in the wild. Mowat himself, a Canadian, was a pioneer in the environmentalist movement and is best known for his adult book, *Never Cry Wolf*. Carl Hiaasen's Hoot is a story about the effects of habitat destruction on wildlife. So, the animal story becomes an excellent vehicle for raising environmental awareness in young readers.

A Word About Verse Novels

In the nineteenth century, it briefly became fashionable to write novels in poetry rather than prose—we call them verse novels. Robert Browning's *The Ring and the Book*, published in installments from 1868 to 1869, is one of the most famous of these early verse novels for adults. Then they fell out of fashion until rather recently. In the 1990s, they began to appear in children's literature. Virginia Euwer Wolf's *Make Lemonade*, appearing in 1993, was one of the first young people's novels to use verse. And Karen Hesse's verse novel *Out of the Dust* won the Newbery Medal in 1998. Verse novels for young readers typically use free verse—in other words, without rhythm or regular rhyme (see Chapter 6). The writing also tends to be sparse, with just a few crisp lines to each page. Consequently, the effective verse novel must rely heavily on suggestive imagery to convey the setting, the character, and the plot details. In many instances, the story is told in the protagonist's words. An interesting variation on the verse novel is the verse biography (biography will be discussed in Chapter 10). Margarita Engle's *The Poet Slave of Cuba* is a biography of a nineteenth-century Cuban poet, Juan Francisco Manzano, an uneducated slave who had a talent for poetry in which he described his difficult life. Engle chose to use her own poems to tell his life story. Books written in verse for young readers reflect the constantly evolving nature of literature for children.

Summary

Realistic fiction, whether historical or contemporary, is enormously diverse, which may be one of the reasons it is so popular with young readers. The subjects and themes of realistic fiction can be both deep and far-reaching. A single novel such as Hiaasen's

Hoot contains numerous themes, including the importance of making new friends, the difficulty of adapting to a new home, the need to protect the environment, and the value of learning to stand up for oneself and for important principles, not to mention the importance of animals in our lives. Realistic fiction can encompass historical settings and themes, which can bring to life the world of the past and pique young readers' curiosity about historical times and places. Contemporary realism, which includes stories set in the author's present, generally assumes the reader is familiar with modern culture and mores—although it can be set in foreign lands or explore cultural groups out of the social mainstream and thereby enrich our experiences.

In both historical and contemporary fiction we find a wide variety of topics, including stories about family, friendship, outsiders, growing up, survival, mysteries, sports, animals, and more. Most address the importance of human connections, assuming personal responsibility, perseverance, and realizing individual potential. Reading a good realistic novel is an excellent way to overcome our narrow prejudices, to get to know people different from us, and to understand human motivation and desire. Ironically, we invariably learn that people, wherever they are, whatever their history or heritage, are very much like us after all.

Works Cited

MacLeod, Anne Scott. "Writing Backward: Modern Models in Historical Fiction." *The Horn Book Magazine* (January/February 1998): 26–33.

Manzoni, Alessandro. *On the Historical Novel.* 1850. Trans. Sandra Bermann. Lincoln: University of Nebraska, 1984.

Reid, Suzanne, and Sharon Stringer. "Ethical Dilemmas in Teaching Problem Novels: The Psychological Impact of Troubling YA Literature on Adolescent Readers in the Classroom." *ALA Review* 24.2 (Winter 1997): 16–18.

Tolstoy, Leo. *Anna Karenina.* Trans. Richard Pevear and Larissa Volokhonsky. London: Penguin, 2000.

Recommended Resources

Alston, Anne. *The Family in English Children's Literature.* New York: Routledge, 2008.

Connelly, Mark. *The Hardy Boys Mysteries, 1927–1979: A Cultural and Literary History.* Jefferson, NC: McFarland, 2008.

Cornelius, Michael G., and Melanie E. Gregg, eds. *Nancy Drew and Her Sister Sleuths: Essays on the Fiction of Girl Detectives.* Jefferson, NC: McFarland, 2008.

Crowe, Chris. *More Than a Game: Sports Literature for Young Adults.* Lanham, MD: Scarecrow, 2003.

Gavin, Adrienne, and Christopher Routledge, eds. *Mystery in Children's Literature: From the Rational to the Supernatural.* New York: Palgrave Macmillan, 2001.

Gillespie, John T. *Historical Fiction for Young Readers (Grades 4–8): An Introduction.* Santa Barbara, CA: Libraries Unlimited, 2008.

Hinton, S. E. "Teenagers Are for Real." *New York Times Book Review* 27 (August 1967): 26–29.

Nixon, Joan Lowry. "Clues to the Juvenile Mystery." *The Writer* 90 (February 1977): 23–26.

Nodelman, Perry. "How Typical Children Read Typical Books." *Children's Literature in Education* 12 (Winter 1981): 177–185.

Paterson, Katherine. *Gates of Excellence: On Reading and Writing Books for Children.* New York: Elsevier/Nelson, 1981.

Rees, David. *The Marble in the Water.* Boston: The Horn Book, 1980.

____. *Painted Desert, Green Shade: Essays on Contemporary Writers for Children and Young Adults.* Boston: The Horn Book, 1984.

Thiel, Elizabeth. *The Fantasy of Family: Nineteenth-Century Children's Literature and the Myth of the Domestic Ideal.* New York: Routledge, 2007.

Townsend, John Rowe. *Written for Children: An Outline of English-Language Children's Literature*, 6th ed. Lanham, MD: Scarecrow, 1996.

Wilkin, Binnie Tate. *Survival Themes in Fiction for Children and Young People*, 2nd ed. New York: Scarecrow, 1993.

Zornado, Joseph. "A Poetics of History: Karen Cushman's Medieval World." *The Lion and the Unicorn* 21, 2 (1997): 251–266.

Historical Realism: A Selected and Annotated Booklist

Very little historical realism is written for children in the lower elementary grades, but some of these titles may appeal to upper elementary readers. No attempt has been made to identify reading levels. An individual's interests and abilities are the best guides.

Anderson, Laurie Halsie. *Chains.* New York: Atheneum, 2008.
- A young black girl's search for freedom during the American Revolution. An excellently researched and powerfully told story. The first in the author's "Seeds of America" trilogy, followed by *Forged* (2010) and *Ashes* (2016).

____. *Fever 1793.* New York: Simon & Schuster, 2000.
- The story of a young girl's survival during a fever outbreak in eighteenth-century America.

Avi. *Crispin: The Cross of Lead.* New York: Hyperion, 2002.
- The story of a fourteenth-century English peasant boy who encounters adventures as he flees punishment for a crime he did not commit.

____. *The True Confessions of Charlotte Doyle.* New York: Orchard, 1990.
- The account of a young girl's harrowing adventures on the high seas in the nineteenth century.

Boyne, John. *The Boy in the Striped Pajamas.* New York: David Fickling, 2006.
- A narrative of the Holocaust, as viewed through the eyes of a 9-year-old boy.

Bradley, Kimberly Brubaker. *The War that Saved My Life.* New York: Dial, 2015.
- A disabled girl escapes London and her abusive mother during a World War II blitz and discovers her own inner strength.

Brink, Carol Ryrie. *Caddie Woodlawn.* 1936. Various modern editions.
- The adventures of a girl on the frontier in nineteenth-century America. Based on the life of the author's grandmother.

Bruchac, Joseph. *Code Talker: A Novel about the Navajo Marines of World War Two.* New York: Penguin, 2005.
- Based on the true story of the use of the Navajo language for secret messages during World War II.

Collier, James Lincoln, and Christopher Collier. *My Brother Sam Is Dead*. New York: Four Winds Press, 1974.
- The story of two brothers finding themselves on opposite sides during the American Revolution.

Conrad, Pam. *Pedro's Journal: A Voyage with Christopher Columbus, August 3, 1492–February 14, 1493*. New York: Scholastic, 1992.
- The experiences and observations of a young boy aboard Columbus's *Santa Maria* on the voyage to the Americas.

Curtis, Christopher Paul. *Bud, Not Buddy*. New York: Delacorte, 1999.
- During the Great Depression, a homeless and destitute African-American boy sets out on his own across Michigan to find his father.

___. *The Watsons Go to Birmingham—1963*. New York: Delacorte, 1995.
- A story in which a 9-year-old African-American boy and his family from Michigan witness racial violence in the Deep South.

Cushman, Karen. *Catherine, Called Birdy*. New York: Clarion, 1994.
- The diary of a thirteenth-century English girl who flouts social norms.

de Angeli, Marguerite. *The Door in the Wall*. New York: Doubleday, 1949.
- The story of a young boy in medieval England who overcomes physical hardships and performs acts of heroism.

Dorris, Michael. *Morning Girl*. New York: Hyperion, 1992.
- A young native girl's account of the devastating effects of the European arrival in the Bahamas in 1492.

Erdrich, Louise. *The Game of Silence*. New York: HarperCollins, 2005.
- Sequel to *Birchbark House* (1999), a story about nineteenth-century Ojibwe people whose way of life is threatened by European settlers.

Estes, Eleanor. *The Moffats*. New York: Harcourt, 1941.
- Adventures of four siblings in Connecticut in the late 1910s.

Forbes, Esther. *Johnny Tremain*. Boston: Houghton Mifflin, 1946.
- A classic story of a patriot boy in Boston during the Revolutionary War.

Fox, Paula. *The Slave Dancer*. New York: Bradbury, 1973.
- A heartbreaking tale of the eighteenth-century African slave trade.

Fritz, Jean. *The Cabin Faced West*. New York: Coward, 1958.
- A story about a young girl who must adjust to life in the frontier in late eighteenth-century Pennsylvania.

Frost, Helen. *Crossing Stones*. New York: Foster/Farrar, 2009.
- A verse novel about a girl wrapped up in American political and social affairs during World War I.

Gray, Elizabeth Janet. *Adam of the Road*. New York: Viking, 1942.
- The adventures of an 11-year-old boy traveling through thirteenth-century England.

Greene, Bette. *Summer of My German Soldier*. New York: Dial, 1973.
- A tragic story of American anti-Semitism during World War II.

Hahn, Mary Downing. *Hear the Wind Blow: A Novel of the Civil War*. New York: Clarion, 2003.
- A story about a Confederate soldier setting off to find his brother during the final days of the Civil War.

Henry, Marguerite. *King of the Wind*. New York: Rand, 1948.
- A story loosely based on the life of Sham, a seventeenth-century Arabian horse who became the ancestor of all future thoroughbreds.

Hesse, Karen. *Letters from Rifka*. New York: Holt, 1992.
- The story of a young Russian Jewish girl immigrating to America in the early twentieth century.

____. *Out of the Dust*. New York: Scholastic, 1997.
- A verse novel about a young girl living in the Dust Bowl during the 1930s.

Ho, Minfong. *The Clay Marble*. New York: Farrar, Straus & Giroux, 1991.
- A story of a young girl separated from her family in war-torn Cambodia in 1980.

Hunt, Irene. *Across Five Aprils*. New York: Follett, 1964.
- The story of a northern family's experiences during the course of the American Civil War.

Kadohata, Cynthia. *Kira-Kira*. New York: Atheneum, 2004.
- A story about a Japanese-American girl growing up in the 1950s who must face the death of her sister.

Lowry, Lois. *Number the Stars*. Boston: Houghton Mifflin, 1989.
- A story about a Danish girl bravely facing the horrors of German occupation and anti-Semitism during World War II.

Kerr, Judith. *When Hitler Stole Pink Rabbit*. New York: Coward McCann & Geoghegan, 1971.
- The adventures of a Jewish girl forced to flee Hitler's Germany.

Kherdian, David. *The Road from Home: The Story of an Armenian Girlhood*. New York: Greenwillow, 1979.
- A powerful memoir of the Armenian holocaust.

Lasky, Kathryn. *The Night Journey*. New York: Warne, 1981.
- The story of a Jewish girl learning about her grandmother's experiences in Czarist Russia.

MacLachlan, Patricia. *Sarah, Plain and Tall*. New York: Harper, 1985.
- A look into the nineteenth-century West, where a brother and sister must adjust to their father's mail-order bride.

Mead, Alice. *Dawn and Dusk*. New York: Farrar, Straus & Giroux, 2007.
- The story of a 13-year-old boy in the Iraq War of the 1980s.

Myers, Walter Dean. *Fallen Angels*. New York: Scholastic, 1988.
- A frankly realistic story of a young man's experiences during the Vietnam War.

O'Dell, Scott. *Island of the Blue Dolphins*. Boston: Houghton Mifflin, 1960.
- A classic survival story about a young American Indian girl alone on a deserted island.

____. *Sing Down the Moon*. Boston: Houghton Mifflin, 1970.
- The story of the cruel relocation of the Navajo in the nineteenth century.

Orlev, Uri. *The Island on Bird Street*. Trans. Hillel Halkin. Boston: Houghton Mifflin, 1984.
- The story of a young Jewish boy in Warsaw, surviving on his own during World War II.

Park, Linda Sue. *A Single Shard*. New York: Dell, 2001.
- The story of a young, determined potter in twelfth-century Korea.

Pearsall, Shelley. *Crooked River*. New York: Knopf, 2005.
- Set in 1812, the story of a young girl who befriends an Ojibwe Indian enslaved by her father. A moving tale of injustice and inhumanity.

Peck, Richard. *A Year Down Yonder*. New York: Dial, 2000.
- Comical adventures of a young boy during the Great Depression.

Pyle, Howard. *Otto of the Silver Hand*. 1888. Various modern editions.
- A classic tale of courage and honor about a young boy in thirteenth-century Germany who earns his way to knighthood.

Richter, Conrad. *Light in the Forest*. New York: Knopf, 1953.
- The story of a white boy kidnapped at age 4 and raised by American Indians who must deal with divided loyalties when, years later, he is returned to his birth parents.

Richter, Hans Peter. *Friedrich*. New York: Holt, 1970.
- The shattering tale of two German boys—a Jew and a Gentile—growing up during Hitler's rise to power.

Ryan, Pam Muñoz. *Esperanza Rising*. St. Louis, MO: Turtleback, 2002.
- The story of a 13-year-old girl from Mexico adjusting to a new way of life during the Depression of the 1930s.

Sayres, Meghan Nuttall. *Anahita's Woven Riddle*. New York: Amulet, 2006.
- A story set in late nineteenth-century Persia, in which four men compete in a battle of wits for the hand of a clever young nomadic woman.

Schlitz, Laura Amy. *A Drowned Maiden's Hair: A Melodrama*. New York: Candlewick, 2006.
- A tale in the gothic vein of an orphaned girl in the early twentieth century unwittingly partaking in fraudulent séances to bilk wealthy clients.

_____. *Good Masters! Sweet Ladies! Voices from a Medieval Village*. New York: Candlewick, 2007.
- Life in thirteenth-century England is described in a series of monologues and dialogues of young people. Ideal for classroom reading aloud and theater.

Schmidt, Gary D. *Lizzie Bright and the Buckminster Boy*. New York: Clarion, 2004.
- The story of a young boy who faces the reality of racism when his family moves to the Maine coast in the early twentieth century.

Speare, Elizabeth George. *The Witch of Blackbird Pond*. Boston: Houghton Mifflin, 1958.
- A young woman's tale of heroism during the witch scares in colonial America.

_____. *The Sign of the Beaver*. Boston: Houghton Mifflin, 1983.
- A survival story of two eighteenth-century boys, one white and one Indian, who become reluctant friends.

Stead, Rebecca. *When You Reach Me*. New York: Wendy Lamb Books, 2009.
- A slice of life from New York in 1979 in which a sixth-grade girl discovers mysterious notes from an unknown person claiming to know the future.

Stevenson, Robert Louis. *Kidnapped*. 1886. Several modern editions.
- The adventures of a youth caught up in the Jacobite rebellion in eighteenth-century Scotland.

Sutcliff, Rosemary. *The Mark of the Horse Lord*. New York: Walck, 1965.
- An ex-gladiator's adventures in Roman Britain in the first century.

Taylor, Mildred. *Roll of Thunder, Hear My Cry*. New York: Dial, 1976.
- A story of an African-American family in the Deep South of the 1930s, facing brutal racial prejudice; the second of a five-book series, along with *The Land*, *Song of the Trees*, *Let the Circle Be Unbroken*, and *The Road to Memphis*.

Vining, Elizabeth Gray. *Adam of the Road*. New York: Viking, 1942.
- The story of an 11-year-old boy in thirteenth-century England who sets out to find his father.

Walsh, Jill Paton. *The Emperor's Winding Sheet*. New York: Farrar, Straus & Giroux, 1974.
- An exciting tale set in 1453, during the fall of Constantinople.

Wilder, Laura Ingalls. *Little House in the Big Woods*. New York: Harper, 1932.
- The first book in a series about growing up in the nineteenth century, followed by *Little House on the Prairie* (1932), *Farmer Boy* (1933), *On the Banks of Plum Creek* (1937), *By the Shores of Silver Lake*

(1939), *The Long Winter* (1940), *Little Town on the Prairie* (1941), *These Happy Golden Years* (1943), and *The First Four Years* (1971).

Wiles, Deborah. *Countdown*. New York: Scholastic, 2010.
- An 11-year-old girl's experiences during the Cuban missile crisis in 1962. A documentary novel that includes actual photos and news clippings from the period to re-create the atmosphere, it is the first in the projected Sixties trilogy.

Williams, Susan. *Wind Rider*. New York: Laura Geringer/HarperCollins, 2006.
- The story of a talented young horsewoman who faces the challenges of living in prehistoric Asia.

Zusak, Marcus. *The Book Thief*. Picador, 2005.
- Powerful story of a young girl, living through the wartime horrors of Nazi Germany, whose life is made palatable through her love of books. A crossover book appealing both to adult and YA readers. (Although narrated by Death, the story itself is tragically realistic.)

Contemporary Realism: A Selected and Annotated Booklist

Most of these books are for readers in about third grade and older. An individual's interests and abilities are the best guides. Look for other titles by these authors and see the booklists at the end of Chapter 2 *for contemporary novels on other cultures.*

Acampora, Paul. *Defining Dulcie*. New York: Dial, 2006.
- The account of a 16-year-old coping with the death of her father.

Alcott, Louisa May. *Little Women*. 1868–1869. Several modern editions.
- The story of the four sisters in the March family living in New England during the Civil War.

Anderson, Laurie Halse. *Speak*. New York: Farrar, Straus & Giroux, 1999.
- A sensitive book that explores the effects of sexual abuse on a teenage girl.

Bauer, Marion Dane, ed. *Am I Blue?: Coming Out of the Silence*. New York: HarperCollins, 1994.
- A collection of short stories by various authors on the subject of gay and lesbian teenagers.

Bennett, James. *I Can Hear the Mourning Dove*. Boston: Houghton Mifflin, 1990.
- A book that explores the healing process in an emotionally disturbed teenage girl.

Block, Francesca Lia. *Weetzie Bat*. New York: HarperCollins, 1989.
- This surrealistic and sympathetic look at alternative lifestyles is the first of a popular series.

Blume, Judy. *Are You There, God? It's Me, Margaret*. New York: Bradbury, 1970.
- A book about a young girl confronting a host of coming-of-age problems, from the onset of menses to seeking answers to religious faith.

____. *Tales of a Fourth Grade Nothing*. New York: Dutton, 1972.
- A long-time favorite about young Peter Hatcher's comic trials and tribulations.

____. *Tiger Eyes*. Scarsdale, NY: Bradbury, 1981.
- A story about a teenage girl coping following a family tragedy and a move across the nation.

Boyne, John. *The Boy in the Striped Pajamas*. Oxford, UK: David Fickling Books, 2006.
- A book about the horrors of life in Auschwitz, as seen through the innocent eyes of a young boy.

Burnett, Frances Hodgson. *The Secret Garden.* 1909. Various modern editions.
- The classic tale of Mary Lennox and her discoveries while living with her mysterious uncle on the Yorkshire moors.

Burnford, Sheila. *The Incredible Journey.* Boston: Little, Brown, 1961.
- An animal survival story about two dogs and a cat journeying together across Canada.

Childress, Alice. *A Hero Ain't Nothin' but a Sandwich.* New York: Coward, 1973.
- The story of an African-American teenager's struggle with drugs, told from multiple viewpoints.

Cisneros, Sandra. *The House on Mango Street.* Houston: Arte Público, 1984.
- A coming-of-age story of a girl growing up in a Hispanic neighborhood in Chicago.

Cleary, Beverly. *Dear Mr. Henshaw.* New York: Morrow, 1983.
- The letters of a young boy coping with his parents' recent divorce.

____. *Henry Huggins.* New York: Morrow, 1950.
- The comic adventures of Henry during his third-grade year. A modern classic.

____. *Ramona the Pest.* New York: Morrow, 1968.
- One of eight books focusing on the adventures of Ramona, a friend of Henry Huggins. A perennial favorite among early elementary readers.

Cleaver, Bill, and Vera Cleaver. *Where the Lilies Bloom.* Philadelphia: Lippincott, 1969.
- A story about orphaned Appalachian children struggling to survive in dire circumstances.

Cormier, Robert. *The Chocolate War.* New York: Pantheon, 1974.
- A dark tale about social corruption pervading a private religious school.

____. *I Am the Cheese.* New York: Bell, 1987.
- The tragic story of an innocent family who become the victims of massive government abuse.

Craven, Margaret. *I Heard the Owl Call My Name.* New York: Bantam, 1973.
- The story of a young priest who comes to a Kwakiutl Indian village in British Columbia, where he faces life's most difficult challenges.

Creech, Sharon. *Walk Two Moons.* New York: Harper, 1994.
- A book narrated by a young girl of American Indian heritage, about the extraordinary events during a difficult year of adjustment.

Crutcher, Chris. *Athletic Shorts.* New York: Greenwillow, 1991.
- A collection of short stories about teenage athletes, including two with gay themes.

Defoe, Daniel. *Robinson Crusoe.* Retold by Steven Zorn. Philadelphia: Running Press, 2002.
- A version of Defoe's classic survival story retold for younger readers.

Donovan, John. *I'll Get There. It Better Be Worth the Trip.* New York: Harper & Row, 1969.
- One of the first young adult novels to deal with homosexuality.

Draper, Sharon. *Out of My Mind.* New York: Atheneum, 2010.
- A moving first-person narrative of a girl with cerebral palsy.

Fama, Elizabeth. *Overboard.* Peru, IL: Cricket, 2002.
- The story of a shipwreck that leaves an American girl and an Indonesian boy struggling to survive in the ocean.

Farley, Walter. *The Black Stallion.* New York: Random House, 1944.
- An adventure classic about a boy and a horse who survive a shipwreck and become inseparable. One of the best horse stories ever written, and the first of a series.

Fitzhugh, Louise. *Harriet the Spy.* New York: Harper, 1964.
- The story of a precocious young girl in New York City who proves too wise for her own good.

Ford, Michael Thomas. *Suicide Notes*. New York: Harper, 2008.
- A 15-year-old gay teenager's examination of his life after a botched suicide attempt; at once irreverent, funny, and poignant.

Fox, Paula. *Eagle Kite*. New York: Orchard, 1995.
- A somber story of a boy wrestling with family secrets as his father is dying of AIDS.

Gantos, Jack. *Dead End in Norvelt*. New York: Farrar, Straus & Giroux, 2011.
- A clever and comical mystery based on the author's own youthful experiences.

George, Jean Craighead. *Julie of the Wolves*. New York: Harper, 1972.
- A survival story of a Yupik girl stranded in the Arctic wilderness.

Gipson, Fred. *Old Yeller*. New York: Harper, 1956.
- The story of the friendship between a Texas boy and his dog.

Green, John. *Looking for Alaska*. New York: Dutton, 2005.
- The story of a 16-year-old who must come to terms with the suicide of her best friend.

Guy, Rosa. *The Friends*. New York: Viking, 1973.
- The story of a difficult friendship between two girls of color, one from the West Indies and one from New York.

Haddon, Mark. *The Curious Incident of the Dog in the Night-time*. New York: Doubleday, 2003.
- A mystery about a boy with an emotionally dissociated mind. The specific condition is never revealed, but traits of the autistic savant or of Asperger's syndrome are suggested.

Hamilton, Virginia. *M. C. Higgins, the Great*. New York: Macmillan, 1974.
- A black teenager in the Appalachian Mountains must choose between tradition and change.

Hest, Amy. *Remembering Mrs. Rossi*. New York: Candlewick, 2007.
- A story in which a third-grade girl and her father cope with the death of her mother.

Hiaasen, Carl. *Hoot*. New York: Bantam, 2005.
- A story with an environmental message that features eccentric characters, including an assortment of animals.

Hinton, S. E. *The Outsiders*. New York: Viking, 1967.
- One of the first novels of new realism, the story of teenage gangs—actually written by a teenager.

Hunt, Irene. *Up a Road Slowly*. New York: Follett, 1967.
- A moving coming-of-age story about an orphaned girl who faces difficult adjustments when she goes to live with her spinster aunt, a teacher.

Kerr, Judith. *When Hitler Stole Pink Rabbit*. New York: Puffin, 1971.
- The semiautobiographical story of a young girl's escape from Nazi Germany.

Kerr, M. E. *Deliver Us from Evie*. New York: Harper, 1994.
- The story of Evie's family adjusting to her announced lesbianism.

Kerrin, Jessica Scott. *Martin Bridge, Ready for Takeoff!* Toronto: Kids Can, 2005.
- The first in a series of books containing short stories about an inventive third-grader's adventures.

Kinney, Jeff. *Diary of a Wimpy Kid*. New York: Amulet, 2007.
- The trials and tribulations of a middle schooler. The first of an immensely popular series, including *Rodrick Rules* (2008) and *The Last Straw* (2009).

Kipling, Rudyard. *Kim.* 1901. Several modern editions.
- A classic tale of life in late nineteenth-century India, through the eyes of a young boy. See also *Captain Courageous*, a coming-of-age story about a boy on the high seas.

Kjelgaard, Jim. *Big Red.* New York: Holiday, 1956.
- The story of the friendship between a boy and his Irish setter.

Knight, Eric. *Lassie Come-Home.* Philadelphia: Winston, 1940.
- The classic tale of a boy and his dog, a prize collie. Set in Great Britain.

Knowles, John. *A Separate Peace.* London: Secker & Warburg, 1959.
- A modern classic about a tragedy at a New England boys' school.

Konigsburg, E. L. *From the Mixed-up Files of Mrs. Basil E. Frankweiler.* New York: Atheneum, 1967.
- A clever mystery story set in the Metropolitan Museum of Art in New York City.

____. *The View from Saturday.* New York: Atheneum, 1996.
- The story of several extraordinary children of varying backgrounds preparing for a quiz contest.

Lin, Grace. *The Year of the Dog.* New York: Little, Brown, 2006.
- A humorous coming-of-age story about the daughter of Taiwanese immigrants living in upstate New York. Followed by the sequels *The Year of the Rat* and *Dumpling Days*.

London, Jack. *The Call of the Wild.* 1903. Many modern editions.
- A classic realistic animal story of a family dog who is stolen from California and lives with a cruel master in Alaska before escaping and returning to the life of his ancestors.

Lord, Cynthia. *Rules.* Scholastic, 2006.
- A sensitive book about a young girl and her relationship with her autistic brother and a paraplegic boy.

Lowry, Lois. *A Summer to Die.* Boston: Houghton Mifflin, 1977.
- The story of a girl coping with the death of her sister.

MacLachlan, Patricia. *Arthur, for the Very First Time.* New York: HarperCollins, 1994.
- The story of 10-year-old Arthur's transformative summer on his great uncle's farm.

____. *Baby.* Logan, IA: Perfection Learning, 1995.
- A moving story of loss and redemption that begins with the discovery of an infant left in a basket in a driveway.

McCloskey, Robert. *Homer Price.* New York: Viking, 1943.
- The comic adventures of an imaginative boy living in small-town Ohio.

Montgomery, Lucy Maude. *Anne of Green Gables.* 1908. Several modern editions.
- The popular tale of a young girl adopted by an elderly brother and sister on Prince Edward Island, Canada.

Morpurgo, Michael. *Kensuke's Kingdom.* New York: Scholastic, 2003.
- The story of an elderly Japanese man, stranded on an island for 40 years, who rescues an 11-year-old boy from the sea.

Mowat, Farley. *Owls in the Family.* Boston: Little, Brown, 1962.
- A comical tale of a boy and his two pet owls.

Myers, Walter Dean. *Scorpions.* New York: Harper, 1988.
- The story of a young African-American boy who is pressured to become a gang member.

____. *Street Love.* New York: HarperCollins, 2006.
- A verse novel about a teenage romance in Harlem.

Na, An. *A Step from Heaven*. Asheville, NC: Front Street, 2001.
- The story of a Korean girl's acculturation after her move to America.

Naylor, Phyllis Reynolds. *Shiloh*. New York: Atheneum, 1991.
- A story about a young West Virginia boy who finds a mistreated beagle pup and faces ethical issues.

Nesbit, E. *The Story of the Treasure Seekers*. London: Unwin, 1899.
- A book about six children who try to recover their family's lost fortune. The first of the Bastable Children trilogy, along with *The Wouldbegoods* (1901) and *The New Treasure Seekers* (1904).

Palacio, R. J. *Wonder*. New York: Knopf, 2012.
- A story about a boy with a physical deformity entering a mainstream fifth-grade class.

Paterson, Katherine. *Bridge to Terabithia*. New York: Crowell, 1977.
- The story of a friendship between a young girl and boy that ends in tragedy.

____. *The Great Gilly Hopkins*. New York: Crowell, 1978.
- The story of a difficult but clever foster child and her efforts to reunite with her mother.

Paulsen, Gary. *Hatchet*. New York: Bradbury, 1987.
- The story of a young boy who must survive on his own after a plane crash, with only a hatchet.

Peck, Richard. *Remembering the Good Times*. New York: Delacorte, 1985.
- A look at teenagers dealing with the suicide of a close friend.

____. *Secrets of the Shopping Mall*. New York: Delacorte, 1979.
- The story of a young boy and girl trying to escape the clutches of a gang by hiding out in a mall.

Peck, Robert. *A Day No Pigs Would Die*. New York: Knopf, 1972.
- The moving story of a 13-year-old boy who must grow up quickly. Set in rural Vermont.

Potok, Chaim. *My Name Is Asher Lev*. New York: Knopf, 1972.
- The story of a Hasidic Jew struggling with his commitment to his faith and to his art.

Ransome, Arthur. *Swallows and Amazons*. 1930. Several modern editions.
- The first of a series of twelve outdoor adventure stories set in the British Isles.

Rawlings, Marjorie Kinnan. *The Yearling*. New York: Scribner's, 1938.
- A powerful tale set in central Florida of a boy who raises a fawn but must make a terrible choice. The only children's book that has ever won the Pulitzer Prize.

Rawls, Wilson. *Where the Red Fern Grows*. New York: Doubleday, 1961.
- A classic, heart-rending tale of a boy and his two dogs in the Ozarks.

Rylant, Cynthia. *Missing May*. New York: Scholastic, 1992.
- The story of a young girl coping with the death of her beloved foster mother.

Sachar, Louis. *Holes*. New York: Farrar, Straus & Giroux, 1998.
- A sort of tragicomedy—verging on fantasy—about a boy who must solve a mystery while he is incarcerated at a detention camp in Texas.

Saeed, Aisha. *Written in the Stars*. Speak, 2016.
- The story of a modern Pakistani girl, living in America, whose parents attempt to force her into an arranged marriage.

Salisbury, Graham. *Lord of the Deep*. New York: Delacorte, 2001.
- The story of a 13-year-old boy coming of age on a deep-sea fishing trip in the Pacific with his stepfather.

Sanchez, Alex. *Rainbow Boys*. New York: Simon & Schuster, 2001.
- A portrayal of the experiences of gay teens. The first book in a trilogy that also includes *Rainbow High* (2003) and *Rainbow Road* (2005).

____. *So Hard to Say*. New York: Simon & Schuster, 2004.
- A sensitive exploration of a young boy's grappling with his own sexuality. One of the few novels on sexual orientation aimed at early teens.

Schmidt, Gary. *Orbiting Jupiter*. New York: Clarion, 2015.
- The moving story of a teenaged foster child who will go to any lengths to find his baby daughter.

Scott, Elizabeth. *Living Dead Girl*. New York: Simon Pulse, 2008.
- The chilling story of a young girl's 5-year abduction by a sex abuser. For older readers.

Sherman, Alexie. *The Absolutely True Story of a Part-Time Indian*. New York: Little, Brown, 2007.
- A teenager from the Spokane Indian Reservation recounts his struggles trying to navigate two worlds—that of his Native American heritage and that of mainstream America.

Smith, Doris Buchanan. *A Taste of Blackberries*. New York: Crowell, 1973.
- A book about a young boy who must come to terms with the death of a friend.

Sobol, Donald. *Encyclopedia Brown, Boy Detective*. 1963. Several later editions.
- The first of a series of popular detective stories for elementary school readers.

Spinelli, Jerry. *Maniac Magee*. Boston: Little, Brown, 1990.
- A tall tale about a boy bringing together a racially divided community.

Staples, Suzanne Fisher. *Shabanu: Daughter of the Wind*. New York: Knopf, 1989.
- The story of a modern Pakistani girl struggling with the conflict between tradition and modernity.

Stevenson, Robert Louis. *Treasure Island*. 1883. Various modern editions.
- A classic pirate tale, complete with buried treasure and a villain with a wooden leg.

Stolz, Joelle. *The Shadows of the Ghadames*. New York: Delacorte, 2004.
- The story of a Muslim girl in nineteenth-century Libya being introduced to a changing world.

Taylor, Theodore. *The Cay*. New York: Doubleday, 1969.
- The story of an 11-year-old white boy, blinded in a wartime accident, who survives with the help of an older black man on a deserted Caribbean island.

Tolan, Stephanie S. *Surviving the Applewhites*. New York: HarperCollins, 2002.
- The story of a troubled 13-year-old boy who finds himself the ward of an eccentric family of artists.

Twain, Mark. *The Adventures of Huckleberry Finn*. 1884. Several modern editions.
- A classic tale about an irascible boy on an adventure down the Mississippi.

____. *The Adventures of Tom Sawyer*. 1876. Several modern editions.
- The classic tale of a boy's life along the Mississippi in the mid-nineteenth century.

Voigt, Cynthia. *Homecoming*. New York: Atheneum, 1981.
- Four siblings abandoned by their mother make a difficult journey to their grandmother's. First of the seven books in the Tillerman cycle.

Wolf, Virginia Euwer. *Make Lemonade*. New York: Holt, 1993.
- A verse novel about a young girl who babysits for the children of an unwed teenage mother and the relationship that develops. The first of a series of three, followed by *True Believer* (2001) and *This Full House* (2009).

Woodson, Jacqueline. *Locomotion*. New York: Putnam, 2003.
- A story in which an 11-year-old orphaned African-American boy reveals his hopes, fears, and frustrations through a series of poems.

Wynne-Jones, Tim. *Some of the Kinder Planets*. New York: Kroupa, 1995.
- A collection of short stories, both serious and amusing, often off-beat, involving a variety of young characters, male and female.

Zindel, Paul. *My Darling, My Hamburger*. New York: Harper, 1969.
- A groundbreaking story in which teenagers confront the issues of premarital sex, rape, and pregnancy.

____. *The Pigman*. New York: Harper, 1968.
- The story of two teenagers forming an unusual bond with a lonely old man.

Nonfiction

Telling It Like It Is

"In nonfiction, you have that limitation, that constraint, of telling the truth."

–Peter Mattheissen. Interview by Michael Sims, *BookPage* (2000)

Introduction

A famous television detective from the 1950s, Joe Friday of *Dragnet*, was fond of remarking, "All we want are the facts, ma'am." In nonfiction, facts are important, of course, but as Dr. P. M. Latham, a nineteenth-century English physician, said, a good book must contain "important facts, duly arranged, and reasoned upon with care" (43). Good nonfiction is not a mere catalogue of information or a list of hard facts. Indeed, the most interesting nonfiction book tells us a story—the story of a natural process, the story of a human life, the story of our past, the story of the universe. It is a book that connects us to the world around us.

The earliest nonfiction for children typically consisted of dreary tomes prepared for use in the schoolroom (see Chapter 1, Figures 1.1, 1.2, and 1.3.) They often contained rather dry catalogues of facts and figures for young readers to absorb, master, or memorize. Beginning in the twentieth century, a new attitude toward nonfiction emerged. This was the notion that a work of nonfiction could be just as interesting, just as beautiful, just as inspiring as a good work of fiction. Among the earliest examples of this new nonfiction were histories for young readers. In fact, the very first winner of the Newbery Medal, in 1922, was Hendrik van Loon's *The Story of Mankind*, an ambitious history of the human race, which was illustrated by van Loon himself (see Figure 10.1). And although nonfiction Newbery Award winners are few and far between, we can take heart that many talented writers are producing high-quality nonfiction for young readers, including books on history, science, nature, the arts, psychology, and sociology. At least two distinguished book awards (the NCTE Orbis Pictus Award and the Robert F. Sibert Informational

FIGURE 10.1 ■ Henrik van Loon made his own illustrations for his account of human history in the Newbery Award-winning *The Story of Mankind* (1922). Here is his topographical map of Europe designed for one of the endcovers. Notice that he even includes the valleys in the ocean floor. The artless drawing possesses a naïve, almost childlike, quality that may make a daunting subject—the history of all of humanity—less intimidating.

Book Award) are reserved exclusively for outstanding works of nonfiction. In fact, the publishing of children's nonfiction has been flourishing in recent years, perhaps in part because of the emphasis placed on nonfiction by the Common Core Curriculum standards (see Chapter 3 and Rosen, 2015). In this chapter, we will examine the world of children's nonfiction—its characteristics, its expansiveness, its rewards.

Characteristics of Nonfiction

Unlike fiction, where we look for engaging characters, a compelling plot, and perhaps excitement and escape, nonfiction is chained to truth. But that does not mean it cannot be fascinating, stimulating, and thought provoking. (And, as they say, truth is often stranger than fiction.) Of course, fiction and nonfiction have very different requirements. We expect nonfiction to have a clear purpose suited to its audience, accurate information that is objective and balanced, and a style and format that are suited to the material. Let's look at these features more closely.

Purpose and Audience

Nonfiction is didactic; it has a specific instructional goal—from teaching the sounds of the alphabet and explaining the cycles of life or the movement of the stars to describing historial events or the life of a famous person. Each work also has a specific audience, ranging from preschoolers and toddlers to young adults and older adults. Naturally, the intended audience will determine the contents and approach of the book. To determine this, we have to answer a few questions: How much do the intended readers know? How much can we expect them to grasp? What is going to keep them interested? What details are appropriate to this audience?

Nonfiction for preschoolers (that is, ages about 5 and younger) often takes the form of the concept book (see Chapter 5). Indeed, an alphabet or counting book is intended to convey certain skills, just as we might find in a nonfiction book for older readers. Sometimes, fiction and nonfiction can intersect—this happens often in alphabet books (see Chris Van Allsburg's *Z Was Zapped*). Or look at *A Medieval Feast* by Aliki, which is a picture book for early elementary readers that describes life in the European Middle Ages. To appeal to this young audience, the author combines a fictional framing story—the king is coming to dine—with colorful illustrations that provide a vivid portrait of medieval life. There is no plot or conflict such as we would find in a fictional tale. Instead, we get a colorful, and fairly accurate, account of one aspect of medieval life. On the other hand, we find books that are filled with straight-forward facts, such as Steve Jenkins' book about comparatives in nature, *Biggest, Fastest, Strongest*, or Ruth Heller's popular *Chickens Aren't the Only Ones*, and about animals who lay eggs. The appeal of both lies in their striking and colorful illustrations and their clear and straightforward textual explanations.

Books for readers in the early grades often rely on humor, which can be conveyed while relying on factual details. Jean Fritz's series of picture-book biographies for children in about third through fifth grade are accurately told, and based on hard facts, and at the same time demonstrate the wonderfully human side of history. Her heroes are not portrayed as sacred relics, but as very vulnerable and engaging people (see *Where Do You Think You Are Going, Christopher Columbus?*; *What's the Big Idea, Benjamin Franklin?*; *Shh! We're Writing the Constitution*; and many others).

As readers reach middle school, they are ready for more deeply penetrating books, but even these need not be dry and stuffy. We all love a good story, and the best nonfiction consists of stories well told. Albert Marrin's *Years of Dust: The Story of the Dust Bowl* relates the history of the devastating dust storms that plagued the Great Plains in the 1930s. A gripping story in itself, Marrin includes not only period photographs but stories of individuals who lived through the disaster, often in their own words. Personal anecdotes remind us that history is not merely dates and facts—it recounts the lives of human beings, in both their struggles and triumphs. Marrin also includes maps, reading lists, and an index—all indications of the high regard in which the author holds his readers.

Factual Information

In fiction, we don't have to worry about the accuracy of facts—most of them are made up anyway. In nonfiction, accuracy is crucial. But "facts" themselves can be tentative things. In *The Reason for a Flower*, first published in 1983, Ruth Heller refers to fungi as plants. But in 2007, fungi were reclassified and put into their own kingdom—neither plant nor animal. In other words, what we think are "facts" may change with new information. (See the discussion below about Pluto.) Moreover, science is not the only field where new discoveries are being made. Historians, for example, also keep uncovering new information—forgotten letters, secret memos, newly discovered artifacts, old photos. For example, it was once popularly believed that the witches in seventeenth-century Salem, Massachusetts, were burned at the stake (in fact, they were hung) or that people in Columbus's day thought the Earth was flat (in fact, both the shape of the Earth and its size have been known since ancient times—the Greek mathematician Pythagoras referred to the spherical shape of Earth in the sixth century BCE and another Greek mathematician, Eratosthenes, calculated its size quite accurately in the late third century BCE). And, by the way, Marie Antoinette never said, "Let them eat cake." History is filled with myths that need to be debunked.

As facts can change, so can attitudes. A good example is seen in a survey of children's biographies of Christopher Columbus. Early books (such as Ingri and Edgar Parin d'Aulaire's *Columbus*, 1955) depict Columbus as a heroic figure braving the unknown and bringing sophisticated European culture to the benighted Indians. But beginning in the later twentieth century, we find books (such as David Adler's *Christopher Columbus, Great Explorer* and Milton Meltzer's *Christopher Columbus and the World Around Him*) that depict Columbus in a less flattering light, emphasizing his mercenary nature as well as his heinous treatment of the native population. It just may be that in some future time, his reputation will be once again re-evaluated. Consequently, we always need to be aware of a nonfiction book's publication date and, as importantly, when it was written—these do matter. On the other hand, this doesn't mean that newer books are always better than the old ones; that is just not true. New books can get it wrong, too.

However, we can generalize that modern nonfiction books for young readers are more likely to offer solid evidence—in the form of figures, data, and charts—to support claims. Two of the most celebrated historical writers are Russell Freedman and Jim Murphy, who began raising the bar for children's nonfiction with their meticulously researched, fact-based historical accounts. And although the period photographs, ample resource lists, and bibliographies can help give integrity to a book (that is, they prove that the writer didn't just make up this stuff), these features also suggest the authors' high regard for their young audience—curious readers who might want to know where the information came from and where they might find more.

Writing Style

Millicent Selsam, a noted science writer for children, once said, "A good science book is not just a collection of facts" (62). A good science book conveys, in Selsam's words, "something of the beauty and excitement of science" (65). She is referring to style—the writer's choice of words, the construction of sentences and paragraphs, and the organization of the material. Perhaps the first rule of style is that the writing be clear. It does not matter how accurate the text is if we cannot understand what it's saying. For example, terms need to be identified in ways young readers can grasp. Here is where the language of metaphor comes in handy (see Chapter 6). When Selsam describes the white spots on a baby deer's coat as looking "like spots of sunlight on the forest floor" (*Hidden Animals*), she is making a comparison (a simile, in fact) to help us visualize the subject.

Jim Arnosky, in *Watching Desert Wildlife*, describes his observations of birds, snakes, lizards, deer, and other desert wildlife. At the conclusion of his work, he sums up his experience and its meaning with these words:

> I went to the desert to feel the heat of the desert sun and breathe the dry air. I went to the desert to see its wide open places. I went with my eyes open wide, watchful for snakes and scorpions, and alert, ready to see all the wonderful wild animals who make their homes amid the thorns and spines.
>
> I came home from the desert with a fresh new outlook on nature and wildlife. I felt bigger and broader, happy in the knowledge that I had discovered another world. (n.p.)

A good writer of nonfiction has a gift for describing complex information in language that is clear, precise, succinct, and beautiful—indeed, the language of science is often quite poetic. But so is the language of history. Albert Marrin's award-winning *Years of Dust: The Story of the Dust Bowl* concludes his story of the ecological disaster of the Great Plains in the 1930s by quoting the great Suquamish Chief Seattle addressing American officials:

> *"Will you teach your children what we have taught our children? That the earth is our mother?" the chief asked. Then Seattle answered his own questions. "What befalls the earth befalls the sons of the earth. . . . The earth does not belong to man, man belongs to the earth. . . . All things are connected like the blood which unites us all. Man did not weave the web of life, he is merely a strand in it. Whatever he does to the web, he does to himself."*
>
> *We should remember the wise chief's words when we think about the Dust Bowl that was and the dust bowls that yet may be.* (122)

Informational Format

Format refers to the physical presentation of material, specifically how the pages and chapters are laid out. In a novel, we typically find just text (that is, words and sentences) divided into chapters. And, except for picture books, we seldom expect to find illustrations in fictional stories. But a nonfiction book is another kettle of fish. A book full of facts can be overwhelming, and some facts are easier explained with pictures than with words alone. A nonfiction book often includes unusual typeface, chapter and division headings, as well as a table of contents, bibliography, index, and illustrations. In other words, an informational book may have a very different look from a work of fiction.

TABLE OF CONTENTS   A table of contents, usually at the front of a book, provides a list of chapter titles along with corresponding page numbers, and serves as an overview of the book's contents. Modern fiction, especially novels, often dispense entirely with a table of contents—it just is not terribly useful (and many readers prefer not to know what's going to happen at the end anyway). But an informational chapter book almost always includes a table of contents. In a nonfiction work, readers usually want to know what to expect and where in the book to find things. A good table of contents gives us a clear sense of what will find inside, listing chapter titles and page numbers (in fact, a table of contents without page numbers is of little use). A helpful table of contents contains clear and accurate headings (rather than merely clever ones) and demonstrates the logic of the book's organization.

EXPLANATORY NOTES   A fictional work really has no need for footnotes or endnotes. But it is fairly common for an informational book to include footnotes, which are placed at the bottom of the page, or endnotes, which are placed at the end of each chapter or at the back of the book. These notes provide additional information the author found interesting and useful but not necessarily crucial to the content of the book. It just may be too awkward to include the additional information in the text. Or perhaps the notes contain suggestions for additional readings or fascinating tidbits of extraneous information. (Footnotes and endnotes are occasionally more interesting than the text!)

GLOSSARY   A glossary is a specialized list of important terms used throughout the book, along with their definitions—in effect, it is a miniature dictionary adapted to a specific book. The glossary (which is never found in fiction) is especially helpful if a book uses a lot of technical terms or uses certain terms in a specialized way. Again, this is something we find only in nonfiction books for older readers and in books that deal with technical topics that use a lot of uncommonly used words or words used in unusual ways. See the glossary at the back of this book for an example.

APPENDIX   An appendix is a section that contains additional information that may not fit so neatly into the body of the text. An example can be found in David Aguilar's *Space Encyclopedia*, which includes a Timeline of the Solar System, a Timeline of the Human Race, and a Timeline of Astronomy, all appended (hence the name "appendix") to the end of the text. An appendix is a great place to include lengthy lists that do not easily fit into paragraphs, and is also excellent for imparting a lot of technical data that would be difficult to incorporate into a typical paragraph. Again, examine the appendices in the back of this book.

BIBLIOGRAPHY   This, of course, is simply a list of resources (books, articles, films, and so forth) on a specific topic. Whenever a student writes a research paper, teachers expect to see a list of the books, papers, essays, articles, and other sources used in the research. But the bibliography is also helpful to readers who want to explore the subject further, which is why so many works of nonfiction contain a bibliography. The bibliography may include not just specific works the author used in the research, but other works on the same topic that might interest the reader. The bibliography is the place to begin if you want to find out more information on a subject. Again, look at the bibliographies that follow each chapter in this book.

INDEX A nonfiction work for older readers (middle school and beyond) is likely to contain an index. Always at the very end of the book, an index is a list of the important subjects discussed in the book, along with the page numbers where readers can find specific information. The purpose of an index is to enable readers to use the book as a reference source. So, if readers want to find out something specific, they can locate the topic in the index without having to read through the entire book. See the index to this book for an example.

ILLUSTRATIONS Young readers—and, I suspect, many adults—enjoy illustrations in a nonfiction book. The illustrations in a nonfiction book may include drawings, photographs, diagrams, graphs, charts, or any other non-textual matter used to explain key ideas. Let's look as some of these in more detail.

Photographs are very popular in nonfiction because of their accuracy and sense of authenticity. History books and biographies may use period photographs that were actually taken during the historical era covered in the book. Russell Freedman's Newbery-award-winning *Lincoln: A Photobiography* makes ample use of period photographs and illustrations. Books about the sciences and arts make effective use of photography as well when they want to convey accurate details.

Sometimes, however, a photograph will just not work. Then the author may turn to drawings. For example, in her book on human reproduction, *Mommy Laid an Egg; Or, Where Do Babies Come From?* Babette Cole uses comical cartoon drawings depicting aspects of human anatomy and sexuality. I am sure you can see why photographs might be problematic in this instance. Tony De Saulles's cartoon drawings for Nick Arnold's *The Body Owner's Handbook* substitute for actual photographs of human internal organs, which could be unsettling. David Macaulay's *Cathedral* describes the process of building a medieval cathedral, and his exquisite pen-and-ink drawings more than make up for the absence of photographs, which of course did not exist in medieval times. David Aguilar is a master of computerization, as can be seen in his illustrations for his books on outer space, including *Space Encyclopedia* and *13 Planets*, where he can help us imagine what is impossible for us to see in the mysterious reaches of the universe (see Figure 10.2).

Seemingly inspired by television and electronic media, the "Eyewitness Juniors" series contains information in small doses on pages filled with an array of illustrations, as in Mary Ling's *Amazing Crocodiles & Reptiles* (see Figure 10.3). These books serve as stimulating introductions and springboards to more sophisticated treatments. Similarly, Seymour Simon's *Out of Sight: Pictures of Hidden Worlds* contains a series of stunning photographs—all produced through technologically sophisticated means—showing us such things as the interior of a living human heart, the head of a ladybug or the formation of new stars in a galaxy 7,000 light years away.

FIGURE 10.2 ■ David Aguilar's stunning drawing from his book *13 Planets* suggests what Uranus might look like from its moon, Miranda, capturing both the majesty and the mystery of the solar system.

Hatching out

Most reptiles lay eggs. Some eggs have leathery shells, and others have hard shells, like hens' eggs. And some reptiles don't lay eggs at all. They give birth to live young, just like humans do.

1 When it's time to break out, the baby hog-nosed viper's egg shrivels, because the baby has used up all the yolk inside.

2 The baby snake makes the first cut in its shell with a special tiny egg tooth. Pushing with its snout, it pokes its head out.

4 The baby snake is a miniature version of its parents. Once it's hatched, it does not need to be looked after by Mom.

3 The snake stays inside its safe shell for hours, or even days, before it finally crawls out.

Empty shell

FIGURE 10.3 ■ In this illustration from Mary Ling's *Amazing Crocodiles & Reptiles*, we see the hatching of a viper, with four stages of the process captured in photography by Jerry Young and carefully labeled.

Maps are very helpful in both history and geography books. Janis Herbert's *The Civil War for Kids*, for example, includes several maps, including battlefield maps. Map reading is an important skill too easily overlooked in this day of global positioning systems, and young readers might need the help of such works as Scot Ritchie's picture storybook *Follow That Map! A First Book of Mapping Skills* and Sara Finelli's *My Map Book*. (See also Figure 10.1)

Charts, diagrams, and tables are used in a wide variety of nonfiction books. A history book might include a timeline that places events in chronological order. A biography might include a genealogy chart or family tree illustrating family relationships. A science book might include a diagram, which is simply a labeled drawing. A book on dance might include a diagram of a dance movement, something that is very difficult to capture in a photograph. A table is a means of organizing information into rows and columns to make it more accessible or to help compare items; for example, a table might be used to show how various kinds of animals differ in their diet, habitat, life span, and so on. Tables can pack a lot of information into a small space. (See the various visual aids in Chapter 4.)

The key to all these visual aids is that they be clear, unambiguous, and easy to follow, and that they help us understand the subject. We want illustrations that are accurately labeled with helpful captions. Illustrations without captions leave us guessing about what we're looking at. What good are they? Finally, each illustration should have a very clear purpose. Illustrations, in other words, should not be mere decoration or window dressing. They should be illuminating and helpful.

Types of Nonfiction

For the sake of convenience, we will divide nonfiction into five types: science and nature; arts and leisure; human growth and development; history, society, and culture; and biography and autobiography. Each of these very broad categories requires a slightly different approach, as you will see.

Science and Nature

Books about science and nature include many topics: the life sciences (animals and plants), the earth sciences (rocks, minerals, the weather, the environment), astronomy, mathematics, and technology.

As might be expected, books about animals are among the most popular of the science books, particularly with younger readers. Even the youngest children find almost any book about animals appealing. In recent years, a number of fine books have been written on unusual and threatened animal species, including the puffin, the panda, and the bald eagle. Series such as *Save Earth's Animals* and *Eye to Eye with Endangered Species* are raising young readers' awareness about the fragility of animal life on our planet. Typically, these books describe the animals' life cycles, habits, and importance in the larger frame of the natural world, and often what is being done to save them. Jim Brandenburg is a noted environmentalist and photographer who has written many books for children, including *Face to Face with Wolves*, an intimate portrait of the threatened Arctic wolf. It is never too early to get children thinking about environmental issues—and it is often the case that the children influence their parents' actions.

Gail Gibbons's *From Seed to Plant* and Ruth Heller's *The Reason for a Flower* (mentioned earlier) illustrate one of nature's most elemental tales—the growth of a plant from a tiny seed—and invite hands-on experiences. It is not only the animal world that is threatened with extinction, and we are beginning to see books alerting young children to the potential disappearance of our plant life as well. Plants, of course, are not naturally cuddly, nor do they have expressive personalities (except possibly for the Venus flytrap). So a writer must emphasize other qualities, such as a plant's beauty, its uniqueness, and its importance to us and to the ecosystem. Richard C. Vogt's *Rain Forests*, one of the *Insiders* series from Simon & Schuster, provides plentiful information about rain forests worldwide, along with three-dimensional illustrations.

Astronomy is an exciting, if challenging, subject for children, and making it understandable for young readers requires a great deal of ingenuity. In *Exploring the Night Sky*, science writer Terence Dickinson describes the immense size of the solar system by using an extended metaphor:

> A model of the solar system gives an idea of its size and the sizes of its various members. Let's use a major-league baseball stadium located in the centre of a large city for the model. The sun, the size of a baseball, rests on home plate. Mercury, Venus, Earth and Mars, each about the dimensions of the ball in a ballpoint pen, are, respectively, 1/8, 1/5, 1/3 and 1/2 of the way to the pitcher's mound. A pea near second base is Jupiter. In shallow centre field is a smaller pea, Saturn. Uranus, the size of this letter O, is at the fence off in deep centre field. Neptune and Pluto, a letter O and a grain of salt in our model, are just outside the park. (26)

He continues with the baseball field metaphor, noting that the nearest star to our solar system "would be a baseball in another city more than 1,000 miles away" (26).

Unlike fictional works, informational books can quickly become outdated. For example, Dickinson's passage, when first published in 1987, was accurate—the solar system contained nine planets. Some 20 years later, the scientific community downgraded Pluto to the status of a dwarf planet, because recent data had revealed Pluto did not possess all the properties to qualify it as a planet; for example, it was not big enough to clear other things out of its orbit. As a result, we had to get used to a solar system of eight planets. Then, just as we were getting accustomed to that view of the solar system, more knowledge was gathered, and new books, such as David Aguilar's *13 Planets: The Latest View of the Solar System*, published in 2011, report the addition of the planets Pluto, Haumea, Ceres, Makemake and Eris bringing the total up to thirteen. (see Figure 10.2.)

An unusual series of science books produced in Great Britain by Nick Arnold is fiendishly called *Horrible Science*. The subject is described in the cover material as "Science with the squishy bits left in!" This series now includes numerous titles on all aspects of science, and each book contains cartoonish and often comically outrageous drawings by Tony De Saulles. The titles themselves are tantalizing, including *Chemical Chaos*, *Fatal Forces*, and *Nasty Nature*. In *The Body Owner's Handbook*, Arnold describes in detail the functions of our organs, what can go wrong, and how to best care for our bodies; it is billed as "the guide you simply can't live without." It reads like a manual for auto care, and the author delights in giving his teen audience the gruesome, the unsavory, and the indelicate details they love so much. Although the texts and illustrations are light-hearted in tone, the subjects and explanations are quite serious, and the books provide a great deal of interesting and useful information.

One book of scientific explanations that is not to be missed is David Macaulay's near monumental *The Way Things Work* (followed by *The New Way Things Work* and, most recently, by *The Way Things Work Now*). These hefty volumes explore all the realms of the earth sciences—mechanics, physics (even nuclear physics), electronics, and chemistry, and each succeeding revision focuses, naturally, more heavily on the digital world. (Have you ever wondered how a pop-up toaster knows when the toast is done?) With amazing clarity and simplicity, and with the help of hundreds of clever drawings, Macaulay explains a phenomenal number of complex ideas and processes. He ties the entire work together by using cartoon figures of woolly mammoths to demonstrate the various properties and scientific principles involved. For example, the mammoths are used to represent "force" or "effort." (The cartoon figures, incidentally, do not trivialize the subject matter in this case; instead, they clarify complex ideas—such as jet propulsion and the operation of computers.) In this way, Macaulay uses metaphor to illustrate an abstract concept and humor to make his explanations understandable and enjoyable. These books have enormous appeal for adults as well as young people.

Arts and Leisure

Unfortunately, modern American society has typically regarded the arts as luxuries, frills, or idle pastimes. When school budgets are cut, art programs are often the first to go. But art feeds the soul as well as the mind, and it should be viewed as an indispensable part of a child's education. As with anything else, most people find art more meaningful when they can participate in it—play the music, perform the dance, act in the play, paint the picture, or mold the sculpture. When participation is not possible, books can help by providing instructions, expanding experiences, piquing curiosity, exploring possibilities, and developing taste. Historical surveys of the various art forms provide essential background information and help broaden our perspectives; it is always important to know what has gone before us. Marc Aronson's *Art Attack: A Short Cultural History of the Avant-Garde*, for example, describes a specific movement in modern art. William Latch's *Can You Hear It?* provides an excellent introduction to classical music for younger readers. Robert Levine's *Story of the Orchestra*, for somewhat older readers, includes material about classical music and orchestral instruments.

But for many young readers, their interest is in participating in art rather than simply reading about it. An essential book for preschoolers, Barney Saltzberg's *Beautiful Oops!* is a clever interactive board book that shows how mistakes in art (spills, tears, and other missteps) can be transformed into something purposeful and lovely. For older readers, Art Roche's contributions to the *Art for Kids* series, including *Cartooning* and *Comic Strips*, are sure to appeal to aspiring graphic artists. And for a general guide to graphic art filled with tips, techniques, and projects, have a look at Fiona Watt's *The Usborne Complete Book of Art Ideas*.

Architecture is both art and technology and inextricably linked to both culture and history. David Macaulay (whom we mentioned above) has created a series of picture books that bridge science, history, and art. Each book focuses on a specific type of building and explains how it is built. The buildings range from an Egyptian pyramid (*Pyramid*) to a medieval castle (*Castle*) and cathedral (*Cathedral*) to a modern skyscraper (*Unbuilding*). Macaulay pays close attention to technical detail and also includes information about the society of the builders. Obviously, his books straddle our categories—and there is nothing wrong with that.

The list of subjects in arts and leisure is seemingly endless. Every conceivable sport, hobby, pastime, and artistic endeavor is covered in children's books. Many of these tend to be how-to or instructional books, but we should not overlook the conceptual and historical accounts of humankind's endeavors at creativity and sport. And, it is not too much of a stretch, in the broadest sense of the term "art," we might even include books on language, which is an interesting amalgam of art and science. For example, Lynn Truss's *Eats, Shoots & Leaves: Why, Commas Do Make a Difference* is a light-hearted way of approaching punctuation. (There actually is an adult version of this book as well.) In addition to these books are biographies of athletes, artists, actors, and writers; we discuss biography and autobiography below.

Human Growth and Development

Books about human growth and development are the most recent additions to nonfiction books for children. They include such psychological and sociological concerns as family relationships, friendship and other human interaction, sexual growth and development, physical and emotional challenges, and death and dying.

As you might imagine, books on sexuality are in high demand. Gail Saltz's *Changing You: A Guide to Body Changes and Sexuality* and Jacqui Bailey's *Sex, Puberty, and All That Stuff: A Guide to Growing Up* both include straightforward text with cartoon drawings. The casual approach and comical illustrations remove the mystery of sex, as well as some of its allure. As children reach puberty, they need books that are addressed specifically to males or females. Jeremy Daldry's *The Teenage Guy's Survival Guide: The Real Deal on Girls, Growing Up and Other Guy Stuff* sets out to assuage some of the teenage angst that plagues every boy. And for teenage girls, there are books such as Debra Beck's *My Feet Aren't Ugly! A Girl's Guide to Loving Herself from the Inside Out*. An important part of growing up is learning that we are fundamentally like everybody else.

Another area that is finally receiving the attention it deserves is the issue of sexual preference. Dan Savage's *It Gets Better: Coming Out, Overcoming Bullying, and Creating a Life Worth Living* is a collection of essays and testimonials from people famous and not-so-famous, including former President Barack Obama; former first lady, senator and presidential candidate Hillary Clinton; and British Prime Minister David Cameron; intended to provide words of encouragement to LGBTQ (lesbian, gay, bisexual, transgender, and questioning) teenagers who are victims of bullying. In Susan Kuklin's *Beyond Magenta: Trans Like Me*, six transgender teenagers reflect on their personal experiences with gender identity. We should be encouraged that so many well-done books on these delicate subjects are becoming available. Knowledge always trumps ignorance. And the best way to overcome bigotry is to heighten awareness and increase knowledge, which will ultimately lead to understanding and empathy.

In Chapter 2, we briefly discussed the treatment of death in books for children, pointing out that sometimes a well-written fictional work can provide comfort and understanding in experiencing loss. And sometimes, young people simply need to hear the facts. Earl A. Grollman's *Straight Talk about Death for Teenagers: How to Cope with Losing Someone You Love* is an example of a thorough and straightforward discussion of the many facets of this very difficult topic. Regardless of the subject matter, young readers need honesty, sensitivity, and accuracy in their nonfiction.

History and Human Society

As mentioned in this chapter's introduction, the winner of the first Newbery Award in 1922 was Hendrik van Loon's *The Story of Mankind,* a history of human civilization (see Figure 10.1). This choice perhaps reflects the importance that should be placed on our grasp of history. Jamaican politician and activist Marcus Garvey said, "A people without knowledge of their past history, origin and culture is like a tree without roots." And philosopher George Santayana famously wrote in *The Life of Reason,* "Those who cannot remember the past are condemned to repeat it." Indeed, if we don't know our past, we can hardly make intelligent choices for our future. There are important things we may learn from those who came before us—and only the very foolish ignore that fact. This is what makes good books about history so important for children, and we might expand this category to include books on politics, society, geography, and culture in general.

As we have seen in the preceding chapters, we can learn a great deal about people and places through well-written fiction (both realistic and fantasy) and even through the traditional folktales. However, along with these fictional works, it is helpful to know the facts to gain a fuller understanding of the world in which we live, of the various human societies, and of individual people. Nor should we think that very young children do not understand the concept of history. Even in their early elementary years, children can be drawn into historical subjects. We have already mentioned Aliki, whose picture books on historical and cultural subjects are ideally suited to young readers. One favorite is *Mummies Made in Egypt*, which describes the complicated process by which the ancient Egyptians embalmed their dead (a subject which seems to captivate almost everyone). Also on an Egyptian subject is James Cross Giblin's *Secrets of the Sphinx*, which includes stunning artwork by Bagram Ibatoulline. It is filled with information about one of the most intriguing monuments of the ancient world, presented for readers in the middle grades.

Books for older readers generally have longer texts and fewer illustrations; most are illustrated books rather than picture books. The best writers of history try to depict the past faithfully, including the unpleasant, the controversial, and the vile along with the good, the glorious, and the inspirational. Of particular note are Milton Meltzer (*The Black Americans: A History in Their Own Word* and *Brother*

Can You Spare a Dime? The Great Depression: 1929–1933), Russell Freedman (*Cowboys of the Wild West*, *The War to End All Wars: World War I*, and *Freedom Walkers: The Story of the Montgomery Bus Boycott*, to name only a few), and Jim Murphy (*An American Plague: The True and Terrifying Story of the Yellow Fever Epidemic of 1793*; *The Long Road to Gettysburg*; *The Great Fire*, the story of the Chicago fire of 1871; and many others). Each of these writers has a lively writing style and provides engaging details; period photographs, news clippings, and other archival materials; and reading lists, endnotes, indexes, and other helpful features for serious readers.

Americans, particularly, can sometimes be a bit myopic when thinking of history—they think their history is the only history that matters. This is not only insensitive, it is unhealthy for society. American history is but a small part of the whole picture of human civilization. We should be encouraging young readers to learn about other people, other places, other ideas. Good historical nonfiction for children about other cultures—Asian, African, South American, European—can be a bit more difficult to find, but it is out there. Some books combine human history and science, such as Catherine Thimmesh's *Lucy Long Ago: Uncovering the Mystery of Where We Came From*, which tells the intriguing tale of the discovery of the one of oldest hominid fossils and what it tells us about the human race. What is so good about many of these works on history—particularly very old history—is that they explain the process of uncovering the mysteries of the past. History is not simply a storehouse of dusty facts, it is a puzzle, perhaps an enigma, to be solved, and with each new discovery, our ideas about what happened those years, centuries and eons ago are continually evolving. Russell Freedman has written a fine study of the great Chinese philosopher Confucius (*Confucius and the Golden Rule*). Adeline Yen Mah's *China: Land of Dragons and Emperors*, an acclaimed history of China for young readers, is an example that needs to be emulated.

We may also include books on religion in this category of human culture. Religion is a sensitive area for many people, and writers on religious subjects are wise to be mindful of the delicate nature of this topic. There is a difference between informing and preaching, however. If approached purely from an informational point of view, books on religion can help children learn about their own heritage as well as about religions and cultures around the world. Mary Pope Osborne's *One World, Many Religions: The Way We Worship* is one example of a book that tries to find the common thread of humanity in the world's many faiths. Unfortunately, this is just one of many areas in children's nonfiction where gaps need to be filled. A continuing need exists for good children's and YA books that introduce readers to the wider world, the world outside the United States, where beliefs, customs, and ways of life are different, where people have different needs and different desires. What we desperately need is a world of mutual and cross-cultural understanding, and a good way to begin is to open a book.

Biography and Autobiography

Related to history—in fact, an indispensible part of history—are biographies and autobiographies. These are, of course, the histories of individual lives. The subjects can be living or dead, famous or infamous, or totally unknown. Technically, a biography is the story of a person's life written by someone else; if a person writes his or her own life story, it's called an autobiography ("auto" comes from the Greek word for "self"). Biographies for young readers began to appear as early as the 1920s and 1930s. These early ones tended to romanticize their subjects. Ingri and Parin d'Aulaire's biographies of Abraham Lincoln and Christopher Columbus, for example, place the subjects on a pedestal, where they appear a bit too perfect and heroic, and consequently lack a flesh-and-blood quality. Today, most biographers prefer to portray their subjects as real-life characters—warts and all. However, rather than debunking the heroes, this approach can make them easier to understand and to like; perhaps we just don't trust someone who seems too perfect.

Take, for example, Russell Freedman's *Lincoln: A Photobiography*, which opens with this anecdote:

> *At first glance, most people thought he was homely. Lincoln thought so too, referring once to his "poor, lean, lank face." As a young man he was sensitive about his gawky looks, but in time, he learned to laugh at himself. When a rival called him "two-faced" during a political debate, Lincoln replied, "I leave it to my audience. If I had another face, do you think I'd wear this one?"* (1)

What sets heroes apart from everyone else is not that they have no weaknesses, but that they succeed despite their weaknesses. Doesn't that make their triumph more impressive?

COMPLETE, PARTIAL, AND COLLECTIVE BIOGRAPHIES   Writers may take one of many possible approaches to biography. A complete biography covers a subject's entire life, from cradle to grave. These can range from simple picture-book biographies (Aliki's *The Story of Johnny Appleseed*, for example) to complex works (such as Freedman's *Lincoln: A Photobiography*). One of the most difficult aspects of writing a biography is the selection of the materials. What should be included, and what omitted? Naturally, this is even tougher in a short book, where a great deal has to be left out. The good biographer has to find not only the most interesting material, but also the most important.

Some biographies cover only one phase of the subject's life. These we can call partial biographies, and they tend to focus on specific themes or periods of the subject's life. One very popular biographical series, *The Childhood of Famous Americans,* includes fictionalized biographies that focus chiefly on the subject's childhood and teen years (Augusta Stevenson's *George Washington: Young Leader*, for example). Presumably, these books will pique the young readers' curiosity so that in time they will want to read full-length biographies of their favorite people. In many cases, this happens, but it really does us little good to read about Washington's boyhood if we have no idea what he contributed to history.

Another type of biography is the collective biography, which includes brief sketches of the lives of several people who are linked by a common thread: scientists, first ladies, sports figures, musicians, and so on. One of the most famous of all collective biographies is President John F. Kennedy's best-selling *Profiles in Courage*, about the lives of some lesser-known American heroes. Originally for adults, it has been edited for younger audiences. Such books make good introductions to the lives of famous people, and may encourage readers to find more thorough biographies.

INDIVIDUAL BIOGRAPHY   It is important to distinguish between an authentic biography, which deals exclusively in facts, and a fictionalized biography, which modifies some facts for the sake of story. We turn again to Freedman's *Lincoln: A Photobiography*. This book contains nothing that cannot be verified by solid evidence. Lincoln's words quoted above are drawn from material of the period—they are not made up. If dialogue is used in an authentic biography (which is not common), it has to be supported by historical documents (such as letters or diaries) or verifiable personal recollections. And all facts, dates, and figures have to come from reliable sources. The best authentic biographies contain reference lists or bibliographies showing us where the information came from. Any book absent these features must be suspect.

On the other hand, we should not think that an authentic biography is just a series of boring facts. Listen to the folksy quality of this passage from Robert Quackenbush's authentic picture-book biography *Mark Twain? What Kind of Name Is That?*:

> *Samuel Langhorne Clemens—river pilot, gold miner, frontier reporter, humorist, and this nation's best-loved author—claimed that two important events took place on November 30, 1835. One was the appearance in the night sky of Halley's Comet—an event that comes only once every seventy-five years—and the other was his birth in Florida, Missouri. Sam loved telling jokes and playing tricks. He claimed that he couldn't remember what his first lie was, but he told his second lie when he was only nine days old. He had pretended that a diaper pin was sticking him, and he'd hollered as loud as he could. This brought him extra loving attention—until his trickery was found out, that is. Sam's mother thought he might get hit by a bolt of lightning one day, on account of all the mischief he caused as he was growing up in Hannibal, Missouri, with his older brother Orion, his older sister Pamela, his younger brother Henry, and nineteen cats.* (9)

Yes, much is omitted about young Sam Clemens's childhood, but in this short paragraph, we learn several facts, and we get a good idea of his character. Most readers will want to read on. It is just what we want from a good biography.

AUTOBIOGRAPHIES AND MEMOIRS   An autobiography is a book written about one's own life—someone else writes our biography, but we write our own autobiographies. Sometimes, an autobiographer will write about only one part of his or her life—childhood and adolescence, for example, or the early adult years, or specific career experiences. (It goes without saying that no autobiography is about the whole life—after all, the subject is still living.) Autobiographies are usually more informal than biographies, often taking the form of memoirs or reminiscences. Many individuals believe they don't have to research their own lives (after all, who should know their lives better than they do?), so they rely on their recollections of events. Consequently, specific dates are frequently missing from autobiographies, and seldom do we find any documentation. Not only are facts suspect in an autobiography, but so is the interpretation. What is more important to the writer of an autobiography—the truth or the subject's image? (Just imagine what you would leave out in telling the story of your life.)

Nevertheless, what famous people say about themselves can be both enlightening and entertaining. An autobiography can also be a great source for discovering an individual's character traits, likes and dislikes, innermost feelings—things that are not so easily hidden. Several children's authors have written their autobiographies for young readers, including Betsy Byars's *The Moon and I*, Phyllis Reynolds Naylor's *How I Came to Be a Writer*, Jean Fritz's *Homecoming: My Own Story*, and Roald Dahl's *Boy: Tales of Childhood*. An autobiography is not so important for what it tells us about the subject's life as what it tells us about the subject's character.

Creative Nonfiction

This discussion of autobiographies and memoirs leads us into one last form of nonfiction that has been getting considerable attention in recent years—some call it "Creative Nonfiction"; others call it "Narrative Nonfiction." This is a work that uses a storytelling format—a narrative—to convey factual information. Like the autobiography, creative nonfiction dispenses with the typical apparatus of a nonfiction work (no index, no list of references, no footnotes, and so on). It works very well for biography, but also for historical accounts—think of a film such as *Apollo 13*, which is based on fact but recreates dialogue and adds human-interest details that are more or less factual. This is akin to what creative nonfiction does.

Truman Capote's blockbuster *In Cold Blood* is often credited with creating this format—although, in fact, children's books have been doing this for years, particularly in the area of biography. Jean Lee Latham's 1956 Newbery Medal-winning *Carry on Mr. Bowditch* is the story of an unlikely hero, Nathaniel Bowditch, a nineteenth-century mathematician/sailor who eventually wrote a landmark handbook on navigation, *The American Practical Navigator*. It would be a stretch to consider as creative nonfiction Robert Lawson's charming fantasies such as *Captain Kidd's Cat* (about the pirate Captain Kidd), *I Discover Columbus*, and *Ben and Me* (about Benjamin Franklin). The narrators in these stories are animals, and many of the events are concocted, but in some ways they serve a similar purpose as creative nonfiction—to get readers interested in the history itself. And creative nonfiction is not confined to biography or history. Kelly Milner's *Albino Animals* is an example for readers in the elementary grades of a science/ecology book written in the style of creative nonfiction. Or we could consider Marianne Berke's poetry collection for very young children, *Over in the Ocean, In a Coral Reef*, illustrated by Jeanette Canyon, a work of biological creative nonfiction.

Creative nonfiction may take certain liberties—perhaps a scene is dramatized, descriptive details are included, dialogue is added—but the essence of the story is real. Some writers will dispute whether or not imagined dialogue should be included in a story; that is, can conversations be reconstructed, or can the inner thoughts of a character be revealed? Creative nonfiction is often described as a form of journalism. In journalism, we never expect to find invented dialogue or made-up quotations—everything the journalist writes must be documented. But conveying the facts is not always the creative nonfiction writer's first priority— the storytelling is paramount. Creative nonfiction has an important role in engaging the reluctant reader, in raising public awareness, and in entertainment. But, needless to say, we really should avoid using creative nonfiction in serious historical research. Pure nonfiction must give us the facts; creative nonfiction will provide the feeling.

Summary

Fiction and nonfiction often have similar ends—to help us understand the world we live in, and to give us pleasure. The difference is that fiction does it through a made-up story, whereas nonfiction sticks to factual evidence. But unlike fiction,

from which we expect primarily a good story, nonfiction is bound to the facts—
it cannot make stuff up. It is judged on the quality of its research, the accuracy
of its facts, and the integrity of its explanations. In other words, it is very
challenging to write a good piece of nonfiction. On the other hand, the topics
are seemingly endless. Nonfiction can include works about science and nature;
arts and leisure; human growth and development; history, society, and culture;
and biography and autobiography. Nonfiction books truly offer something for
everyone.

Once thought of as chiefly dull, utilitarian works, nonfiction books have risen
to a higher stature in recent years. Some have even received children's literature's
most prestigious awards, and they have prizes of their own (see the Children's Book
Awards lists in Appendix A). The best nonfiction gives us facts in a way that sparks
our interest and stirs our imagination. Facts themselves are not dull, but how they
are presented may be. The good nonfiction writers combine the spellbinding skills
of the storyteller with the knowledge of the scholar and researcher. They know that
truth, as the old expression goes, is "stranger than fiction."

Works Cited

Arnosky, Jim. *Watching Desert Wildlife.*
    Washington, DC: National Geographic
    Society, 1998.
Dickinson, Terence. *Exploring the Night Sky.*
    Willowdale, Ontario: Firefly, 1987.
Freedman, Russell. *Lincoln: A Photobiography.*
    New York: Clarion, 1987.

Latham, P. M. *The Collected Works.* Vol. II.
    London: New Sydenham Society, 1877.
Selsam, Millicent E. "Writing about Science for
    Children." In *Beyond Fact: Nonfiction for
    Children and Young People.* Ed. Jo Carr.
    Chicago: American Library Association,
    1982, 61–65.

Recommended Resources

Aiken, Joan. "Interpreting the Past." *Children's
    Literature in Education* 16 (Summer 1985):
    67–83.
Atkinson, T. S., M. N. Matusevich, and L. Huber.
    "Making Science Trade Book Choices for
    Elementary Classrooms." *The Reading
    Teacher* 62.6 (2009): 484–497.

Bamford, R. A., J. V. Kristo, and A. Lyon.
    "Facting Facts: Nonfiction in the Primary
    Classroom." *The New England Reading
    Association Journal* 23.2 (2002): 8–15.
Barnatt, Joan. "The Power of Nonfiction: Using
    Informational Text to Support Literacy
    in Special Populations." *Reaching Every*

Learner: Differentiating Instruction in Theory and Practice. Chapel Hill, NC: University of North Carolina-Chapel Hill, n.d. Online source: *Learn NC.*

Baxter, Kathleen A., and Marcia Agness Kochel. *Gotcha Good! Nonfiction Books to Get Kids Excited about Reading.* Santa Barbara, CA: Libraries Unlimited, 2008.

Burton, Hester. "The Writing of Historical Novels." In *Children and Literature: Views and Reviews.* Ed. Virginia Haviland. Glenview, IL: Scott, Foresman, 1973: 299–304.

Carr, Jo, ed. *Beyond Fact: Nonfiction for Children and Young People.* Chicago: American Library Association, 1982.

Carter, Betty. "A Universe of Information: The Future of Nonfiction." *The Horn Book* 74.4 (2000): 697–707.

Carter, Betty, and Richard F. Abrahamson. *Nonfiction for Young Adults: From Delight to Wisdom.* Phoenix, AZ: Oryx Press, 1991.

Cianciolo, Patricia. *Informational Picture Books for Children.* Chicago: American Library Association, 2000.

Dillard, Annie, and Lee Gutkind, eds. *In Fact: The Best of Creative Nonfiction.* New York: W. W. Norton & Co., 2005.

Epstein, William H. "Introducing Biography." *Children's Literature Association Quarterly* 12 (Winter 1987): 177–179.

Ford, Danielle. "More Than the Facts: Reviewing Science Books." *The Horn Book Magazine* 78. 3 (May/June 2002): 265–271.

Fraser, Elizabeth. *Reality Rules! A Guide to Teen Nonfiction Reading Interests.* Santa Barbara, CA: Libraries Unlimited, 2008.

Garfield, Leon. "Historical Fiction for Our Global Times." *The Horn Book* (November/December 1988): 736–742.

Gill, Sharon Ruth. "What Teachers Need to Know about the 'New' Nonfiction."

Gottlieb, Robin. "On Nonfiction Books for Children: Tradition & Dissent." *Wilson Library Journal* (October 1974): 174–177.

Gutkind, Lee. *The Art of Creative Nonfiction: Writing and Selling the Literature of Reality.* New York: Wiley, 1997.

Lounsberry, Barbara. *The Art of Fact: Contemporary Artists of Nonfiction.* Westport, Conn: Greenwood Press, 1990.

Mallet, Margaret. *Making Facts Matter: Reading Non-fiction 5–11.* London: Paul Chapman, 1992.

Marcus, Leonard. "Life Drawing: Some Notes on Children's Picture Book Biographies." *The Lion and the Unicorn* 4 (Summer 1980): 15–31.

Moore, Ann W. "A Question of Accuracy: Errors in Children's Biographies." *School Library Journal* 31 (February 1985): 34–35.

Moss., Barbara. *Exploring the Literature of Fact: Children's Nonfiction Trade Books in the Elementary Classroom.* New York: Guilford, 2003.

Rosen, Judith. "Is Children's Nonfiction Having Its Moment?" *Publishers Weekly,* 17 July 2015. publishersweekly.com.

Saul, E. W., and D. Dieckman. "Choosing and Using Information Trade Books." *Reading Research Quarterly* 40.4 (2005): 502–513.

Segel, Elizabeth. "In Biographies for Young Readers, Nothing Is Impossible." *The Lion and the Unicorn* 4 (Summer 1980): 4–14.

Webster, P.S. "Exploring the Literature of Fact." *The Reading Teacher* 62(8) (2009): 662–671.

Weinberg, Steve. "Biography: Telling the Untold Story." *The Writer* (February 1993): 23–25.

Wilms, Denise M. "An Evaluation of Biography." In *Jump Over the Moon.* Ed. Pamela Barron and Jennifer Burley. New York: Holt, Rinehart & Winston, 1984, pp. 220–225.

Wilson, S. "Getting Down to Facts in Children's Nonfiction Literature: A Case for the Importance of Sources." *Journal of Children's Literature* 321 (2006): 56–63.

Nonfiction: A Selected and Annotated Booklist

The following list does not even scratch the surface of what is available in nonfiction for children, and is only intended to suggest the wide variety of quality books available. Reading levels are only suggestions. An individual's interests and abilities are the best guides. The dates are generally for the most recent edition.

Science and Nature

PRE-K—GRADE 4

Arnosky, Jim. *Thunder Birds: Nature's Flying Predators.* New York: Sterling, 2011.
- A picture book about the great birds of prey by a celebrated naturalist.

____. *Watching Desert Wildlife.* Washington, DC: National Geographic, 2002.
- Stunning illustrations and a text for beginning readers.

Bang, Molly. *Common Ground: The Water, Earth, and Air We Share.* New York: Scholastic, 1997.
- A picture book that argues for conservation of our natural resources.

Batten, Mary. *Hungry Plants.* Illus. Paul Mirocha. New York: Random House, 2004.
- A story of carnivorous plants, illustrated from the insect's viewpoint.

Berke, Marianne. *Over in the Ocean, In a Coral Reef.* Illustrated by Jeanette Canyon. Nevada City, CA: Dawn Publications, 2004.
- In lyrical short poems, inhabitants of a coral reef are introduced, with colorful illustrations.

____. *Over in the Jungle: A Rainforest Rhyme.* Illustrated by Jeanette Canyon. Nevada City, CA: Dawn Publications, 2007.
- Another addition to a charming series of illustrated books introducing very young children to the natural world through lyricism and pictures.

Bland, Celia. *Bats.* Chicago: Kidsbooks, 1997.
- Photographs capture the life of bats; a book in the *Eyes on Nature* series on various animals.

Brandenburg, Jim. *Face to Face with Wolves.* Washington, DC: National Geographic, 2010.
- Photographs accompany an intimate look at the Arctic wolf.

Branley, Franklyn. *The Air Is All Around You.* Illus. John O'Brien. New York: HarperCollins, 2006.
- One of many in a popular series of picture books on science (*Let's-Read-and-Find-Out Science*); for younger readers and with hands-on projects.

Brown, Laurie Krasny, and Marc Brown. *Dinosaurs to the Rescue! A Guide to Protecting Our Planet.* Boston: Little, Brown, 1992.
- An ecological guidebook for the very young.

Cobb, Vicki. *I Face the Wind.* Illus. Julia Gorton. New York: HarperCollins, 2003.
- One of a series of accessible science books by Cobb, this one on the science of wind.

Cole, Joanna. *The Magic School Bus and the Climate Challenge.* Illus. Bruce Degen. New York: Scholastic, 2010.
- One of the popular and long-running series of Magic School Bus adventures.

Floca, Brian. *Moonshot: The Flight of* Apollo 11. New York: Atheneum, 2009.
- A handsomely illustrated and well-told story of a historic space mission.

George, Jean Craighead. *Galápagos George.* Illus. Wendell Minor. New York: HarperCollins, 2014.
- The true story of the giant tortoise who was the last of his species, along with an introduction to other unusual inhabitants of the Galápagos Islands, beautifully illustrated.

Gibbons, Gail. *From Seed to Plant*. New York: Holiday, 1993.
- One of Gibbons' many accessible nonfiction picture books about nature.

Heller, Ruth. *Chickens Aren't the Only Ones*. St. Louis, MO: Turtleback, 1999.
- A fascinating look at egg-laying animals, colorfully illustrated; from the *World of Nature* series.

____. *The Reason for a Flower*. New York: Puffin, 1999.
- A colorful introduction to the makeup of flowers.

Henderson, Douglas. *Asteroid Impact*. New York: Penguin, 2001.
- A dramatically illustrated story of the asteroid scientists believe may have destroyed the dinosaurs.

Hopkinson, Deborah. *Sky Boys: How They Built the Empire State Building*. Illus. James F. Ransome. New York: Schwartz & Wade, 2006.
- Part science, part history, describing the building of the world's tallest building in 1931.

Hughes, Catherine D. *Little Kids First Big Book of Dinosaurs*. Illus. Franco Tempesto. Washington, DC: National Geographic, 2011.
- One of a series of *Little Kids* books by National Geographic, notable for their dynamic illustrations and sound texts.

Jenkins, Steve. *Biggest, Strongest, Fastest*. Boston: Houghton Mifflin, 1995.
- Extreme facts about animals, depicted in collage illustrations.

____. *Life on Earth: The Story of Evolution*. Boston: Houghton Mifflin, 2002.
- A good introduction to evolution, illustrated with Jenkins's characteristic collages.

____. *Actual Size*. Boston: HMH, 2011.
- Collages capture texture and color of various animals, along with their size compared to human beings.

Lyon, George Ella. *All the Water in the World*. Illus. Katherine Tillotson. New York: Atheneum, 2011.
- An explanation for young readers of the complexities of the water cycle with stunning art and beautiful language.

McCarthy, Meghan. *Astronaut Handbook*. New York: Knopf, 2008.
- An informative and funny book about the science of space travel—for toddlers.

Miche, Mary. *Nature's Patchwork Quilt: Understanding Habitats*. Illus. Consie Powell. Nevada City, CO: Dawn Publications, 2012.
- A book of lively illustrations and good explanations of various animal habitats.

Schwartz, David M. *Millions to Measure*. Illus. Steven Kellogg. New York: HarperCollins, 2003.
- A book whose playful illustrations help explain the concept of measuring.

Selsam, Millicent. *Hidden Animals*. New York: Harper & Row, 1967.
- A book with fascinating nature photography that demonstrates the camouflage of animals. Unfortunately out of print.

Simon, Seymour. *Guts: Our Digestive System*. New York: HarperCollins, 2005.
- An excellent introduction for young readers.

____. *Our Solar System*, rev. ed. New York: HarperCollins, 2007.
- A tour of the solar system with full-color photographs. One of dozens of fine science books by Simon for younger children.

____. *Out of Sight: Pictures of Hidden Worlds*. New York: Chronicle Books, 2002.
- Imaginative photographs of nature.

Tara, Stephanie Lisa. *Snowy White World to Save*. Illus. Alex Walton. CreateSpace, 2013.
- Picture-book treatment of the effects of global warming on the polar ice caps.

Vogt, Richard C. *Rain Forests*. New York: Simon & Schuster, 2009.
- Packed with information and three-dimensional illustrations.

FOR GRADES 4 AND ABOVE

Aguilar, David. *13 Planets: The Latest View of Our Solar System*. Washington, DC: National Geographic, 2011.
  • A book illustrated with computer art that is based on the most recent scientific data.

____. *Space Encyclopedia: A Tour of Our Solar System and Beyond*. Washington, DC: National Geographic, 2013.
  • Another striking book with Aguilar's stunning computer art, this one exploring the universe beyond the solar system.

Arnold, Nick. *The Body Owner's Handbook*. Illus. Tony De Saulles. New York: Scholastic, 2002.
  • Hilarious explanations of how the body works. Also see the many other science titles by Arnold and De Saulles in the *Horrible Science* series.

Broom, Jenny. *Animalium: Welcome to the Museum*. Illus. Katy Scott. Big Picture Press, 2014.
  • Beautiful pen-and-ink drawings and a fine text introduces the animal kingdom—an exquisite volume for children and adults.

Bryson, Bill. *A Really Short History of Nearly Everything*. New York: Delacorte, 2009.
  • A book filled with amazing scientific facts and richly illustrated.

Dickinson, Terry. *NightWatch: A Practical Guide for Viewing the Universe*, 4th ed. Illus. Adolf Schaller. Richmond Hill, Ontario: Firefly, 2006.
  • A very good introduction to astronomy.

Farrell, Jeanette. *Invisible Enemies: Stories of Infectious Disease*, rev. ed. New York: Farrar, Straus & Giroux, 2005.
  • A book filled with interesting facts about seven major killers.

Hague, Bradley. *Alien Deep: Revealing the Mysterious Living World at the Bottom of the Ocean*. Washington, DC: National Geographic, 2012.
  • A fascinating explanation of underwater exploration.

Kerrod, Robin, and David Hughes. *Visual Encyclopedia of Space*. New York: DK Children, 2006.
  • A compact book filled with hundreds of illustrations covering all aspects of space.

Krautwurst, Terry. *Night Science for Kids: Exploring the World after Dark*. Asheville, NC: Lark Books, 2005.
  • An interactive approach to discovering nature in the nighttime.

Kurlansky, Mark. *World without Fish*. Illus. Frank Stockton. New York: Workman, 2011.
  • A book about the interconnections between biology, economics, politics, climate, and so on.

Macaulay, David. *The Way Things Work Now*. Boston: Houghton Mifflin Harcourt, 2016.
  • Meticulously illustrated explanations of the workings of everything from pop-up toasters to computer chips and beyond.

Masoff, Joy. *Oh, Yuck! The Encyclopedia of Everything Nasty*. Illus. Terry Sirrell. New York: Workman, 2000.
  • A well-researched book that appeals to young teenagers.

McCutcheon, Chuck. *What Are Global Warming and Climate Change? Answers for Young Readers*. Albuquerque: University of New Mexico Press, 2010.
  • An objective approach to a still controversial subject.

Murray, Elizabeth A. *Death: Corpses, Cadavers, and Other Grave Matters*. Minneapolis, MN: Twenty-First Century Books, 2010.
  • A book filled with fascinating details, written by a forensic scientist.

Pringle, Laurence. *Billions of Years, Amazing Changes: The Story of Evolution*. Illus. Steve Jenkins. Honesdale, PA: Boyds Mill Press, 2011.
  • A lively explanation of evolution by a celebrated science writer. Look for the many other titles by Pringle.

Ride, Sally, and Susan Okie. *To Space and Back.* New York: Lothrop, 1986.
- The personal experiences of the first American woman in space.

Rubino, Michael. *Bang! How We Came to Be.* Prometheus Books, 2011.
- A stunningly illustrated history of the universe for readers in the middle grades.

Spangler, Steve. *Naked Eggs and Flying Potatoes: Unforgettable Experiments That Make Science Fun.* Austin, TX: Greenleaf, 2010.
- A lively collection of a wide variety of experiments suited to middle schoolers.

St. George, Judith. *The Brooklyn Bridge: They Said It Couldn't Be Built.* New York: Putnam, 1982.
- A book that's part history and part engineering, with period photographs.

Taylor-Butler, Christine. *The Digestive System.* New York: Children's Press, 2008.
- A very good introduction to this subject.

Turner, Pamela S. *The Frog Scientist*, reprint ed. New York: Sandpiper, 2011.
- A book about the scientist who discovered the ill effects of pesticides on frogs.

Walker, Sally M. *Fossil Fish Found Alive: Discovering the Coelacanth.* Minneapolis, MN: Carolrhoda, 2002.
- The story of finding a fish once thought to be extinct, illustrated with color photographs.

Arts and Leisure

FOR PRE-K TO GRADE 4

Aliki. *William Shakespeare and the Globe.* New York: HarperCollins, 1999.
- A picture-book introduction to the Elizabethan theater.

Banks, Kate. *Max's Words.* Illus. Boris Kulikov. New York: Farrar, Straus & Giroux, 2006.
- A book about a little boy who decides to collect words.

Brown, Marc. *Your First Garden Book.* New York: Trumpet, 2009.
- Gardening projects for beginners.

Burleigh, Robert. *Edward Hopper Paints His World.* Illus. Wendell Minor. New York: Holt, 2014.
- An award-winning picture-book biography of a great American artist, with illustrations reminiscent of Hopper's own works.

Herzog, Brad. *Little Baseball.* Illus. Doug Bowles. Ann Arbor, MI: Sleeping Bear, 2011.
- A board book that introduces baseball to the youngest readers. See also *Little Football.*

Latch, William. *Can You Hear It?* New York: Abrams, 2006.
- An introduction to classical music for children from about second grade and up, with an accompanying CD. Produced with the Metropolitan Museum of Art.

Lipsey, Jennifer. *My Very Favorite Art Book: I Love to Paint.* Asheville, NC: Lark, 2005.
- A practical approach to art for elementary school children. One of a series by Lipsey, including *I Love to Draw*, *I Love to Collage*, and others.

Pulver, Robin. *Punctuation Takes a Vacation.* Illus. Lynn Rowe Reed. New York: Holiday, 2003.
- A comical picture-book story that illustrates the use of punctuation.

Raimondo, Joyce. *Imagine That: Activities and Adventures in Surrealism.* New York: Watson-Guptill, 2008.
- A great introduction to surrealism for young children, including hands-on activities. The first in the Art Explorers series, including *Express Yourself* (expressionism), *What's the Big Idea?* (abstract art), *Make It Pop* (pop art), and *Picture This* (impressionism), all by the same author.

Saltzberg, Barney. *Beautiful Oops!* New York: Workman Publishing, 2010.
- Highly acclaimed interactive book for very young children showing how artistic mistakes can be turned into art.

Truss, Lynn. *Eats, Shoots & Leaves: Why, Commas Do Make a Difference.* Illus. Bonnie Timmons. New York: Putnam, 2006.
- Picture-book fun with punctuation; great for early elementary language study. A popular adult version, with the same author and title, also exists.

FOR GRADES 4 AND ABOVE

Ancona, George. *Cutters, Carvers, and the Cathedral.* New York: Lothrop, 1995.
- A book about the building of St. John the Divine, the largest cathedral in the United States.

Aronson, Marc. *Art Attack: A Short Cultural History of the Avant-Garde.* New York: Clarion, 1998.
- An introduction to twentieth-century art.

Berman, Len. *The Greatest Moments in Sports.* New York: Sourcebooks Jabberwocky, 2009.
- Twenty-five episodes in modern sports, selected by a sportscaster whose personal biases are reflected. One of a series of interesting sports books by this author.

Bierhorst, John. *A Cry from the Earth: Music of the North American Indians.* Santa Fe, NM: Ancient City Press, 1992.
- An introduction to American Indian music, song, and dance.

Crisfield, Deborah W. *The Everything Kids' Soccer Book: Rules, Techniques, and More about Your Favorite Sport.* New York: Adams Media, 2009.
- One of the *Everything Kids* series of informative books about children's sports, including Bob Schaller's book on baseball, Schaller and Dave Harnish's on basketball, and Greg Jacobs's on football.

Dance. New York: DK, 2012.
- A composite book covering all aspects of dance, from history to dance movements.

Evans, Dilys. *Show and Tell: Exploring the Fine Art of Children's Book Illustration.* San Francisco: Chronicle Books, 2008.
- An excellent introduction for children and adults.

Helsby, Genevieve. *Those Amazing Musical Instruments! Your Guide to the Orchestra Through Sounds and Stories.* New York: Sourcebooks Jabberwocky, 2007.
- An exploration of the various musical instruments in the orchestra; includes a CD.

Hughes, Langston. *The First Book of Jazz.* New York: Ecco, 1997.
- Originally written in 1955, still a fine introduction by a great poet.

LeBoutillier, Nate. *The Best of Everything Baseball Book.* Mankato, MN: Capstone, 2011.
- A compendium of facts about baseball. The same author has a companion book on basketball.

Levine, Robert. *The Story of the Orchestra: Listen while You Learn about the Instruments, the Music and the Composers Who Wrote the Music!* Illus. Meredith Hamilton. New York: Black Dog & Leventhal, 2000.
- An introduction to classical music and musical instruments.

Macaulay, David. *Cathedral: The Story of Its Construction.* Boston: Houghton Mifflin, 1973.
- Just one of many informative picture books, including *Castle*, *Mosque*, and *Pyramid*, on the art and science of architecture.

Metropolitan Museum of Art. *Monet's Impressions.* New York: Chronicle Books, 2009.
- An introduction to Monet, using the artist's own words and paintings.

____. *Vincent's Colors.* New York: Chronicle Books, 2005.
- An introduction to van Gogh, using the artist's own words and paintings.

Roche, Art. *Comic Strips: Create Your Own Comic Strips from Start to Finish.* (*Art for Kids* series) New York: Sterling, 2011.
- A superb introduction for children. See also the author's *Cartooning*.

Temple, Kathryn. *Drawing: The Only Drawing Book You'll Ever Need to Be the Artist You've Always Wanted to Be.* (*Art for Kids* series) Asheville, NC: Lark, 2005.
  • An excellent resource for young artists.

Watt, Fiona. *The Usborne Complete Book of Art Ideas.* United Kingdom: Usborne Publishing, 2011.
  • A large book filled with helpful advice, including ideas, techniques, and projects covering a wide variety of artistic media; helpful for both home and classroom.

Wenzel, Angela. *13 Art Techniques Children Should Know.* New York: Prestel, 2013.
  • An introduction for children from about grades three through six, with very fine illustrations. Part of the *Children Should Know* series (including *13 Artists Children Should Know, 13 Architects Children Should Know*, and others by various authors).

Human Growth and Development

FOR PRE-K TO GRADE 4

Bang, Molly. *When Sophie Gets Angry.* New York: Blue Sky Press, 1999.
  • A picture-book story of a child dealing with anger that is frank and realistic.

Bausum, Ann. *Breaking Out in the Fight for Gay Rights.* New York: Penguin/Viking, 2015.
  • A well-documented history of the origin of the gay rights movement.

Brown, Laurie Krasny, and Marc Brown. *What's the Big Secret? Talking about Sex with Girls and Boys.* Illus. Marc Brown. Boston: Little, Brown, 1997.
  • A good introduction for very young children with cartoon illustrations and accurate information. One of many similar books by this husband-and-wife team; see also *Dinosaurs Divorce, How to Be a Friend: A Guide to Making Friends and Keeping Them*, and *When Dinosaurs Die: A Guide to Understanding Death.*

Carlson, Nancy. *How to Lose All Your Friends.* New York: Puffin, 1997.
  • A humorous look at bratty behavior—and how to avoid it.

Cole, Babette. *Mommy Laid an Egg! Or Where Do Babies Come From?* New York: Chronicle, 1996.
  • A light-hearted but factually accurate introduction to sex and reproduction.

Ekster, Carol Gordon. *Where Am I Sleeping Tonight?* Illus. Sue Rama. Weaverville, CA: Boulden, 2008.
  • A picture book describing the initial struggles and confusion facing two children when their parents divorce.

Goodman, Susan E. *The Truth about Poop.* Illus. Elwood H. Smith. New York: Viking, 2004.
  • Perhaps more than we wanted to know about bodily elimination, but young readers will be captivated.

Harris, Robie H. *It's Not the Stork! A Book about Girls, Boys, Babies, Bodies, Families and Friends.* Illus. Michael Emberley. New York: Candlewick, 2008.
  • About those sensitive issues parents have so much trouble discussing.

____. *Who Has What? All about Girls' Bodies and Boys' Bodies.* Illus. Nadine Bernard Westcott. New York: Candlewick, 2011.
  • Accurate yet accessible answers to all those questions young people ask that many grownups wish they didn't.

Jeffers, Oliver. *The Heart and the Bottle.* New York: Philomel, 2010.
  • A powerful exploration of grief and overcoming it, told with moving symbolism.

Kaplow, Julie, and Donna Pincus. *Samantha Jane's Missing Smile: A Story about Coping with the Loss of a Parent.* Illus. Beth Spiegel. Washington, DC: Magination, 2007.
- A realistically presented story of a young girl's coping with the death of her father.

Levins, Sandra. *Was It the Chocolate Pudding? A Story for Little Kids about Divorce.* Illus. Bryan Langdo. Washington, DC: American Psychological Association, 2005.
- A discussion about divorce for young children.

Meiners, Cheri J. *Cool Down and Work through Anger.* Minneapolis, MN: Free Spirit, 2010.
- Practical ways for children to cope with anger. One of the books in the *Learning to Get Along* series by the same author, which also includes *Join In and Play* and *Talk and Work It Out.*

Mills, Joyce C. *Gentle Willow: A Story for Children about Dying.* Illus. Michael Chesworth. Washington, DC: Magination, 1993.
- A book about accepting death—one's own and that of a loved one.

Newman, Lesléa. *Daddy, Papa, and Me.* Illus. Carol Thompson. Berkeley, CA: Tricycle Press, 2009.
- A toddler spends a day with its two dads, a gay couple; a companion book, *Mommy, Mama, and Me*, describes similar experiences, but with a lesbian couple.

Riggs, Shannon. *Not in Room 204: Breaking the Silence of Abuse.* Illus. Jaime Zollars. New York: Whitman, 2007.
- A well-told story that raises awareness of child abuse at home—a difficult subject, but one not to be ignored.

Rosen, Michael. *Michael Rosen's Sad Book.* Illus. Quentin Blake. New York: Candlewick, 2005.
- A moving book about dealing with grief; it is sad but very insightful.

Saltz, Gail. *Changing You: A Guide to Body Changes and Sexuality.* Illus. Lynn Avril Cravath. New York: Puffin, 2009.
- A factual but informal approach for readers about 6 and older.

Spelman, Cornelia Maude. *When I Miss You.* Illus. Kathy Parkinson. New York: Whitman, 2000.
- An animal family is used to explore human emotions. One of the *Way I Feel* series by this author, including *When I Feel Scared, When I Feel Jealous,* and others.

Stickney, Doris. *Water Bugs & Dragonflies: Explaining Death to Children.* Cleveland, OH: Pilgrim Press, 2004.
- Death is explained through the allegory of metamorphosis.

FOR GRADES 4 AND ABOVE

Bailey, Jacqui. *Sex, Puberty, and All That Stuff: A Guide to Growing Up.* Illus. Jan McCafferty. Hauppauge, NY: Barron's Educational, 2004.
- A humorous, but accurate and honest, approach with cartoon illustrations.

Beck, Debra. *My Feet Aren't Ugly! A Girl's Guide to Loving Herself from the Inside Out,* rev. ed. New York: Beaufort Books, 2011.
- An amusing book designed to build self-confidence.

Belge, Kathy, and Marke Bieschke. *Queer: The Ultimate LBGT Guide for Teens.* San Francisco: Zest Books, 2011.
- A humorous, personal, and honest approach to the subject.

Bode, Janet. *Death Is Hard to Live with: Teenagers and How They Cope with Loss.* New York: Delacorte, 1993.
- A collection of personal stories written by teenagers.

Daldry, Jeremy. *The Teenage Guy's Survival Guide: The Real Deal on Girls, Growing Up and Other Guy Stuff.* Boston: Little, Brown, 1997.
- Frank and occasionally irreverent; the American version of a British book titled *Boys Behaving Badly.*

Dee, Catherine. *The Girls' Guide to Life: Take Charge of Your Personal Life, Your School Time, Your Social Scene, and Much More!* 2nd ed. Boston: Little, Brown, 2005.
- Information and accompanying activities on a wide variety of subjects of interest to girls about 10 and older.

Grollman, Earl A. *Straight Talk about Death for Teenagers: How to Cope with Losing Someone You Love.* Boston: Beacon Press, 1993.
- A book that deals with a wide variety of issues, such as accidental death, suicide, long-term illness, and the death of a parent or a friend.

Harris, Robie H. *It's Perfectly Normal: Changing Bodies, Growing Up, Sex, and Sexual Health.* Illus. Michael Emberley. New York: Candlewick, 2009.
- An excellent introduction for upper elementary readers.

Huegel, Kelly. *GLBTQ: The Survival Guide for Gay, Lesbian, Bisexual, Transgender, and Questioning Teens*, rev. ed. Minneapolis, MN: Free Spirit, 2011.
- A valuable resource for teenage readers.

Kuklin, Susan. *Beyond Magenta: Transgender Teens Speak Out.* Candlewick, 2014.
- Interviews with six transgender teens describing their thoughts and experiences.

Pardes, Bronwen. *Doing It Right: Making Smart, Safe, and Satisfying Choices about Sex.* New York: Simon Pulse, 2013.
- Frank discussions from a sex educator.

Savage, Dan. *It Gets Better: Coming Out, Overcoming Bullying, and Creating a Life Worth Living.* New York: Plume, 2012.
- A collection of essays directed toward LGBTQ teens.

Stout, Glen. *Able to Play: Overcoming Physical Challenges.* New York: Sandpiper, 2012.
- Personal stories of four professional athletes who have physical disabilities.

History, Society, and Culture

FOR PRE-K TO GRADE 4

Alexander, Heather. *A Child's Introduction to the World: Geography, Cultures, and People.* Illus. Meredith Hamilton. New York: Black Dog and Leventhal, 2010.
- A colorful introduction to world cultures.

Aliki. *A Medieval Feast.* New York: HarperCollins, 1986.
- Lively illustrations and interesting facts about a great occasion during the Middle Ages.

____. *Mummies Made in Egypt.* New York: Crowell, 1979.
- A factual account of mummification, complete with detailed drawings.

Amery, Heather. *Then and Now*, rev. ed. Illus. Peter Firmin. London: Usborne, 2008.
- A picture-book explanation of how things change over time.

Coombs, Rachel. *A Year in a Castle.* Minneapolis, MN: First Avenue, 2009.
- A book illustrated in great detail and filled with interesting facts about medieval life; part of the *Time Goes By* series that also includes Nicholas Harris's *A Day in the City* and *A Year at a Farm* and Elizabeth Havercroft's *A Year on a Pirate Ship*, among many others.

Fowler, Alan. *Africa.* New York: Children's Press, 2002.
- One of several books by this author for the *Rookie Read-About Geography Series* for very young children, including *Antarctica, Asia, Australia, Europe, North America,* and *South America.*

Frank, John. *The Tomb of the Boy King.* Illus. Tom Pohrt. New York: Farrar, Straus & Giroux, 2001.
- A picture-book account of the discovery of King Tutankhamen's tomb.

Knowlton, Jack. *Geography from A to Z: A Picture Glossary*. Illus. Harriet Barton. New York: HarperCollins, 1997.
- Arranged like a dictionary, but with geographical terms; useful for early elementary readers. See also Knowlton's *Maps and Globes*, an introductory geography for very young children.

Mara, Will. *The Seven Continents*. New York: Children's Press, 2005.
- Geography for the very young; part of the *Rookie Read-About Geography* series.

Millard, Anne. *A Street Through Time*. New York: DK Children, 1998.
- Young children watch history unfold as the panorama of history is revealed at a single riverside site over 12,000 years.

Ritchie, Scot. *Follow That Map! A First Book of Mapping Skills*. Toronto: Kids Can Press, 2009.
- A good introduction to maps and how to use them.

Smith, David J. *If the World Were a Village: A Book about the World's People*. Illus. Shelagh Armstrong. Toronto: Kids Can, 2002.
- A fascinating book that imagines the world's population as a village of 100 people. A good introduction to thinking about ecology.

FOR GRADES 4 AND ABOVE

Bartoletti, Susan Campbell. *Black Potatoes: The Story of the Great Irish Famine*. Boston: Houghton Mifflin, 2001.
- The story of a bleak episode in nineteenth-century history.

Bascomb, Neal. *The Nazi Hunters: How a Team of Spies and Survivors Captured the World's Most Notorious Nazi*. New York: Arthur A. Levine Books, 2013.
- Its formidable title aside, an excellent narrative of the exhausting search for Adolf Eichmann, one of the most ruthless of the Nazi leaders.

Bealer, Alex W. *Only the Names Remain: The Cherokees and the Trail of Tears*. Boston: Little, Brown, 1972.
- The tragic tale of the forced Cherokee relocation in the 1830s.

Bowker, John. *World Religions: The Great Faiths Explored and Explained*, rev. ed. New York: DK Publishing, 2006.
- A fully illustrated examination of many of the world's great religions.

Chang, Ina. *A Separate Battle: Women and the Civil War*. New York: Dutton, 1991.
- The seldom-told story of the contributions of women during this national tragedy.

Colman, Penny. *Corpses, Coffins, and Crypts: A History of Burial*. New York: Holt, 1997.
- The intriguing survey of an unusual, and often ignored, subject.

____. *Rosie the Riveter: Women Working on the Home Front in World War II*. New York: Crown, 1995.
- A book about the contributions of women during World War II.

Cooper, Ilene. *The Dead Sea Scrolls*. Illus. John Thompson. New York: Morrow, 1997.
- A good introduction to the discovery and meaning of these ancient Jewish documents.

Deary, Terry. *Horrible History of the World*. Illus. Martin Brown. New York: Scholastic, 2007.
- Especially appealing to middle-school readers. Part of the popular *Horrible Histories Handbooks* series; great fun, if not always entirely accurate.

Fleming, Candace. *The Family Romanov: Murder, Rebellion & the Fall of Imperial Russia*. New York: Schwartz & Wade, 2014.
- The fascinating story of the last emperor of Russia and his family, thoroughly researched and complete with period photos.

Freedman, Russell. *Cowboys of the Wild West*. New York: Tickner & Fields, 1985.
- One of many fine works of historical nonfiction by this writer.

Giblin, James Cross. *Secrets of the Sphinx*. Illus. Bagram Ibatoulline. New York: Scholastic, 2004.
- An award-winning exploration of the theories surrounding a mysterious Egyptian sculpture.

Gombrich, E. H. *A Little History of the World*. Illus. Clifford Harper. New Haven, CT: Yale University Press, 2008.
- First written in German in 1935; still a remarkable feat, a brief overview of all human history.

Greenfeld, Howard. *The Hidden Children*. New York: Clarion, 1993.
- A gripping account of children saved from the Holocaust of World War II.

Hopkinson, Deborah. *Titanic: Voices from the Disaster*. New York: Scholastic, 1912.
- An exciting telling of a familiar story, thoroughly researched and illustrated with period photos.

Ippisch, Hanneke. *Sky: A True Story of Resistance During World War II*. New York: Simon & Schuster, 1996.
- A book about the heroic efforts to rescue the Jews from the Holocaust, written by a member of the Dutch resistance. A moving work despite some stylistic impediments.

Kantar, Andrew. *29 Missing: The True and Tragic Story of the Disappearance of the* S.S. Edmund Fitzgerald. East Lansing: Michigan State University Press, 1998.
- The story of one of the most famous shipwrecks on the Great Lakes.

Levine, Ellen. *Darkness Over Denmark: The Danish Resistance and the Rescue of the Jews*. New York: Holiday House, 2000.
- A good nonfiction companion to Lois Lowry's award-winning *Number the Stars*.

Leyson, Leon. *The Boy on the Wooden Box: How the Impossible Became the Possible . . . on Schindler's List*. New York: Atheneum, 2013.
- Memoir of the Holocaust from one of the youngest people on Schindler's famous list.

Marrin, Albert. *Year of Dust: The Story of the Dust Bowl*. New York: Puffin, 2009.
- An excellent description of the 1930s, with both back story and warnings for the future. Superbly illustrated with period photographs.

McWhorter, Diane. *A Dream of Freedom: The Civil Rights Movement from 1954 to 1968*. New York: Scholastic, 2004.
- A book movingly illustrated with period photographs.

Meltzer, Milton, ed. *The Black Americans: A History in Their Own Words, 1619–1983*. New York: Crowell, 1984.
- A book filled with moving personal accounts.

____. *Brother, Can You Spare a Dime? The Great Depression: 1929–1933*. New York: New American Library, 1977.
- Powerful personal stories that recount the period.

Miller, Sarah. *The Borden Murders: Lizzie Borden and the Murder of the Century*. New York: Random/Schwartz & Wade, 2016.
- A thrilling account of one of the most famous (and unsolved) crimes of the nineteenth century.

Morimoto, Junko. *My Hiroshima*. 1987. New York: Puffin, 1990.
- The author's personal experiences as a youth in Hiroshima when the atomic bomb was dropped.

Murphy, Jim. *An American Plague: The True and Terrifying Story of the Yellow Fever Epidemic of 1793*. New York: Clarion, 2003.
- The story of a tragic and little-known episode.

____. *The Great Fire*. New York: Scholastic, 1995.
- An account of the great Chicago fire of 1871.

Myers, Walter Dean. *Now Is Your Time! The African-American Struggle for Freedom*. New York: HarperCollins, 1991.
- A book that recounts the individual stories of people involved in the civil rights movement.

Osborne, Mary Pope. *One World, Many Religions: The Way We Worship*. New York: Knopf, 1996.
- An overview of the beliefs and practices of seven major world religions.

Shetterly, Margot Lee. *Hidden Figures (Young Readers' Edition)*. Stanley, Jerry. New York: Harper Collins, 2016.
- The story of four African-American women mathematicians who worked in the original NASA space program (subsequently made into an excellent film).

Stanley, Jerry. *I Am an American: A True Story of Japanese Internment*. New York: Crown, 1994.
- A book about racial prejudice that resulted in the abuse of Japanese Americans during World War II.

Thimmesh, Cathering. *Lucy Long Ago: Uncovering the Mystery of Where We Came From*. Boston: HMH, 2009.
- The story of the discovery in Africa of the remains of the earliest-known hominid, nicknamed Lucy, and what it means in our quest to understand the origins of humans.

Yen Mah, Adeline. *China: Land of Dragons and Emperors*. 2004. New York: Delacorte, 2009.
- An overview of China's long and turbulent history.

Yousafzai, Malala, with Patricia McCormick. *I Am Malala: How One Girl Stood Up for Education and Changed the World*. Little, Brown, 2014.
- Celebrated memoir of life in Pakistan under the Taliban by the youngest Nobel Prize winner.

Biographies and Autobiographies

FOR PRE-K TO GRADE 4

Adler, David A. *Lou Gehrig: The Luckiest Man Alive*. Illus. Terry Widener. New York: Harcourt, 1997.
- A picture-book biography of the great baseball player.

Aliki. *The Story of Johnny Appleseed*. New York: Perfection Learning, 1971.
- The life of the man who planted apple trees and good will all over the Midwest in the early nineteenth century.

Anderson, M. T. *Handel, Who Knew What He Liked*. Illus. Kevin Hawkes. Cambridge, MA: Candlewick, 2001.
- A picture-book biography of the great eighteenth-century composer.

Bauer, Marion Dane. *Martin Luther King, Jr.* Illus. Jamie Smith. New York: Scholastic, 2009.
- One of a series of picture-book biographies.

Borden, Louise. *A. Lincoln and Me*. Illus. Ted Lewin. New York: Scholastic, 2009.
- A clever introduction to Abraham Lincoln through the eyes of a modern-day boy who shares his birthday.

Brown, Don. *Odd Boy Out: Young Albert Einstein*. Boston: Houghton Mifflin, 2004.
- A picture-book story of the famous scientist's early years.

Bryant, Jen. *River of Words: The Story of William Carlos Williams*. Illus. Melissa Sweet. Grand Rapids, MI: Eerdmans, 2008.
- A picture-book story about the life of a famous American poet.

Fritz, Jean. *Bully for You, Teddy Roosevelt!* New York: Putnam, 1991.
- The life of the president told for younger readers; one of many picture-book biographies of American figures by Fritz.

Giovanni, Nikki. *Rosa*. Illus. Bryan Collier. New York: Holt, 2005.
- A brief, richly illustrated biography of Rosa Parks.

Greenfield, Eloise. *Mary McLeod Bethune*. 1977. Illus. Jerry Pinckney. New York: Crowell, 1994.
- A picture-book biography of a great African-American educator.

Hill, Laban Carrick. *Dave the Potter*. Illus. Bryan Collier. New York: Little, Brown, 2010.
- A beautifully told story of the life of a slave in nineteenth-century South Carolina who became a celebrated potter.

Lawrence, Jacob. *Harriet and the Promised Land*. New York: Windmill, 1968.
- A picture-book biography of one-time slave and heroine of the Underground Railroad, Harriet Tubman.

McCarthy, Meghan. *The Incredible Life of Balto*. New York: Knopf, 2011.
- A lively biography of the great Alaskan sled dog.

McDonnell, Patrick. *Me . . . Jane*. New York: Little, Brown, 2011.
- A brief picture-book biography of Jane Goodall, the celebrated primate expert.

Quackenbush, Robert. *Mark Twain? What Kind of a Name Is That?* New York: Aladdin, 1990.
- A picture-book biography of the famous writer, appropriately light-hearted.

Raboff, Ernest. *Pablo Picasso*. New York: Doubleday, 1968.
- A picture-book biography of the celebrated artist; one of a series.

Sis, Peter. *Starry Messenger: Galileo Galilei*. New York: Farrar, Straus & Giroux, 1996.
- A picture book about the life of the great astronomer.

____. *The Tree of Life: Charles Darwin*. New York: Farrar, Straus & Giroux, 2003.
- A picture book about the life of the scientist who articulated the theory of evolution.

Stanley, Diane, and Peter Vennema. *Good Queen Bess: The Story of Elizabeth I of England*. Illus. Diane Stanley. New York: Four Winds, 1990.
- A picture-book biography of the great English queen; one of many biographies from this husband-and-wife team.

____. *Shaka: King of the Zulus*. Illus. Diane Stanley. New York: Morrow, 1988.
- A picture-book biography of a famous African warrior-king.

Steig, William. *When Everybody Wore a Hat*. New York: HarperCollins, 2003.
- A picture-book autobiography of a popular children's author and illustrator.

Venezia, Mike. *The Beatles*. New York: Scholastic, 1997.
- A picture-book biography of the famed band.

FOR GRADES 4 AND ABOVE

Allen, Thomas B. *Harriet Tubman, Secret Agent: How Daring Slaves and Free Blacks Spied for the Union During the Civil War*. Washington, DC: National Geographic, 2006.
- A book filled with fascinating information about the Underground Railroad.

Andronik, Catherine M. *Wildly Romantic: The English Romantic Poets: The Mad, the Bad and the Dangerous*. New York: Henry Holt, 2007.
- A lively collective biography of Wordsworth, Coleridge, Byron, Shelley, and Keats.

Bitton-Jackson, Livia. *I Have Lived a Thousand Years: Growing Up in the Holocaust*. New York: Simon & Schuster, 1997.
- The personal account of a Holocaust survivor.

Bruchac, Joseph. *A Boy Called Slow: The True Story of Sitting Bull*. New York: Philomel, 1995.
- An engaging account of the great Lakota chief.

____. *Pocahontas*. New York: Harcourt, 2003.
- The story of the Powhatan princess, told from two points of view—hers and John Smith's.

Byars, Betsy. *The Moon and I*. New York: Harper Collins, 1996.
- The autobiography of an award-winning children's author.

Dahl, Roald. *Boy: Tales of Childhood*. New York: Farrar, Straus & Giroux, 1984.
- Lively reminiscences of the author of *Charlie and the Chocolate Factory*.

Engle, Margarita. *The Poet Slave of Cuba: A Biography of Juan Francisco Manzano*. New York: Holt, 2006.
- A verse biography of a celebrated Cuban poet, who was also a slave.

Ferris, Jeri. *Native American Doctor: The Story of Susan La Flesche Picotte*. Minneapolis, MN: Carolrhoda, 1991.
- A book about the first American Indian woman to graduate from medical school.

Fleischman, Sid. *Escape! The Story of the Great Houdini*. New York: Greenwillow, 2006.
- A book about the life of the fascinating escape artist.

Fleming, Candace. *The Family Romanov: Murder, Rebellion, and the Fall of Imperial Russia*. York: Schwartz & Wade, 2014.
- A gripping account of the last years of the Russian Empire, with photographs and first-person accounts.

Frank, Anne. *The Diary of a Young Girl: The Definitive Edition*. Ed. Otto H. Frank and Mirjam Pressler. Trans. Susan Massotty. New York: Doubleday, 1995.
- A young girl's candid reflections on her life while hiding from the Nazis in Amsterdam during World War II; perhaps the most famous personal memoir to come out of the war.

Freedman, Russell. *Confucius and the Golden Rule*. New York: Clarion, 2002.
- Life and thought of the great Chinese philosopher.

____. *Eleanor Roosevelt: A Life of Discovery*. New York: Clarion, 1993.
- The life of the famed first lady; one of many illustrated biographies by Freedman.

____. *Lincoln: A Photobiography*. New York: Clarion, 1987.
- The life of the great Civil War president, illustrated with archival material.

Fritz, Jean. *The Double Life of Pocahontas*. New York: Puffin, 1983.
- The story of the life of the famous Powhatan princess who was torn between two worlds.

____. *Homesick: My Own Story*. New York: Putnam, 1982.
- A children's author recounts her own childhood.

Gerstein, Mordicai. *What Charlie Heard*. New York: Farrar, Straus & Giroux, 2002.
- The story of the life of American classical composer Charles Ives.

Gibbin, James Cross. *Charles A. Lindbergh: A Human Hero*. New York: Clarion, 1998.
- The story of the celebrated first pilot to fly solo over the Atlantic.

Heiligman, Deborah. *Charles and Emma: The Darwins' Leap of Faith*. New York: Holt, 2009.
- The story of the personal and professional life of Charles Darwin.

Jennings, Jazz. *Being Jazz: My Life as a Transgender Teen*. New York: Random House, 2016.
- A bold, first-person account of a teenager's transition from male to female.

Kherdian, David. *The Road from Home: The Story of an Armenian Girl*. New York: Greenwillow, 1979. (Later re-issued with the subtitle *A True Story of Courage, Survival and Hope*.)
- A book about the childhood experiences of the author's mother, a survivor of the Armenian holocaust of 1915.

Krull, Kathleen. *Lives of the Artists: Masterpieces, Messes (and What the Neighbors Thought)*. Illus. Kathryn Hewitt. Orlando, FL: Harcourt, 1995.
• A lively collection of brief biographies.

____. *Lives of the Presidents: Fame, Shame (and What the Neighbors Thought)*. Illus. Kathryn Hewitt. Orlando, FL: Harcourt, 1998.
• Another lively collection of brief biographies.

Lanier, Shannon, and Jane Feldman. *Jefferson's Children: The Story of One American Family*. New York: Random House, 2000.
• A book about the multiracial family legacy of the third president.

Latham, Jean Lee. *Carry On, Mr. Bowditch*. New York: Houghton Mifflin, 1955.
• A fictionalized biography of an unlikely hero, an American colonial mathematician.

Matthews, Elizabeth. *Different Like Coco*. New York: Candlewick, 2007.
• The story of the life of famed fashion designer Coco Chanel.

Mora, Pat. *A Library for Juana: The World of Sor Juana Inéz*. Illus. Beatriz Vidal. New York: Knopf, 2002.
• A biography of an unusual seventeenth-century female scholar in Mexico.

Myers, Walter Dean. *At Her Majesty's Request: An African Princess in Victorian England*. New York: Scholastic, 1999.
• The life of an orphaned African princess raised in England under the protection of Queen Victoria.

Naylor, Phyllis Reynolds. *How I Came to Be a Writer*. New York: Atheneum, 2001.
• The memoir of the author of *Shiloh*, focusing on her writing.

Parks, Rosa, with Jim Haskins. *I Am Rosa Parks*. Illus. Will Clay. New York: Dial, 1997.
• An autobiographical account of the life of the famous civil rights leader.

Rappaport, Doreen. *John's Secret Dreams: The Life of John Lennon*. Illus. Bryan Collier. New York: Hyperion, 2004.
• A book about the life of the most controversial member of the Beatles.

Redsand, Anna. *Viktor Frankl: A Life Worth Living*. New York: Clarion, 2006.
• The biography of a Holocaust survivor and renowned psychiatrist.

Reich, Susanna. *Clara Schumann: Piano Virtuoso*. New York: Clarion, 1999.
• A book about one of the few celebrated female composers and musicians of the nineteenth century.

Reiss, Johanna. *The Upstairs Room*. New York: HarperCollins, 1972.
• A stark autobiographical account of a Dutch girl's survival during World War II.

Severance, John B. *Gandhi: Great Soul*. New York: Clarion, 1997.
• A book about the life of Mahatma Gandhi.

Siegal, Aranka. *Upon the Head of a Goat: A Childhood in Hungary, 1939–1944*. New York: Farrar, Straus & Giroux, 1985.
• An autobiographical account of a Jewish girl's life during World War II.

Singer, Isaac Bashevis. *A Day of Pleasures: Stories of a Boy Growing Up in Warsaw*. New York: Farrar, Straus & Giroux, 1969.
• Reminiscences of a Nobel Prize–winning author.

Stevenson, Augusta. *George Washington: Young Leader*. New York: Aladdin, 1971.
• A fictionalized biography focusing on the first president's youth; part of the *Childhood of Famous Americans* series.

Szabo, Corinne. *Sky Pioneer: A Photobiography of Amelia Earhart*. Washington, DC: National Geographic, 1997.
• The story of the adventurous life of the pioneering woman pilot.

Thomas, Jane Resh. *Behind the Mask: The Life of Queen Elizabeth I*. New York: Clarion, 1998.
- A handsome biography of the great English queen.

Tillage, Leon Walter. *Leon's Story*. Illus. Susan L. Roth. New York: Farrar, Straus & Giroux, 1997.
- An autobiographical account of an African American's struggle in the mid-twentieth century.

Van der Rol, Ruud, and Rian Verhoeven. *Anne Frank: Beyond the Diary*. New York: Viking, 1993.
- Richly illustrated with photographs, an excellent companion to the famous diary.

Yates, Elizabeth. *Amos Fortune, Free Man*. New York: Dutton, 1950.
- The story of a nineteenth-century American slave who managed to buy his freedom.

Yousafzai, Malala, with Christina Lamb. *I Am Malala: The Story of the Girl Who Stood Up for Education and Was Shot by the Taliban*. New York: Little, Brown, 2013. (First published 2012.)
- The story of a young Pakistani girl's brave struggle against overwhelming odds to become the world's youngest Nobel Peace Prize winner.

Children's Book Awards

American Awards

The Newbery Medal

The Newbery Medal is named for John Newbery, a British entrepreneur who pioneered children's book publishing in the eighteenth century. The award is, however, an American award, presented annually by the American Library Association to the most distinguished contribution to children's literature published in the United States. Runners-up are given Newbery Honor Awards, but in the interest of space, Honor books have been omitted from here, except for those from 2000 and beyond; the complete list is readily found at the Newbery Award online site. As with any other such award, there has not always been general agreement with the decisions. However, the list does include some of the finest writing for young people in the past century.

1922   *The Story of Mankind* by Hendrik Willem van Loon, Liveright

1923   *The Voyages of Doctor Dolittle* by Hugh Lofting, Lippincott

1924   *The Dark Frigate* by Charles Hawes; Little, Brown

1925   *Tales from Silver Lands* by Charles Finger, Doubleday

1926   *Shen of the Sea* by Arthur Bowie Chrisman, Dutton

1927   *Smoky, the Cowhorse* by Will James, Scribner's

1928   *Gay Neck, the Story of a Pigeon* by Dhan Gopal Mukerji, Dutton

1929   *The Trumpeter of Krakow* by Eric P. Kelly, Macmillan

1930   *Hitty, Her First Hundred Years* by Rachel Field, Macmillan

1931   *The Cat Who Went to Heaven* by Elizabeth Coatsworth, Macmillan

1932   *Waterless Mountain* by Laura Adams Armer; Longmans, Green (McKay)

1933   *Young Fu of the Upper Yangtze* by Elizabeth Foreman Lewis, Winston

1934   *Invincible Louisa: The Story of the Author of* Little Women by Cornelia Meigs; Little, Brown

1935   *Dobry* by Monica Shannon, Viking

1936   *Caddie Woodlawn* by Carol Ryrie Brink, Macmillan

1937   *Roller Skates* by Ruth Sawyer, Viking

1938   *The White Stag* by Kate Seredy, Viking

1939   *Thimble Summer* by Elizabeth Enright; Holt, Rinehart & Winston

1940   *Daniel Boone* by James Daugherty, Viking

1941   *Call It Courage* by Armstrong Sperry, Macmillan

1942   *The Matchlock Gun* by Walter D. Edmonds; Dodd, Mead

1943   *Adam of the Road* by Elizabeth Janet Gray, Viking

1944   *Johnny Tremain* by Esther Forbes, Houghton Mifflin

1945   *Rabbit Hill* by Robert Lawson, Viking

1946   *Strawberry Girl* by Lois Lenski, Lippincott

1947   *Miss Hickory* by Carolyn Sherwin Bailey, Viking

1948   *The Twenty-One Balloons* by William Pène du Bois, Viking

1949   *King of the Wind* by Marguerite Henry, Rand McNally

1950   *The Door in the Wall* by Marguerite de Angeli, Doubleday

1951   *Amos Fortune, Free Man* by Elizabeth Yates, Aladdin

1952   *Ginger Pye* by Eleanor Estes, Harcourt Brace Jovanovich

1953   *Secret of the Andes* by Ann Nolan Clark, Viking

1954   *. . . and Now Miguel* by Joseph Krumgold, Crowell

1955   *The Wheel on the School* by Meindert DeJong, Harper

1956   *Carry On, Mr. Bowditch* by Jean Lee Latham, Houghton Mifflin

1957   *Miracles on Maple Hill* by Virginia Sorensen, Harcourt Brace Jovanovich

1958   *Rifles for Watie* by Harold Keith, Crowell

1959   *The Witch of Blackbird Pond* by Elizabeth George Speare, Houghton Mifflin

1960   *Onion John* by Joseph Krumgold, Crowell

1961   *Island of the Blue Dolphins* by Scott O'Dell, Houghton Mifflin

1962   *The Bronze Bow* by Elizabeth George Speare, Houghton Mifflin

1963   *A Wrinkle in Time* by Madeline L'Engle; Farrar, Straus & Giroux

1964   *It's Like This, Cat* by Emily Cheney Neville, Harper

1965   *Shadow of a Bull* by Maia Wojciechowska, Atheneum

1966   *I, Juan de Pareja* by Elizabeth Borten de Trevino; Farrar, Straus & Giroux

1967   *Up a Road Slowly* by Irene Hunt, Follett

1968   *From the Mixed-up Files of Mrs. Basil E. Frankweiler* by E. L. Konigsburg, Atheneum

1969   *The High King* by Lloyd Alexander; Holt, Rinehart & Winston

1970   *Sounder* by William H. Armstrong, Harper

1971   *Summer of the Swans* by Betsy Byars, Viking

1972   *Mrs. Frisby and the Rats of NIMH* by Robert C. O'Brien, Atheneum

1973   *Julie of the Wolves* by Jean Craighead George, Harper

1974   *The Slave Dancer* by Paula Fox, Bradbury

1975   *M. C. Higgins, the Great* by Virginia Hamilton, Macmillan

1976   *The Grey King* by Susan Cooper, Atheneum

1977   *Roll of Thunder, Hear My Cry* by Mildred D. Taylor, Dial Press

1978   *Bridge to Terabithia* by Katherine Paterson, Crowell

1979   *The Westing Game* by Ellen Raskin, Dutton

1980   *A Gathering of Days: A New England Girl's Journal 1830–32* by Joan Blos, Scribner

1981   *Jacob Have I Loved* by Katherine Paterson, Cromwell

1982   *A Visit to William Blake's Inn: Poems for Innocent and Experienced* by Nancy Willard, Harcourt

1983   *Dicey's Song* by Cynthia Voigt, Atheneum

1984   *Dear Mr. Henshaw* by Beverly Cleary, Morrow

1985   *The Hero and the Crown* by Robin McKinley, Greenwillow (Morrow)

1986   *Sarah, Plain and Tall* by Patricia MacLachlan, Harper

1987   *The Whipping Boy* by Sid Fleischman, Greenwillow (Morrow)

1988   *Lincoln: A Photobiography* by Russell Freedman, Clarion/Houghton Mifflin

1989   *Joyful Noise: Poems for Two Voices* by Paul Fleischman, Harper

1990   *Number the Stars* by Lois Lowry, Houghton Mifflin

1991   *Maniac Magee* by Jerry Spinelli; Little, Brown

1992   *Shiloh* by Phyllis Reynolds Naylor, Atheneum

1993   *Missing May* by Cynthia Ryland, Orchard

1994   *The Giver* by Lois Lowry, Houghton Mifflin

1995   *Walk Two Moons* by Sharon Creech, HarperCollins

1996   *The Midwife's Apprentice* by Karen Cushman, Houghton Mifflin

1997   *The View from Saturday* by E. L. Konigsburg, Atheneum

1998   *Out of the Dust* by Karen Hesse, Scholastic

1999   *Holes* by Louis Sachar; Farrar, Straus & Giroux

2000   *Bud, Not Buddy* by Christopher Paul Curtis, Delacorte
Honor Books: *Getting Near to Baby* by Audrey Couloumbis, Putnam; *26 Fairmount Avenue* by Tomie de Paola, Putnam; *Our Only May Amelia* by Jennifer L. Holm, HarperCollins

2001   *A Year Down Yonder* by Richard Peck, Dial
Honor Books: *Hope Was Here* by Joan Bauer, Putnam; *The Wanderer* by Sharon Creech, HarperCollins; *Because of Winn-Dixie* by Kate DiCamillo, Candlewick; *Joey Pigza Loses Control* by Jack Gantos, Farrar, Straus & Giroux

2002   *A Single Shard* by Linda Sue Park, Houghton Mifflin
Honor Books: *Everything on a Waffle* by Polly Horvath, Farrar, Straus & Giroux; *Carver: A Life in Poems* by Marilyn Nelson, Front Street

2003   *Crispin: The Cross of Lead* by Avi, Hyperion
Honor Books: *The House of the Scorpion* by Nancy Farmer, Atheneum; *Pictures of Hollis Woods* by Patricia Reilly Giff, Random House; *Hoot* by Carl Hiaasen, Knopf; *A Corner of the Universe* by Ann M. Martin, Scholastic; *Surviving the Applewhites* by Stephanie S. Tolan, HarperCollins

2004   *The Tale of Despereaux: Being the Story of a Mouse, a Princess, Some Soup, and a Spool of Thread* by Kate DiCamillo, Candlewick
Honor Books: *Olive's Ocean* by Kevin Henkes, Greenwillow; *An American Plague: The True and Terrifying Story of the Yellow Fever Epidemic of 1793* by Jim Murphy, Clarion

2005   *Kira-Kira* by Cynthia Kadohata, Atheneum
Honor Books: *Al Capone Does My Shirts* by Gennifer Choldenko, Putnam; *The Voice that Challenged a Nation: Marion Anderson and the Struggle for Equal Rights* by Russell Freedman, Clarion; *Lizzie Bright and the Buckminster Boy* by Gary D. Schmidt, Clarion

2006   *Criss Cross* by Lynne Rae Perkins, Greenwillow
Honor Books: *Whittington* by Alan Armstrong, Random House; *Hitler Youth: Growing Up in Hitler's Shadow* by Susan Campbell Bartoletti, Scholastic; *Princess Academy* by Shannon Hale, Bloomsbury; *Show Way* by Jacqueline Woodson, Putnam

2007   *The Higher Power of Lucky* by Susan Patron, Simon & Schuster
Honor Books: *Penny from Heaven* by Jennifer L. Holm, Random House; *Hattie Big Sky* by Kirby Larson, Delacorte; *Rules* by Cynthia Lord, Scholastic

2008   *Good Masters! Sweet Ladies! Voices from a Medieval Village* by Laura Amy Schlitz, Candlewick
Honor Books: *Elijah of Buxton* by Christopher Paul Curtis, Scholastic; *The Wednesday Wars* by Gary D. Schmidt, Clarion; *Feathers* by Jacqueline Woodson, Putnam

2009   *The Graveyard Book* by Neil Gaiman, illustrated by Dave McKean, HarperCollins
Honor Books: *The Underneath* by Kathi Appelt, illustrated by David Small, Atheneum; *The Surrender Tree: Poems of Cuba's Struggle for Freedom* by Margarita Engle, Henry Holt; *Savvy* by Ingrid Law, Dial/Walden Media; *After Tupac & D Foster* by Jacqueline Woodson, G. P. Putnam's Sons

2010   *When You Reach Me* by Rebecca Stead, Random House
Honor Books: *Claudette Colvin: Twice Toward Justice* by Phillip Hoose, Farrar, Straus & Giroux; *The Evolution of Calpurnia Tate* by Jacqueline Kelly, Henry Holt; *Where the Mountain Meets the Moon* by Grace Lin, Little, Brown; *The Mostly True Adventures of Homer P. Figg* by Rodman Philbrick, Scholastic, Inc.

2011   *Moon over Manifest* by Clare Vanderpool, Delacorte Press
Honor Books: *Turtle in Paradise* by Jennifer L. Holm, Random House; *Heart of a Samurai* by Margi Preus, Amulet Books; *Dark Emperor and Other Poems of the Night* by Joyce Sidman, Houghton Mifflin; *One Crazy Summer* by Rita Williams-Garcia, Amistad

2012   *Dead End in Norvelt* by Jack Gantos, Farrar, Straus & Giroux
Honor Books: *Inside Out & Back Again* by Thanhha Lai, HarperCollins; *Breaking Stalin's Nose* by Eugene Yelchin, Henry Holt

2013   *The One and Only Ivan* by Katherine Applegate, HarperCollins
Honor Books: *Splendors and Glooms* by Laura Amy Schlitz, Candlewick; *Bomb: The Race to Build—and Steal—the World's Most Dangerous Weapon* by Steve Sheinkin, Roaring Brook Press; *Three Times Lucky* by Sheila Turnage, Dial Books

2014   *Flora & Ulysses: The Illuminated Adventures* by Kate DiCamillo, Candlewick Press
Honor Books: *Doll Bones* by Holly Black, Margaret K. McElderry Books, an imprint of Simon & Schuster Children's Publishing; *The Year of Billy Miller* by Kevin Henkes, Greenwillow Books, an imprint of HarperCollins Publishers; *One Came Home* by Amy Timberlake, Alfred A. Knopf, an imprint of Random House Children's Books; *Paperboy* by Vince Vawter, Delacorte Press, an imprint of Random House Children's Books

2015   *The Crossover* by Kwame Alexander, Houghton Mifflin Harcourt
Honor Books: *El Deafo* by Cece Bell, Amulet Books, an imprint of ABRAMS; *Brown Girl Dreaming* by Jacqueline Woodson, Nancy Paulsen Books, an imprint of Penguin Group LLC

2016   *Last Stop on Market Street* by Matt de la Peña, G. P. Putnam's Sons/Penguin
Honor Books: *The War that Saved My Life* by Kimberly Brubaker Bradley, Dial Books for Young Readers/Penguin; *Roller Girl* by Victoria Jamieson, Dial Books for Young Readers/Penguin; *Echo* by Pam Muñoz Ryan, Scholastic Press/Scholastic Inc.

2017   *The Girl Who Drank the Moon* by Kelly Barnhill, Algonquin Young Readers, an imprint of Algonquin Books of Chapel Hill, a division of Workman Publishing
Honor Books: *Freedom Over Me: Eleven Slaves, Their Lives and Dreams Brought to Life* by Ashley Bryan, Atheneum Books for Young Readers, an imprint of Simon & Schuster Children's Publishing Division; *The Inquisitor's Tale: Or, The Three Magical Children and Their Holy Dog* by Adam Gidwitz, illustrated by Hatem Aly, Dutton Children's Books, Penguin Young Readers Group, an imprint of Penguin Random House LLC; *Wolf Hollow* by Lauren Wolk, Dutton Children's Books, Penguin Young Readers Group, an imprint of Penguin Random House LLC

The Caldecott Medal

Named for British illustrator Randolph Caldecott, the Caldecott Medal has been awarded annually since 1938 by the American Library Association for the most distinguished picture book published in the United States. Runners-up are given Caldecott Honor Awards, but in the interest of space, Honor books have been omitted here, except for those from 2000 and beyond; the complete list is readily found at the Caldecott Award website. The Caldecott Award is given to the illustrator, not the writer. Unless indicated otherwise, the illustrator is the author.

1938   *Animals of the Bible* by Helen Dean Fish, illustrated by Dorothy P. Lathrop, Stokes

1939   *Mei Li* by Thomas Handforth, Doubleday

1940   *Abraham Lincoln* by Ingri and Edgar Parin d'Aulaire, Doubleday

1941   *They Were Strong and Good* by Robert Lawson, Viking

1942   *Make Way for Ducklings* by Robert McCloskey, Viking

1943 *The Little House* by Virginia Lee Burton, Houghton Mifflin

1944 *Many Moons* by James Thurber, illustrated by Louis Slobodkin, Harcourt Brace Jovanovich

1945 *Prayer for a Child* by Rachel Field, illustrated by Elizabeth Orton Jones, Macmillan

1946 *The Rooster Crows . . .* , illustrated by Maud and Miska Petersham, Macmillan

1947 *The Little Island* by Golden MacDonald, illustrated by Leonard Weisgard, Doubleday

1948 *White Snow, Bright Snow* by Alvin Tresselt, illustrated by Roger Duvoisin, Lothrop

1949 *The Big Snow* by Berta and Elmer Hader, Macmillan

1950 *Song of the Swallows* by Leo Politi, Scribner's

1951 *The Egg Tree* by Katherine Milhouse, Scribner's

1952 *Finders Keepers* by William Lipkind, illustrated by Nicholas Mordvinoff, Harcourt Brace Jovanovich

1953 *The Biggest Bear* by Lynd Ward, Houghton Mifflin

1954 *Madeline's Rescue* by Ludwig Bemelmans, Viking

1955 *Cinderella, or the Little Glass Slipper* by Charles Perrault, translated and illustrated by Marcia Brown, Scribner's

1956 *Frog Went A-Courtin',* edited by John Langstaff, illustrated by Feodor Rojankovsky, Harcourt Brace Jovanovich

1957 *A Tree Is Nice* by Janice May Udry, illustrated by Marc Simont, Harper

1958 *Time of Wonder* by Robert McCloskey, Viking

1959 *Chanticleer and the Fox,* adapted from Chaucer and illustrated by Barbara Cooney, Crowell

1960 *Nine Days to Christmas* by Marie Hall Ets and Aurora Labastida, illustrated by Marie Hall Ets, Viking

1961 *Baboushka and the Three Kings* by Ruth Robbins, illustrated by Nicolas Sidjakov, Parnassus

1962 *Once a Mouse . . .* by Marcia Brown, Scribner's

1963 *The Snowy Day* by Ezra Jack Keats, Viking

1964 *Where the Wild Things Are* by Maurice Sendak, Harper

1965 *May I Bring a Friend?* by Beatrice Schenk de Regniers, illustrated by Beni Montresor, Atheneum

1966 *Always Room for One More* by Sorche Nic Leodhas, illustrated by Nonny Hogrogian; Holt, Rinehart & Winston

1967 *Sam, Bangs & Moonshine* by Evaline Ness; Holt, Rinehart & Winston

1968 *Drummer Hoff* by Barbara Emberley, illustrated by Ed Emberley, PrenticeHall

1969 *The Fool of the World and the Flying Ship* by Arthur Ransome, illustrated by Uri Shulevitz; Farrar, Straus & Giroux

1970 *Sylvester and the Magic Pebble* by William Steig; Windmill, Simon & Schuster

1971 *A Story A Story* by Gail E. Haley, Atheneum

1972 *One Fine Day* by Nonny Hogrogian, Macmillan

1973 *The Funny Little Woman* retold by Arlene Mosel, illustrated by Blair Lent, Dutton

1974 *Duffy and the Devil* by Harve Zemach, illustrated by Margot Zemach; Farrar, Straus & Giroux

1975 *Arrow to the Sun,* adapted and illustrated by Gerald McDermott, Viking

1976 *Why Mosquitoes Buzz in People's Ears* retold by Verna Aardema, illustrated by Leo and Diane Dillon, Dial Press

1977 *Ashanti to Zulu: African Traditions* by Margaret Musgrove, illustrated by Leo and Diane Dillon, Dial Press

1978 *Noah's Ark* by Peter Spier, Doubleday

1979 *The Girl Who Loved Wild Horses* by Paul Goble, Bradbury

1980 *Ox-Cart Man* by Donald Hall, illustrated by Barbara Cooney, Viking

1981   *Fables* by Arnold Lobel, Harper

1982   *Jumanji* by Chris Van Allsburg, Houghton Mifflin

1983   *Shadow* by Blaise Cendrars, illustrated by Marcia Brown, Scribner's

1984   *The Glorious Flight: Across the Channel with Louis Blériot July 25, 1909* by Alice and Martin Provenson, Viking

1985   *Saint George and the Dragon* by Margaret Hodges, illustrated by Trina Schart Hyman; Little, Brown

1986   *The Polar Express* by Chris van Allsburg, Houghton Mifflin

1987   *Hey, Al* by Arthur Yorinks, illustrated by Richard Egielski; Farrar, Straus & Giroux

1988   *Owl Moon* by Jane Yolen, illustrated by John Schoenherr, Philomel (Putnam)

1989   *Song and Dance Man* by Karen Ackerman, illustrated by Stephen Gammell, Knopf

1990   *Lon Po Po: A Red-Riding Hood Story from China* by Ed Young, Philomel (Putnam)

1991   *Black and White* by David Macaulay, Houghton Mifflin

1992   *Tuesday* by David Wiesner, Clarion

1993   *Mirette on the High Wire* by Emily Arnold McCully, Putnam

1994   *Grandfather's Journey* by Allen Say, Houghton Mifflin

1995   *Smoky Night* by Eve Bunting, illustrated by David Diaz, Harcourt

1996   *Officer Buckle and Gloria* by Peggy Rathmann, Putnam

1997   *Golem* by David Wisniewski, Clarion

1998   *Rapunzel* by Paul O. Zelinsky, Dutton

1999   *Snowflake Bentley* by Jacqueline Briggs Martin, illustrated by Mary Azarian, Houghton Mifflin

2000   *Joseph Had a Little Overcoat* by Simms Taback, Viking
       Honor Books: *Sector 7* by David Wiesner, Clarion; *The Ugly Duckling* by Jerry Pinkney, Morrow; *When Sophie Gets Angry—Really, Really Angry . . .* by Molly Bang, Scholastic; *A Child's Calendar* by John Updike, illustrated by Trina Schart Hyman, Holiday

2001   *So You Want to Be President?* by Judith St. George, illustrated by David Small, Philomel
       Honor Books: *Casey at the Bat* by Ernest Thayer, illustrated by Christopher Bing, Handprint; *Click, Clack, Moo: Cows That Type* by Doreen Cronin, illustrated by Betsy Lewin, Simon & Schuster; *Olivia* by Ian Falconer, Atheneum

2002   *The Three Pigs* by David Wiesner, Clarion/Houghton Mifflin
       Honor Books: *The Dinosaurs of Waterhouse Hawkins* by Barbara Kerley, illustrated by Brian Selznick, Scholastic; *Martin's Big Words: The Life of Dr. Martin Luther King, Jr.* by Doreen Rappaport, illustrated by Bryan Collier, Hyperion; *The Stray Dog* by Marc Simont, HarperCollins

2003   *My Friend Rabbit* by Eric Rohmann, Roaring Brook
       Honor Books: *The Spider and the Fly* by Mary Howitt, illustrated by Tony DiTerlizzi, Simon & Schuster; *Hondo and Fabian* by Peter McCarty, Holt; *Noah's Ark* by Jerry Pinkney, Seastar/North-South

2004   *The Man Who Walked Between the Towers* by Mordicai Gerstein, Roaring Brook Press
       Honor Books: *Ella Sarah Gets Dressed* by Margaret Chodos-Irvine, Harcourt; *What Do You Do with a Tail Like This?* by Steve Jenkins and Robin Page, Houghton Mifflin; *Don't Let the Pigeon Drive the Bus* by Mo Willems, Hyperion

2005   *Kitten's First Full Moon* by Kevin Henkes, Greenwillow
       Honor Books: *The Red Book* by Barbara Lehman, Houghton Mifflin; *Coming on Home Soon* by Jacqueline Woodson, illustrated by E. B. Lewis, Putnam; *Knuffle Bunny: A Cautionary Tale* by Mo Willems, Hyperion

2006   *The Hello, Goodbye Window* by Norton Juster, illustrated by Chris Raschka, Hyperion
       Honor Books: *Rosa* by Nikki Giovanni, illustrated by Bryan Collier, Henry Holt; *Zen Shorts* by Jon J. Muth, Scholastic; *Hot Air: The (Mostly) True Story of the First Hot-Air Balloon Ride* by Marjorie Priceman, Simon & Schuster; *Song of the Water Boatman and Other Pond Poems* by Joyce Sidman, illustrated by Beckie Prange, Houghton Mifflin

2007   *Flotsam* by David Wiesner, Clarion
Honor Books: *Gone Wild: An Endangered Animal Alphabet* by David McLimans, Walker; *Moses: When Harriet Tubman Led Her People to Freedom* by Carole Boston Weatherford, Hyperion

2008   *The Invention of Hugo Cabret* by Brian Selznick, Scholastic
Honor Books: *Henry's Freedom Box: A True Story from the Underground Railroad* by Ellen Levine, illustrated by Kadir Nelson, Scholastic; *First the Egg* by Laura Vaccaro Seeger, Roaring Brook/Neal Porter; *The Wall: Growing Up Behind the Iron Curtain* by Peter Sis, Farrar, Straus & Giroux/Frances Foster; *Knuffle Bunny Too: A Case of Mistaken Identity* by Mo Willems, Hyperion

2009   *The House in the Night* by Susan Marie Swanson, illustrated by Beth Krommes, Houghton Mifflin
Honor Books: *A Couple of Boys Have the Best Week Ever* by Marla Frazee, Harcourt; *How I Learned Geography* by Uri Shulevitz, Farrar, Straus & Giroux; *A River of Words: The Story of William Carlos Williams* by Jen Bryant, illustrated by Melissa Sweet, Eerdmans

2010   *The Lion & the Mouse* by Jerry Pinkney; Little, Brown
Honor Books: *All the World* by Liz Garton Scanlon, illustrated by Marla Frazee, Beach Lane Books; *Red Sings from Treetops: A Year in Colors* by Joyce Sidman, illustrated by Pamela Zagarenski, Houghton Mifflin Harcourt

2011   *A Sick Day for Amos McGee* by Philip C. Stead, illustrated by Erin E. Stead, Roaring Brook Press
Honor Books: *Dave the Potter: Artist, Poet, Slave* by Laban Carrick Hill, illustrated by Bryan Collier, Little, Brown; *Interrupting Chicken* by David Ezra Stein, Candlewick

2012   *A Ball for Daisy* by Chris Raschka, Random House
Honor Books: *Blackout* by John Rocco, Disney; *Grandpa Green* by Lane Smith, Roaring Brook Press; *Me ... Jane* by Patrick McDonnell, Little, Brown

2013   *This Is Not My Hat* by Jon Klassen, Candlewick
Honor Books: *Creepy Carrots!* by Aaron Reynolds, illustrated by Peter Brown, Simon & Schuster; *Extra Yarn* by Mac Barnett, illustrated by Jon Klassen, HarperCollins Publishers; *Green* by Laura Vaccaro Seeger, Roaring Brook Press; *One Cool Friend* by Toni Buzzeo, illustrated by David Small, Dial Books; *Sleep Like a Tiger* by Mary Logue, illustrated by Pamela Zagarenski, Houghton Mifflin

2014   *Locomotive* by Brian Floca, Atheneum Books for Young Readers, an imprint of Simon & Schuster Children's Publishing
Honor Books: *Journey* by Aaron Becker, Candlewick Press; *Flora and the Flamingo* by Molly Idle, Chronicle Books; *Mr. Wuffles!* by David Wiesner, Clarion Books

2015   *The Adventures of Beekle: The Unimaginary Friend* by Dan Santat, Little, Brown and Company
Honor Books: *Nana in the City* by Lauren Castillo, Clarion Books, an imprint of Houghton Mifflin Harcourt; *The Noisy Paint Box: The Colors and Sounds of Kandinsky's Abstract Art,* illustrated by Mary GrandPré, written by Barb Rosenstock, Alfred A. Knopf, an imprint of Random House Children's Books; *Sam & Dave Dig a Hole*, illustrated by Jon Klassen, written by Mac Barnett, Candlewick Press; *Viva Frida* by Yuyi Morales, Roaring Brook Press; *The Right Word: Roget and His Thesaurus*, illustrated by Melissa Sweet, written by Jen Bryant, Eerdmans Books for Young Readers; *This One Summer*, illustrated by Jillian Tamaki, written by Mariko Tamaki, First Second

2016   *Finding Winnie: The True Story of the World's Most Famous Bear*, illustrated by Sophie Blackall, written by Lindsay Mattick; Little, Brown and Company
Honor Books: *Trombone Shorty*, illustrated by Bryan Collier, written by Troy Andrews, Abrams Books for Young Readers, an imprint of ABRAMS; *Waiting* by Kevin Henkes, Greenwillow Books/HarperCollins; *Voice of Freedom: Fannie Lou Hamer, Spirit of the Civil Rights Movement*, illustrated by Ekua Holmes, written by Carole Boston Weatherford, Candlewick Press; *Last Stop on Market Street*, illustrated by Christian Robinson, written by Matt de la Peña, G. P. Putnam's Sons/Penguin

2017   *Radiant Child: The Story of Young Artist Jean-Michel Basquiat* by Javaka Steptoe; Little, Brown and Company, a division of Hachette Book Group, Inc.
Honor Books: *Leave Me Alone!* by Vera Brosgol, Roaring Brook Press/Holtzbrinck; *Freedom in Congo Square*, illustrated by R. Gregory Christie, written by Carole Boston Weatherford, Little Bee Books/Bonnier; *Du Iz Tak?* by Carson Ellis, Candlewick Press; *They All Saw a Cat* by Brendan Wenzel, Chronicle Books

The Mildred L. Batchelder Award

Presented annually by the American Library Association, this award recognizes the most outstanding children's book published in the preceding year and originally translated from a language other than English.

1968　*The Little Man* by Erich Kastner, translated by James Kirkup, illustrated by Rich Schreiter (Knopf)

1969　*Don't Take Teddy* by Babbis Friis-Baastad, translated by Lise Somme McKinnon (Scribner)

1970　*Wildcat Under Glass* by Alki Zei, translated by Edward Fenton (Holt, Rinehart & Winston)

1971　*In the Land of Ur: The Discovery of Ancient Mesopotamia* by Hans Baumann, translated by Stella Humphries, illustrated by Hans Peter Renner (Pantheon Books)

1972　*Friedrich* by Hans Peter Richter, translated by Edite Kroll (Holt, Rinehart & Winston)

1973　*Pulga* by Siny Rose Van Iterson, translated by Alexander and Alison Gode (Morrow)

1974　*Petros' War* by Alki Zei, translated by Edward Fenton (Dutton)

1975　*An Old Tale Carved Out of Stone* by Aleksandr M. Linevski, translated by Maria Polushkin (Crown)

1976　*The Cat and Mouse Who Shared a House* by Ruth Hurlimann, translated by Anthea Bell (Walck)

1977　*The Leopard* by Cecil Bodker, translated by Gunnar Poulsen (Atheneum)

1978　No award given

1979　*Konrad* by Christine Nostlinger, translated by Anthea Bell, illustrated by Carol Nicklaus (Watts) and *Rabbit Island* by Jorg Steiner, translated by Ann Conrad Lammers, illustrated by Jorg Muller (Harcourt Brace Jovanovich)

1980　*The Sound of Dragon's Feet* by Alki Zei, translated by Edward Fento (Dutton)

1981　*The Winter When Time Was Frozen* by Els Pelgrom, translated by Raphael and Maryka Rudnik (Morrow)

1982　*The Battle Horse* by Harry Kullman, translated by George Blecher and Lone Thygesen-Blecher (Bradbury)

1983　*Hiroshima No Pika* by Toshi Maruki, translated by the author (Lothrop)

1984　*Ronia, the Robber's Daughter* by Astrid Lindgren, translated by Patricia Crampton (Viking)

1985　*The Island on Bird Street* by Uri Orlev, translated by Hillel Halkin (Houghton Mifflin)

1986　*Rose Blanche* by Christophe Gallaz and Roberto Innocenti, translated by Martha Coventry and Richard Graglia, illustrated by Roberto Innocenti (Creative Education)

1987　*No Hero for the Kaiser* by Rudolf Frank, translated by Patricia Crampton, illustrated by Klaus Steffans (Lothrop)

1988　*If You Didn't Have Me* by Ulf Nilsson, illustrated by Eva Ericksson, translated by Lone Thygesen-Blecher and George Blecher (McElderry)

1989　*Crutches* by Peter Hartling (Lothrop)

1990　*Buster's World* by Bjarne Reuter, translated by Anthea Bell (Dutton)

1991　*A Handful of Stars* by Rafik Schami, translated by Rika Lesser (Dutton)

1992　*The Man from the Other Side* by Uri Orlev, translated by Hillel Halkin (Houghton Mifflin)

1993　No award given

1994　*The Apprentice* by Pilar Molina Llorente, translated by Robin Longshaw, illustrated by Juan Ramón Alonso (Farrar, Straus & Giroux)

1995　*The Boys from St. Petri* by Bjarne Reuter, translated by Anthea Bell (Dutton)

1996　*The Lady with the Hat* by Uri Orlev, translated by Hillel Halkin (Houghton Mifflin)

1997　*The Friends* by Kazumi Yumoto, translated by Cathy Hirano (Farrar, Straus & Giroux)

1998　*The Robber and Me* by Josef Holub, edited by Marc Aronson, translated by Elizabeth D. Crawford (Holt)

1999　*Thanks to My Mother* by Schoschana Rabinovici, edited by Cindy Kane, translated by James Skofield (Dial)

2000   *The Baboon King* by Anton Quintana, translated by John Nieuwenhuizer (Walker)

2001   *Samir and Yonaton* by Daniella Carmi, translated by Yael Lotan (Scholastic)

2002   *How I Became an American* by Karin Gündisch, translated by James Scofield (Cricket/Carus)

2003   *The Thief Lord* by Cornelia Funke, translated by Oliver Latsch (Scholastic)

2004   *Run, Boy, Run* by Uri Orlev, translated by Hillel Halkin (Houghton Mifflin)

2005   *The Shadows of Ghadames* by Joëlle Stolz, translated by Catherine Temerso (Delacorte)

2006   *An Innocent Soldier* by Josef Holub, translated by Michael Hofmann (Arthur Levine Books)

2007   *The Pull of the Ocean* by Jean-Claude Mourlevat, translated by Y. Maudet (Delacorte)

2008   *Brave Story* by Miyuki Miyabe, translated by Alexander O. Smith (VIZ Media)

2009   *Moribito: Guardian of the Spirit* by Nahoko Uehashi, translated by Cathy Hirano (Scholastic)

2010   *A Faraway Island* by Annika Thor, translated by Linda Schencd (Delacorte Press)

2011   *A Time of Miracles* by Anne-Laure Bondoux, translated by Y. Maudet (Delacorte)

2012   *Soldier Bear* by Bibi Dumon Tak, illustrated by Philip Hopman, translated by Laura Watkinson (Eerdmans)

2013   *My Family for the War* by Anne C. Voorhoeve, translated by Tammi Reichel (Dial)

2014   *Mister Orange,* written by Truus Matti, translated by Laura Watkinson (Enchanted Lion Books)

2015   *Mikis and the Donkey,* written by Bibi Dumon Tak, illustrated by Philip Hopman, translated by Laura Watkinson (Eerdmans)

2016   *The Wonderful Fluffy Little Squishy,* written and illustrated by Beatrice Alemagna, translated from the French by Claudia Zoe Bedrick (Enchanted Lion Books)

2017   *Cry Heart, But Never Break* by Glenn Ringtved, illustrated by Charlotte Pardi, translated by Robert Moulthrop (Enchanted Lion Books)

The Laura Ingalls Wilder Award

This award is named in honor of the beloved author of the "Little House" books, who was also its first recipient. The Association for Library Service to Children of the American Library Association presents this award to the individual, either author or illustrator, whose work has over the years proved to be a significant contribution to children's literature. Originally awarded every five years, it was awarded every three years from 1980 to 2001. It is now awarded every two years.

1954   Laura Ingalls Wilder

1960   Clara Ingram Judson

1965   Ruth Sawyer

1970   E. B. White

1975   Beverly Cleary

1980   Theodore Geisel (Dr. Seuss)

1983   Maurice Sendak

1986   Jean Fritz

1989   Elizabeth George Speare

1992   Marcia Brown

1995   Virginia Hamilton

1998   Russell Freedman

2001   Milton Meltzer

2003   Eric Carle

2005   Laurence Yep

2007   James Marshall

2009   Ashley Bryan

2011   Tomie dePaola

2013   Katherine Paterson

2105   Donald Crews

2016   Jerry Pickney

2017   Nikki Grimes

The Coretta Scott King Award

Presented annually by the Social Responsibilities Round Table of the American Library Association, this award recognizes an African American author and, from 1974, an illustrator who have made an outstanding contribution to literature for children in the preceding year. The award is named for the widow of civil rights leader and Nobel Peace Prize winner Dr. Martin Luther King, Jr., and it acknowledges the humanitarian work of both Dr. and Mrs. King.

1970   Lillie Patterson, *Martin Luther King, Jr., Man of Peace* (Garrard)

1971   Charlemae Rollins, *Black Troubadour: Langston Hughes* (Rand)

1972   Elton C. Fax, *17 Black Artists* (Dodd)

1973   Jackie Robinson and Alfred Duckett, *I Never Had It Made* (Putnam)

1974   Author: Sharon Bell Mathis, *Ray Charles* (Crowell)
        Illustrator: George Ford, *Ray Charles* by Sharon Bell Mathis (Crowell)

1975   Author: Dorothy Robinson, *The Legend of Africana* (Johnson)
        Illustrator: Herbert Temple, *The Legend of Africana* by Dorothy Robinson (Johnson)

1976   Author: Pearl Bailey, *Duey's Tale* (Harcourt)
        Illustrator: No award given

1977   Author: James Haskins, *The Story of Stevie Wonder* (Lothrop)
        Illustrator: No award given

1978   Author: Eloise Greenfield, *Africa Dream* (Day/Crowell)
        Illustrator: Carole Bayard, *Africa Dream* by Eloise Greenfield (Day/Crowell)

1979   Author: Ossie Davis, *Escape to Freedom* (Viking)
        Illustrator: Tom Feelings, *Something on My Mind* by Nikki Grimes (Dial)

1980   Author: Walter Dean Myers, *The Young Landlords* (Viking)
        Illustrator: Carole Bayard, *Cornrows* by Camille Yarbrough (Coward)

1981   Author: Sidney Poitier, *This Life* (Knopf)
        Illustrator: Ashley Bryan, *Beat the Story-Drum, Pum-Pum* (Atheneum)

1982   Author: Mildred Taylor, *Let the Circle Be Unbroken* (Dial)
        Illustrator: John Steptoe, *Mother Crocodile: An Uncle Amadou Tale from Senegal* adapted by Rosa Guy (Delacorte)

1983   Author: Virginia Hamilton, *Sweet Whispers, Brother Rush* (Philomel)
        Illustrator: Peter Mugabane, *Black Child* (Knopf)

1984   Author: Lucile Clifton, *Everett Anderson's Good-Bye* (Holt)
        Illustrator: Pat Cummings, *My Mama Needs Me* by Mildred Pitts Walter (Lothrop)

1985   Author: Walter Dean Myers, *Motown and Didi* (Viking)
        Illustrator: No award given

1986   Author: Virginia Hamilton, *The People Could Fly: American Black Folktales* (Knopf)
        Illustrator: Jerry Pinkney, *Patchwork Quilt* by Valerie Flournoy (Dial)

1987   Author: Mildred Pitts Walter, *Justin and the Best Biscuits in the World* (Lothrop)
        Illustrator: Jerry Pinkney, *Half Moon and One Whole Star* by Crescent Dragonwagon (Macmillan)

1988   Author: Mildred D. Taylor, *The Friendship* (Dial)
        Illustrator: John Steptoe, *Mufaro's Beautiful Daughters: An African Tale* (Lothrop)

1989   Author: Walter Dean Myers, *Fallen Angels* (Scholastic)
        Illustrator: Jerry Pinkney, *Mirandy and Brother Wind* by Patricia McKissack (Knopf)

1990   Author: Patricia and Fredrick McKissack, *A Long Hard Journey* (Walker)
        Illustrator: Jan Spivey, *Nathaniel Talking* by Eloise Greenfield (Black Butterfly Press)

1991   Author: Mildred D. Taylor, *Road to Memphis* (Dial)
        Illustrator: Leo and Diane Dillon, *Aida,* retold by Leontyne Price (Harcourt)

1992   Author: Walter Dean Myers, *Now Is Your Time! The African-American Struggle for Freedom* (HarperCollins)
        Illustrator: *Tar Beach* by Faith Ringgold (Crown)

1993   Author: Patricia McKissack, *The Dark-Thirty: Southern Tales of the Supernatural* (Knopf)
        Illustrator: Kathleen Atkins Smith, *Origins of Life on Earth: An African Creation Myth* by David A. Anderson (Sight Productions)

1994   Author: Angela Johnson, *Toning the Sweep* (Orchard)
        Illustrator: Tom Feelings, *Soul Looks Back in Wonder* (Dial)

1995   Author: Patricia and Fredrick McKissack, *Christmas in the Big House, Christmas in the Quarters,* illustrated by John Thompson (Scholastic)
        Illustrator: James E. Ransom, *The Creation* by James Weldon Johnson (Holiday)

1996   Author: Virginia Hamilton, *Her Stories,* illustrated by Leo and Diane Dillon (Scholastic)
        Illustrator: Tom Feelings, *The Middle Passage: White Ships, Black Cargo* (Dial)

1997   Author: Walter Dean Myers, *SLAM!* (Scholastic)
        Illustrator: Jerry Pinkney, *Minty: A Story of Young Harriet Tubman* by Alan Schroeder (Dial)

1998   Author: Sharon M. Draper, *Forged by Fire* (Atheneum)
        Illustrator: Javaka Steptoe, *In Daddy's Arms I Am Tall: African Americans Celebrating Fathers* (Lee & Low)

1999   Author: Angela Johnson, *Heaven* (Simon & Schuster)
        Illustrator: Michele Wood, *I See The Rhythm* (Children's Book Press)

2000   Author: Christopher Paul Curtis, *Bud, Not Buddy* (Delacorte)
        Illustrator: Brian Pinkney, *In the Time of the Drums* by Kim L. Siegelson (Hyperion)

2001   Author: Jacqueline Woodson, *Miracle's Boys* (Putnam)
        Illustrator: Brian Collier, *Uptown* (Holt)

2002   Author: Mildred D. Taylor, *The Land* (Penguin)
        Illustrator: Jerry Pinkney, *Goin' Someplace Special* by Patricia McKissack (Atheneum)

2003   Author: Nikki Grimes, *Bronx Masquerade* (Dial)
        Illustrator: E. B. Lewis, *Talkin' About Bessie* (Scholastic)

2004   Author: Angela Johnson, *The First Last Part* (Simon & Schuster)
        Illustrator: Ashley Bryan, *Beautiful Blackbird* (Atheneum)

2005   Author: Toni Morrison, *Remember: The Journey to School Integration* (Houghton Mifflin)
        Illustrator: Nadir Nelson, *Ellington Was Not a Street* by Ntozake Shange (Simon & Schuster)

2006   Author: Julius Lester, *Day of Tears: A Novel in Dialogue* (Hyperion)
        Illustrator: Bryan Collier, *Rosa* (Holt)

2007   Author: Sharon Draper, *Copper Sun* (Simon & Schuster)
        Illustrator: Kadir Nelson, *Moses: When Harriet Tubman Led Her People to Freedom* (Hyperion)

2008   Author: Christopher Paul Curtis, *Elijah of Buxton* (Scholastic)
        Illustrator: Ashley Bryan, *Let It Shine* (Atheneum)

2009   Author: Kadir Nelson, *We Are the Ship: The Story of Negro League Baseball* (Disney)
        Illustrator: Floyd Cooper, *The Blacker the Berry* by Joyce Carol Thomas (HarperCollins)

2010   Author: Vaunda Micheaux Nelson, *Bad News for Outlaws: The Remarkable Life of Bass Reeves, Deputy U.S. Marshal* (Carolrhoda)
Illustrator: Charles R. Smith, Jr., *My People* by Langston Hughes (Atheneum)

2011   Author: Rita Williams-Garcia, *One Crazy Summer* (Amistad)
Illustrator: Bryan Collier, *Dave the Potter: Artist, Poet, Slave* by Laban Carrick Hill (Little, Brown)

2012   Author: Kadir Nelson, *Heart and Soul: The Story of America and African Americans* (Balzer + Bray)
Illustrator: Shane W. Evans, *Underground: Finding the Light to Freedom* (Roaring Book Press)

2013   Author: Andrea Davis Pinkney, *Hand in Hand: Ten Black Men Who Changed America* (Disney)
Illustrator: Bryan Collier, *I, Too, Am America* (Simon & Schuster)

2014   Author: Rita Williams-Garcia, *P.S. Be Eleven* (Amistad)
Illustrator: Bryan Collier, *Knock, Knock: My Dad's Dream for Me* by Daniel Beatty (Little, Brown)

2015   Author: Jacqueline Woodson, *Brown Girl Dreaming* (Nancy Paulson Books)
Illustrator: Christopher Myers, *Firebird* by Misty Copeland (Putnam/Penguin)

2016   Author: Rita Williams-Garcia, *Gone Crazy in Alabama* (Amistad)
Illustrator: Bryan Collier, *Trombone Shorty* by Troy Andrews and Bill Taylor (Abrams)

2017   Author: John Lewis and Andrew Aydin, *March: Book Three* illustrated by Nate Powell (Top Shelf Productions)
Illustrator: Javaka Steptoe, *Radiant Child: The Story of Young Artist Jean-Michel Basquiat* (Little, Brown and Company)

National Council of Teachers of English Award for Excellence in Poetry for Children

This award is now presented biennially (from 1977 through 1982, it was awarded annually, and until 2009, triennially) by the National Council of Teachers of English. The award was established to recognize a living poet's lifetime contribution to poetry for children.

1977   David McCord
1978   Aileen Fisher
1979   Karia Kuskin
1980   Myra Cohn Livingston
1981   Eve Merriam
1982   John Ciardi
1985   Lilian Moore
1988   Arnold Adoff
1991   Valerie Worth
1994   Barbara Juster Esbensen
1997   Eloise Greenfield
2000   X. J. Kennedy
2003   Mary Ann Hoberman
2006   Nikki Grimes
2009   Lee Bennett Hopkins
2011   J. Patrick Lewis
2013   Joyce Sidman
2015   Marilyn Singer
2017   Marilyn Nelson

The Scott O'Dell Award for Historical Fiction

Established by noted children's novelist Scott O'Dell and administered by the Advisory Committee of the Bulletin of the Center for Children's Books, this award is presented to the most distinguished work of historical fiction set in the New World and written by a citizen of the United States.

1984   *The Sign of the Beaver* by Elizabeth George Speare (Houghton Mifflin)

1985   *The Fighting Ground* by Avi (Harper)

1986   *Sarah, Plain and Tall* by Patricia MacLachlan (Harper)

1987   *Streams to the River, River to the Sea: A Novel of Sacagawea* by Scott O'Dell (Houghton Mifflin)

1988   *Charlie Skedaddle* by Patricia Beatty (Morrow)

1989   *The Honorable Prison* by Lyll Becerra de Jenkins (Lodestar)

1990   *Shades of Gray* by Carolyn Reeder (Macmillan)

1991   *A Time of Troubles* by Pieter van Raven (Scribner's)

1992   *Stepping on the Cracks* by Mary Downing Hahn (Clarion)

1993   *Morning Girl* by Michael Dorris (Hyperion)

1994   *Bull Run* by Paul Fleischman (Harper)

1995   *Under the Blood Red Sun* by Graham Salisbury (Delacorte)

1996   *The Bomb* by Theodore Taylor (Flare)

1997   *Jip: His Story* by Katherine Paterson (Lodestar)

1998   *Out of the Dust* by Karen Hesse (Scholastic)

1999   *Forty Acres and Maybe a Mule* by Harriette Gillem Robinette (Atheneum)

2000   *Two Suns in the Sky* by Miriam Bat-Ami (Front Street)

2001   *The Art of Keeping Cool* by Janet Taylor Lisle (Atheneum)

2002   *The Land* by Mildred Taylor (Dial)

2003   *Trouble Don't Last* by Shelley Pearsall (Knopf)

2004   *River Between Us* by Richard Peck (Dial)

2005   *Worth* by A. LaFaye (Simon & Schuster)

2006   *The Game of Silence* by Louise Erdrich (HarperCollins)

2007   *The Green Glass Sea* by Ellen Klages (Viking)

2008   *Elijah of Buxton* by Christopher Paul Curtis (Scholastic)

2009   *Chains* by Laurie Halse Anderson (Simon & Schuster)

2010   *The Storm in the Barn* by Matt Phelan (Candlewick)

2011   *One Crazy Summer* by Rita Williams-Garcia (Amistad)

2012   *Dead End in Norvelt* by Jack Gantos (Farrar, Straus & Giroux)

2013   *Chickadee* by Louise Erdrich (HarperCollins)

2014   *Bo at Ballard Creek* by Kirkpatrick Hill (Henry Holt)

2015   *Dash* by Kirby Larson (Scholastic)

2016   *The Hired Girl* by Laura Amy Schlitz (Candlewick)

2017   *Full of Beans* by Jennifer L. Holm (Random House)

NCTE Orbis Pictus Award for Outstanding Nonfiction for Children

This award is given annually by the National Council of Teachers of English to the best works of nonfiction published in the preceding year. The award is named for Johannes Amos Comenius' *Orbis Pictus—The World in Pictures*, an illustrated Latin vocabulary book published in 1657 and considered the first picture book actually intended for children. Although several honor books and recommended titles are included each year, only the winners are listed here. See the NCTE website for a complete list.

1990   *The Great Little Madison* by Jean Fritz (Putnam)

1991   *Franklin Delano Roosevelt* by Russell Freedman (Clarion)

1992   *Flight: The Journey of Charles Lindbergh* by Robert Burleigh, illustrated by Mike Wimmer (Philomel Books)

1993   *Children in the Dust Bowl: The True Story of the School at Weedpatch Camp* by Jerry Stanley (Crown)

1994 *Across America on an Emigrant Train* by Jim Murphy (Clarion)

1995 *Safari Beneath the Sea: The Wonder World of the North Pacific Coast* by Diane Swanson (Sierra Club Books)

1996 *The Great Fire* by Jim Murphy (Scholastic)

1997 *Leonardo da Vinci* by Diane Stanley (Morrow Junior Books)

1998 *An Extraordinary Life: The Story of a Monarch Butterfly* by Laurence Pringle (Orchard Books)

1999 *Shipwreck at the Bottom of the World: The Extraordinary True Story of Shackleton and the Endurance* by Jennifer Armstrong (Crown)

2000 *Through My Eyes* by Ruby Bridges and Margo Lundell (Scholastic)

2001 *Hurry Freedom: African Americans in Gold Rush California* by Jerry Stanley (Crown)

2002 *Black Potatoes: The Story of the Great Irish Famine, 1845–1850* by Susan Campbell Bartoletti (Houghton Mifflin)

2003 *When Marian Sang: The True Recital of Marian Anderson: The Voice of a Century* by Pam Munoz Ryan, illustrated by Brian Selznick (Scholastic)

2004 *An American Plague: The True and Terrifying Story of the Yellow Fever Epidemic of 1793* by Jim Murphy (Clarion)

2005 *York's Adventures with Lewis and Clark: An African-American's Part in the Great Expedition* by Rhoda Blumberg (HarperCollins)

2006 *Children of the Great Depression* by Russell Freedman (Clarion)

2007 *Quest for the Tree Kangaroo: An Expedition to the Cloud Forest of New Guinea* by Sy Montgomery, photos by Nic Bishop (Houghton Mifflin)

2008 *M.L.K.: Journey of a King* by Tonya Bolden (Abrams Books)

2009 *Amelia Earhart: The Legend of the Lost Aviator* by Shelley Tanaka, illustrated by David Craig (Abrams Books)

2010 *The Secret World of Walter Anderson* by Hester Bass, illustrated by E. B. Lewis (Candlewick)

2011 *Ballet for Martha: Making Appalachian Spring* by Jan Greenberg and Sandra Jordan, illustrated by Brian Floca (Roaring Brook Press)

2012 *Balloons Over Broadway: The True Story of the Puppeteer of Macy's Parade* by Melissa Sweet (Houghton Mifflin)

2013 *Monsieur Marceau: Actor without Words* by Leda Schubert, illustrated by Gérard DuBois (Roaring Brook Press)

2014 *A Splash of Red: The Life and Art of Horace Pippin* by Jen Bryant, illustrated by Melissa Sweet (Alfred A. Knopf)

2015 *The Family Romanov: Murder, Rebellion & the Fall of Imperial Russia* by Candace Fleming (Schwartz & Wade)

2016 *Drowned City: Hurricane Katrina & New Orleans* by Don Brown (Houghton Mifflin Harcourt)

2017 *Some Writer!: The Story of E. B. White* by Melissa Sweet (Houghton Mifflin Harcourt)

Robert F. Sibert Informational Book Award

This annual award was established by the American Library Association in 2001 to honor the most distinguished information book published in English in the preceding year. It is named for the one-time president of Bound to Stay Bound Books, Inc., of Jacksonville, Illinois, which sponsors the award.

2001 *Sir Walter Raleigh and the Quest for El Dorado* by Marc Aronson (Clarion)

2002 *Black Potatoes: The Story of the Great Irish Famine, 1845–1850* by Susan Campbell Bartoletti (Houghton Mifflin)

2003 *The Life and Death of Adolf Hitler* by James Cross Giblin (Clarion)

2004 *An American Plague: The True and Terrifying Story of the Yellow Fever Epidemic of 1793* by Jim Murphy (Clarion)

2005 *The Voice That Challenged a Nation: Marian Anderson and the Struggle for Equal Rights* by Russell Freedman (Clarion)

2006 *Secrets of a Civil War Submarine: Solving the Mysteries of the H. L. Hunley* by Sally M. Walker (Carolrhoda)

2007 *Team Moon: How 400,000 People Landed* Apollo 11 *on the Moon* by Catherine Thimmesh (Houghton)

2008 *The Wall: Growing Up Behind the Iron Curtain* by Peter Sis (Farrar, Straus & Giroux)

2009 *We Are the Ship: The Story of Negro League Baseball* by Kadir Nelson (Disney)

2010 *Almost Astronauts: 13 Women Who Dared to Dream* by Tanya Lee Stone (Candlewick)

2011 *Kakapo Rescue: Saving the World's Strangest Parrot* by Sy Montgomery, photographs by Nic Bishop (Houghton Mifflin)

2012 *Balloons Over Broadway: The True Story of the Puppeteer of Macy's Parade* by Melissa Sweet (Houghton Mifflin)

2013 *Bomb: The Race to Build—and Steal—the World's Most Dangerous Weapon* by Steve Sheinkin (Roaring Brook Press)

2014 *Parrots Over Puerto Rico* by Susan L. Roth and Cindy Trumbore, illustrated by Susan L. Roth (Lee & Low Books, Inc.)

2015 *The Right Word: Roget and His Thesaurus* by Jen Bryant, illustrated by Melissa Sweet (Eerdmans)

2016 *Funny Bones: Posada and His Day of the Dead Calaveras* by Duncan Tonatiuh (Abrams)

2017 *March: Book Three* by John Lewis and Andrew Aydin, illustrated by Nate Powell (Top Shelf)

International Awards

The Carnegie Medal

Awarded by the British Library Association to an outstanding book first published in the United Kingdom, this medal has been awarded annually since it was established in 1937 (the first award being presented to a book published in the preceding year). The date given is the date of publication. (This should not be confused with the Carnegie Medal awarded by the Association for Library Service to Children for contributions to children's video.)

1936 *Pigeon Post* by Arthur Ransome (Cape)

1937 *The Family from One End Street* by Eve Garnett (Muller)

1938 *The Circus Is Coming* by Noel Streatfield (Dent)

1939 *Radium Woman* by Eleanor Doorly (Heinemann)

1940 *Visitors from London* by Kitty Barne (Dent)

1941 *We Couldn't Leave Dinah* by Mary Treadgold (Penguin)

1942 *The Little Grey Men* by B. B. (Eyre & Spottiswoode)

1943 No award given

1944 *The Wind on the Moon* by Eric Linklater (Macmillan)

1945 No award given

1946 *The Little White Horse* by Elizabeth Goudge (Brockhampton Press)

1947 *Collected Stories for Children* by Walter de la Mare (Faber)

1948   *Sea Change* by Richard Armstrong (Dent)

1949   *The Story of Your Home* by Agnes Allen (Transatlantic)

1950   *The Lark on the Wind* by Elfrida Vipont Foulds (Oxford)

1951   *The Woolpack* by Cynthia Harnett (Methuen)

1952   *The Borrowers* by Mary Norton (Dent)

1953   *A Valley Grows Up* by Edward Osmond (Oxford)

1954   *Knight Crusader* by Ronald Welch (Oxford)

1955   *The Little Bookroom* by Eleanor Farjeon (Oxford)

1956   *The Last Battle* by C. S. Lewis (Bodley Head)

1957   *A Grass Rope* by William Mayne (Oxford)

1958   *Tom's Midnight Garden* by Philippa Pearce (Oxford)

1959   *The Lantern Bearers* by Rosemary Sutcliff (Oxford)

1960   *The Making of Man* by I. W. Cornwall (Phoenix)

1961   *A Stranger at Green Knowe* by Lucy Boston (Faber)

1962   *The Twelve and the Genii* by Pauline Clarke (Faber)

1963   *Time of Trial* by Hester Burton (Oxford)

1964   *Nordy Banks* by Sheena Porter (Oxford)

1965   *The Grange at High Force* by Philip Turner (Oxford)

1966   No award given

1967   *The Owl Service* by Alan Garner (Collins)

1968   *The Moon in the Cloud* by Rosemary Harris (Faber)

1969   *The Edge of the Cloud* by K. M. Peyton (Oxford)

1970   *The God Beneath the Sea* by Leon Garfield and Edward Blishen (Kestrel)

1971   *Josh* by Ivan Southall (Angus & Robertson)

1972   *Watership Down* by Richard Adams (Rex Collings)

1973   *The Ghost of Thomas Kempe* by Penelope Lively (Heinemann)

1974   *The Stronghold* by Mollie Hunter (Hamilton)

1975   *The Machine Gunners* by Robert Westall (Macmillan)

1976   *Thunder and Lightnings* by Jan Mark (Kestrel)

1977   *The Turbulent Term of Tyke Tiler* by Gene Kemp (Faber)

1978   *The Exeter Blitz* by David Rees (Hamish Hamilton)

1979   *Tulku* by Peter Dickinson (Dutton)

1980   *City of Gold* by Peter Dickinson (Gollancz)

1981   *The Scarecrows* by Robert Westall (Chatto & Windus)

1982   *The Haunting* by Margaret Mahy (Dent)

1983   *Handles* by Jan Mark (Kestrel)

1984   *The Changeover* by Margaret Mahy (Dent)

1985   *Storm* by Kevin Crossley-Holland (Heinemann)

1986   *Granny Was a Buffer Girl* by Berlie Doherty (Methuen)

1987   *The Ghost Drum* by Susan Price (Faber)

1988   *Pack of Lies* by Geraldine McCaughrean (Oxford)

1989   *My War with Goggle-Eyes* by Anne Fine (Joy Street)

1990   *Wolf* by Gillian Cross (Oxford)

1991   *Dear Nobody* by Berlie Doherty (Hamish Hamilton)

1992   *Flour Babies* by Anne Fine (Hamish Hamilton)

1993   *Stone Cold* by Robert Swindells (Hamish Hamilton)

1994   *Whispers in the Graveyard* by Theresa Breslin (Methuen)

1995   *Northern Lights* by Philip Pullman (Doubleday) (U.S. title: *The Golden Compass*)

1996   *Junk* by Melvin Burgess (Andersen/Penguin)

1997   *River Boy* by Tim Bowler (Oxford)

1998   *Skellig* by David Almond (Hodder)

1999   *Postcards from No Man's Land* by Aidan Chambers (Bodley Head)

2000   *The Other Side of Truth* by Beverley Naidoo (Puffin)

2001   *The Amazing Maurice and His Educated Rodents* by Terry Pratchett (Doubleday)

2002   *Ruby Holler* by Sharon Creech (Bloomsbury)

2003   *A Gathering of Light* by Jennifer Donnelly (Bloomsbury)

2004   *Millions* by Frank Cottrell Boyce (Macmillan)

2005   *Tamar* by Mal Peet (Walker)

2007   *Just in Case* by Meg Rosoff (Penguin)

2008   *Here Lies Arthur* by Philip Reeve (Scholastic)

2009   *Bog Child* by Siobhan Dowd (David Fickling)

2010   *The Graveyard Book* by Neil Gaiman (Bloomsbury)

2011   *Monsters of Men* by Patrick Ness (Walker)

2012   *A Monster Calls* by Patrick Ness (Walker)

2013   *Maggot Moon* by Sally Gardner (Hot Keys)

2014   *The Bunker Diary* by Kevin Brooks (Penguin)

2015   *Buffalo Soldier* by Tanya Landman (Walker Books)

2016   *One* by Sarah Crossan (Bloomsbury Children's)

2017   *Salt to the Sea* by Ruta Sepetys (Penguin)

The Kate Greenaway Medal

Named for the celebrated nineteenth-century children's illustrator, this medal is awarded annually by the British Library Association to the most distinguished illustrated work for children first published in the United Kingdom during the preceding year. (Unless otherwise noted, the author is also the illustrator. The date given is the year of publication.)

1956   *Tim All Alone* by Edward Ardizzone (Oxford)

1957   *Mrs. Easter and the Storks* by V. H. Drummond (Faber)

1958   No award given

1959   *Kashtanka and a Bundle of Ballads* by William Stobbs (Oxford)

1960   *Old Winkle and the Seagulls* by Elizabeth Rose, illustrated by Gerald Rose (Faber)

1961   *Mrs. Cockle's Cat* by Philippa Pearce, illustrated by Anthony Maitland (Kestrel)

1962   *Brian Wildsmith's ABC* by Brian Wildsmith (Oxford)

1963   *Borka* by John Burningham (Jonathan Cape)

1964   *Shakespeare's Theatre* by C. W. Hodges (Oxford)

1965   *Three Poor Tailors* by Victor Ambrus (Hamilton)

1966   *Mother Goose Treasury* by Raymond Briggs (Hamilton)

1967   *Charlie, Charlotte & the Golden Canary* by Charles Keeping (Oxford)

1968   *Dictionary of Chivalry* by Grant Uden, illustrated by Pauline Baynes (Kestrel)

1969   *The Quangle-Wangle's Hat and the Dragon of an Ordinary Family* by Helen Oxenbury (Heinemann)

1970   *Mr. Gumpy's Outing* by John Burningham (Jonathan Cape)

1971   *The Kingdom Under the Sea* by Jan Pienkowski (Jonathan Cape)

1972   *The Woodcutter's Duck* by Krystyna Turska (Hamilton)

1973   *Father Christmas* by Raymond Briggs (Hamilton)

1974   *The Wind Blew* by Pat Hutchins (Bodley Head)

1975   *Horses in Battle* by Victor Ambrus (Oxford)

1976   *The Post Office Cat* by Gail E. Haley (Bodley Head)

1977   *Dogger* by Shirley Hughes (Bodley Head)

1978   *Each Peach Pear Plum* by Janet and Allan Ahlberg (Kestrel)

1979   *The Haunted House* by Jan Pienkowski (Dutton)

1980   *Mr. Magnolia* by Quentin Blake (Jonathan Cape)

1981   *The Highwayman* by Alfred Noyes, illustrated by Charles Keeping (Oxford)

1982   *Long Neck and Thunder Foot* by Michael Foreman (Kestrel); *Sleeping Beauty and Other Favorite Fairy Tales* by Michael Foreman (Gollancz)

1983   *Gorilla* by Anthony Browne (Julia McRae Books)

1984   *Hiawatha's Childhood* by Errol LeCain (Faber)

1985   *Sir Gawain and the Loathly Lady* by Selina Hastings, illustrated by Juan Wijngaard (Walker)

1986   *Snow White in New York* by Fiona French (Oxford)

1987   *Crafty Chameleon* by Adrienne Kennaway (Hodder & Stoughton)

1988   *Can't You Sleep, Little Bear?* by Martin Waddell, illustrated by Adrienne Kennaway (Hodder & Stoughton)

1989   *War Boy: A Country Childhood* by Michael Foreman (Arcade)

1990   *The Whale's Song* by Dyan Sheldon, illustrated by Gary Blythe (Dial)

1991   *The Jolly Christmas Postman* by Janet and Allan Ahlberg (Heinemann)

1992   *Zoo* by Anthony Browne (Julie MacRae Books)

1993   *Black Ships Before Troy* retold by Rosemary Sutcliff, illustrated by Alan Lee (Frances Lincoln)

1994   *Way Home* by Libby Hawthorne (Anderson)

1995   *The Christmas Miracle of Jonathan Toomey* by Susan Wojciechowski, illustrated by P. J. Lynch (Candlewick)

1996   *The Baby Who Wouldn't Go to Bed* by Helen Cooper (Doubleday)

1997   *When Jessie Came Across the Sea* by Amy Hest, illustrated by P. J. Lynch (Doubleday)

1998   *Pumpkin Soup* by Helen Cooper (Doubleday)

1999   *Alice's Adventures in Wonderland* by Lewis Carroll, illustrated by Helen Oxenbury (Walker)

2000   *I Will Not Ever Eat a Tomato* by Lauren Child (Orchard)

2001   *Pirate Diary* by Chris Riddell (Walker)

2002   *Jethro Byrde: Fairy Child* by Bob Graham (Walker)

2003   *Ella's Big Chance* by Shirley Hughes (Bodley Head)

2004   *Jonathan Swift's "Gulliver"* by Marti Jenkins, illustrated by Chris Riddell (Walker)

2005   *Wolves* by Emily Gravett (Macmillan)

2007   *The Adventures of the Dish and the Spoon* by Mini Grey (Jonathan Cape)

2008   *Little Mouse's Big Book of Fears* by Emily Gravett (Macmillan)

2009   *Harris Finds His Feet* by Catherine Rayner (Little Tiger Press)

2010   *Harry & Hooper* by Freya Blackwood (Scholastic)

2011   *FArTHER* by Graham Baker-Smith (Templar)

2012   *A Monster Calls* by Patrick Ness, illustrated by Jim Kay (Walker)

2013   *Black Dog* by Levi Pinfold (Templar)

2014   *This Is Not My Hat* by John Klassen (Walker)

2015   *Shackleton's Journey* by William Grill (Flying Eye)

2016   *The Sleeper and the Spindle* by Chris Riddell (Bloomsbury)

2017   *There Is a Tribe of Kids* by Lane Smith (Two Hoots)

The Hans Christian Andersen Award

This medal, named for the great Danish storyteller, is presented every two years by the International Board on Books for Young People to a living author and (since 1966) a living illustrator whose works have made a significant international contribution to children's literature.

1956   Eleanor Farjeon (Great Britain)

1958   Astrid Lindgren (Sweden)

1960   Erich Kastner (Germany)

1962   Meindert DeJong (United States)

1964   René Guillot (France)

1966   Author: Tove Jansson (Finland)
        Illustrator: Alois Carigiet (Switzerland)

1968   Authors: James Krüss (Germany) and José Maria Sanchez-Silva (Spain)
        Illustrator: Jirí Trnka (Czechoslovakia)

1970   Author: Gianni Rodari (Italy)
        Illustrator: Maurice Sendak (United States)

1972   Author: Scott O'Dell (United States)
        Illustrator: Ib Spang Olsen (Denmark)

1974   Author: Maria Gripe (Sweden)
        Illustrator: Farsid Mesghali (Iran)

1976   Author: Cecil Bødker (Denmark)
        Illustrator: Tatjana Mawrina (U.S.S.R.)

1978   Author: Paula Fox (United States)
        Illustrator: Svend Otto S. (Denmark)

1980   Author: Bohumil Riha (Czechoslovakia)
        Illustrator: Suekichi Akaba (Japan)

1982   Author: Lygia Gojunga Nunes (Brazil)
        Illustrator: Zbigniew Rychlicki (Poland)

1984   Author: Christine Nostlinger (Austria)
        Illustrator: Mitsumasa Anno (Japan)

1986   Author: Patricia Wrightson (Australia)
        Illustrator: Robert Ingpen (Australia)

1988   Author: Annie M. G. Schmidt (Netherlands)
        Illustrator: Dusan Kállay (Yugoslavia)

1990   Author: Tormod Haugen (Norway)
        Illustrator: Lisbeth Zwerger (Austria)

1992   Author: Virginia Hamilton (United States)
Illustrator: Keveta Pacovská (Czechoslovakia)

1994   Author: Michio Mado (Japan)
Illustrator: Jörg Müller (Switzerland)

1996   Author: Uri Orlev (Israel)
Illustrator: Klaus Ensikat (Germany)

1998   Author: Katherine Paterson (United States)
Illustrator: Tomi Ungerer (United States)

2000   Author: Ana Maria Machado (Brazil)
Illustrator: Anthony Browne (Great Britain)

2002   Author: Aidan Chambers (Great Britain)
Illustrator: Quentin Blake (Great Britain)

2004   Author: Martin Waddell (Ireland)
Illustrator: Max Velthuijs (Netherlands)

2006   Author: Margaret Mahy (New Zealand)
Illustrator: Wolf Erlbruch (Germany)

2008   Author: Jürg Schubiger (Switzerland)
Illustrator: Roberto Innocenti (Italy)

2010   Author: David Almond (Great Britain)
Illustrator: Jutta Bauer (Germany)

2012   Author: Maria Teresa Andruetto (Argentina)
Illustrator: Peter Sis (Czech Republic)

2014   Author: Hahoko Uehashi (Japan)
Illustrator: Roger Mello (Brazil)

2016   Author: Cao Wenxuan (China)
Illustrator: Rotraut Susanne Berner (Germany)

The Astrid Lindgren Memorial Award

Named in honor of the beloved author of *Pippi Longstocking,* this international award from the Swedish government carries a prize of 5 million Swedish crowns, second only to the Nobel Prize among literature prizes in the world. The award (one or two a year) may be given to an individual or organization whose work has promoted children's and youth literature.

2003   Christine Nöstlinger (Austria) and Maurice Sendak (United States)

2004   Lygia Bojunga (Brazil)

2005   Ryôji Arai (Japan) and Philip Pullman (United Kingdom)

2006   Katherine Paterson (United States)

2007   Banco del Libro (Venezuela)

2008   Sonya Harnett (Australia)

2009   The Tamer Institute for Community Education (Palestine)

2010   Kitty Crowther (Belgium)

2011   Shaun Tan (Australia)

2012   Guus Kuijer (Netherlands)

2013   Isol (Argentina)

2014   Barbro Lindgren (Sweden)

2015   Project for the Study of Alternative Education in South Africa (PRAESA) (South Africa)

2016   Meg Rosoff (United States)

2017   Wolf Erlbruch (Germany)

Glossary

Alliteration The repetition of similar sounds at the beginnings of words in close proximity, as in "Billy Button bought a buttered biscuit"

Anachronism Anything that is out of place for the time period—any tale of time travel is necessarily anachronistic, such as Philippa Pearce's *Tom's Midnight Garden* and Penelope Farmer's *Charlotte Sometime,* in which the protagonists travel back in time. Sometimes, an anachronism is simply the result of an author's carelessness (such as the striking clock in Shakespeare's *Julius Caesar*)

Anapest A poetic metrical foot consisting of two unstressed syllables followed by a stressed syllable, as in the phrase "in the **still** of the **night**"

Antagonist The main character in opposition to the protagonist (or hero) in a literary work—often termed the villain, although the antagonist need not be human (a hurricane or forest fire, for example)

Anthropomorphism Giving human qualities (such as speech or emotions) to something nonhuman—e.g., a talking animal, a plant, or a machine—Mickey Mouse or Thomas the Tank Engine, for example

Artistic medium The material an artist uses to produce an illustration—oil paints, watercolors, pencil, ink, and so on

Art Nouveau An artistic style developed in the late nineteenth century characterized by fluid, sinuous lines and florid designs

Assonance The repetition of similar vowel sounds within words of close proximity—as the long *a* sounds in *slate* and *grey* and *lake* in this line: "The surface of a slate-grey lake is lit" (Seamus Heaney)

Autobiography The life story of an individual written by the person himself or herself

Ballad A narrative poem typically of folk origin, in four-line stanzas, and intended to be sung (*see also* Narrative poem)

Bibliotherapy The treatment of psychological or emotional problems through the use of selected reading materials

Biography The life story of an individual written by someone else (in contrast to the *autobiography*)

Border In book illustration, the framing element for a picture, usually consisting of white space, but sometimes decorated

Cartoon art An artistic style characterized by simple, grossly exaggerated figures, usually for humorous or satirical effect

Censorship The act of restricting the public's access—through speech or the written word—to what certain authorities deem to be objectionable ideas

Cinquain A poem consisting of five lines, usually containing two, four, six, eight, and two syllables, respectively, with the first and last lines often echoing each other

Climax The high point of a dramatic plot when all the threads come together—usually the turning point of the story

Collage An artistic composition made up of a variety of materials, usually nonpainterly, such as fabric, paper, wood, and metal

Coming-of-age story A story in which the protagonist, through a variety of experiences, undergoes personal growth and development, a tale of maturing

Concrete poetry See "Visual poetry"

Consonance The repetition of similar consonant sounds within words of close proximity—such as the *l* sounds in "Afternoon light falling beautifully into the room" (Richard Jones)—as opposed to alliteration when the repeated sound occurs at the beginning of a word

Cubism An artistic movement of the early twentieth century characterized by abstract drawings emphasizing the geometric shape and structure of an object rather than pictorial representation

Cumulative plot A story consisting of an accumulation of events, which in its telling repeats the entire sequence with each addition—used most commonly in folktales such as *The Gingerbread Man*, and usually for comic effect

Dactyl A poetic metrical foot consisting of one stressed syllable followed by two unstressed syllables, as in the word "**beau**-ti-ful"

Dénouement Literally, the "unraveling" or "untying," applied to the final outcome of a dramatic plot when everything is explained and resolved

Dialogue The words spoken between two or more characters in a literary work

Didactic Literature that is intended to teach a concept or deliver a moral or ethical lesson

Digital art Art generated by a computer program

Dramatic plot A story consisting usually of a single major conflict, chronologically organized and leading up to a climax and a concluding dénouement

Dynamic character A fictional character—always a round one—who undergoes a significant change or emotional growth in the course of the action

Episodic plot A story, usually told in chapters, describing a series of adventures, tied together by characters, setting, or theme

Exposition The information provided in a literary work to supply needed background information to the audience—setting the stage, as it were

Expressionism In picture book art, a style that evokes the artist's emotional response to the subject rather than a realistic portrayal, characterized by unusual distortions

(elongated figures, for example), unrealistic use of colors, shapes that only suggest objects, and so on

First-person narrator A storyteller who is a character in the story and refers to himself or herself as I

Flashback In a narrative, a shift backward in time to reveal events that happened earlier; chiefly used as a means of explaining character motivation

Flat character A one-dimensional fictional character without depth or complexity; common among minor characters and always a static character

Foil character A fictional character whose personality traits sharply contrast with those of another character in the work

Folk art In picture book art, a style associated with a specific folk culture, usually identified by uncomplicated drawings and the use of cultural symbols and culturally specific colors, patterns, or designs

Foreshadowing In a narrative, hints of what is to come; a device used to create suspense and avoid what might otherwise seem incredible.

Found poetry A poem created from an ordinary piece of prose—an advertisement or a passage from a book, newspaper, or magazine—that retains the original language but has the sentences rearranged to resemble a poetic form

Free verse Poetry that observes no strict rules about rhythm, rhyme or stanza length—but most free verse still uses such devices as simile, metaphor, personification, and so on

Functionary character A minor character whose role is to perform specific necessary functions—as a servant, for example, or an official

Graphic novel A book-length work that uses both text and art, usually in comic book format, to tell the story (*manga* refers specifically to Japanese graphic novels)

Graphic technique A method by which a graphic artist creates images through the use of blocks, plates, or type, including woodblocks, linocuts, and so on

Gutter In a book, the crease caused by the binding—an important consideration in picture books that use double-page spreads

Haiku A Japanese poetic form usually consisting of 17 syllables in three lines and reflecting on nature

Iamb A poetic metrical foot consisting of one unstressed syllable followed by one stressed syllable, as in the word "a-**rise**"

Illustrated book A book that uses illustrations to highlight or support specific points in the text—as opposed to a picture book, in which the pictures share equally with the text

Irony Literary incongruity—a difference between what is said and what is meant, or between what happens and what we would normally expect to happen

Limerick A humorous five-line poem, with an *a-a-b-b-a* rhyme scheme and a regular rhythm

Limited narrator A third-person storyteller who is not a character in the story but tells the story from just one character's point of view

Lyric poem A poem that expresses the poet's personal feelings or thoughts about a subject (rather than telling a story), often following a verse pattern, sometimes intended to be sung; sonnets, odes, cinquains, and so on are examples

Metaphor An implied comparison, giving the attributes of one thing to another—for example, "All the world's a stage" (Shakespeare)

Meter A pattern of stressed and unstressed syllables (called metrical feet) in a line of poetry (*see also* "Anapest," "Dactyl," "Iamb," and "Trochee")

Montage A visual composition created by artfully arranging graphic images such as photographs in contrast with a collage, which combines various non-painterly materials

Motif A recurring thematic or plot element in literature, such as the recurring plot devices found throughout folktales

Motivation In a fictional story, what it is that causes a character to behave in a certain way or do certain things

Naïve art An artistic style that is deliberately made to resemble childlike drawings, often disproportioned and without depth of perspective

Narrative poem A story, complete with characters, setting, and plot, told in verse

New realism A type of fiction begun in the 1960s characterized by more realistic portrayal of social and personal issues confronting teenagers, including sexuality, drugs, gangs, and similar matters

Nonsense verse Comical verse featuring outlandish characters, absurd actions, and often made-up words and rollicking rhyme and rhythm

Omniscient narrator A third-person storyteller who is not a character in the story and is usually both all-seeing and all-knowing

Painterly technique A method by which an artist creates images by applying a medium (paint, ink, gouache, tempera, and so on) to a surface (usually paper), in contrast with digital art or woodblocks, for example

Panel In a picture book, a framed illustration, usually combined with others, that permits the simultaneous depiction on a single page of varying perspectives or time passing

Parallel plot A story consisting of two or more dramatic plots, often interwoven, operating simultaneously

Parody A literary work that imitates another to poke fun

Personification Giving inanimate objects human qualities—"around us the trees full of night lean hushed in their dreams" (W. S. Merwin)

Picture book A book in which the illustrations share equally with the text in conveying the story or information

Playground poetry The traditional oral verses that children themselves both share and invent, including playground games, camp songs, and so on

Plot The interrelated sequence of events making up a story (*see also* "Cumulative plot," "Dramatic plot," "Episodic plot," and "Parallel plot")

Problem novel A type of realistic fiction developed in the 1960s that focuses on a specific psychological or social issue confronting the protagonist

Protagonist The principal sympathetic character in a literary work, the main character

Reader-response theory A reading theory (sometimes called "transactional analysis") which proposes that each reader derives something personal from reading a text based on past experiences and knowledge, and that rereading a text will result in a still different response

Realism In picture book art, representational drawing or painting that attempts to give lifelike detail to objects

Renaissance In European history, the time period from about 1400 to 1650 that experienced a flowering of art and culture; based on a revived interest in the civilizations of ancient Greece and Rome

Round character A fictional character with a fully developed personality that has numerous facets

Satire A literary work that pokes fun, often through the use of irony, at some human folly or vice

Scanimation Originally a term used to describe analog computer animation (which gave way to digital animation), now applied to a technique, developed by Rufus Seder Butler, by which scrambled images are passed behind a transparent film marked with thin stripes, giving the images the illusion of motion

Sentimentalism A literary tone that expresses excessive emotion—overly sweet, overly mournful, overly passionate—that seems disproportionate to the circumstances

Setting The time and place in which the action of a story occurs

Simile An explicit comparison that uses the word *like* or *as*—for example, "His breath hung in the air like a white balloon" (Baron Wormser)

Static character A fictional character—either flat or round—who does not undergo any significant change throughout the work

Stock character A fictional character—always a flat one—who represents a type rather than an individual: the boor, the buffoon, the ingénue, the penny-pincher, the prude, and so on

Stylized intensification In folk narratives, the exaggeration of a repeated plot element for dramatic purposes—for example, each of the three little pigs building a slightly sturdier house

Surrealism In picture book art, a style that is drawn with realistic detail but with unrealistic, even unsettling, subject matter, often with a dreamlike or nightmarish quality

Tabula rasa Latin for "blank slate," a term philosopher John Locke used to describe his notion of a child's intellectual capacity at birth—in other words, the child's mind was like a blank slate awaiting the addition of concepts and information; the theory (which has since been disproven) inspired a multitude of didactic children's books in the eighteenth century

Theme The principal subject or idea of a specific literary work; the fundamental concept the author is attempting to convey

Tone The author's attitude—comical, satirical, cynical, and so on—toward the subject of a literary work

Transactional analysis *See* "Reader-response theory"

Trochee A poetic metrical foot consisting of one stressed followed by one unstressed syllable, as in the word "**hap-py**"

Typography The way in which letters are designed (including size and shape), and their arrangement on a page

Urchin poetry Poetry that deliberately appeals to a young reader's fixation on the disgusting and gross, as in some of the poetry of Shel Silverstein

Verse novel A novel written in poetry rather than prose, usually in free verse and from a first-person viewpoint; popular in nineteenth-century adult fiction, the form has gained prominence in modern children's fiction

Vignette In a picture book, a small picture integrated into a larger illustration to supply additional information or perhaps to add humor

Visual poetry Also called concrete poetry or shape poetry; poetry in which the text is designed to resemble a shape on the page, usually illustrative of the poem's subject—for example, a poem about a butterfly shaped like a butterfly

Zone of proximal development (ZPD) A term created by the psychologist Lev Vygotsky to refer to the difference between what a person can learn on his or her own and what the person can learn with the assistance of others

Children's Literature Resources

General Reference Works

These publications provide background information on a multitude of topics in children's literature and are excellent places to begin research. They can be found in large libraries and online.

Children's Literature Review (1976–). Detroit: Gale.
A series devoted to assembling critical commentary on children's authors, with each volume focusing on approximately 10 individuals. Excerpts are taken from scholarly journals, book reviews, and similar sources. A good place to find out what critics are saying about a specific work.

Dictionary of Literary Biography (1978–). Detroit: Gale.
A multivolume series that includes extensive scholarly essays on literary figures; each volume focuses on a specific type of writing, and several volumes deal with children's writers and illustrators. A good place to find biographical material as well as some in-depth critical commentary on an individual's work.

Oxford Encyclopedia of Children's Literature. Jack Zipes, ed. New York: Oxford University Press, 2006.
A four-volume set that includes articles on writers, illustrators, works, and topics important in the field of children's literature—all written by specialists in the field.

Something about the Author (1971–). Detroit: Gale.
A multivolume series that includes biographical entries on children's authors and illustrators. A good place to find an introductory overview of an individual's life and work.

Periodicals

Some of the many periodicals that publish articles on children's literature are listed here. Notice that some publications are devoted largely to book reviews and are most helpful for book selection. Other publications feature scholarly essays on topics in children's literature or literacy, and these are most helpful for academic research.

ALAN Review—A publication of the Assembly on Literature for Adolescents of the National Council of Teachers of English that features articles on adolescent literature.

Bookbird—A quarterly publication of International Board on Books for Young People (IBBY) that is devoted to international children's literature.

Booklist—The review journal of the American Library Association; includes recommended books for both children and adults, and reviews some 7,500 books a year.

Bulletin of the Center for Children's Books—A monthly publication featuring reviews of the latest books for children.

Children's Literature—An annual publication of the Children's Literature Association, with scholarly articles on the entire range of children's literature.

Children's Literature Association Quarterly—A quarterly publication of the Children's Literature Association that has scholarly articles on the entire range of children's literature and reviews of recent scholarly books on children's literature.

Children's Literature in Education—A quarterly publication featuring scholarly articles of special interest to educators, including both pedagogy and literary analysis.

The Horn Book Magazine—A bimonthly publication with informal articles on children's books and a lengthy section devoted to brief reviews of the most recently published children's books.

Jeunesse: Young People, Texts, Cultures—An interdisciplinary journal, international in scope and with a particular interest in Canadian works, publishing studies on various issues, including literature, film, art, and other cultural productions by, for, and about young people.

Journal of Early Childhood Literary—A quarterly publication for scholarly research on the history, development, and teaching of childhood literacy.

Language Arts—A bimonthly publication of the National Council of Teachers of English featuring scholarly articles of particular interest to elementary and middle-school teachers, featuring current research on classroom theory and practice, and reviews of books for children.

The Lion and the Unicorn—A triennial publication featuring scholarly articles on the entire range of children's literature, also emphasizing international literature and reviews of recent scholarly books on children's literature; awards the annual *The Lion and Unicorn Poetry Award* for the year's best poetry publication.

School Library Journal—A monthly publication of book reviews intended, as the name implies, for libraries, but very helpful for educators as well.

Professional Organizations

Many professional organizations related to the field of children's literature exist, each with a slightly different focus. The following are only some of the most prominent. (Notice that professional associations are fond of acronyms.)

Children's Literature Association (ChLA)—For those interested in the scholarly pursuit of children's literature, especially educators and scholars.

International Board on Books for Young People (IBBY)—For those interested in international children's literature.

International Reading Association (IRA)—For those interested primarily in the instruction and scholarship of reading skills.

Modern Language Association (MLA)—For those interested in the scholarly pursuit of literature in general; MLA includes a children's literature section.

National Council of Teachers of English (NCTE)— For those interested in the profession of language arts education at all levels, from elementary through high school.

Popular Cultural Association—For those interested in the broader issues of popular culture, including music, art, and media.

Index

Credits

Image Credits

Page 5, By permission of the Folger Shakespeare Library. *Page 6*, Illustration from "Orbis Sensualium Pictus" (1659), John Comenius. Woodcut. *Page 7*, Illustrations from the "New England Primer" (1727). *Page 10*, British Library. *Page 12*, "The Man in the Moon" from "Mother Goose's Melodies" (1833), Abel Bowen. Woodcut. *Page 14*, "Jack and Jill" from "The Baby's Opera" (1877), Walter Crane. *Page 15*, Illustration from "The Frog He Would A-Wooing Go" (1883), Randolph Caldecott. *Page 30*, HarperCollins Publishers. *Page 31*, Illustrations copyright © 2013 Fred Marcellino. First published in 1899. Used by permission of HarperCollins Publishers. *Page 98*, From Good Two- Shoes, 1888 by McLoughlin Bros New York. *Page 100*, Project Gutenberg. *Page 106*, From "Perrault's Fairy Tales" (1867), illustrated by Gustave Doré. *Page 119*, From MY FRIEND RABBIT © 1999 by Eric Rohmann. Reprinted by permission of Roaring Brook Press, a division of Holtzbrinck Publishing Holdings Limited Partnership All Rights Reserved. *Page 120*, From "Tuesday" by David Wiesner. Copyright © 1991 by David Wiesner. Reprinted by permission of Clarion Books, an imprint of Houghton Mifflin Harcourt Publishing Company. All rights reserved. *Page 121*, "The Tiger Who Came to Tea" copyright © 1968 by Kerr-Kneale Productions Ltd. Reproduced by permission of the publishers, Candlewick Press, Somerville, MA and HarperCollins Publishers Ltd. *Page 125*, Illustration from "The Tale of Peter Rabbit" (1901), Beatrix Potter. *Page 126*, Illustrations from MADELINE by Ludwig Bemelmans, copyright 1939 by Ludwig Bemelmans; copyright renewed © 1967 by Madeleine Bemelmans and Barbara Bemelmans Marciano. Used by permission of Viking Children's Books, an imprint of Penguin Young Readers Group, a division of Penguin Random House LLC. All rights reserved. *Page 127*, Excerpt(s) from EL CUENTO DE FERDINANDO by Munro Leaf, illustrated by Robert Lawson, translated by Pura Belpre, Copyright 1936 by Munro Leaf and Robert Lawson, renewed © 1964 by Munro Leaf and John W. Boyd. Translation copyright © 1962 by Munro Leaf and Nina Forbes Bowman. Used by permission of Viking Children's Books, an imprint of Penguin Young Readers Group, a division of Penguin Random House LLC. All rights reserved. *Page 128*, Illustration from "Jumanji" by Chris Van Allsburg. Copyright © 1981 by Chris Van Allsburg. Reprinted by permission of Houghton Mifflin Harcourt Publishing Company. All rights reserved. *Page 130*, From MR. GUMPY'S OUTING © 1971 by John Burningham. Reprinted by permission of Roaring Brook Press, a division of Holtzbrinck Publishing Holdings Limited Partnership All Rights Reserved. *Page 157*, Illustration from "Mother Goose's Melodies" (1833). Wood engraving. Munroe & Francis, Boston. *Page 158*, Illustration from "The Nursery Rhyme Book" (ca. 1897), by Andrew Lang. Illustrated by L. Leslie Brooke. *Page 159*, Illustration from "The Real Mother Goose" (1916), Blanche Fisher Wright. *Page 160*, Illustration from "Mother Goose or the Old Nursery Rhymes" (ca. 1881), Kate Greenaway. *Page 161*, "Little Miss Muffet" (1913), Arthur Rackham. *Page 192*, From "Household Stories by the Brothers Grimm" (1886), translated by Lucy Crane, illustrated by Walter Crane. *Page 193*, From "Household Stories by the Brothers Grimm" (1886), translated by Lucy Crane, illustrated by Walter Crane. *Page 196*, Grimm, Jacob and Wilhelm. The Fairy Tales of the Brothers Grimm. Mrs. Edgar Lucas, translator. Arthur Rackham, illustrator. London: Constable & Company Ltd, 1909.). *Page 197*, From "The Red Fairy Book" (1890), edited by Andrew Lang, illustrated by H.J. Ford. *Page 198*, Ivan Bilibin. *Page 202*, Rapunzel by Paul O. Zelinsky. Copyright 1997 by Paul O. Zelinsky. Used by permission of Dutton Children's Books, a division of Penguin Readers Group, a member of Penguin Group (USA) Inc., 345 Hudson Street, New York, NY 10014. All rights reserved. *Page 203*, "The Twelve Dancing Princesses" in Powder and Crinoline, illustrated by Kay Nielsen, London, Hodder & Stoughton, 1913. *Page 204*, Taken from Walter Crane's Aesop. *Page 211*, From ANANSI THE SPIDER: A TALE FROM THE ASHANTI © 1972 by Gerald McDermott. Reprinted by permission of Henry Holt Books for Young Readers. All Rights Reserved. *Page 223*, From "Alice's Adventures in Wonderland" (1865), by Lewis Carroll, illustrated by Sir John Tenniel. *Page 226*, From "The Wonderful Wizard of Oz" (1900), by L. Frank Baum, illustrated by W.W. Denslow. *Page 228*, From The Tale of Peter Rabbit by Beatrix Potter. London: Warne, 1901. *Page 229*, From "The Wind in the Willows" (1931), by Kenneth Grahame, illustrated by Ernest H. Shepard. *Page 231*, Created for Walt Disney's 1940 animated musical film. *Page 238*, Based on Jules Verne's popular From the Earth to the Moon. *Page 240*, Ivy Close Images/Alamy Stock Photo. *Page 251*, From "Otto of the Silver Hand" (1888), written and illustrated by Howard Pyle. *Page 261*, From "Little Women" (ca. 1900), by Louisa May Alcott, illustrated by J. S. Eland. *Page 263*, There were Trees . . . and a Large Pool with an Old Grey Fountain in its Midst" Charles Robinson (1870-1937). Colour lithograph. Private Collection/© Look and Learn/The Bridgeman Art Library. *Page 266*, Library of Congress. *Page 267*, Blind Pew - N.C. Wyeth - WikiArt.org. *Page 286*, Henrik van Loon. *Page 294*, Hatching out" from "Amazing Worlds: Crocodiles and Reptiles" by Mary Ling, photographs by Jerry Young. Copyright © 1991 Dorling Kindersley. Reproduced by permission of Dorling Kindersley Ltd.